Mary

I am so pleased that you
should have been honoured
in the same way as my
father.

Happy Christmas and
very best wishes for the
coming year.

Desmond
December 2003.

KELLY'S BURMA CAMPAIGN

Frontispiece: *Caricature of Norman Kelly in 1942 by George Long*
('A small whisky for the Master!').

KELLY'S BURMA CAMPAIGN

Letters from the Chin Hills

Desmond Kelly

TIDDIM PRESS

LONDON

Tiddim Press
PO Box 28958
Mortlake
London
SW14 8XE
E-mail: TiddimPress@aol.com
Website: www.tiddimpress.com

A CIP catalogue record for this book is available from the British
Library.

ISBN 0-9540238-1-1

Maps by Technical Art Services
Indexer: Ursula Caffrey
Designed and produced by the Short Run Book Company Ltd
St Stephen's House
Arthur Road
WINDSOR
Berkshire
SL4 1RY

To the memory of my father, Norman Kelly,
my mother Betty,
and the loyal peoples of the Chin Hills

CONTENTS

LIST OF ILLUSTRATIONS

Frontispiece: Caricature of Norman Kelly in 1942 by George Long.
Page 24   Panoramic drawing of the Chin Hills. (The Illustrated London News *Picture Library*)

Between pages 16 and 17

1. Ripon Grammar School 1st XV, 1922.
2. Norman Kelly, as a Cambridge undergraduate, with his father.
3. Betty Megarry and Norman Kelly on the doorstep of 'Walnutvale'.
4. Norman Kelly in the Shan States.
5. Betty and Norman Kelly on their wedding day.
6. The bungalow in Loilem, Shan States.
7. Norman with Desmond.
8. The Kelly family.
9. Maeve with Desmond.
10. Norman in the uniform of the Burma Frontier Service.
11. The Wild Wa headhunters of the Shan States.
12. A 'skull grove' in 1937. (The Illustrated London News *Picture Library*)

Between pages 80 and 81

13. Betty Kelly at a garden party in 1939.
14. A Haka Chin with hair tied in a topknot by Yatanabon Mg Su. (*Ken Shaw*)
15. A Chin headhunter's sword. (*Nigel Robson*)
16. A Chin girl drinking from a *zu* pot.
17. Norman on tour.
18. The Kelly family before the trek out of Burma.
19. Tiddim village in the Chin Hills. (*Imperial War Museum*).
20. A pre-war suspension bridge over the Manipur River. (*Lieutenant-Colonel Patrick Cardwell Moore*)
21. A country boat on the Dhaleswari River.
22. Chin Levies at No. 2 Stockade. (*Imperial War Museum*)
23. A village headman and his Levies. (*Imperial War Museum*)
24. Falam, Chin Hills: Captain Carlyle Seppings, Captain Kenny Fraser and Captain Bryan Watt-Smyth with his Haka batman and battalion riflemen. (*Carlyle Seppings*)
25. The crest of the Burma Frontier Force. (*Anne Smith*)

LIST OF MAPS

Colour contour maps are included in the colour section between pages 144 and 145. No. 27 shows the Tiddim front; no. 28 shows the Tonzang area and the Battle of Tonzang in 1944 (both courtesy of Major-General Ian Lyall Grant).

FOREWORD

by

Major-General Ian Lyall Grant, MC

Norman Kelly was one of that select band of young men at the universities, both athletically and academically prominent who, before the Second World War, were offered the chance of joining Britain's colonial service. The task for many would be to win the hearts and minds of isolated communities and to introduce them to the benefits of education, modern medicine, and law and order.

Kelly, a natural leader with a warm-hearted personality, clearly thrived on the challenge of this life, and before the Second World War had already made his mark among the headhunting tribes on Burma's north-eastern border. In 1939 he was posted to the north-west, to the northern part of the Chin Hills district, based at Tiddim, where he soon became devoted to the Chins. In the dark days of 1942, when the Japanese invasion seemed unstoppable, he succeeded in persuading them to throw in their lot with the British rather than the Japanese. He quickly realised that the Chins, and the terrain in which they lived, were ideally suited for guerrilla warfare so he then raised, armed and personally led a most successful force of Chin guerrillas who, for more than a year, dominated the hills down to the Burmese plain. The confidence they engendered enabled a motor road to be completed from Imphal to Tiddim.

In late 1943 a large British force moved into the Tiddim area, so Kelly handed over his military command and resumed his civil and intelligence-gathering role. When, in March 1944, the Japanese launched a major advance through Kelly's fiefdom and the British forces were withdrawn to concentrate at Imphal, Kelly himself, refusing to abandon the Chins, stayed on in the hills and resumed his military role. Although the Japanese placed a large price on his head, he continued to travel widely among the villages and was never betrayed. When the Japanese retreated back through Tiddim, they suffered heavily at the hands of his now much-reinforced guerrillas.

Kelly's contribution to the Japanese defeat was widely recognised at the time. He was promoted, but sadly fell victim to ill-health stemming from the continual strain to which he had been subject and worries about the welfare in India of his family, to whom he was devoted. He never returned to the Chin Hills but is still well remembered there, as Dr Desmond Kelly – who has recently revisited his former home in Tiddim – shows in this absorbing biography of his father.

Dr Kelly has researched his book widely, and it forms a valuable addition to the history of the Burma campaign. More importantly, in telling this story and its sequence, with great frankness and from many angles, he preserves the memory of a most enterprising and courageous man who, at a critical time, upheld to the full the high standards for which the British were once famous.

Ian Lyall Grant

ACKNOWLEDGEMENTS

This book would not have been written if my mother, Betty, had not had the foresight to keep my father's letters through the turmoil of war. My sister Maeve Reid has made her own inspired contribution. Nicholas Greenwood has been a Burmese literary guru and persuaded the authorities to let me visit the normally forbidden Chin Hills; he edited the early manuscript and I have sought his advice throughout.

Numerous people have provided their own stories – too many to mention all by name but Major-General Ian Lyall Grant, who has written the Foreword, has allowed me to use two of his colour maps and has helped in innumerable ways. The late Professor Kenny Fraser was a source of insight into the characters of the major players in the drama; he was a true friend. Major Stephen Khup Chin Pau and Colonel Khen Za Moong have provided unique material. Dr Go Za Kham, his brother T. H. Go Khan Pau and Leo Deng Hau are but a few of the Chins who have made very important contributions. Dr Vum Ko Hau, PhD, and his daughter Diana deserve special mention.

Mrs Prue Brewis lost her husband, Alison Anne Whiting her brother, Rachel Brown her boyfriend and Bernard Bird his brother – they all gave me permission to quote from their letters and allowed their photographs to be used. I am most grateful, especially, for the late Jack Oats' account of his Chin Hills experience, provided by Prue. Lieutenant-Colonel Patrick Cardwell Moore, Tom Barton and Fergus West, all sons of veterans, have also furnished material. Lieutenant-Colonel Patric Emerson, Secretary of the Indian Army Association, has educated me in military ways and been of the greatest assistance.

All the black and white maps were drawn by David Hoxley, Technical Art Services, who deserves special recognition. Patricia Herbert of the British Library and Prospect Burma has been a constant source of information and encouragement and Dr Andrew Cook found British Library maps for me that few others could have located. The late Ken Shaw, a Levy officer, lent me the maps he had used during the campaign and John Nunneley, another veteran, was constructively creative.

Paul Strachan, on RV *Pandaw I* of the Irrawaddy Flotilla Company, was responsible for getting me up the Chindwin to Kalewa – an experience I shall never forget. The staff of the National Archives Department in Yangon (Rangoon) could not have been more helpful.

Dr John Ford, John Wall (the former head boy of the Hallett War School in Naini Tal) and Major General Robert Staverley read the manuscript and gave most valuable advice.

I am grateful to the following for their permission to use material in the book: The Gurkha Museum, Winchester, for permission to quote from *The Story of Gurkha VCs* by Maurice Briggs, 1993; David Higham Associates for permission to quote from *Defeat into Victory* by Field Marshal Sir William Slim (Cassell, 1956; Macmillan, paperback edition, 1999); *The Illustrated London News* Picture Library; The Imperial War Museum Photographic Archive. In a few cases I have been unable to trace copyright holders and would be pleased to rectify any omissions at the earliest opportunity.

Sophacles Alexiou reproduced the old family photographs that survived the trek out of Burma. I owe a great deal to the dedication of Dorothy White who typed the numerous drafts so carefully. Linda Cecil of the Short Run Book Company designed the jacket and the layout of the photographs and the text. I am deeply indebted to Miranda Stonor, managing editor, for her attention to detail and endless patience.

My wife Angela has gallantly survived the long gestation period required for the completion of this task – she deserves a great deal more than 'mentioned in despatches'!

Note

The text contains documentary material, much of it originally handwritten. This has been reproduced verbatim as far as possible, although minor errors have been corrected for clarification where necessary.

INTRODUCTION

When I retired from the Priory Hospital, Roehampton, where I had been a Consultant Psychiatrist and the Medical Director for many years, the project to which I was most looking forward was writing about my father's wartime experiences. My father Norman went out to the Orient in 1927 to join the Burma Frontier Service and was posted to the Chin Hills in 1939 as war broke out in Europe (see map no. 1 on p. 2). This book, which describes events of 60-odd years ago, came about through good fortune.

I was born in the Shan States of Burma in 1934, near the Golden Triangle. It was when I was living in Tiddim with my father, mother Betty and sister, Maeve Patricia, that the advance of the Japanese shattered our world in May 1942. The British Army was in the midst of its longest retreat in history. The enemy was about to penetrate my father's territory, where he was Assistant Superintendent. So it was that my mother, sister and I were forced to trek out to India. I was only seven years old but clearly remember, on crossing the boundary of the Tyao River, looking back at Burma and resolving to return one day. My mother, luckily, kept the letters my father wrote to her from Tiddim and they are the inspiration for this book. Reading them made me appreciate how much they loved each other and the strain that the war put on their relationship, as it did for millions of others.

My first return to Burma was in 1986. In those days a seven-day tourist visa was the only one allowed. On my second visit, in 1997, I met Vum Ko Hau, who had been my father's stenographer during the war. He gave me a copy of his PhD thesis *Profile of a Burma Frontier Man*. He had been downstairs in the Secretariat in Rangoon, now called Yangon, when General Aung San and six other members of his cabinet were assassinated on the floor above on 17 July 1947. My father had worked in the same building in 1946, as Additional Secretary to the Governor of Burma, before independence in 1948.

In 1998 I travelled as far as Kalewa on the Chindwin River, the gateway to the Chin Hills. We were on the RV *Pandaw I's* maiden voyage (see photograph no. 32). A former paddle steamer of the Irrawaddy Flotilla Company, she was built in Scotland in 1947 especially for the rivers of Burma. Our engines required urgent repairs. Amazingly, Inland Water Transport had cannibalised a spare piston rod from a vessel in the Arakan on the west coast of Burma, flown it to Rangoon,

1

1. Burma in 1942

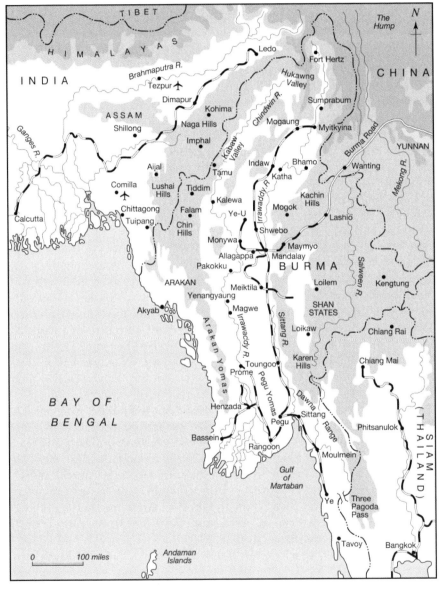

then Mandalay, then driven it up to Monywa – all in the space of twenty-four hours. Eight mechanics worked on replacing the propeller shaft. However, the power was still limited and the post-monsoon current was running strongly as we battled upstream. Below Kalewa it was so strong that it kept sweeping us back. The black thought went through my head that I had come so far and yet might not make it to Kalewa. I prayed to the *Nats* (Burmese spirits) to let us through and we succeeded at the fourth attempt. We were the first group of travellers to explore this part of Burma since the Second World War. I could see the Chin Hills, but most of all I longed to return to Tiddim.

Meeting Nicholas Greenwood, who is the author of an excellent guidebook on Burma and an expert on the country's culture and customs, was invaluable. He said he could arrange for me to get back to the Chin Hills. When he had first said this, it was difficult to believe that such an expedition would be possible. There are no hotels, no infrastructure for tourists, an insurgency problem and foreigners are forbidden. The roads, which are battered by the monsoon from May until August, are very rough and subject to landslides.

In spite of all these obstacles an interview was set up with the Burmese (Myanmar) Embassy in London, who were in contact with Rangoon. I passed the investigation and was then granted a visa to revisit Tiddim in 1999, provided a military officer accompanied me for my own safety. Major Myo Khaing waited for me at Rangoon Airport. A happy coincidence was that his best friend at the Military Academy was Major Min Lwin Oo, Commanding Officer responsible for Chin State, and he arranged for me to meet Chins who had known my father.

So it was that I was able to revisit the house in Tiddim where I had been so happy as a child – it had been rebuilt on the original foundation after it was burnt down during the war. The local theological college put on a 'Sing Spiration' as a fundraising concert before Christmas. The retired Education Officer, U Neng Khen Thang, who remembered Norman Kelly and our family, made a speech: '…he was our leader'. The sincerity of their welcome was touching. On leaving, he said two things: 'You are the first white man to visit Tiddim since the war' and 'If you cannot come back and see us, send your son.' Videos of that trip were sent to all the veterans or their relatives that I had been able to locate. My research was a race against time.

As a consequence of that adventure, which in addition also took me to Falam and Haka, I met several Chins, including Leo Deng Hau (the photographer) and Stephen Khup Chin Pau, son of the Tiddim headman, who was eight years old in 1942 and remembered my nickname 'Desi-men' (the Chins had trouble pronouncing Desmond). He it was who gave me a treasured copy of my father's address to the Chin chiefs, headmen, elders and villagers in Tiddim on 25 April 1942. The address includes these words:

In the first place the British brought you peace and freedom. Freedom from fear, freedom from want... I cannot believe that after fifty years of peace and progress you will surrender your homes, your women and your lands to the Japanese who will burn your villages, plunder your houses, rape your women, steal your crops and make you slaves...

This war is not a war fought by soldiers alone. It is a war in which every man must be ready to fight for the protection of his own family and home when danger approaches. The people of France depended only on their soldiers and are now enslaved by the enemy. Let us rather follow the example of Russia where every civilian man or woman is ready to go forth to repel the enemy and, moreover, these efforts have been crowned with the success of halting the greatest fighting machine the world has seen...

Let there then be no hesitation amongst us. Let us decide that we shall keep the Japanese from our hills, and that having once taken up our guns, we shall not lay them down again until he is driven back to his own land.

After much debate they agreed to fight with the British and the Chin Levies were formed.

Major-General Ian Lyall Grant's book, *Burma: The Turning Point*, was published in 1993. We corresponded and he mentioned my father in his second book, with co-author Kazuo Tamayama, *Burma 1942: The Japanese Invasion* (1999). Professor Kenny Fraser, who had been the medical officer of the Chin Hills Battalion, and had won the Military Cross, read it; he had known my father well and contacted me. During our lengthy correspondence, for he lived in Scotland, he published *'Don't Believe a Word of It!'* (1999), under his Chin name 'Sii Boi-pa' (Doctor Sahib). It is a little gem, dedicated to the Chins. I took copies of it with me when I visited them. We were to meet just a year before he died, aged 84, in 2001. Ours had been a very special relationship. I knew that he was not well and had sent him a chapter, hoping that it would cheer him up. It was returned unopened with one word, 'Deceased'. In that way I learned of the parting of a very dear and courageous friend.

My last expedition to Burma was in 2001. I very much wanted to visit the National Archives in Rangoon (Yangon) but this is no easy matter and requires a written application to the Director General. The staff could not have been more helpful. The records of the British administration are beautifully catalogued and through them the missing parts of my father's tale fell into place.

War brings out the best and worst in humanity. This is the story of a moment in history long forgotten by the British. As one of the last children of the Raj, it has been my privilege to meet some of the men who took part in the Burma campaign.

...Still through chaos
Works on the ancient plan,
And two things have altered not
Since first the world began –
The beauty of the wild green earth
And the bravery of man.

> T. P. Cameron Wilson, from 'Magpies in Picardy',
> in *Other Men's Flowers*, ed. A. P. Wavell

PROLOGUE

by my sister Maeve Patricia

Norman Wilson Kelly was born in Liverpool on 4 July 1904. His parents were Irish; his father was a customs officer, and he was the youngest in a family of twin brothers, Harold and George, and sister Lily. The Kellys originated in the west of Ireland and, thanks to centuries of invasions from the Mediterranean, were dark-haired, dark-eyed and of a fiery disposition. So was Norman.

Mrs Lily Kelly senior had a fine voice and sang in concerts and choirs in and around Liverpool. She doted on my father and was reluctant for him to go to school. He recalled being hidden behind her skirts (or more likely in some better place of household concealment) when the school inspector called. Desmond and I never knew our paternal grandparents.

'Kelly the Customs' was posted to West Hartlepool during the First World War and Pa remembered with horror, as a boy, watching a German Zeppelin being shot down over the sea. What upset him most, apart from identifying with the agony of the burning crew, was the loud and jingoistic rejoicing of the local people at this human tragedy. But war is war. Later in life he, like others, had to make fine-tuned moral decisions; the power of life and death he also found in his hands, not actually having sought them.

Pa had many talents – painting, writing and music, among others – and was also left-handed. His father used to tie his left hand behind his back and forced him to use his right as often as possible, but to no avail. Modern neuropsychologists might argue that this coercing of the left–right brain activity could have had damaging consequences on the child's personality. These subtleties were not yet considered during the early decades of the twentieth century; people were still getting to grips with Freud's and Einstein's revolutionary theories.

My father's education, when he finally embarked upon it, led him to Ripon Grammar School, Yorkshire, between 1917 and 1923. He passed his Junior and Senior Cambridge Certificates with Honours as well as his Higher School Certificate (A levels), being awarded the County Major and the de Grey scholarships. He was captain of school. He was also captain of the 1st XV rugby (see photograph no. 1) and the 1st XI cricket for two years and hockey for one year. He was secretary of the Debating and Scientific Societies and belonged to the Union and Law Societies. He played the organ in Ripon Cathedral and all his life enjoyed playing the piano whenever there was one around. In 1923 he went up to St Catharine's College, Cambridge, as a Crabtree Exhibitioner (see photograph no. 2). He achieved a Part I History Tripos in 1925 and Part II Law Tripos, for which he was awarded a BA degree in 1926.

We gather that he also played rugger and cricket for his college but the main tales that Mother recounted were more to do with his pranks with a lifelong friend called Ian Wallace, who had rowed for Bedford School. Ian was in the same college and later distinguished himself by passing out eighth in the Indian Civil Service examination in 1927. His first option was Bengal, because he had an uncle there. His second was Burma, because his friend Norman Kelly had gone there that year. Another distinguished St Catharine's student was Tunku Abdul Rahman, later to become Prime Minister of Malaya.

Ian Wallace was an important member of the exclusive five-membered Quincunx Club at Cambridge. He was named, by Norman, 'the Wily Scot, Keeper of all the Privy Purses if he gets the chance'. The President was W. M. Knight, 'the White-haired Boy'. R. O. Anderson and C. Casson were also comrades in wickedness! There was the occasion when these spirited young men set the college chapel bell ringing in the middle of the night and the time when my father inadvertently set his bedclothes on fire (Pa was an ardent smoker as well as inheriting the Irish propensity for alcohol intake). And then there was the episode when he was rusticated – sent down for the rest of the term – for one or other of these pranks or mishaps. By this time 'Kelly the Customs' had been posted from Yorkshire to Harwich, Essex, and the family had a house in Dovercourt, an elegant resort nearby. His son cycled the 50-odd miles from Cambridge to the coast in disgrace – his father was reputedly a tartar. However, rustication turned out to be a fortunate circumstance, for this is how our parents met.

Mother, Annie Elizabeth Megarry, was born on 16 February 1904 in the family home, 'Walnutvale', near Lisburn, Northern Ireland. She was fourth in an early-orphaned gentleman farming family of eight (the Megarrys had been awarded lands following the Battle of the Boyne in the seventeeth century). Mother was working for her degree at Queen's University, Belfast, and had been feeling peaky during that summer of 1925 so she had been sent over to holiday with an aunt who also happened to have taken a house in Dovercourt.

Betty Megarry and a girl cousin were strolling along the Dovercourt esplanade by the sea and passed two young men on a bench who were also viewing the passing parade that afternoon. My father's rustication had turned out to be a blessing in disguise. He looked at Betty and liked what he saw and the way in which she walked. She was slim, hazel-eyed, and her Eton-cropped hair, all the rage in the Roaring Twenties was, as he recalled, the colour of corn. Betty was also of a lively disposition and not short of suitors. Indeed, some of those that she refused in marriage later became senior figures in Irish political and literary circles. Norman began courting Betty, but mostly at a distance. He was still reading for his degree and was one of the many undergraduates who volunteered to drive trucks during the General Strike of 1926.

Oxford and Cambridge undergraduates were influenced by tutors who had served in, or had connections with, India and Burma. At Oxford a leading historian and author of *The History of Burma* was G. E. Harvey. He had previously served in the Indian Civil Service (ICS). Many of those who returned to the universities after service abroad had a nostalgic affection for Burma and its peoples. Before 1937 Burma was treated as a province of India and there were two main routes of entry for young graduates wishing to become administrators in the East – the ICS, which held competitive examinations, and the Burma Frontier Service (BFrS), where selection was by interview. The Burma Frontier Service, as its name implies, administered the wild frontier areas of Burma, such as the Shan States and the Chin Hills, where headhunting had been prevalent. Its brief was to maintain law and order, dispense justice, provide medical and social welfare, ensure the rights of the indigenous people and raise taxes. A law degree or a flair for languages, self-sufficiency and leadership were what the Burma Frontier Service was looking for. Physical prowess, stamina, being an 'all-rounder' and the ability 'to put oneself into other men's shoes' were what was required. For my father the challenge of the Burma Frontier Service was irresistible.

By 1927 my father had been appointed to the Burma Frontier Service and for the next twenty-one years dedicated himself to the service of Great Britain and Burma. In 1928 – during his probationary year – he wrote to his parents about life in Burma, which gives an enlightening description of what it was like for a young trainee in those days. He was stationed in Bassein, 118 miles from Rangoon in the Irrawaddy Delta. The following extract recounts the story of a holiday with a friend.

> I have cast about for an appropriate title to cover this record of our adventure, and considering all the facts and our too frequent anguish of body and mind, I can think of nothing better than to inscribe it as

A record of our trip to Sin-ma
or
On the Road to Ruin, Mother

(In extenuation of the weakness of the pun I can only plead with the patient reader to be indulgent and to realise that such trials as are hereinafter recorded are sufficient to blunt even the most powerful wit. Incidentally, Sinma actually means a female elephant and has no connection with Sin or with this plebeian term of maternal endearment.)

Thursday, April 12th 1928

I had been looking forward keenly to this time, and for several days I was busy with Beadon, the District Assistant Superintendent of Police, who was to accompany me, making all the necessary arrangements. We had written to Sinma to tell the Headman to prepare a shelter for us and to Ngakwa about the provision of a camping ground in the jungle where we could rest for breakfast during the long march over the hills. The job of arranging the coolies was a great joke for we had no idea how many we should want, and the more we argued the point the greater the number became as we thought of further articles which were essential to our comfort. We had laid in all the stores by Wednesday night, and Thursday morning saw the commencement of the fun, for Beadon was to collect me at the Bungalow Jetty, in a small police motor launch at 8 a.m.

I was up by 5 a.m. in order to get my bedding packed and after breakfast Beadon turned up, twenty minutes late, since the engine had been misbehaving on the way down the river. Had we but realised we might have known that the beastly launch intended to play some pranks but, full of optimism, we overlooked this obviously bad omen. By 8.30 a.m. I had got the launch pretty completely filled with our gear, in fact it seemed almost in the nature of a complete furniture removal. Nevertheless, although it certainly appeared to weigh several tons we had the satisfaction that we were not carrying superfluous gear and at 8.30 a.m. we got away, to the great amusement of the Scottish twin who seemed quite morbid at the prospect of having to send out a party to collect the bodies if we collapsed in the jungle from exhaustion during the march!

And so down the Bassein river (Ngawun) in high glee. At 1.30 p.m. we left the Ngawun and headed into a smaller creek, the Thandwe River. Nothing remarkable so far although the launch became frightfully stuffy with the fumes of the exhaust gases as the day grew hotter. We had to use this small launch owing to the numerous sandbars in this smaller river so we just had to endure the increasing discomfort of being penned up among the gear, hardly able to move at all to relieve the cramped condition of our legs. Needless to say I took the opportunity to revile a Police Force which provides such poor accommodation for its officers. One up on Beadon!

About this time (10.30) we decided to have some food. My boy, Po Si, unearthed the food supply and the luncheon outfit. What a sight! We got the plates laid out on one of the boxes, and the next thing I saw was Po Si diving a grimy hand into the box where he stores all the sooty cooking pots, to produce a cold chicken which, being a bit greasy, slipped out of his dirty fingers and was momentarily lost between a uniform-case and my valise. It was retrieved, not much the worse for the wear and tear. Some cold roasted potatoes were also produced by Po Si by the same 'sleight of hand'.

We both decided that we didn't exactly like such crude conjuring tricks with the food we were expected to eat. But since there was nothing else for it, we just wired in and tried to forget that the chicken had attempted suicide in the bilge water or that the potatoes had acquired an added flavour from contact with the unclean hands of my *lugale* [young man]. These little things are surely sent to try one on any camping adventure, and the fact remains that we did full justice to the damaged victuals. After this unorthodox meal we dozed fitfully but owing to our cramped positions and the vibration of the engine it was not much of a success, for one can't find great comfort in using the sharp edge of a camping basket as a pillow. Consequently we sought solace in reading for a while.

At 1 p.m. we were aroused by a gasping cough from the engine, and a complete cessation of all activity when we were five miles from our destination – Ngakwa. All things considered, we displayed commendable self-restraint and treated the matter with philosophic calm. We continued to read, although I must admit I cast occasional furtive glances at the *serang* [boatman] to see what hope there was of getting under way soon. For two hours the *serang* fooled around trying to put things right, but by 3 p.m. our patience had worn so thin that we held a council of war, and decided that since the *serang* seemed bent on taking the engine to pieces, and since he didn't look to know much about it, we might render valuable aid and do the dread deed in much less time. Trading on a youthful knowledge of motor engines we started in, thinking that this beastly marine engine would not present any great difficulty…

There's a slight hiatus here since it is undesirable to record our remarks on the incompetence of government *serangs* and the inefficiency of government launches. However, we were not to be beaten by this stubborn product of HM Dockyard, and entered the lists manfully. What an epic struggle! We wrestled and prayed with a myriad of refractory nuts and bolts, and had the occasional satisfaction of seeing another limb of the enemy removed. At 4 p.m. we were still here, but the enemy was vanquished. Nuts, bolts, washers, exhaust pipes, valve springs and other debris of the fray lay scattered on the floorboards and were callously kicked into the bilge beyond hope of recovery. In the meantime, we had lost an enormous amount of perspiration, and were thoroughly covered with grease and oil. The trouble lay in the crankcase and still we couldn't get it free. However, since the order of the day seemed to be the complete crippling of the engine, I was convinced that no one on board could have done the job half so effectively as us. We also had the satisfaction of knowing that the beastly thing was at least rendered incapable of causing trouble to other intrepid voyagers on the waters of adventure for some time. Incidentally, the launch was still lying at Ngakwa on our return ten days later, and the *serang* was still looking for the missing parts, which had disappeared below the floorboards!

In the meantime, word had been sent to the village-headman at Ngakwa to come and tow us in, and we arrived there at 5.15 p.m. I'm afraid our arrival was not so dignified as I could have wished, for there's a subtle difference between puffing up in state and being hauled in at the end of a towrope.

Our gear was unloaded and the villagers made themselves generally useful in decorating the local *zayat* or rest-house for our convenience.

We stayed here for the night, sleeping in the shadow of an immense Buddha, which stood at one end of the open hut. After a comforting dinner, and a pipe, which restored my equanimity, I talked to the Headman and the elders on general matters of administration and checked the village registers. Everything seemed OK. Very little crime, no contagious disease, crops fairly good and no dangerous shortage of water. So far so good.

At 9 p.m. the Headman came with a request that we honour the village by attending an *Anyein Pwè* [variety show] which they had organised for us. We endured for half an hour the high-pitched screeching of the village girls, wriggling round in their native dances, and then we stole back to an early bed.

Friday, April 13th
Might have known that this was our unlucky day. We were up at 4 a.m. and after a wash and cup of tea we packed up. The moon was still high but by 5.20 a.m., when we had got all the coolies fixed up, dawn was breaking and we moved off; an impressive cavalcade of 19 coolies, 2 police constables, 2 *lugales* and ourselves, together with the hound from the monastery which insisted on coming too. Two hours march saw us through the paddy fields and into the jungle where Beadon got a green pigeon. Unfortunately, I only had my express rifle in case we met anything bigger. We were already pretty hot by the time we reached the first great hill. My shirt was thoroughly soaked and perspiration was streaming down to the knees of my breeches. On descending the far side of the hill we arrived at Kywè Sakan – a deep glen on the right of the precipitous path, through which flowed a mountain stream. By this time we were so hot that we just scrambled down recklessly and threw ourselves into the stream. In a few minutes we pressed on from this, our first halt.

About 9.45 a.m. we reached the camping ground where we intended to breakfast – Michaunggon Sakan. What a relief! We had been walking 4 ½ hours with only one sign of water. The day was getting much hotter as the sun rose, and even though it did not penetrate the jungle, everything was frightfully still and stuffy. Here I changed into open shorts and discarded my leggings. We attacked the basket where the soda water was stored and thoroughly enjoyed this refresher, since the river water was unsafe.

While the boys were preparing breakfast we rested quietly in the shade and comparative coolness of a *dhani*-leaf shelter which had been erected for our convenience. I rigged up my camp bed and had only lain down for a few minutes before Beadon butted in to tell me there was a beastly great snake among the leaves forming the wall of the hut. The brute was not more than a couple of feet from my bed. I got such a fright that I took one frantic leap to the other side of the hut. In fact I moved so quickly that I very nearly tripped over myself in the rush! I seized my rifle, but a snake's head doesn't present a good target, and in the excitement I missed it with my first bullet. Beadon let fly some No. 4 shot with no better result. We had clearly stirred the brute's ire for it slithered up the wall and across the roof to the centre post of the hut where it coiled preparatory to springing down. I didn't bother to shoot for the head this time, but hit it in the coils of the body, blowing it into three pieces. The head was severed about six inches down the neck and lay with its jaw snapping wickedly. The other portions were each over two feet in length. I never knew there was so much blood in a snake. The odd bits lay writhing on the ground and it was awfully funny to watch the frantic wriggling of the tail, when it happened to touch on the lighted end of a cigarette, which one of us had dropped in the excitement.

We made enquiries as to whether it was a poisonous brute and received the laconic reply, 'Had the *Thakin* ['Master'] been bitten he would have no use for medicine' – a beastly fatalistic way of saying that everything would be all up. Somehow I didn't feel quite so keen on our little shelter after that, but nevertheless we packed a useful meal – the inevitable curried chicken – despite the pressing attentions of some fierce ants fully ¾ inches in length.

At 11 a.m. we prepared to move on. You will see by the snap that the sun was now pretty well vertical and was beating down relentlessly through the trees. We were quite hopeful, though, for our deluded guide told us we had covered about half the distance. Of course we still had the main mountain pass to negotiate, but we fully expected to reach Sinma by about 2.30 p.m. instead of 5 p.m. as we had been previously told. Blind optimism!

After the restart, we didn't make such good pace as in the first few hours, for as we climbed the ground became rougher, the jungle thicker, and the sun even hotter. Nothing exciting happened save for a dreadful clamouring among a school of monkeys, which declaimed in no uncertain language our intrusion upon their privacy. By this time we were beginning to feel the heat sadly. Somehow the enterprise didn't seem so funny to us now; all attempts at joking and light banter were abandoned and we plodded along silently, grim and travel-stained. At 1.30 p.m. we reached another water-pool – Botènga Sakaw. Here we emptied our flasks of cold tea, thinking another hour or so would bring us to our goal.

And thus, having done the things we ought not to have done, we met our Waterloo! We had crossed the main ridge by this time and the ground fell away precipitously. We expected to find Sinma at the foot of the hills but at 2.30 p.m. we were still in the jungle and as yet there was no sign of the sea or Sinma. By this time my temper was wearing somewhat thin, and Beadon was labouring along disconsolately, having stubbed his toe pretty badly in sliding over some boulders. I asked the guide how far we had to go and nearly collapsed when the scurvy knave said it was about 9 more miles – 3 hours march! And here we were already feeling as though we'd just done the London to Brighton stunt. That guide will surely remember us, though not so much by the things we left unsaid. Soon after this we left the jungle behind and came out on a flat expanse of paddy fields, stretching for miles. At 3 p.m. we were met by the village headman and elders of Ywathit. They brought a gift of coconuts and the refreshing juice was most acceptable. In fact, we just guzzled like cannibals using the great gourds as a drinking vessel. These strange gurglings over, we enquired of Sinma and learnt that we were two miles from Ywathit, and another three to Sinma. I think the old headman must have seen the despair written on our faces, and thoughtfully lessened the distance for us, for actually it was another two hours before we reached our destination. By 3.30 p.m. we had reached Ywathit and changed coolies. Haggled over the cost and got away with Rupees 33¼ for twenty men. Poor blighters, one can't grudge them Rs 1¾ for such a day's work. I wonder what British workmen would do it for 3 shillings? Having got the new coolies we moved on again, and at 4.15 p.m. reached Magyikmaw, by which time we were convinced that Sinma was a mere mirage. We were told it was still 3 miles, and on hearing this, had to be revived with more coconut juice. Meanwhile all the female villagers turned out in festival garb; it being the season of the Burmese New Year, the Water Festival was in full progress. We were presented with bowls of scented water and had to go round sprinkling the village belles. They were frightfully braced, and even our jaded spirits revived miraculously. It was great fun until they got their own back by completely deluging us.

Having satisfied the villagers in this respect we carried on, muttering strange thoughts against Burma, its jungles, its hills, its paddy-fields [rice], its villages, its festivals…and its still invisible coast. In the open paddy-fields the heat was terrific and we were choked with dust from the dry ground. And still, far away, are more trees but no sea.

Quite suddenly at 5 p.m. we came upon it, but by this time our minds were so completely obsessed with the seemingly endless vista of trees and paddy fields that for some seconds we simply couldn't realise that the blue Bay of Bengal faced us at last. We had to follow the shores of the bay south to Sinma, so we just took off our boots and paddled along in the sea where the sand was somewhat firmer. At 5.30 p.m. we arrived at Sinma, after fording a creek waist deep and, only waiting to don bathing costumes, we threw our tired bodies into the sea. This latter half of the journey, across the Arakan Yomas, had nearly killed us, but cynical and short-tempered as we were, we couldn't but admire this delightful spot shaded by tall palm trees, with its endless silver strand and sapphire blue sea.

A hut had been erected and furnished for us under the fringe of palms, about 50 feet from the sea. It was great, and well worth every step of the 27-mile march. We just lazed about in camp chairs until the boys had straightened the hut and produced dinner but after that, healthily tired, we were glad to crawl into bed, thankful for the cool sea breeze after our energetic day's trek. We might have known that the 13th and a Friday at that could have no other end for us than sore feet, and tired and aching bones! But why worry? It's good to sleep and after all...we had arrived.

Saturday, April 14th
Having enjoyed a good night's rest we were up early and straight down for a bathe, although we were both so stiff that we did little more than laze about in the water.

In fact we were much too tired to do any great amount of work, and after breakfast we determined to spend the whole afternoon in siesta. We weren't allowed much peace, however, for at 2 p.m. we were roused by the din of a Burmese band outside, and learned that the villagers wanted us to join in the Water Festival. We told them to come back later but they wouldn't hear of it, and were so insistent that eventually we had to turn out and submit to the ordeal. It was good fun and after half an hour's strenuous splashing we won the day and routed the villagers.

In the evening we went for a walk and on our return were met by a crowd from a neighbouring village, which had come over for the revels. Had to submit to the same procedure again, but these people being obviously more 'high church' the ceremony was somewhat gentler and very much more dignified. Being pretty thoroughly wet, we completed the deal with a bathe.

After dinner I had a long pow-wow with the Headman and checked his registers. The village tract is free from criminals and quite peaceful. The revenue is nearly all collected, the health of the villagers is good, there is no cattle disease, and the crop is of good quality, though below normal in quantity owing to scanty rains and the depredations of wild elephants. The villagers are embarrassingly hospitable in the gifts of rice, eggs, chickens, etc. – certainly no food shortage.

Sunday, April 15th
Our day of rest and gladness. The villagers had put a dug-out canoe at our disposal, so after *chota-hazri* [little breakfast] we decided to paddle off to one of the neighbouring islands for amusement, clad

only in bathing costumes and topees. An edifying spectacle. Great fun. We found great difficulty in preventing the beastly canoe from moving in circles and a few yards from the shore it got broadside on to a wave and washed us out. However, with half an hour's practice in shallow water we became more expert and ventured out. We got to the island eventually, although Beadon nearly capsized it again in his enthusiasm, by trying to look over the side at the deep, clear blue water. The island was covered with thick jungle and since we had no shoes, we had to restrict ourselves to climbing over the rocks on the beach. The rocks were uncomfortably warm, and the sands positively burning. Consequently we soon abandoned our attempt to walk right round the coast, and retraced our steps. Paddled back to breakfast and slept in the afternoon.

Couldn't rest since we found the sun had played havoc with our exposed arms and shoulders. In the evening we watched the villagers fishing with a seine net. Retired early to spend a restless night. We were so burned that we did not bathe in the evening.

Monday, April 16th
This day it struck me that I really ought to do a spot of work. Hence I set out at 7 a.m. to walk round the coast to Thibyu to check things there and to make some general enquiries. Six miles, which proved very heavy going over the hot loose sand. Arrived there at 9 a.m. to find that the Headman had gone away to Bassein to pay his revenue into the Treasury. Most annoying! However, I made some general enquiries and set off back. By this time it was frightfully hot, and since there was no shade on the beach I arrived back about 11.30 a.m. very heated and exhausted. Lazed about in the afternoon, bathed in the evening and after dinner sat in the open while Beadon played his ukulele. Early to bed, but were disturbed about 10.30 p.m. by a heavy shower which penetrated our *dhani*-leaf roof in places. Fortunately it soon stopped, but not before a persistent stream of rain had penetrated my mosquito curtain.

Tuesday, April 17th
Went down to the police station and made my inspection. Beadon took the parade while I sat and laughed, as he became more and more purple at the ineffectual efforts of the men to execute the drill orders. Spent all this day and Wednesday in inspecting all the registers and enquiring into a case of assault against a police constable.

Thursday and Friday I spent mainly in novel reading, and having learnt from my fruitless walk on Monday I just sat quietly and sent out to the neighbouring villages requiring the various Headmen to appear before me. A case of Mohammed and the mountain.

Saturday, April 21st
Up at 4 a.m., packed and away by 5 a.m. Nothing of interest on the return march. We were pretty hardened by this time and didn't feel

so exhausted after the march, as we had done on our arrival. Breakfasted at the old hut Michaunggon Sakan. No more excitement with snakes. Arrived at Ngakwa 5 p.m. My mail was waiting for me and that revived my spirits wonderfully. After dinner we sat and watched the fireflies playing all round a magnolia – topping sight, but the mosquitoes were troublesome so we turned in early.

Sunday, April 22nd
Left Ngakwa at 7.15 a.m. towing the old launch which was still lying here unrepaired. Nothing of note. Arrived at Bassein about 1 p.m. to find the Scottish twin enjoying a siesta. However, I soon raked him out and he was greatly delighted to hear of our experiences. And so ended a ten day holiday which we had thoroughly enjoyed and which has just braced us up sufficiently to endure the heat of Bassein. It has been well worth all the discomfort of the march, and the only trouble is that this is the last glimpse of the sea that I shall get for years, until I get my first great leave.

During those years in the Far East my father's further training had included all aspects of law and a detailed working knowledge of all the local dialects of those varied peoples among whom he worked. After two years' training he was a session's judge with special powers in criminal cases to impose a capital sentence subject to High Court confirmation.

Betty became a teacher in Belfast and fended off the romantic opposition, one supposes, as this high-spirited young Irishman must have captured her heart. His letters had kept Betty in touch with all he did in that remote part of the Empire. He had also sent a beautiful emerald ring set in gold, and another to her younger sister Berta. They married during my father's next home leave, which was not until three years later in August 1931, and had a splashy society wedding in Belfast (see photograph no. 5). Their honeymoon began at the Ritz Hotel, Piccadilly, en route to Le Touquet. They had travelled from Ireland on the Belfast–Liverpool ferry.

Lavish as always when he had spending money, my father had treated his bride's family with characteristic generosity before and during the champagne wedding but, faced with the Ritz bill, funds had evidently faded. Honest as always, with his words no less than his feelings, my father had to say: 'Sorry, Betty dear, do you think you could sort this out till I've had a word with my bank?' And Betty duly did, the first but far from the last time she bailed out the two of them and, subsequently, the family of 'temporary fiscal difficulties'.

By the time he took his young bride out to Burma in 1932 my father was Assistant Superintendent of the north-eastern and south-eastern subdivisions of the southern Shan States bordering China and Thailand – then known as Siam (see map no. 2 on p. 18). The voyage took several weeks via the Suez Canal. Mother recalled her arrival in Loilem, a village

16

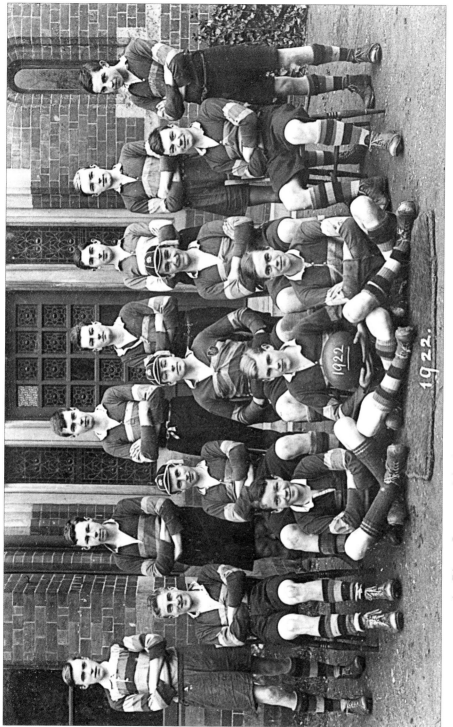

1. *Ripon Grammar School 1st XV in 1922. Norman Kelly (Captain) is seated centre.*

2. *Norman Kelly with his father William outside St Catharine's College, Cambridge, in 1923.*

3. Above: *Betty Megarry and Norman Kelly on the doorstep of 'Walnutvale', Betty's home in Northern Ireland, in 1926.*

4. Right: *Norman Kelly in the Shan States, wearing his St Catharine's blazer and with his topee under his arm.*

5. *Betty and Norman Kelly on their wedding day, 15 August 1931, in Belfast.*

6. *The bungalow in Loilem, Shan States, where Maeve and Desmond were born.*

7. Left:
Norman with Desmond.

8. Below:
The Kelly family and Toby the dog on 9 June 1938 at Taunggyi, before Desmond's illness.

9. Above:
Maeve with Desmond.

10. *Norman in the uniform of the Burma Frontier Service, with sword, as Headquarters Assistant, Taunggyi, in 1938.*

11. The Wild Wa headhunters of the Shan States.

12. A 'skull grove' in 1937, showing the typical wooden pillars with their niches, one with two skulls and the others with a single skull each. There was a semi-religious aspect to the headhunting of the Wild Wa.
(Courtesy of The Illustrated London News Picture Library)

in the southern Shan States where my father was stationed from 1932, moving later to Taunggyi as Burma Frontier Service Headquarters Assistant. She had been partially prepared for life in the backwoods but to a young Irish lady – as with other European women who followed their men to far-flung corners of the earth – reality was still something of a culture shock.

The Kelly home was a bungalow with a wonderful view through silver birch to the little pine-shaded lake (see photograph no. 6). The garden was full of roses, jasmine and cannas, and bordered the jungle. Elephants, monkeys, snakes, poisonous plants, insects and infectious diseases were all part of the wild scenario. Loilem was a 'one-man' station 60 miles to the east of Taunggyi. It was here that Desmond and I were born. The local people were gentle and fun-loving, for the most part Buddhist or pantheistic (when they hadn't been converted to Christianity), but mostly Roman Catholic or Baptist when they had – there were intrepid missionaries all over the Empire. Where their gods were those of nature, such as the *Nats*, these often required propitiation when times were hard, flattery, placation and sacrifice being a matter of course on the 'just-in-case' principle. Burma in those days also had everything in the way of natural resources: oil, teak, rubber, gold, silver and gems including jade, rubies and emeralds. It was the biggest exporter of rice in the world, there was a host of wild life, and it had a beauty that was unlike that of any other country.

Pa once described to us how he shot a leopard, spending all night in a *basha* – a wooden platform high up a tree – watching for the predator to take his bait, a live tethered goat. The leopard skin subsequently became part of a smart pillbox hat and a pair of gloves for Mother. He also shot other game, including a tiger, which became a rug. Now, in these conservation-minded days, killing these beautiful animals seems sacrilege but in the earlier part of the twentieth century it was considered an honourable sport in which man pitted his wits against beast. Often enough he had to, for man-eating tigers were not uncommon and bore off children and domestic animals from many a village in jungles and hills. Certainly Pa had no blood lust for these sports. Though he rode and played polo, I feel his preferred activity was trekking on foot whenever he could between those wild provinces, towns and villages or driving sometimes, when necessary, in battered motor vehicles over rutted earth tracks. At one point he had a Ford V8 motor car which must have been brought up the Irrawaddy by paddle steamer, as were many of our provisions.

Mother had a pretty hazy idea about childbirth when I, the firstborn, was on the way in January 1933. Her own mother had died when Betty was in her teens and sex education was not part of a young woman's repertoire even in the more liberated twenties and thirties. What she knew came out of novels, most of which, she later told me, involved women in labour screaming and pulling on sheets tied to the bedposts.

2. The Shan States in the 1930s

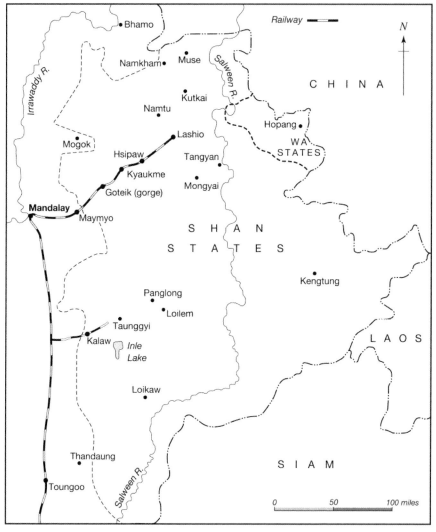

A British midwife was engaged at great expense, including her travel for hundreds of miles up the Irrawaddy from Rangoon. As I eventually arrived one night, a week later than expected, it was perhaps no wonder that Pa was under stress, to say nothing of my mother. He shouted at the poor midwife to do something about Mother's pain. Chloroform was the only analgesia in those days, and women in labour could hardly have had much of that, as it would have been a knockout and no good when they were asked to push. Maybe the local women had herbal concoctions or smoked opium. I was healthy and well, and Ian Wallace became my godfather. Not so with Desmond, born six weeks prematurely eighteen months later. His birth was rather more touch and go. He spent his early weeks wrapped in cotton wool soaked in olive oil. However, in celebration of the birth of a son, all the Shan chiefs (*Sawbwas*) gathered for a tribal ritual of monumental proportions. My own birth had been commemorated with the gift from a Shan princess of a silver mug emblazoned with monkeys, tigers and elephants. I have carried this round on all my life's travels, including the wartime flight from the Japanese, and it is with me now, 70 years later.

We had a Burmese *ayah* (nanny). From her I learned the local language and dances; in many ways, with hindsight, I related better to her than to my own mother, who apologised to me many times later in life for that early distance between us. 'I had no choice,' she said, 'European women were not expected to rear their own children. As it was, some wives pretended to look down on me because of my Irish accent.' Our parents, however, were not snobbish themselves. 'Always,' I remember them advising Desmond and me, 'treat everyone politely and with courtesy, not least of all those who may be our so-called servants.'

It was the nature spirits our servants summoned up when Desmond, in 1938, fell ill with diphtheria and hovered for three weeks on the borders of death. In the early 1930s Dr MacAdam, the Scottish doctor, did not have the benefit of modern medicine. He tried what he could but in the end, he told my parents, mortality's fate lay in loving nursing and the lap of the gods. 'There'll be a crisis in the fever,' he said, 'and it could go one way or the other.' The servants asked permission to pray to the *Nats*. 'There will be a death,' they were told by their priest, 'whose, we cannot say.' In the event it was Toby, Pa's dearly beloved springer spaniel, who had followed him faithfully all his years in Burma, who unaccountably died (see photograph no. 8).

My mother had wondered, on her arrival in the wilds, why such a dearth of furniture? But who needed it when bamboo provided comfortable seating, flooring, roofing and shelter for most people, even the cultivated Europeans who lived in brick-built homes. However, there were plenty of parties; alcohol and tobacco were part of the social way of life and people entertained each other, notably for Sunday brunches. I remember crisp and tasty roast snipe, mulligatawny soup, luscious curries prepared by our servants, who were constantly singing and laughing. And often the men played a graceful form of football – known as *chinlon* – with a wicker ball kicked skilfully in all directions, especially back behind their heads.

Later are hazy memories of Taunggyi, administrative capital of the Shan States, and watching polo; of being a bridesmaid at the wedding of one of Mother's Girl Guide friends, wearing a long ivory satin dress (how one remembers clothes, even at the age of five or six!). Desmond wore a satin pageboy's outfit. The scents of wood and bamboo come powerfully back; of incense, perfumes, exotic flowers, dust and cooking smells; and of coconut oil used everywhere to dress those Burmese-black gleaming coils of glossy-haired women.

In 1936 we had a home leave in England. I broke an arm tangling with a dog while running on the beach at Bournemouth. We'd been staying with relatives, the medical missionaries who'd been in China, Mother's Davidson uncle, aunt and cousins. On the way back to Rangoon, sweltering in the heat of the bowels of the ship sailing through the Red Sea, I developed chickenpox. Our crying, homesick *ayah* was not helpful. The ship was flying the yellow flag meaning 'contagious disease' as we sailed into Rangoon; I felt as though I had the plague. Desmond was emotionally traumatised by a *gully-gully* man (magician) who came aboard the ship at Port Said, put his hand up Desmond's trouser leg and pulled out a day-old chick! It was all too much of a shock and there were copious tears.

I remember visiting Mandalay and the royal palace of the old Burmese kings, its massive teak pillars and gleaming gold leaf everywhere, as on the thousands of pagodas up and down the land. Alas, it was to be shattered during the war, like our childhood world.

Chapter 1

SHAN STATES TO THE CHIN HILLS

In 1932 Norman Kelly was Assistant Superintendent on Special Duty in Loilem and then in Taunggyi, where he was responsible for the north-eastern and south-eastern subdivisions of the Shan States. He was seconded, as Civil Officer, to the Boundary Commission in 1935. This had been set up by the League of Nations to map and investigate the boundary between the Wa States and the Chinese province of Yunnan.

The Sino-British Boundary Commission

Sir George Scott had delineated the Wa/China boundary in the convention of 1894 to which the Yunnan government was co-signatory. Now the Chinese, hoping to gain mineral deposits, especially silver, were threatening to occupy the territory inhabited by the Wa between the Scott Line and the Liachen Line. The police had to be reinforced in Hopang and Lufang. Sir John Clague CMG, CIE (ICS retired) was one of the Frontier Commissioners (and the other was F. S. Grose)[1] who chose Norman to help with their work.

The Wild Wa were the most dangerous tribesmen in Burma. They held the religious conviction that they needed human heads to guarantee a good harvest (see photographs nos. 11 and 12). No white man until that time had witnessed their headhunting ceremony – anyone who may have seen it had never lived to tell the tale. There were other tribes, known as the Tame Wa, who did not hold the same views and were peaceful. Various efforts by the British had not changed the unsavoury practice of the Wild Wa, who kept one skull in the village until the successful completion of the harvest, while skulls of human victims of previous years were displayed in special groves.

In his book *The Trouser People* Andrew Marshall wrote: 'The Wa coveted the heads of foreigners, believing that foreign ghosts did not know their way out of the hills and so could not stray far from the rice fields they were meant to safeguard.'[2] Andrew Marshall had followed in the footsteps of Sir George Scott, who had described how heads had been bought and sold in the 1890s. The skulls of the un-warlike Lem Shans were least valued while those of the La'hu, who used poisoned arrows and crossbows, were worth three times as much, and those of an Englishman were the greatest prize. The *Gazetteer of Upper Burma and the*

Shan States also contains the following description: 'When the head, or heads are brought home, there is great rejoicing. The big wooden gong is frantically beaten. All the bamboos of rice-spirit in the village are tapped, the women and children dance and sing and the men become furiously drunk.' [3]

By the 1930s Wa customs had not changed at all and Norman Kelly's task was, to say the least, a delicate one. Not only did he negotiate with the Wa, but his duties also took him to Lashio, Maymyo and, from 7 to 15 November 1936, the Home and Political Department of the Secretariat in Rangoon. The Commissioner of the Shan States, Harold Nichols, in his confidential report on Norman of 1 February 1936, wrote:

> Mr. F. S. Grose of the Burma Frontier Service noted that Mr. Kelly is the best Assistant Superintendent in the Federated Shan States. He has been attached to the Boundary Commission since my arrival here.
>
> My assistant, since his return from the Wa States in May 1937, has been of the greatest assistance to me: competent, hard working, shrewd and honest. Gets on well with everybody. An excellent Magistrate and Civil Judge. Plenty of ability. Did very well in the Wa States where his tact, patience and firmness (Mr. Grose) averted trouble on many occasions.
> Federated Shan States Commissioner, 15.3.38.

The Boundary Commission was not without its physical dangers. As a result of his enhanced reputation Norman was appointed the HQ Assistant in Taunggyi, with the powers of a Deputy Commissioner, and became Secretary of the Federal Council of Shan Chiefs on 31 December 1937. For his work on the commission he was awarded the OBE. This must have been a great thrill for his young wife. The citation from the *London Gazette* of 9 June 1938 states:

> The King has been graciously pleased on the occasion of the Celebration of His Majesty's Birthday to give orders for the appointment to the Most Excellent Order of the British Empire: – To be an Officer of the Civil Division of the said Most Excellent Order:– Norman Wilson Kelly, Esq., Burma Frontier Service, headquarters Assistant, Taunggyi.

In 1938 I contracted diphtheria in Taunggyi. This was to produce a crisis in my father's career, reflected in his next confidential report.

> Normally a really excellent officer. As I noted in March 1938 – competent, hard working, shrewd and honest. Plenty of ability and tact. Keen on exercise and games. His work as Magistrate and Civil Judge is admirable – up to the best standard of the Judicial Service. Went to pieces completely in 1938 as a result of his child's serious illness – so serious that the Civil Surgeon slept in Mr. Kelly's house for three weeks on end. The strain left him a nervous wreck and he was no use to me for three or four months. He has since made steady, recently rapid progress to recovery and is now almost back again to his former high standard of competent disposal of

work. The change to a largely outdoor post should complete his recovery speedily.

Harold Nichols, Commissioner F.S.S. 4/5/1939.

On 28 January 1939 Norman was invested with his OBE at Taunggyi by the Governor of Burma, His Excellency The Honourable Sir Archibald Douglas Cochrane. My mother Betty, who entertained Lady Cochrane, the Chief Girl Guide of Burma, to tea (see photograph no. 13), described the State visit of His Excellency at Taunggyi:

> We were in the parade, with members of the Town Committee. I am glad it is all over, for there were weeks of Council work included when bed wasn't until 2 to 5 a.m. Norman was terribly busy as he had all the arrangements to make for H.E.'s visit as well as his own work. The banquet was held in the Council House and 120 guests sat down to a six-course dinner. I did the flowers and you can guess the amount of glass, cutlery and china that was required. We had champagne – but I didn't take enough!

Norman was posted as Assistant Superintendent, Tiddim (Chin Hills District), with effect from 27 May 1939.

Arrival in Tiddim

On 3 September 1939 we were on an Irrawaddy Flotilla boat steaming up the Chindwin. My father had been transferred from the Shan States, on the eastern border of Burma, to Tiddim in the Chin Hills on the western frontier (see illustration on p. 24). Momentous world events were taking place and the adults were gathered around the ship's wireless listening to Chamberlain's declaration of war against Germany. Meanwhile, I was on deck with my sister – Maeve was six and I was five – heedlessly playing hopscotch with the fillings from lemon cream biscuits.

We said goodbye to the romantic paddle steamer at Kalewa, where General Sir George White VC had landed his men in 1889 during his conquest of the Chins. Then, with the rhythmic chugging still in our ears, we left the riverbank and passed through hills of brilliant green to arrive in the flat, fertile Kale plain.

At Kalemyo we had our first sight of 'Chinland' and the towering heights of Kennedy Peak, which at nearly 9,000 feet was the highest vantage point. We were to follow in the footsteps of General White past Stockade No. 2, where his troops, building the road in 1889, had erected fortifications of logs to protect themselves from the hostile tribes. Then we were to go to Stockade No. 3 further up the hill, until we reached Fort White, named after the general. We stayed at a rest house overnight, 25 miles from Tiddim.

By now we were climbing into the clouds on ponies, with our belongings on mules – there were no cars or jeeps in the Chin Hills. Earlier in the year it had taken my father nine days to make the journey from Kalewa to Tiddim. Had we climbed Kennedy Peak, we might have

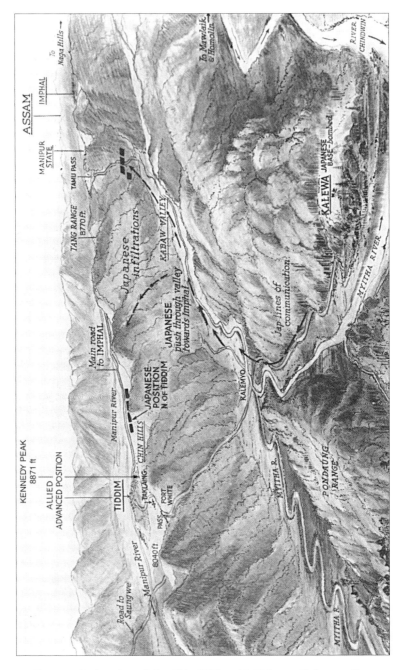

Panoramic drawing of the Chin Hills with Kalewa, Kalemyo, Fort White, Tiddim and Kennedy Peak, showing the Manipur River and the Tiddim Road back to Imphal. The Japanese advanced up the Kabaw Valley in March 1944 and cut the Tiddim Road north of Tiddim.
(Courtesy of *The Illustrated London News* Picture Library)

looked down through gaps in the clouds and seen a ridge at 5,600 feet which was Tiddim, the little village we would call home.

Our bungalow, with its grassy compound surrounded by pine trees and cosmos flowers, was high above the village and looked out on Kennedy Peak (see photograph no. 19). Who could have guessed that war would touch us in this remote outpost of Empire? Or that our home would become the headquarters for the British, then Japanese, forces?

For two and a half years our Tiddim childhood was idyllic. It's true that we didn't have other European children to play with but the servants spoiled us dreadfully, especially our *ayah*, a Sino-Chin called Mei Ngook. My father had a Wendy house made for us, with a wooden frame and bricks painted on the canvas. We named it Red Rose Cottage, and grandly entertained our parents to tea. As the Chins had problems pronouncing Desmond I was 'Desi-men' to them. To my parents I was 'Tigger', perhaps due to the hyperactive, bouncy child that I was or perhaps to the fact that there was a tiger under my bed. Everyone thought I imagined him but he and I knew he was there! My sister Maeve was known as Patricia or 'Rabbit'. We had no electricity and hurricane lamps lit our evenings. My father or a servant would pedal a stationary bicycle powering the dynamo so that we could receive the 9 o'clock news from London. Listening to the sonorous tones of Big Ben in such a setting, while shadows danced across the room, is something I shall never forget.

Once a month papers, books and comics were delivered with other stores, via Rangoon, by boats and coolies. Mother taught Maeve to read and she started writing endlessly in little notebooks. It would be a long time before my dyslexia (unknown in the 1940s) was diagnosed and at last I would have an excuse for my seemingly wayward efforts. Puppies besotted me and when our fox terrier, Patch, gave birth to Musso and Lini (one fat, one thin), I never wanted to forget the smell of newborn puppies in straw. Maeve loved Mickie, a wild Siamese cat, who scratched her all the time. She can still remember when my mother doused one particular scratch down her face with neat peroxide, the only disinfectant available. The scar faded only years later but it didn't get infected, which was the object of this summary first aid. She also adored Jacko, a red-furred rhesus monkey who rode around on her shoulder.

To communicate with the Chins, about forty-four tribes in all, my father had mastered some of the dialects. This was quite an achievement; even Tiddim Chins couldn't understand Falam Chins. The best times were when my father took us with him on tours of his territory to administer justice (see photograph no. 17). It was a great thrill to stay with him in the rest house beside the Manipur River at Tuibel, which had been built by the Public Works Department (PWD) at the turn of the century. After a long day's walking or riding we would be lulled to sleep by the crashing waves in flood tide, very tired but feeling very grown up. Our parents were devoted to each other and very much in love. 'Marmaduke', as my father affectionately called my mother, was wonderfully warm and very pretty. She was also full of ingenuity and common sense – essential qualities if you were married to a man in the Burma Frontier Service.

We were the only British family living in Tiddim, which, before the war, had less than 200 inhabitants. There were two American Baptist missionaries, Frank and Phil Nelson, and a very courageous French Catholic priest, Father Blivet.

Tiddim was the second most important village in the Chin Hills. Falam, about 75 miles to the south, was where L. B. Naylor (BFrS), the Deputy Commissioner, Chin Hills District, was stationed. He was approaching retirement age and my father was his deputy. The Chin Hills Battalion also had their headquarters at Falam. The Chins were effectively cut off from the rest of the world by their mountains and the biggest river, the mighty Manipur, became a roaring torrent dangerous to man and beast during the monsoon season. It was at the bottom of the ridge upon which Tiddim was situated and there was a suspension bridge across it, which could carry about six mules at a time (see photograph no. 20). There were no motor roads in the Chin Hills before the war, only tracks between villages, and not all of these were wide enough to allow a loaded mule to pass. Hairpin bends would punctuate the zigzag trail up the side of the mountain. Occasionally a vertical shortcut would reduce the distance, but increase the chance of getting lost in the dense undergrowth of bamboo.

My father's career got off to a good start and he impressed the Chief Justice, who wrote on 16 October 1939: 'On transfer. This officer arrived in the Chin Hills in May and since then has toured systematically and has picked up a great deal of the work of his subdivision. A very capable officer.' L. B. Naylor was later to write, on 4 January 1940: 'A very keen officer who should do well in his present post. Is learning the local dialect and is liked by the Chins. Believed honest and sober. Judicial work good.' Naylor had himself served as Assistant Superintendent, Tiddim, from 1923 to 1930 and had written a book on the Chin language.[4]

The Chins

The Chins are a hill race, vigorous, warm-hearted and very hospitable – the name 'Chin' is said to mean 'comrade'. They were loyal and tough, and my father had great respect for them. He understood the importance of their customs and culture, and their pride in their traditions. They were originally headhunters and a warrior race that had given the British a tough time between 1888 and 1894. Among the tribes (see Appendix A) the most prominent were the Kamhau (or Kamhow), Sokte (or Sukte), Sihzang, Siyin, Thado (known in Assam and Manipur as Kuki), Tashon, Haka, Whelngo, Khongsai and Zahau (or Zahow).

The Chins should not be confused with the 'Chindits' of the Second World War. The latter was a long-range penetration group, originally led by General Orde Wingate, who were dropped behind Japanese lines in 1943/44. They did contain some Chins but they took their name from the Burmese mythical lion (*chinthe*) that often stands guard at pagodas.

The Chins have many features in common with the Lushais of Bengal and Assam to the west, and the Kukis of Manipur to the north (see map no. 3 on p. 28). Their methods of cultivation, manners and customs, beliefs and traditions all point to one origin. Their form of government was also similar, like the Nagas of Assam (who were also headhunters before the British arrived). It is thought that they may have come from the same stock in Tibet.

In contrast, Kalemyo in the valley is much more Burmese. The Shans founded the fortress city of Kale, now called Kalemyo, in AD 1397. It is at the foot of the Chin Hills, and it is probable that the Chins used to farm the Chindwin Valley by 'slash and burn' methods before retreating to the safety of their hills, where malaria is much less of a problem. Kennedy Peak looks down on the Chindwin–Kale–Kabaw–Myittha valley, the Chindwin being 'the river from the Chin Hills'. The northern Chins comprise nearly all those who live in the Tiddim, Falam and Haka areas. They do not include the people known as Kuki in the Chittagong Hill tracts, Assam, Manipur and Tripura.

The Chins used to come down from their hills to raid the Burma plains, especially after 1700, and often took war captives back with them to become slaves. Booty obtained by this means helped provide a new flow of luxury goods into the hills. In *The Structure of Chin Society* F. K. Lehman wrote: 'The Chin preferred his own hill country, owing to its cold climate, relative freedom from tropical fevers, and its beauty, but he was also vividly aware of its relative poverty and of the difficulties of his existence there.' [5] (The Kabaw Valley, to the north of Kalemyo, was known as 'The Valley of Death' because of its reputation for lethal malaria.)

The Haka people made a special sword (*khin khot naam*), which was used to cut off trophy heads from enemies in war, and it played a part in the ceremonial dances that marked the event. The steel blade had a handle of cast and polished brass, wrapped with red-dyed leather or cane, and was capped with a plume of red-dyed goats' hair (see photograph no. 15). The British outlawed its use soon after their arrival. In the past, if an old chief died, Chin custom required a human head for the adornment of his grave, so a headhunting party would be sent out.[6] *Ngal-ai* was a special victory feast, complete with hornbill feathers, red-dyed goats'-hair plumes, reed *phiit* pipes, gongs and drums. It had been used by ancient Chin warriors as a ritual of songs and dancing to ward off the *gal gau* curse that resulted from the taking of a human life, and was a very rare event.[7]

3. The Chin Hills

There was no alphabet for the different Chin dialects before American missionaries came to the Chin Hills. History was passed down by word of mouth. In addition, Chins often have three names – sometimes the spelling of these differ, and some villages even have two names! The father does not pass his last name to his son. This makes it more difficult to understand how different people are related.

Noel Stevenson, who had worked in the Chin Hills before the war as Assistant Superintendent Falam 1934–6 [8] and had married a Chin, made some astute observations about the Chins:

> The total population is approximately a quarter of a million. All of the northern and central tribes are closely related to each other and their neighbours in the Lushai Hills of Assam to the west. The northerners from Tiddim tie their hair in a bun at the nape of the neck, wear a broad cloth round the waist, and are known as *Mar*, while the Falam and Haka Chins wear a long narrow loin-cloth, tie their hair in a top-knot and are called *Pawi* [see illustration no. 14].
>
> Some of the numerous Chin tribes have hereditary tribal chiefs and an aristocracy, others have democratic political organisations.
>
> The clothing of Chin women differs little in its modesty from north to south, except in the length of the skirt; but even the shortest skirt is never immodest, so expert are the wearers. The dress of the men can be said to dwindle from little in the north to still less in the south, and the sex exhibits a magnificent resistance to the wide climatic variations to which it is exposed. [9]

Noel Stevenson's return to the Chin Hills in 1943 is described later in Chapter 9.

The British started their Chin Hills expedition in 1888/89, and had a number of skirmishes with the Chins. From Kale the British had advanced through Tulsuk and Phatzang, and a big battle took place at Leisan. The Chins fought with flintlocks and *dahs* (long Burmese knives), using guerrilla tactics. The British burned villages, including Tiddim in 1889, and occupied it in 1891. General White was in charge when a road-making party was attacked by a small number of Siyins in 1889. He estimated that a thousand rounds of ammunition were used against the British that day. He later described the Chins to the Chief Commissioner of Burma, as the 'most difficult enemy to see or hit I ever fought.' [10] (General White was later to command the garrison at the siege of Ladysmith during the Boer War.) In 1891 the Tashon tribe also held out against General White at Falam and he had required a considerable force to win the day.

The Chins were often armed with muzzle-loading flintlocks and they manufactured their own gunpowder. This was made out of soil, which had been impregnated with goats' urine or bats' dung (saltpetre), and mixed with charcoal and the beans of the *gataam* plant, which contained sulphur. Saltpetre could also be obtained from the filth heaps under the houses, occupied by pigs. The barrel of a gun was half-filled with gunpowder and then loaded with nuts and bolts or sharp stones and, later, telegraph wire. Guns were prized possessions, passed down from father to son; in 1943 a flintlock was found dated 1796!

Lieutenant-Colonel Ferdinand S. Le Quesne, of the Royal Army Medical Corps, won the Victoria Cross for gallantry in the fight with the Siyins at Tartan (Taitan) on 4 May 1889. He was attending Lieutenant Michel, who was mortally wounded under heavy fire. Stockade No. 2, at the bottom of the Chin Hills, and Stockade No. 3, halfway up the road, remained as strategic points during the Second World War, 50 years later, as did Fort White, Tiddim and Kennedy Peak.

On 31 March 1891, Captain Rundall handed over political as well as military charge of the northern Chin Hills to Captain Hugh Rose. He arranged for the Kamhau chief, How Chin Khup, and four Siyin chiefs to visit Mandalay and Rangoon to see the benefits of British rule. They returned suitably impressed and pleased with the kind treatment they had received on their travels. Captain Rose held a Durbar at Fort White on 23 June 1891, where Chief How Chin Khup and all the elders of the clan took the oath of allegiance to the British government and swore to abstain from raiding in Burma.[11] The signatories, who vowed to render aid in times of war (*sial ban*), dipped the tail of a *mithun sial* (ox) in the blood and sprinkled one another with it, calling on a curse that anyone who broke the treaty would fall like the hair of a moulting *sial*.[12] Eventually the Chin Hills were brought under control and the remaining guns were collected.[13] This nineteenth-century British expedition is best described in *The Image of War or Service on the Chin Hills 1894* by Surgeon-Captain Arthur Newland. The author later married the daughter of Chun Kai, a famous Chin chief, and lived in Haka. His son Sammy's contribution to the 1942–4 Chin Hills campaign is discussed later. Both father and son were held in the highest regard by the Chins.

During the First World War, the Chin Labour Corps, comprising 1,000 men, 500 from the Sokte and Sihzang tract and 500 from the Kamhau, were conscripted and sent to France. The Burma Military Police provided basic training for three months in Tiddim. The corps left on 27 May 1917 and went by steamer from Kalewa to Myingyan, where they were issued with military equipment. From Rangoon they passed through Calcutta, Bombay, Aden and Suez, and reached Marseille on 15 August, where they received warm clothes. They were then sent to camps near the front line on the Belgium border where they stayed from October to January 1918, in the depths of winter. Everything was frozen, even the raindrops from the eaves of the roof; in *Tedim to Yangon* Khen Za Moong wrote that 'One had to use eight to ten blankets and still shiver'.[14]

The hard-working Tiddim group distinguished themselves to such a degree that King George V in London expressed his desire to meet a delegation of Chins. The ten-man group was led by Captain E. O.

Foular; they met the King in London and returned to France on 27 March 1918. The Sokte, and then the Tiddim group of Chins, arrived back home in August 1918. Armistice was declared on 11 November 1918 and five members of the Tiddim contingent were each presented with a silver *dah* for their good services. One of them, Tong Za Kai, returned to his old post, as interpreter in the Deputy Commissioner's Office, Falam.

In 1921, in recognition of the good work done during the First World War, the government recruited one company each from the Tiddim, Falam and Haka areas to form the 4/70th Chin Rifles. Tong Za Kai became a Jemedar (one small star); in 1925 he was posted to 1/20th Burma Rifles and rose to the rank of Subedar Major (one small crown). (For an explanation of military ranks in Burma and India, see Appendix B.) He retired after sixteen years in the Army in 1937. In July 1942 he was recalled from retirement and appointed Inspector of Police Tiddim. He retired for the second time in 1946 and died in 1951. His son Khen Za Moong wrote *Tedim to Yangon*, which contains the early history of the Chins and Tiddim. In the past the Chins would take slaves – *shillas* – back to the hills after raids on the Kale Valley. In 1910 the British government had established a policy of non-interference in the *shilla* system. Pau Khen, the grandfather of Khen Za Moong, had petitioned for the abolition of slavery and it had then died a natural death.

A feudal regime still operated in the Chin Hills in 1939 and it was common for taxes to be paid by weaker villages for protection to landlords, generally collected once a year. These varied from a basket of grain per house to a pig per house per annum. A full-grown *mithun* would cover three years. *Ramsa* was another method by which chiefs and headmen could benefit from animals killed by villagers. This Chin custom could be restricted to certain animals, for example bison and *saing*, but not others such as *gyi* (Barking deer), *serow* (jungle goat) or *ghooral* (antelope). A portion of the *ramsa* animal would be given to the chief or landlord. Kamhau chiefs would receive a shoulder and the whole leg, including *gamsa liang* (hoofs).

The steep hills made growing food a constant battle. The high altitude and the cold added to their difficulties. The Chins used the method of cultivation known as 'slash and burn' (*taungya*), which had served them well since time immemorial. A portion of land would be cleared of trees and undergrowth – a laborious process – and burned to enrich the soil with nitrogen. The crop would then be sown, and a satisfactory yield resulted in the *taungyas* being used for a second year. When the earth was exhausted, they would move on to another site, further from the village.

Most of the dwellings were on the upper part of the hills, where hopefully there was a spring or where bamboo irrigation pipes could be used to bring water closer to their houses. These were often built on stilts on the sides of the hills, since flat land was so rare (see illustration no. 23). Growing rice was difficult, if not impossible, but maize and millet were less of a problem. Arthur Newland introduced giant corn (maize) from California, which was so successful that it became the Chins' staple food – *Newland Fawn-voi* or Newland corn. They could easily grow sweet potatoes, peas, beans, pumpkins, melons, oranges and coffee.

They made their own beer – *zu* – from millet or rice, in large earthenware pots. After fermentation it would be drunk through straws. *Zu* was central to their feasts, when songs would be sung, dancing would take place and guests in turn would be invited to the *zu* pot, and to suck until a prearranged mark on the narrow bamboo pipe (*peeng*) had been reached (see illustration no. 16). The common Tiddim Chin dance *Lamgui* is a long line of dancers led by a drum-man and a gong-man moving rhythmically to the beat of the drum. Boys and girls are in alternate positions, making up a line by joining their hand over the shoulders of the next person.[15]

Chicken was the most readily available form of meat but a type of ox common to the Chin Hills, known as *mithun*, would be killed for a big feast. For a smaller feast, a black pig would do. Meat, sugar and milk were scarce. Honey was in short supply and, because of the lack of iodine in the hills, thyroid problems and goitre were endemic.

Before 1942 in the Chin Hills there were elephants, rhinoceroses, black Himalayan bears, tigers, leopards, wild boars, various types of monkey, flying squirrels, Barking deer and mountain goats. The hornbill and its highly prized feathers had its own ritual significance for the Chins and the flights of various birds, such as the Indian cuckoo and shrike, were taken as omens. The hovering, gliding birds of prey used to circle as they were lifted by a thermal from the valley below, and some even attacked domestic fowl. The scarlet minivet cocks and their orange-coloured hens are the most dramatic of the soothsayer birds; there is also a white bird like a magpie, but with a red bill, which has a call resembling iron screeching against iron and could be a tree pie. Nuthatch, jay and woodpecker are still commonly seen. Birdsong in the wooded ravines, from the hoopoe, would bring back memories of Britain.

The British Administration in Burma

The Governor of Burma in Rangoon had a small number of councillors, in charge of departments, reporting to him. Then there were Commissioners, one for each geographical division, such as the Federated Shan States, Mandalay and Sagaing. Under him would be a Deputy Commissioner – L. B. Naylor, for example – who was responsible for a 'District' like the Chin Hills. The subdivisions, such as Falam, Tiddim and Haka, each had an Assistant Superintendent, sometimes simply called Superintendents, who reported to the Deputy Commissioner.

Just before Norman Kelly reached the Chin Hills a very rare event had taken place. The Governor of Burma, Sir Archibald Cochrane, GCMG, KCSI, DSO, had decided to hold a Durbar in Falam on 21 April 1939. At the last moment his speech had to be read by Charles Pearce because 'circumstances of extreme importance prevented him from carrying out his intention'. The speech is a good account of the British view of their relationship with the Chins.

Mr Deputy Commissioner, Chiefs and Elders of the Chin Tribes.
His Excellency the Governor of Burma planned, as you have no doubt been informed, to pay a personal visit to your Hills to acquaint himself with local conditions, to ascertain your requirements, and to declare to you the policy in pursuance of which he has acted and will continue to act in matters concerning your Hills. Unfortunately at the last moment circumstances of extreme importance prevented him from carrying out his intention and he has deputed me, his Counsellor, to represent him and to deliver to you his message. He has instructed me to convey to you all his sincere regret that he has been unable to come himself. For my own part I am glad to have this opportunity of meeting the officers and the Chiefs of the Chin Hills and of discussing your problems; and I shall convey to His Excellency the results of these discussions. His Excellency's message is as follows:–

Chiefs and Elders of the Chin Hills,
My desire to hold a Durbar at Falam arises from the fact that it is many years since the Head of the Government was able to visit the Chin Hills. In addition, it has been my particular wish to meet you in view of the important changes in the constitution of the Government of Burma brought into effect two years ago when the Government of Burma Act of 1935 came into force.

I am aware that many of you have undertaken long journeys in order to be present at this Durbar, and I extend to you all a hearty welcome.

No doubt many of you will be feeling regret that Col. Burne [the former Deputy Commissioner][16] who was the friend and the adviser of the Chin people for so many years is not here today, but I know that in Mr. Naylor you have an officer who is equally determined to do all in his power to bring prosperity to the Chin Hills. The welfare of the people of the Chin Hills is a direct responsibility of the Governor of Burma and, while as Governor I look to you yourselves to conduct your affairs wisely and to be energetic in making the hills healthier, more prosperous and better to live in, I wish you to know that your interests are my interests and that your efforts at betterment will always receive the help and encouragement of the officers of Government who serve under my direction.

In the sphere of administration practical effect is being given to these ideals and a Conference on Education was held recently at Rangoon. I am satisfied that when the proposals made at this Conference are put into effect they will provide greater facilities for the education of the Chin people and for the improvement of vocational training in the Chin Hills. I am glad to inform you also that a Chin graduate, who was until recently a Senior Master of the Government Anglo-Vernacular School, Falam, has been selected for training in Rangoon and that when he has successfully passed his test he will receive an appointment as Assistant Inspector of Schools for the Chin Hills.

I am also aware of the need for greater medical facilities in the Chin Hills and it is intended to re-open the travelling dispensary centred on Haka, which was closed down some years ago owing to financial stringency. Proposals are also under consideration for the improvement of the Civil Hospital here at Falam and for the establishment of a dispensary at Fort White.

The losses which villagers have suffered from the death of their cattle owing to periodical outbreaks of cattle disease have been brought to my notice, and arrangements are now being made to train Chin Veterinary Assistants at the Veterinary School at Insein for service in each of the three Subdivisions of the Chin Hills.

You will be interested to know that over 200 Chin recruits are being taken every year into the Burma Defence Force and that in course of time an equivalent number will be returning to their homes having earned either their pensions or gratuities and acquired a wider knowledge of the world. It is my hope that after retirement Governor's Commissioned Officers and other ranks will make use of the education, training and discipline which they acquired while serving with the Burma Defence Force for the benefit of the whole community when they return home.

I take this opportunity of congratulating the Chiefs concerned on the considerable improvements effected in inter-village communications of recent years especially as regards the provision of wire rope bridges. I am glad to announce that it has been possible for Government to pay a general subvention towards the construction and maintenance of wire rope bridges, which are maintained by the Chiefs for purposes of inter-village communication.

Your Deputy Commissioner [L. B. Naylor] has brought to my notice the immense damage that is done every year by unnecessary jungle burning. I recognised that your agricultural customs make burning for *taungya* and perhaps for grazing necessary, but the burning of jungle beyond what is necessary is, you will yourselves realise, contrary to the general interests of the community. I am informed that some Chiefs already recognised the importance of carefully controlled burning and that the Superintendent has been trying to extend this system of control. I would urge you all to consider this question carefully and to assist your Deputy Commissioner by preventing unnecessary burning and by punishing those of your villagers who neglect to take reasonable precautions to this end.

All these improvements will materially benefit life in the hills, and it will be my particular care to see that these improvements shall be maintained. This is in accordance with the desire of His Majesty that peace, justice and fair dealing should prevail throughout His Empire, and in the administration of the Chin Hills I bear these ideals constantly in mind.

It must also be realised that the application of these ideals must have an effect on customary law; customary law[17] is not static and cannot be made rigid; it had its basis in reciprocity, service being given in return for protection, and it varies with the passage of time in accordance with the benefits given and received. Where the benefit to the tribesman arising from the Chiefs' protective power has decreased owing to the occupation of the Hills by the British Government and the establishment in the Hills of the Pax Britannica it is in full accordance with custom that the services rendered by tribesmen to their Chiefs should also decrease. This has been set out in my declaration of 1936.

Customs relating to the ownership or occupation of land are also matters of importance and I must remind you that according to the custom of the Hills, a custom which is recognised by the payment of tribute in the form of house tax, Government has become overlord and protector of the Chin Hills and the Chins. While maintaining this position Government has no intention of interfering with the customary rights of the people in regard to the land or with the customary right and obligations of the Chiefs in allocating and administering the tribal lands in accordance with custom, and has no intention of interfering with rights of private occupation where such rights have been created or become established; but it must be clearly understood that all these rights which Government intends to recognise and uphold are only valid because they are recognised by Government which is overlord both of the Chiefs and the people in all the Chin Hills. I would impress it upon you that this declaration is in full accordance with ancient usage and custom and involves no change or innovation, and that as the customary rights and privileges of the tribal communities in their lands and of the Chiefs in administering them have in the past been recognised and upheld by Government as overlord so they will continue to be recognised and upheld by Government as overlord in the future.

It is with pleasure that I recognise the deep loyalty which you have towards His Majesty the King, a loyalty which is highly valued and which is so amply displayed by the number of men anxious to serve in the forces of the Crown. I wish to you, Chiefs and Elders assembled in this Durbar, and to all the people of the Chin Hills a steady advance in your prosperity and well being, and I assure you that I, and the officers of Government who serve in the Chin Hills, will continue to take a personal interest in your affairs and to do everything possible to promote the welfare of the people of the Chin Hills.[18]

The speech was followed by a Tattoo organised by the Chin Hills Battalion – with a parade of Chin heroes of the past, wearing their full Chin war kit of their time and tribe. There were tribal dances and a torchlight display by the recuits, 'The Retreat' by the pipes, drums and bugles, the march past, a firework display and the singing of 'God Save the King'.[19] The timing of the Governor's Durbar was perfect. Little did Sir Archibald Cochrane know that in three years' time the loyalty of the Chins, in this distant corner of Burma, would be put to the ultimate test.

In 1939, when Norman Kelly arrived in Tiddim, the village was made up of government buildings consisting of offices, schools, the hospital and the military barracks. The bazaar row, as it was called, began from the football field side, where the headman Pau Za Kam lived, as well as Gurkhas, shopkeepers, the Army recruiter, Vung Za Chin, and the tailor, Gin Thual. The house of the Tonzang chief was in front of Mang Za Chin's home. On the road to the school the vaccinator, Kham Khen Pau, resided. Below the bazaar the carpenters had their dwelling. Big *hiang* trees grew inside the town area and around the outskirts pine trees grew so thickly that pine needles formed a thick carpet that was difficult to walk on, because the needles were so slippery. All the Chins knew everybody else and formed a big extended family.[20] In 1939 one of Norman's first tasks was to adjudicate over land disputes between several Siyin villages. These were Buanman, Tuklai, Lophei and Khuasak. When a new boundary had been drawn, he arranged that it should be demarcated on the ground in his presence and witnessed by the chiefs concerned.

Norman toured the Chin Hills and managed to visit most of the 135 villages and hamlets of the Kamhau as well as those in Sokte and Sihzang tracts by November 1941. Chief Pum Za Mang was the chief of the Kamhau and the most powerful Chin in the Tiddim area. His main home was in Tonzang but he also had a house in Tiddim. Salt was in short supply in the Chin Hills. In early 1942, Norman and Chief Pum Za Mang had six mining wells dug 60 miles north of Tonzang at Cikha (which means 'bitter salt' in Chin). They were named after Norman Kelly and Pum Za Mang.

Norman's subdivision extended for 90 miles east–west and 120 miles north–south. Now the Japanese were approaching his north–south border and their 33rd Division had so far been unstoppable... Anxious days lay ahead.

4. The British Army's Withdrawal from Burma, May 1942

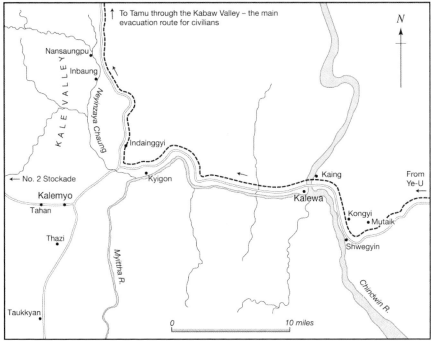

Chapter 2

A LONE OUTPOST OF THE EMPIRE

The Japanese bombed Pearl Harbor on 7 December 1941 and Rangoon on Christmas Day 1941, resulting in a considerable loss of life, panic and chaos, and they marched through Burma leaving a trail of devastation in their wake. The Army proved no match for them, for the Japanese had been planning their invasion of Burma for some years. The Prime Minister had said that Japan was unlikely to enter the war unless the Germans made a successful invasion of Britain and, unfortunately, this had effectively prevented any preparation for war being made in Burma. On 12 December General Sir Archibald Wavell was made Theatre Commander for Burma, but the country was not at all ready for the grim reality that was to come. It was hoped that the Japanese could be stopped at the Sittang River as they advanced from Siam but the Sittang Bridge was blown, with two brigades of Allied forces still on the wrong side of the river, on 23 February 1942. By 4 March Rangoon was a lifeless city. The massive exodus of civilians was in full swing – some 100,000 refugees were in camps in Mandalay and, later that same month, 30,000 had reached Imphal. Many had perished on the way (see map no. 1 on p.2).

On 5 March General Sir Harold Alexander arrived in Rangoon to take command. At the end of April, General 'Punch' Cowan's 17th Indian Division was strung out along the banks of the Irrawaddy River between Sagaing, near Mandalay, and Allagappa. The 1st Burma Division was 4 miles south of Monywa on the Chindwin, being pursued by the Japanese 33rd Division who had progressed up the river in boats. General Slim's Burma Corps was involved in a bloody, fighting withdrawal. Alexander's Burma Army had lost 13,000 men – killed, wounded or missing, and he took the decision to move the Burma Army back into India on 26 April 1942. The last stand took place at Shwegyin on the east bank of the Chindwin on 10 May. The 17th Division, with General Cowan in command, was, after a great gun battle, able to make its way 6 miles to the north where they crossed the river to Kalewa (see map no. 4 opposite). The Japanese 33rd Division appeared to have suffered more casualties in that battle than in any other in the 1942 campaign. Alexander took his men towards Kalemyo and north to Tamu, near the Indian border (see map no. 5 on p. 70). Kalewa was occupied by the Japanese on 12 May.[1] Under orders from the Prime

Minister, the Governor of Burma flew from Myitkyina, in the far north of Burma, to India on 4 May. The British were in full retreat and the Burmese had offered little resistance to the Japanese as they swept north through Burma. The question was whether the Chins would fight for the British. They had a choice, and Norman Kelly knew this only too well.

Before Alexander's momentous decision, Norman had met some Chin chiefs in Tiddim on 13 and 14 April. He sent a secret minute of that meeting by special messenger to his superior, the Deputy Commissioner, Chin Hills District.

Letter from Norman Kelly
to Deputy Commissioner L. B. Naylor, Esq., Chin Hills District

Tiddim, 14/4/42

<u>SECRET</u> No. 459

Dear Mr. Naylor,

Reference your telegram No. 164 dated the 13th, I am sending by special messenger a copy of a minute I have made of the meeting I have just held with certain of the Chiefs on the question of the Levies.

In your covering letter to McCall's scheme[2] you suggested I should call in my *trusted* Chiefs. In view of your recent information I do not know if I have done right in including Pum Za Mang, but I have no personal proof that he is untrustworthy, and as the bulk of our Levy must be made up from his [Kamhau] tract, he could not well be omitted. Nor can I say that I place much trust in some of the Siyin Chiefs whom I invited to meet me; at the same time they, too, could not well be omitted.

You will see that I am holding another meeting on a wider basis on the 25th to enlist the active fighting men for the Levy.

In your No. 209/213 regarding the Lushai scheme, you say you sanction Rupees 20 as pay for our Chiefs. Am I to infer from this that the other rates referred to in McCall's para 2(f) have also been sanctioned? If not, I suggest in accordance with the views of my Chiefs that the house payment of Rs. 2 should be dropped completely and that scales of pay be fixed for section commanders, platoon commanders, company commanders and that the basic rate for fighting men be increased to bring it more into line with the rates paid to previous Levies in this area. There are 8341 houses in the Subdivision and this proposed house payment would amount to a considerable sum. I expect to enlist 830 active fighting men, plus a reliable intelligence corps of probably 50 men. I would therefore have about 83 section commanders, some 21 to 28 platoon commanders and some 5 or 7 company commanders, depending on whether there are 8 or 4 sections to a platoon and 3 or 4 platoons to a company. Scales of pay commensurate with rank are, I consider, essential, and I think McCall's flat-rate scheme should be modified accordingly.

At this confidential meeting the scheme has been well received by the Chiefs, but you will notice they are not anxious to risk annoying the enemy by active resistance at his first approach unless they are confident of keeping him out of the hills completely. I have already informed you that I do not share this view. I think the earliest opportunity should be seized to test the calibre of our Levy in action. My idea is to let them have one crack at the enemy and then disperse for the time being until we reorganise for later harrying raids, ambushes, etc. I do not favour the idea of having the Levy organised on village group lines and lying doggo in the village until called out untried for a harrying raid after the enemy occupation has already become a fait accompli. If they haven't struck a blow before the enemy arrives, they are much less likely to do so after he has established himself and organised his own system of espionage by bribery.

Yours sincerely,

N.W. Kelly

CONFIDENTIAL
Minute of a meeting of certain Chiefs, etc. Held in the office of the Assistant Superintendent, Tiddim, on the 13th and 14th April 1942, to consider formation of Levies in a defence scheme.
(N. W. Kelly, Assistant Superintendent)

***

1. Present
   The Assistant Superintendent, Tiddim
   Pum Za Mang, A.T.M., Kamhau Chief (Tonzang)
   Thuam Za Mang, Mualbem Chief
   Lam Kho Mang, Tuklai Chief
   Suang Hau Thang, Lophei Chief
   Pau Kam, Limkhai Chief
   Thian Pum, Buanman Chief
   Lian Thawng, Khuasak Chief
   ex-Sub. Major Thong Za Kai
   ex-Sub. Thuam Chin
   ex-Sub. Za Suan
   Thawng Za Khup, Saizang Chief
   (Hau Za Nang of Heilei, who had been invited to attend, was absent)

2. The Asst. Supt. observed that the meeting would be of a strictly confidential nature and had been called by him in order to consider the present situation arising out of the invasion of Burma by the Japanese so far as it concerns this subdivision. He said the time had come for all to realise clearly that a very real danger of enemy occupation would become imminent if the enemy advance continued, and that it would be fatal to wait until it was too late before deciding what action to take in

emergency. He suggested that plans should be laid now and the necessary organisation arranged in advance, which would be put into operation as and when required to deal with a situation which envisaged the possibility of temporary enemy occupation of the area. He explained that he had received orders to organise Levies, which would operate under him in the defence of the lives and lands of the villagers, and that similar schemes were also being evolved in neighbouring hill areas, notably in the Lushai Hills. He said the facts must be faced squarely and that the Chiefs must have plans ready to meet if necessary the worst contingency that could be foreseen, i.e. that of enemy occupation. If such a contingency never arose, so much the better, but preparations should nevertheless be made. He outlined the steps that were being taken in the Lushai Hills.

As for Tiddim he did not anticipate that the area would, even at worst, be occupied by more than a nominal column of the enemy and that there was considerable hope that successful resistance could be offered in the initial stages by local Levies favoured both by the terrain and by their own knowledge of it.

Assuming that the enemy would enjoy superior firepower, he did not contemplate direct frontal attack but thought much could be done by adopting Chin tactics of guerrilla warfare.

3. The Chiefs present re-affirmed their loyalty to government and their determination to support the present regime throughout the ups and downs of the fortunes of war. In return they expected government to do all it could to assist the Chins. The Asst. Supt. gave them an assurance on this point.

4. The meeting agreed that a scheme for the formation of Levies was a good one and should be organised now. It was thought, however, that resistance ab initio would only anger the enemy, and would lead to a more ruthless occupation than might otherwise be contemplated by the enemy. Unless they could be certain of repelling the enemy successfully before he entered Tiddim, the Chiefs thought their ill-armed resistance would be non-effective. They therefore proposed that the Levy organisation should remain secret and should only be put into operation to harass the enemy after occupation had occurred. In other words, that the policy to be followed should be not so much one of active resistance to an invader as subsequent rebellion against the occupying power.

5. Detailed discussion of ways and means of forming the Levies followed. The Asst. Supt. pointed out that there were within the subdivision at the moment about 830 guns of all types – Chin flintlocks, cap guns, breech-loading double and single-barrelled guns, and a few rifles and revolvers. It was not thought that the Lushai scheme of the gunmen providing their own local ammunition would prove practicable. It was urged that the Asst. Supt. should arrange to lay in as large stocks as possible of ammunition, powder, shot, dynamite and flints. If possible, it should also be his responsibility to obtain more arms.

6. Method of raising the Levies
It was thought that in the first place all guns in the subdivision should be called in. Simultaneously with this calling in of the guns, a wider meeting

should be called as it was considered necessary that the people must be told then of the scheme to call out Levies. Each person in whose charge a gun has normally been kept – whether a communal gun or privately owned – should be given the opportunity to elect to enlist in the Levy. The names of people so enlisting would be recorded and the guns would be re-issued to them provided they satisfy the Asst. Supt. as Levy Commander that they are sufficiently able-bodied to put the gun to the best use in the general defence scheme. 'Caretakers' of guns who do not wish to enlist in the Levy will hand in their guns to the Asst. Supt. for redistribution. Volunteers will then be called for to take over these guns in the prosecution of the defence scheme.

7. There was considerable discussion regarding the fixation of a date for the meeting at which the scheme should be made public. The Asst. Supt. said every day was of importance and proposed that meetings be held at once in the Sokte and Siyin areas while the more distant Huites, Zoes and Thadoes were being called in to suitable centres where meetings could be held later. The majority of the meeting, however, considered that the matter was of such importance that all tribes should be simultaneously present at the meeting so that there would be no distrust on the part, say, of the Huites or Thadoes as to what the Siyins and Soktes had already previously agreed upon in the absence of the former. It was therefore arranged that notices be issued at once requiring all headmen and elders to come to Tiddim on April 25th, and to bring with them all guns in their villages together with the caretakers or owners of the same, and such other villagers as care to attend the meeting. The notices will merely explain primarily that a check of all arms in the subdivision is being made.

8. Rates of remuneration for Levies
The Lushai proposals were discussed in confidence. It was not considered necessary that a payment of Rs 2 be made to each house in connection with the scheme. The practice on this side is that the gunmen carry their own rations or take their food where they can, as they are seldom away on raids or ambushes, etc., for more than four or five days at a time. It was thought that instead of making this payment to each house enlisted in the scheme, this money would be better utilised in providing higher scales of pay for the actual fighting men. It was pointed out that in the case of the Labour Corps Levy and the Kuki Rebellion Levy, men were paid Rs 20, and that to obtain the most suitable men on this occasion some better inducement than a flat rate of Rs 5 must be offered. The Asst. Supt. undertook to represent this to the D.C. [Deputy Commissioner] In any case he did not favour a flat rate throughout the proposed force, as this would be detrimental to discipline. There must be subordinate commanders in the Levy and their position must be recognised by higher scales of pay. The meeting agreed on this point but pressed for a higher basic rate of pay for the gunmen.

9. Organisation
It was agreed that, as far as possible, this should be by village groups. The Levy should be organised in sections of 10 men with 3 or 4 sections to each platoon and 3 or 4 platoons to each company as expediency

demands. By organising the section units by village groups, it was thought that a healthy competitive spirit of bravery would be stimulated, whereas the closer bonds existing between village neighbours would be thus preserved. Suitable scales of pay should be fixed for section commanders, platoon commanders, and company commanders. The strategy to be followed would be worked out by the Asst. Supt. in consultation with his company commanders and the Chiefs.

10. Payment

Though not discussed in the meeting, it should be noted that before the Asst. Supt. found it necessary to leave Tiddim, arrangements must be made for the safe custody of the treasury. Supplies of cash will have to be maintained, and these could best be safeguarded by entrusting them to the Chiefs in the interior. Cash would presumably have to be obtained from Imphal or Aijal. Policy regarding the continued payment of pensioners, schoolmasters, etc., also requires to be considered.

11. Intelligence

It was agreed that it would also be necessary to have, apart from the fighting men, a corps of specially selected men to spy on the enemy's dispositions and to keep the Levy Commander fully informed of the enemy's movements in order to enable him to seize every opportunity to harass them. These men of the intelligence corps would be unarmed, must be utterly reliable, good linguists and versatile. As whole-time men they should be on a paid scale, but their pay should be supplemented by suitable rewards from secret service funds according to the value of information brought in by them.

14/4/42   Asst. Supt., Tiddim

Address delivered to the Chiefs, Headmen, Elders and Villagers Assembled at Tiddim on April 25th 1942
by Norman Kelly

On April 13th I had a meeting with the Chiefs of Tiddim. At that private meeting I spoke to them of the situation arising from the unprovoked attack which the Japanese have made upon Burma. I spoke to them of the possibility of the war being brought to our very boundaries in the Tiddim area and suggested to them certain plans which should be made without delay in order to prepare for the defence of our lands and our homes. The Chiefs agreed to the proposals but suggested that the situation should be first explained fully to the people at a larger representative meeting of the headmen and elders.

I have therefore called here today all the headmen and elders of the whole Kamhau, Huite, Thado, Zo, Sokte and Siyin. I have called you all here in order that no one tribe can say that they were not informed of what was being done by the other tribes. Let not the Thadoes or the Zoes say that they did not know what the Siyins were being called on to do.

I have been with you for the last three years, and in that time I have always tried my best to help you in all possible ways. I have naturally been unable to please everybody but I have always tried to be scrupulously fair and my orders have always aimed at doing the greatest good to the greatest number. I have not tried to hide things from you. I have not tried to help one at the expense of another. I have tried solely to treat you all as my friends and to help *you*. I ask you now to help *me*.

It is your custom always to settle your debts. You cannot deny that you owe a debt to the government for all the blessings that have come to you since first the British brought peace among you. You have now the opportunity to acknowledge that debt and to settle it by helping me in the manner which I expect from you.

When the British first came here you fought them and tried to keep them out of your Hills. You have since learnt that the British did not come here to plunder your villages, to take away your crops, to outrage your women, to make slaves of you or to destroy your ancient customs.

In the first place the British brought you peace and freedom. Freedom from fear, freedom from want. They gave you peace and freedom from fear of attack by your tribal neighbours. For the first time in your history you were able to live freely. You were able to keep your lands and to cultivate them. You were able to settle your disputes according to your ancient customs without recourse to fighting. You have enjoyed the benefits of British justice. I cannot believe that after fifty years of peace and progress you will surrender your homes, your women and your lands to the Japanese who will burn your villages, plunder your houses, rape your women, steal your crops and make you slaves.

The Japanese have attacked Burma, Japan is far distant from Burma, and the Burmese people have never done any harm to the Japanese. Why then should they make this war? They have attacked Burma in order to steal the lands and to enslave the people. They might also try to conquer our Hills and to enslave the Chins. We must be ready to defend our land and our homes against any such attack. It is useless to wait until the enemy crosses our boundaries. We must decide at once the steps we shall take to expel him if he should gain a footing in our hills.

These were the plans which your Chiefs discussed with me on April 13th. These plans I shall explain to you all, since I shall require your assistance in carrying them out in the defence of your homes and lands. I want your help and it is therefore only fair that you should understand exactly the nature of the help I shall require from you, before the necessity arises to call upon you to render it.

Every gun in your villages must be placed in the hands of the bravest and strongest of your people. I have just returned from Kalemyo, where I have been trying and am still trying to get more guns and more ammunition for you. This was in accordance with an undertaking I had given to your Chiefs on April 13th. I made an agreement with them that I would obtain as many extra guns and as much extra ammunition as possible, if they would provide the villagers to use them. I have already carried out my part of the agreement for I have obtained for your use 100 rifles and much ammunition, which is already being carried up to Fort White. It is your part of the agreement to find all the best possible villagers to make the best possible use of every gun now in the Subdivision.

It is for this reason that I have ordered you today to bring in all the guns, in order to place them in the best hands. If a gun owner or caretaker is unable to take up arms actively himself in the defence of our hills, he must nominate a brave and strong friend who will agree to carry the gun on his behalf and to use it in defence as required by me. If the gun owner is unable to nominate a suitable agent of his own who is approved by his Chief and his elders, I shall hand the gun over temporarily to any suitable man who volunteers to use it in the defence of your hills and your homes.

I want you to understand that this arrangement is only a temporary one and will only remain in force until such time as the Japanese enemy is utterly defeated and driven from our land. When all threat from the enemy has been removed, the guns will be returned to their original owners or caretakers, as the case may be. It is of paramount importance that our Defence Levy should consist of the bravest and strongest of our villagers, and thus each of them should be armed with a gun. I shall want additional volunteers to man the new rifles I have obtained for your defence.

Our Defence Levy will be organised as far as possible into village groups so that if and when he should be called on to fight, a man will be fighting side by side with his own village friends, and not with people from another village or tribe whom he does not know. The Levy would also be organised in sections of about 10 men each. These will be in the charge of a section leader. Three or four sections will be formed into a platoon under a platoon commander. Three or four platoons will be formed into a Company under a Company Commander. I myself will be your Levy Commander and I pledge myself to remain with you no matter what happens, and to do all I am capable of doing in your best interests. Any operation which I consider can be profitably undertaken by the Defence Levy for the protection of the people and the discomfiture of the enemy, will be undertaken only after the most careful consideration with the Chiefs of the area and with the Company Commanders. I shall remain in close and constant communication with the Chiefs, and for this purpose will require a force of runners.

In order to assist the movements and actions of the Levy it will be essential to watch the enemy at all points and to have full information of his movements. For this purpose we will require a force of watchers.

As there is no immediate threat to Tiddim, the men to whom the guns are handed over on undertaking to fight under my command in the defence of their homes and lands, will take the guns back to their villages. They will remain there until they are required for active defence purposes. While in their home villages, they will be required to maintain their guns in instant readiness and in good fighting order.

If and when the Defence Levy is called out to fight, men will be paid from the date they leave their homes. Every man employed in the active defence of these hills against the enemy will be paid Rs 20 per month from the time his active service commences. Section Leaders, Platoon and Company Commanders will be paid proportionately higher rates. For every rifle captured from the enemy, you will receive a bounty of Rs 50. Larger sums will be given for the capture of more important weapons.

I know that at present you are having great difficulty owing to the shortage of food. I will do all I can to assist you by obtaining supplies for our Levies. I have already secured a reserve stock of food, which will be issued free to our fighting men, if and when they are required to fight. I shall try to obtain further supplies, but I have already laid in 1,000 baskets of rice, 500 baskets of dhall, 500lbs. of salt and more than 800 blankets for the use of our men.

The Japanese are fighting so far away from their homes that they cannot obtain their food directly from Japan save with the greatest difficulty. They will therefore try to steal our food if they are allowed to enter these hills. We cannot live in these hills unless we can produce food for our own use. If the Japanese take our food we shall die. We must therefore stop the Japanese from reaching our villages. We must also stop every rebel Burman from coming up to our hills.

In doing this we shall not be without other help. Our Chin Hills Battalion has gone down to the plains to fight for us. If the Japanese approach our hills, the Battalion will be with us and will help us. You will have help too from the surrounding district, for a Levy of 2,000 has already been formed in the Lushai Hills.

Tiddim has up to now always had a high reputation for sending men to the Burma Rifles and to the Frontier Force. Let us now make an even greater name for ourselves. Let us all stand together in the defence of our homes, our women and our children. Never before has war come so close to our doors. It is on this occasion that we must prove not only to ourselves but to the whole world, our determination and capacity to defend our own hills.

This war is not a war fought by soldiers alone. It is a war in which every man must be ready to fight for the protection of his own family and home when danger approaches. The people of France depended only on their soldiers and are now enslaved by the enemy. Let us rather follow the example of Russia where every civilian man or woman is ready to go forth to repel the enemy and moreover these efforts have been crowned with the success of halting the greatest fighting machine the world has seen.

We must all be prepared to help. We must fight each for his own existence, for in that way only shall we conquer and be worthy of our victory. Let there there be no hesitation amongst us. Let us decide that we shall keep the Japanese from our hills, and that having once taken up our guns, we shall not lay them down again until he is driven back to his own land. We will kill him wherever we find him and the *Ngal-Ai* [victory celebration] will again be held in the Hills.

We will not fight him face to face, but we will ambush him at every opportunity. We will shoot and run; run to return to hit him again another day. We will steal his food supplies for our own use. We will cut his telegraph lines and destroy his wireless instruments so that he cannot summon further aid. We will wait for him beside our streams so that he will either fall to our guns or die of thirst in a hostile land. We will remove our food to the jungle and if necessary burn our villages so that he gets no food or house in which to sleep. We will destroy our roads to hinder his progress. In these and other ways we will keep him out of our hills, so that we can be left to cultivate our fields in the peace and freedom which the British government brought to the hills 50 years ago.

And now, I have told you frankly of the danger in which we stand. I have told you of the steps you should and must take if that danger is to be averted. I have told you how your Levy would be organised under your own leaders. I have told you of the help which government will give you both in money and goods, and of the plunder which will be yours for the taking from every Japanese or Burman rebel who tries to enter our hills.

I ask you therefore to consider carefully all that I have said, and to give me your answer tomorrow. The sole question is: will you or will you not fight in the defence of your hills and your homes? If you are true to your forebears and to your own sons, there can be but one answer. Thereafter, let us return to our villages to carry on our ordinary lives, knowing what we are expected to do, and ready at an instant's call to do it.

Signed: N.W. Kelly, OBE, B.FR.S.

Asst. Superintendent, Tiddim

25/4/1942

Norman must surely have felt that this was a pitifully short time for the headmen. In the next few hours they would have to reflect, consider and decide on an issue that would undoubtedly affect the rest of their lives.

Replies of the tribal spokesmen after consideration of the Assistant Superintendent's address, 26th April 1942

KAMHAUS

Spokesmen: Thawng Za Kham, headman of Muizawl

Chin Za Lian, elder of Tonzang

Thual Za Kham, headman of Lezang

Have helped government in the past – Labour Corps, Haka Rebellion, Kuki Punitive Column, etc. and have helped now with recruits.

They will resist the enemy if he comes to the hills, but the Siyins [west of Fort White] and Soktes should first resist him at No. 2 and No. 3 Stockades. If the enemy still advanced, the Kamhaus would defend their own lands.

They want to retain their guns for the time being for crop protection. They do not think they can get volunteers to use the guns, but if and when emergency arises, if volunteers come forward, let the guns be requisitioned then for their use. They think compensation should be given for privately owned guns which arc taken for the use of other fighting men, in cases where the owner cannot make use of the weapon himself.

They (the Lithu) say that unless the private ownership of land is recognised it cannot be said in the true sense of the word that they are being called on for the defence of their own lands. They want the same rights in land as are recognised among the Siyins and the Soktes.

HUITES[3]

Spokesmen: Mang Za Thang, headman of Tuimui

Thong Thang, elder of Selbung

They relate the help they have given to government in the past – Labour Corps, etc.

The Huite headmen formerly ate the grain due. The influence of the Huite headmen has been undermined by taking away the grain due, and they do not think that, on this account, they can get support of the people for the Levy. If government wants assistance, they will assist when the enemy actually enters the hills, but the arrangements should be made through the Chief, since all authority over the tribe has now been centred in him and not in the tribal headmen.

They do not think they can find the men to man their guns. In many cases they had bought their guns with mithun [Chin ox]. They want to know if compensation will be paid if their guns are taken away for the use of other fighting men or whether their guns will be taken and recognised as being their contribution to the common defence scheme.

ZOES:
Spokesmen: Vum Lian Kham, son of Gelmual headman
Sel Chin Pau, Phuntong headman

Relate the help previously given to government. They will fight if given private sale rights in land and if Siyins and Soktes first resist the enemy in their areas. They will fight in defence of their own women and children if the enemy should cross the Gawmual range.

They enquire whether compensation will be given on account of those who lose their lives in the defence of their homes. If we fight will government say we are fighting in defence of our *own* land? Following the tactics adopted against the British they think each tribe should fight in defence of its own lands only. As only the elders and gun-holders are present there may be better men in the village who might be ready to man the guns in the defence scheme.

They want fuller information about the fates of their sons now fighting in the Burma Rifles.

THADOES:
Spokesmen: On Kho Mang, headman of Hiangzang
On Kho Let, son of Hangken headman

Relate help previously given to government.

Cannot assist as no fighting men are left in the villages.

They want to retain their guns for their own protection if the enemy reaches their doors.

SOKTES:
Spokesmen: Khai Khaw Hau, elder of Mualbem
Son Kho Hau, ditto
Tual Kam, villager of Phunom
Dong Kam, headman of Zung
Son Khai, headman of Suangpi
Tuang Hau, elder of Kaptel
Tun Thual, ditto
Khoi Kho Hau, elder of Heilei

They speak jointly for all the Soktes — Mualbem, Saizang, Kaptel and independents, apart from Vangte and Dimpi villages, which are not yet in agreement with the other Soktes and will speak separately.

Will assist in fighting in defence of their wives and children.

Are not prepared to go beyond the hills with only inferior Chin guns.

Are not prepared for frontal attack on the enemy.

Will use Chin tactics of ambush.

Want no payment except rations, clothing and ammunition.

Do not favour conscription but will call for volunteers and will get them, though they cannot say at once how many they will get.

They want to resist the enemy jointly and not by separate tribes.

In recognition of their assistance on this occasion, government should continue to recognise their private ownership of land as they have hitherto done, and house tax should be reduced to Rs 1 and fixed forever at that figure. These two conditions to be observed after the war has been won.

They want Rs 300 compensation for death arising out of defence action.

They want written agreement as they were let down over the Labour Corps.

They say method of acquisition of land was practically the same throughout the Sokte tracts and therefore want uniform recognition of private ownership rights in land throughout the tract.

They want more information of their sons now fighting in the army and want to discuss the matter more fully at their villages.

SIYINS
Spokesman: Lian Thawng, Chief of Khuasak

His remarks centre around two main points: first, their willing determination to help and, secondly, to voice the grievances under which they still labour. Deals first with their grievances and says:

1. Labour Corps: People who entered this corps were promised preferential treatment in the issue of teak and gun licenses, etc. Were also promised exemption from house-tax. These promises were not fulfilled.
2. They have always been the first to help government yet preference is now being given to Hakas in appointment to government jobs in the hills, on the ground that there are already many Tiddims employed by government and few Hakas, despite the fact that the Siyins were always friendlier while the Hakas in the rebellion were the enemies of government. Claim that as they are the more enlightened, they should not be handicapped in obtaining these appointments.
3. Education: They are dissatisfied at the attempt to reduce their standard of education, and claim that higher education will not spoil the people.
4. Motor road: This request has always been refused on the grounds that the Burma Ministry would not spend the money. So long as the Chins and the Burmans are under the same British government they are like sons under the same father, and it is unfair that equal treatment should not be meted out to both.
5. The Tamu road: Their villagers were badly treated under contractors by the cutting of rates, etc., when they were recently asked to send labour to help on the road. In future they want to work under their own coolie-*gaungs* [supervisors] and contractors.
6. Fort White dispensary: They are aggrieved that this project has been dropped.

They want a written agreement and copies of this to be given to them, because verbal promises re the Labour Corps were never fulfilled. They want this agreement to embody the terms on which they are prepared to help in the present instance.

Secondly. They are quite prepared to help as much as they can.

They do not want to go beyond No. 2 Stockade to fight the enemy.

They want no frontal attack, but will follow Chin tactics.

They want no payment and say they would not be rendering assistance in the true sense of the word if they were paid.

They want government, however, to arrange to ration the Levy and to arrange food supplies which the families of the Levies could purchase on payment. This is due to the present shortage of food and the difficulty their families are experiencing in buying food at Kalemyo.

They do not want to be placed under the control of any military officer, and want to be under the command only of their Assistant Superintendent and their chiefs.

They think all gun owners or caretakers should enter the Levy. If anyone is unable to join, he should nominate an agent to carry his gun and to use it in the defence scheme. If he cannot find an agent he must hand in his gun and the Asst. Supt. must try to find a man to use it.

After the war is won, the guns should be given permanently to those who have used them in the defence of the hills. This should be the case no matter what the nature of the gun – private or communal. The present owner should be ignored. If he doesn't use his gun himself, it should be assumed that its surrender is his contribution to the common defence effort.

They want suitable pensions for bereaved families.

They want quicker, reliable information regarding the fate of their sons in the Burma Rifles. If they knew, they avenge their deaths if the enemy seeks to enter the hills.

They will have difficulty in getting suitable men to man the extra rifles which the A.S. has obtained for them. They aim at getting men to man the guns they already have. All their best men are already away in the Burma Frontier Force.

They ask that since deductions for the General Provident Fund of government servants have now been stopped, they should be permitted to withdraw the whole of the amounts at their credit.

After the war they want no further enquiries to be made as to the nature of their land tenure, and want full recognition of the present position without government contemplating any change therein in future.

VANGTE & DIMPI:
Spokesmen: Tun Za Sing, headman of Vangte
Hawi Hen, elder of Vangte
Sing Tuam, villager of Vangte
Zel Tiao, headman of Dimpi
Pum Dai, elder of Dimpi

Thought meeting was called merely for a check of guns and did not know this question of defence was to be discussed. Have therefore come unprepared to give full answer.

Have always helped government in the past and will now defend their homes and lands as government will help them in this. They want all the tribes to resist jointly. They have more than 80 men away from the village in the forces. They want these men to come back to assist in village defence. They will endeavour to produce a man for every gun, but cannot give the names at the moment and must arrange this at the village. If unable to man all the guns they will hand in the balance. They will fight in the Chin style of ambush. The Dimpi spokesmen agree with what has been said by the Vangte people.
    Signed: N. W. Kelly, O.B.E., B.Fr.S.
    26/4/42.

Further address by the Asst. Supt. on the remarks made by the Tribal spokesmen
April 26th 1942

The Asst. Supt. noted that all the tribes had referred to the help they had given to government on previous occasions, notably, in the formation of the Labour Corps, in service rendered during the Haka Rebellion and the Kuki Punitive Column, and in sending their sons to the Burma Rifles and the Frontier Force. He acknowledged these services with appreciation and said that in view of their past record he had never entertained any doubts as to the loyalty they would again display on this occasion.

At the same time he pointed out that most of the tribal spokesmen had in the course of their remarks adopted the mistaken attitude that on this occasion government was asking for their assistance, and appeared to be making this an opportunity for driving various bargains in return for help. He deprecated this attitude. This was no time for bargaining or for haggling over grievances – real or supposed. In fact, it was not government which was asking for help. Government was quite capable of looking after itself with the regular armed forces at its command. All that the Asst. Supt. was urging them to do was to organise themselves into a Levy for the sole purpose of helping *themselves* in the defence of their homes and lands. In this government would assist them, but it was up to them to make the decision whether or not they were prepared to fight if necessary in defence of their hills.

He was both sorry and ashamed that they were only *conditionally* prepared to enter into this scheme of self-defence. It was not his home they were being asked to protect. He had simply pointed out to them the danger in which *they* stood and had suggested the steps they should take and the plans they should make to meet this danger and to ensure an early return to the peaceful conditions they had enjoyed under British rule. If they were not prepared unconditionally to pledge themselves to defend their women and children against the Japanese aggressor, his mission among them would be at an end with the arrival of the enemy since he himself had no intention of surrendering to them. If, on the other hand, having learnt the facts from him, they were decided wholeheartedly to fight for their hills and their homes, he would take pleasure in remaining among them to do all he could in the direction of their defence effort. He would, in fact, become one of themselves. In doing so he was prepared to come to an agreement with them as to the main principles to be followed in the conduct of their defence scheme, but they must understand that as their Asst. Supt. he was in no position to make promises, the fulfilment of which he could not guarantee himself, and as for their grievances in the administrative sphere he would go no further than to place these on record as being matters which the people would represent for the consideration of government on the victorious conclusion of the war.

He thought it advisable to clarify the situation at once with regard to the grievances they had voiced.

In the first place they appeared not to be wholly satisfied with the land question. The Kamhaus wanted recognition of the same rights of private ownership as the Siyins and certain of the Soktes, while the latter wanted an undertaking that, after the war, government would continue to recognise the right to sell land as hitherto. The Asst. Supt. said he was not the Governor and could not, with a mere stroke of the pen, give them any final answer on this point.

He gave them an assurance, however, that government had expressed the intention to observe Chin custom and he had no reason to believe that any alteration in this policy was contemplated. It followed therefore that government would presumably continue to recognise existing custom with regard to land, as in other matters. If government had recognised private rights in the sale of land in certain areas in the past, he thought they would continue to do so in the future, and he would be prepared to support the people in any representation they might wish to make to government after the war on these lines. In the case of the Kamhau Tract and certain Sokte villages, no custom of selling land had been followed in the past. Government had undertaken to observe custom, and with regard to the land question in the Kamhau tract, was fulfilling this undertaking by recognising the communal nature of the land tenure system which had been customary among the people. At the same time government had recognised that custom was fluid and could be changed. Such changes in custom, however, were not to be imposed by government, but if the people as a whole wished to change their custom, they could petition to have the change recognised. This presumably applied equally to customs with regard to the land. He therefore suggested that if the people wished to change their land custom to the extent of permitting sales of land, there was nothing to prevent them after the war from petitioning to have such a change of custom recognised by government.

The spokesmen had also referred to their grievances arising out of the organisation of the Labour Corps in the last war.[4] He regretted that it appeared that certain promises had been made to them on that occasion which were not fulfilled later. It was to avoid a repetition of any such misunderstandings on this occasion that he was determined to make no offers unless he was certain they would be implemented to the full later. He had told them plainly that he was not in a position to give written agreements on points of administrative policy which he did not control. Such promises would not be worth the paper on which they might be written, and he therefore did not propose to give any. He did not wish them in the future to look upon his name as that of one who cajoled them with specious promises which were later broken.

The Asst. Supt. thought that the Huite reference to the transference of the grain due from their headmen to the Chiefs voiced merely the personal grievance of the Tuimui headman, and pointed out that the commoners generally had benefited by the standardisation of dues.

The Asst. Supt. undertook to place on record the other matters raised by the spokesmen, namely:

1. Their dissatisfaction at the proposal to close the Tiddim Anglo-Vernacular [native tongue] School and reopen it on different lines.
2. Their demand for a motor road.
3. Their dissatisfaction at the treatment of Chin labour under contractors employed on the Tamu Road. In this connection he said he had taken steps on this occasion fully to safeguard their interests in this matter.
4. Siyin regret that the proposal to build a dispensary at Fort White was being held in abeyance.

As for the withdrawal of General Provident Fund accounts of government servants, each of these would be dealt with on its merits as and when application was made by the people concerned. With regard to the question of pensions for vernacular schoolmasters, he fully realised that the present position might be construed as indicating an undesirable discrimination on the part of government toward this class of its servants as against other services under its control, and said he would be prepared to support their representations in this matter, after the war.

The Asst. Supt. then referred to the remarks which had been made regarding the actual organisation of the contemplated Levy, and of the operations it was likely to undertake.

He could not subscribe to the Kamhau and Zo plan of resistance by tribal units as and when the danger approached a particular area, and he deprecated the suggestion of these tribes that they would only resist the enemy if the Siyins and Soktes first offered resistance. He instanced the lessons to be taken from the experiences of the smaller countries in Europe, which had been swallowed up one after the other merely because each had stood alone. He thought the only hope for Tiddim lay in concerted joint action by all the tribes. It would be useless for the Kamhaus to wait merely by reason of their geographical position, until the Siyins and the Soktes had been overrun, before doing anything to help themselves. If he wanted to keep the enemy out of the hills the place to hit him was below Fort White and on the other paths leading up the eastern slopes [of the Letha Range] from the plains. We should try to hit him there, and if we could not succeed in turning him back, we should return to our villages and bide our time for harrying him at every possible opportunity.

He assured them that it was not contemplated that they should engage the enemy in frontal attack and he would give them a written undertaking on this point. The enemy would possess greater firepower than the Tiddim Levy, and he did not intend to throw away unnecessarily either his own life or that of any of the fighting men. They would follow their own Chin tactics of ambush and quick retirement, and the Asst. Supt. would not ask the Levy to undertake any operation which had not been decided on without the fullest consultation with the leading Chiefs and the Company Commanders of the Levy.

He would give them a written assurance that full compensation would be paid in the event of a man being killed while on service with the Levy. Some of the tribes were asking for compensation of Rs 300. Others suggested, in addition, that pensions should be paid to families bereaved as a result of the Levy's operations. These were points on which he could not give an immediate undertaking, but he would discuss them with Col. Haswell who was shortly to visit Tiddim in connection with the organisation of the Levy.

He sympathised with their desire not to operate beyond the Hills, and on their behalf he would resist any suggestion that they should be called on to operate in the plains against their will. He presumed, however, that this decision would not preclude their desire to raid an adjacent plains village held by the enemy or by rebel Burmans, if a favourable opportunity presented itself (this remark met with a buzz of applause).

He noted with pride their desire to fight only under their Asst. Supt. and their Chiefs. He undertook strenuously to resist any attempt to place them under Army control or discipline, but he had no doubt they would be glad to have the advice of such an experienced and gallant officer as Col. Haswell, who was well known to many of them, during the time he had served with the Chin Hills Battalion.

The Asst. Supt. regretted that it was unlikely that the desire of the Vangte people could be met to the extent of calling back for the defence of the village all the men they had serving with the Burma Rifles. These sons of the village would be doing their utmost to keep the enemy from the hills by their operations in the plains, and would there be even more usefully employed than with the Levy. In addition, the Asst. Supt. understood now that the Levy would have the support of the Chin Hills Battalion. This was more than he had hoped for when he laid his appreciation of the situation before the Chiefs at the confidential meeting on April 13th and 14th.

<u>Pay or supplies?</u> Spokesmen had stated that they wanted no pay in connection with the Levy, but wanted only rations, clothing and ammunition. In this the Asst. Supt. must consult Col. Haswell and would make known to him the wishes of the meeting. Supplies were being obtained but the question of transport was particularly difficult this year, and some solution to this must be found immediately. This matter was receiving the full attention of the Asst. Supt.

Supplies would be coming up in bulk and must be distributed to suitable storage centres. He would undertake to supply the families of those serving men who had no other male member left at home fit enough to look after the food supply of the family. Headmen and elders must assist evacuees whose menfolk were all on service with the Levy, and the Asst. Supt. would assist such people with food if necessary.

The Siyins had stated they did not wish to deny their houses to the enemy by burning, as their buildings were valuable. The Asst. Supt. sympathised with this attitude and would not press the point provided the villagers undertook to remove all food stocks, pack animals, etc., to a place of safety, so that the enemy at best would get nothing more than the unfurnished building. He asked, however, what the fighting man would think of the enemy sleeping in comfort in his house while his women and children shivered in the damp jungle during the rains.

There remained the question of the disposal of the guns at the conclusion of the war. The Asst. Supt.'s plan was that every gun should be handed in and then handed back to those who undertook to use them in the defence of their homes. Any owner or caretaker of a gun was at liberty, if he could not for any reason carry his own gun, to find an agent to carry it on his behalf. Otherwise the guns would be forfeited and would be distributed by the Asst. Supt. to any volunteer who came forward. The Kamhaus and the Huites wanted compensation for their guns. The Siyins suggested that unless the present owners or caretakers entered the Levy or arranged their agents, their claims to a gun should be ignored and that after the war the weapons should remain permanently with the persons who had actually carried them in the defence of the hills. The Asst. Supt.'s personal opinion favoured the Siyin view. If a man was not prepared to use his gun in the defence of his home or could not arrange to have it used for this purpose, he did not think he deserved to hold a gun licence or to be in charge of the weapon, and should therefore be required to forfeit it for ever. He did not think any compensation should be paid, and suggested that the value of the gun should be set off as the owner's cash contribution to the defence effort in lieu of his taking a more active part therein. As for allowing the people who used the guns on the present occasion to keep them permanently after the war, the Asst. Supt. could not give a final answer to this question as this involved a matter of policy beyond his control. He favoured the idea, however, and would fight on behalf of the people for recognition of this principle after the war, if he was still entrusted with the administration of the subdivision then.

Dissatisfaction has been expressed at the lack of news regarding the Tiddim Chins serving with the Army in Burma. The Asst. Supt. explained the disorganisation which must inevitably result in war, particularly when our Army has so far had to fall back. Units were broken up and it was difficult for Army headquarters to obtain accurate information quickly as to the fate of individuals. Their task had been complicated by the regrettable fact that some of our own Chins had deserted and returned to their homes.[5] In addition, communications had been delayed and disrupted as a result of the Japanese bombing of the non-military city of Mandalay. He assured the meeting that the Army authorities were doing all they could to keep the next-of-kin informed of casualties, but that delay was inevitable and in the meantime the people could not do other than to bear the suspense and to bear it in patience.

At the request of the tribesmen further time was given for more private discussion and it was resolved that they would meet the Asst. Supt. again at 5 p.m. in the evening.

26/4/42   Asst. Supt. Tiddim

Further remarks by the Tribal spokesmen at the resumed meeting at 5 p.m.
on April 26th 1942

KAMHAU TRACT: The Kamhau Chief [Pum Za Mang] said they had not yet reached a decision on all points. He said there was a difficulty in asking every owner or caretaker to man his own gun. There were some 80 guns in Tonzang alone but there were not 80 suitable men to man them. They had some 100 men away in the Burma Rifles. Even if conscription were applied and a man was taken from every house possessing a gun and two male members, there would still be a shortage of men to man the remainder. He asked for the opinion of the Ast. Supdt. (A.S.) and the other Chiefs as to what was to be done if we could not get enough men to man all our guns. He suggested that those who were willing to volunteer for the Levy should give their names to the Asst. Supdt. tomorrow. Others should hand in their guns and go home to arrange their agents if possible. A date should be fixed for the final acceptance of the volunteers or gun owners' agents. Those who cannot man their guns or find a suitable agent should forfeit their guns and these should be distributed as the Asst. Supdt desires. Forfeitures should be for ever. He said the tribes would speak separately but urged that decision should be reached now and the meeting closed tomorrow.

KAMHAU spokesmen. Having heard the full explanations of the Asst. Supdt. they have agreed to enter the Levy and to call for volunteers. They will hand in their guns tomorrow. Those who volunteer will be listed and can take back their arms at once. If the owners cannot come forward they want time to consider the matter or to find their agents. They agreed to all the proposals put forward regarding the organisation of the Levy and all details regarding pay, compensation, supplies, pensions and connected matters which have been put forward. They want to be commanded only by the A.S. and their Chief. As the supply of rations is likely to be alternative to pay, they agree to whichever the A.S. and the Chiefs consider the best method. They do not want military command. They now agree to joint resistance but only as far as No.2 Stockade. They perforce agree to the permanent forfeiture of guns if they can't get the men to man them, since otherwise there will be few volunteers.

THADOES. The A.S. has said he was ashamed that yesterday we had no will to defend our homes. Our difficulty is shortage of men, but in love for our guns and love for our homes, we now agree to do whatever the other tribes do in this matter of defence. As is the case with the other tribes they do not want pay but want rations, clothing and ammunition. Also compensation for death. They agree to joint resistance wherever and whenever decided best, but only in the hills. Let the cowards lose their guns and after the war let them be forfeited to the men who used them.

HUITES: Were unprepared for this discussion so will leave all guns with the Asst. Supdt. for the time being. They will go back to their villages to make their arrangements. They agree to do whatever the Kamhaus do and what the other Kamhau tribes do. If no volunteers come forward, let our guns be forfeited forever to the Asst. Supdt. to be disposed of in the best way he thinks fit.

ZOES: Agree to all proposals put forward and will do as all other tribes do. They want government help for the families of those who follow their own guns and have no males left at home to provide food.

SIYINS: Chief Lian Thawng of Khuasak. For them the question of the disposal of guns after the war does not arise as they have already agreed that every owner of a gun, if he is not willing to man it, should forfeit it forever. If they have been allowed to purchase guns, this permission has been in recognition of good service to government. It is up to them to realise this and to come forward now. If possible they want not only compensation for death but also pensions for bereaved families. They do not want the cultivating season upset by being called in for training. They want government help in supplies for those families whose sole male member is serving with the Levy, but the family concerned should pay for this. They want arrangements to be made for headmen and villagers generally to assist evacuees who have no male left at home. They will not burn their houses but undertake to remove all of value. If hostilities first break out in Tiddim they want the support of the Falam and Haka Levies. They mutually agree to give the same assistance to Falam or Haka if those places should be the first attacked by the enemy, but only offer this help if the other Levies reciprocate. They want the Asst. Supdt to suggest to Col. Haswell that in active service the Levy should be eligible for decorations for bravery on the same lines as the Regular Forces.

The Chief expressed the following personal view to which the other Siyin Chiefs and elders did not subscribe:-

Those who have benefited best from British rule are the Chiefs, headmen, elders, government servants in all branches, and pensioners. We should therefore make it a rule that if any of these classes of persons fail to help now, they should be promptly punished. Chiefs, headmen and elders, should be dealt with as government directs i.e. removed from their posts. Government servants or pensioners who do not help should lose their pay or pensions.

SOKTES. Thuam Za Mang.

They agree that if a fit man does not follow his own gun he should forfeit it. If a man is ill or unable to go on active service, or if a widow owns a gun, they should find an agent to carry it on service. If they do so these guns should be returned to the owners at the end of the war and should not be given to the agent. Any damage to a gun during the fighting should be borne by the owner and not by the agent. If a gun is lost in the war, government should compensate the original owner. If an agent is killed on service, the compensation or pension should go to his family and is no concern of the gun owner. There should be pensions for disablement. Government should support the families of those who leave no male members at home when they go on service. Where a man owns more than one gun and joins the Levy, if his other guns are used by others, they should all be returned to him after the war. (This is agreed to also by the Kamhaus). They want a written agreement.

Signed: N. W. KELLY   26/4/42.
A. S. Tiddim.

REMARKS OF THE ASST. SUPDT., IN CONCLUSION.

The Asst. Supdt. said they had given him the answer he had expected from them. He would call for all guns at 8 a.m. tomorrow and would return them directly to those who volunteered to enrol in the Levy. Other guns would remain with him until the owners or caretakers decided what they would do, or found agents to carry them. All other guns remaining with him, would be distributed to suitable volunteers, and if there was a balance of guns in excess of the men willing to fight in the Levy, he would retain these. In order to deny them to the enemy, it might even become necessary for him to destroy them, and he was therefore not prepared to give any undertaking in regard to the ultimate disposal of such arms after the war. He suggested that the final date for the acceptance of volunteers or gun owners' agents should be May 15th. Every day was of importance, but time had to be given for the more distant villages to discuss the matter thoroughly in the light of what had been said at this meeting. The Asst. Supdt undertook to draw up an agreement regarding the terms of service in the Levy and other connected matters, after he had seen Col. Haswell.

He would also draft a statement to be placed on record regarding the various administrative matters to which his attention had been drawn by the various spokesmen in the course of these meetings. He trusted that tomorrow's enrolment would prove fully the unanimity which had been reached among the tribes as the result of these deliberations.

Signed: N. W. KELLY, O.B.E.
26/4/1942   ASSISTANT SUPERINTENDENT, TIDDIM.

It was agreed that Rs 300 should be paid as compensation to the relatives of those who lost their lives while serving in the Levy, and there would be a pension for those who were wounded. There would be no compulsion to join the Levy as there had been in the efforts to recruit the Labour Corps in the First World War. A Pony Levy would also be set up at the same time to carry food and ammunition to the Levy outposts; Rs 30 would be paid per pony per month along with Indian rations. There were two main pathways into the Chin Hills to be defended. The traditional one was from the south via Kalemyo, No. 2 Stockade, Fort White and Tiddim (see map no. 6 on p. 74); the other was from the east, across the Letha Range from Yazagyo via Phaidim to Mimbil, Phaitu and Tonzang. The terms of the agreement are set out in *Sukte Beh Leh Tedimgam Tangthu*, which encapsulates the history of 'Tiddimland'.[6]

After the agreement, as was the Chin custom, there was a big feast, with the slaughter of ten *mithun* and the consumption of innumerable pots of *zu*. The dancing, merrymaking and singing of Chin folk songs went on all night – and could have lasted for days. The warrior code of the Chin was never to abandon a comrade in battle. This made him a dependable soldier and was to earn the admiration of the British officers who fought with them. Tiddim was now, as General Slim said later, 'a lone outpost of the Empire'.[7]

On 30 April Norman sent a letter to L. B. Naylor in Falam telling him about the talks that had been held, outlining his plans and voicing his concerns.

Letter from N. W. Kelly, Assistant Superintendent, to Deputy Commissioner, Falam

D.O. No. 529

Tiddim
30/4/42

Dear Mr. Naylor,

In accordance with your letter dated at Rih Lake the 16th April, I am sending a messenger to meet you there on May 3rd.

I have gone ahead with my Levy scheme and held a mass meeting of the tribes here on the 25th, 26th and 27th. I enclose copies of the proceedings. After addressing the tribes on the 25th morning they asked for time for private discussion, and they met me again at 5 p.m. the same evening when they spent three hours setting forth their replies (copies attached). The next morning I replied to their remarks and we spent four hours in full discussion. They again held a private meeting in the afternoon and in another evening meeting on that day they expressed their willingness to form a Levy. They have set out the terms on which they were prepared to do so. On the 28th morning I enrolled 400 men who volunteered at once. These 400 have been given back their guns. The remainder have gone back to their villages to consider the matter and to arrange for the men who will carry their guns. In the meantime, I have kept the balance of the guns with me. In fact the subdivision has been disarmed and is being re-armed as volunteers come forward.

Since my last report to you the situation has completely changed. Col. Haswell has been appointed Area Commander for these Levies and has just arrived here. He is paying Rs 20 a month for category A men, with proportionately higher rates for section leaders, etc. He has agreed to my proposed organisation by sections, platoons and companies, on a tribal basis. He is putting in supplies to Fort White and Tiddim for the rationing of the men, and I have obtained already 100 service rifles and 10,000 rounds of ammunition.

The Soktes and Siyins have come in almost solidly, but so far I have only got 82 volunteers from the Kamhau area. I have fixed May 15th as the last day for enrolment in the Levy, and I hope to get another 300 men. Haswell has also been over to Haka and Falam and though things are not so far forward there, he is hopeful of the results.

A party of Commandos are being sent to Tiddim. I personally think these British troops are likely to cause no little trouble – these bushwhackers earned a pretty poor reputation in Maymyo last year, and I have told their commander Col. Musgrave that I won't have them here unless their discipline is strictly enforced.

I am getting ahead with the No. 3 hospital, and in this connection I was down in Kalemyo on the 20th. The Area Commander – Col. Goss at Kalewa – then asked for a hospital of 500 beds, but I told him this was entirely impossible.

I have been unable to get any appreciable amount of labour for the Tamu road, as people are busy buying up their own food supplies. This has complicated the transport problem, too, with regard to the Levy supplies, but I am doing the best I can. Haswell is giving me a clerical officer to assist in the work.

One important point of policy must be decided at once and that is the disposal of the guns after the war. You will see that the Kamhaus and Siyins favour the idea that the men who man the guns should keep them and that present owners' rights should be ignored unless they follow their own weapon in the Levy.

I personally support this proposal. As you know the communal ownership of the village guns was nothing more than a fiction in fact, and I see no reason why outright ownership of guns should not be recognised once and for all after the war. I have, however, not committed myself on this point, nor on the land question which was also raised by the tribes.

I trust you are satisfied with the progress so far made here in this matter. I understand the Commissioner has moved to Pakokku and that Myitkyina is now the headquarters of govt. As communications below are so impossible, I am just going ahead with my own organisation.

Yours sincerely,

N. W. Kelly

Norman must have wondered what his boss was doing at the beautiful Rih Lake, not far from Tiddim, during this time of crisis. It was not until the first week in May that he arrived back at his headquarters in Falam. On 7 May 1942 Naylor issued the following document:

Instructions for the Guidance of Assistant Superintendents

It is proposed to raise 2 classes of Levies. Class A will be composed of men who are prepared to take an offensive role outside their own tracts and including the valley immediately east of the Chin Hills district boundary.

Class B will be those who will function in their own locality. With regards to class A it may be found that whilst many are willing to take an offensive role in the Chin Hills they may fear going down into the plain. The idea of going down in the plain is that if reliable information is obtained that a very small and vulnerable party of the enemy were, say, guarding stores, that these could then be attacked and considerable loot both in arms and rations obtained.

If the opposition to the recruitment of these A men is strong on the grounds that they don't want to go into the valley but are willing for general service in the hills then do not press them to give their promise and enrol them for general service in the hills. No doubt later, if you get a tempting bait in the valley and the specific purpose is put to them, then they will seize the opportunity. With regards to arms for these class A men, a number have already arrived at Fort White and will be distributed to each subdivision as soon as the necessary transport can be obtained. These arms consist of approximately 300 .303 rifles with ammunition and also some shotguns.

The composition of both class A and class B should be in group A of approximately 50. Each group will be under a leader and each 25 will be under a sub-leader. Their pay will be as follows:-

Group leader	Rs 50–0–0}	
Each sub-leader	25–0–0}	Class A
Each gunman	20–0–0}	

To some extent these men have to ration themselves but every endeavour is being made at the present moment to bring up a simple ration and to make dumps of this at suitable places. Arrangements for bringing up these rations have already been made but owing to false rumours transport from No. 2 and Natchaung has been delayed.

Class B men will be composed in similar groups and will operate in their own tribal area but will not be called out until the enemy is close to their area. The group leader will be paid Rs 20, sub-leaders Rs 15 and gunmen Rs 10. They will ration themselves as they will not be far distant from their own villages. Discretion is left to the Asst. Supt. in the raising of these B class groups, to modify the size of the group to suit local conditions.

Guns

The policy which has been approved by all the Tiddim subdivision with regard to guns is that if the owner or keeper of a gun refuses or is unable to join the Levy then he must either provide someone who will join the Levy and carry his gun or surrender his gun to the Asst. Supt., chief or headmen for issue to another volunteer for the Levy who has not a gun and, in the case of Tiddim, they further passed a resolution: once the war is won the Levyman who has carried the gun during the war shall retain that gun without the payment of compensation or any liability to the previous owner as such owner failed to come up to the mark and employ his gun in the defence of the village. This resolution may give rise ultimately to some cases of injustice, for example the owner of a gun may be already serving in the armed forces and therefore cannot use his gun in the defence of his village. Such cases must be settled later with due consideration to equity and justice.

Role to be played by Levies:
It must be understood from the first that the Levies are not expected to resist or attempt to resist, face to face, like regular troops in battle. Their duty is:
1. to snipe and bolt to safety
2. to ambush and again bolt before the enemy can counter-attack them
3. to destroy roads and bridges immediately in front of the enemy
4. to deny all local supplies and transport
5. to set *panjis* [concealed, sharpened bamboo stakes] in the enemy's line of advance
6. to construct booby traps
7. in accordance with Chin ancient custom in fighting to delay the enemy's advance and the advance of any ration or supply column by every means found possible

Lieutenant-Colonel F. W. [Jack] Haswell [Indian Army] is the Commandant of the Western Area Levies which includes the Chin Hills, or in other words will be the Chief Guerrilla Warfare Officer of the Chin Hills. Under him will be a number of officers whom he will assign to each subdivision to assist the Asst. Supt. who will be local commandant of the Levy. Each Asst. Supt. should arrange for the collection of information and pass all information on to the Deputy Commissioner at Falam who will act as chief intelligence officer to the Levy Commander. Each Asst. Supt. is authorised to employ either permanent intelligence agents or odd men for specific jobs and to fix their rate of pay or reward according to the value of their work.

Denials
It is most essential that in the event of the enemy advancing into these hills that all sources of food supplies and transport should be denied to them. If this is thoroughly done his advance will be delayed as he will have to bring up his rations by supply columns and this again will become most vulnerable to the attacks of the Levies. It is therefore most necessary to enlist the aid of all the Chiefs and Headmen and the Asst. Supt. is authorised to put the Chiefs on a monthly pay comparable with their importance and to place subordinate headmen on a pay of Rs 20 a month. Attached is a list of a number of the Chiefs of the 3 subdivisions with the amount against each which I consider is suitable.

Besides denying all material help as above to the enemy it will be the duty of these chiefs to receive the pay of the village headmen and the Levies and to distribute it through the village headmen to the payee. Each Asst. Supt. is being given a considerable amount of treasury coins and it will be his duty, if necessary, to remove these coins from his subdivisional headquarters and hide it in various parts of his subdivision from where payments can be made to the areas through which the enemy may have already passed and thus keep alive the Levies in the enemy's rear. The Asst. Supts. will of course be able to draw their own pay and all expenses in connection with this Levy scheme from these sources.

Stragglers

There are a number of men from the army who will have found their way back to the hills. All these men should be roped in and placed in class A and used to instruct the rest of the class A Levies in the use of .303 rifles. The maximum of 10 rounds may be expended in practice shooting but where a man shows proficiency the whole ten rounds should not be used.

Explosives

A small number of British personnel trained in the use of explosives and demolition work, booby traps, et cetera have been placed at Colonel Haswell's disposal and he will attach these to each subdivision. It is also hoped that a further supply of explosives, Mills bombs, poison for anointing *panjis*, etc., including medical stores which have been promised from Assam, will arrive for distribution without undue delay.

> Deputy Commissioner,
> Chin Hills District

After the bombing of Rangoon it had taken the Japanese a mere four months to arrive at the Chin Hills. This was the only strategic part of Burma that remained in British hands. They had been able to recruit the Burma Independence Army (BIA), which had accelerated their triumphal advance north. The two small British divisions were unable to defend a country much bigger than France. The Japanese were professional, well trained and battle hardened after fighting the Chinese for many years. They had been planning their campaign for years and were masters of infiltration. General Slim[8] watched his Burma Corps men arrive in Imphal on the last day of their 900-mile retreat. They were in very bad shape. Tiddim, with the Chin Levies, and Falam with the Chin Hills Battalion, 164 miles to the south, were now in the front line. They were facing the Japanese 33rd Division, and defending not only India but also the Burma Corps, who were utterly exhausted.

No wonder Norman Kelly took three days to persuade the Chins to fight with the British against an enemy that appeared invincible. Fortunately, the myth that the Japanese soldier was a superman in the jungle had never taken root in the Chin Hills. The Japanese did, however, possess a massive advantage in firepower and military organisation. The Chins had never been engaged in modern warfare – air bombardment to them was a new and terrible thing.

The Chin Hills Battalion

When expeditions by the British from 1889 to 1894 had finally brought peace to the Chin Hills (see Chapter 1) the government had decided to withdraw one of the regular regiments from Tiddim and replace it with a new battalion of military police. The purpose was twofold: to support the political officers administering the hills, and to protect the frontier with India. It was at first referred to as the 'Chin Levy', but it evolved into the Chin Hills Battalion.

In 1937, when Burma separated from India, the Chin Hills Battalion joined the Burma Frontier Force. The battalion was comprised mainly of

Chins of different tribes: the Hakas in the south; the Siyins from villages west of Fort White; and the Kamhaus, who occupied the Chin Hills north of Fort White. The Kamhaus' proper Chin name was Sokte and Tiddim was their principal village.

On 1 January 1942 there was one company each of Hakas, Siyins, Khongsais, Whelngos and three platoons of Kamhaus. There were also Gurkhas, a few Sikhs and clerks, who were mainly Indian. Each tribe had its own dialect, but the common language was Urdu, which everybody was taught to read in English script. The Commanding Officer, or Commandant as he was known, was from the Indian Army, and was Major A. C. Moore. The other British officers who had served in 1941 were Lieutenant T. T. (Tommy) West, 2nd Lieutenant A. K. Scott; 2nd Lieutenant W. P. B. Smart and 2nd Lieutenant J. F. (Jack) Oats. All these were Army Burma Reserve Officers (ABRO). Lieutenants Bobbie Peebles and Syd Hyde rejoined the battalion in Kalewa in April 1942.

Major Moore, who was forty-four, had done a very good job in organising the battalion in peacetime. It had assisted in the withdrawal of General Alexander's army as well as the flood of refugees fleeing from the Japanese up the Kalewa–Tamu Road. The Chins in the Burma Rifles and the battalion had experienced the chaos of headlong retreat. The congestion was overwhelming; malaria and dysentery were rife and most of the civilian population had come all the way from Rangoon or Mandalay, so were exhausted by the time they reached Kalewa. They now had to face the malaria of the Kabaw Valley, known as 'The Valley of Death', as they headed north on foot for India (see the illustration on p. 24).

The battalion, as part of the Burma Frontier Force (see illustration no. 25), was commanded ultimately by its Inspector General, Brigadier Roughton, but he had died of heat exhaustion in the vital oil fields on the Irrawaddy at Yenangyaung during the retreat and had been succeeded by John Bowerman. Moore had to act on his own initiative and, to his eternal credit, had decided that his men would remain in Burma and defend the Chin Hills. It was the only unit of the army defending Burma that did not vacate the country. It remained behind voluntarily and without orders until it later came under the command of 4 Corps with its HQ at Imphal, 164 miles north of Tiddim. At that time there was no road of any kind linking the Chin Hills to Imphal. Moore was handicapped by not having direct access to Army Command as a source of supply. He was responsible for getting food out of the plains and up into the Chin Hills to feed his battalion and the Chins of Falam and Haka. There was no battalion medical officer, which added to its difficulties.

When Moore, now a lieutenant-colonel, met General Alexander in Kalemyo in May 1942 he expressed the view that he had initially voiced in April: that Naylor should be replaced by his predecessor as Deputy Commissioner, Colonel Burne,[9] who had been very popular with the

Chins. Burne was now retired and in England, but Moore complained that Naylor was absent from his district during April 1942 and did not return until May. This had left a vacuum of civilian leadership in Falam during the greatest emergency in the history of the Chin Hills British administration. Colonel Burne CBE, CIE, had been Deputy Commissioner of the Chin Hills 1909–1914 and 1920–1937, when Naylor took over. General Alexander said he would relay Moore's request to Army HQ in India.

Naylor suspected that Moore had reported against him to General Alexander and collected some information against Moore which Vum Ko Hau, who was the Deputy Commisssioner's Chief Clerk, detailed in *Profile of a Burma Frontier Man*: 'It was a fact that both Naylor and Moore were very unpopular with the people [Chins].' It was an absurd situation that the Deputy Commissioner and Battalion Commandant in Falam were unable to cooperate with each other with the Japanese in Kalewa and possibly about to invade the Chin Hills.

Lieutenant-Colonel Jack Haswell, a former Commandant of the Chin Hills Battalion, was the most senior professional soldier in the Chin Hills, and was based in Falam. He later oversaw the Levy organisation and had direct communication by radio with 4 Corps at Imphal and the HQ of Eastern Army Command, at Ranchi in India. Norman Kelly was Zone Commander, Tiddim, in addition to his civilian duties. On 17 May the retreating Army evacuated Kalemyo and the battalion retired to Webula in the southern Chin Hills on the night of 27/28 May. Major Duguid, second in command, was posted to Falam to be in charge of the depot.

The Japanese had been very clever and had released Chins whom they had captured during the retreat and encouraged them to return to their homes. They said they were not the enemies of the Chins and that in due course they would take the whole of the hills as well as India. The former prisoners brought only good news about the behaviour of the Japanese troops. This had a bad effect on the battalion and many Chins deserted. This trend was not helped by the overbearing manner of Moore, and the rift between Moore and Naylor clearly affected on the morale of the Chins and their subordinates. In both cases their administrations were not communicating with one another. With Falam in disarray and the most powerful Tashon chief convinced that the Japanese would win, during the critical months of April, May and June it fell to Norman Kelly and Peter Bankes – the 'old Burma hands' – to hold the fort until the capital of the Chin Hills put its house in order.

Peter Bankes (see photograph no. 41) had been educated at Oundle and Christ Church, Oxford, where he read forestry and anthropology. He was 6 feet 4 inches in height, with curly fair hair, and had rowed for three years in the Blue Boat against Cambridge, up to that time the heaviest man to do so. As a student he had also run a camp for unemployed men from the East End of London. He had gone out to

Burma in 1936 to join the Bombay-Burmah Trading Corporation (known as Bombine), extracting teak. J. H. Williams, who was later to achieve fame as the author of *Elephant Bill*, became one of his mentors. After four and a half years he had his first home leave and married his fiancée Prue in England; on the voyage back to Rangoon he met Peter and Dodie Courtenay (it was Peter Courtenay who was to accompany my mother, Maeve and myself on our trek to India). They sailed up the Irrawaddy, then the Chindwin to Homalin and trekked 20 miles to the east to their final destination, Pyinmana, through beautiful mountains, rivers and plains. Peter Bankes was then back on the job as a jungle *wallah*, with his own area and a troop of elephants to organise (see map no. 3 on p. 28).

Prue Bankes had joined the Women's Auxiliary Service Burma,[10] known as WAS(B), when it was formed on 16 January 1942. She and her best friend Dodie Courtenay were evacuated from Maymyo by train when Army Headquarters were told they had to leave. Their train was strafed by Japanese planes on the slow journey to Shwebo, where they looked after civilian casualties in the hospital for two to three weeks. They were bombed and machine-gunned and, the day after the WASBIES left, the hospital took a direct hit. They travelled on a single-track railway line at night to avoid aerial attacks and at Myitkyina caught the last plane out before the runway was captured. Their Dakota flew them to Dibrugarh in northern Assam, and their party reached Simla in May 1942.

In February 1942 Peter Bankes had joined the 9th Burma Rifles, commanded by Colonel Dick Musgrave in Maymyo, and was posted to Tiddim on 18 April 1942, where he was Norman's first British Levy officer. He was in command of a Levy detachment at Fort White. It was a precarious situation in April 1942 and, if the Chins had not trusted Norman Kelly, it would not have been possible to keep them in the field. With hindsight, it was a close-run thing.

Chapter 3

THE TREK OUT OF BURMA

My sister and I knew the war was approaching the Chin Hills but we couldn't comprehend how it would change our lives. I recall seeing a plane flying overhead; it might have been the first aeroplane I had ever seen, and certainly we had never seen one fly over the Chin Hills during the previous three years. Maeve and I assumed it must be the RAF. We had heard on the wireless the exploits of the Battle of Britain. As children do, we waved enthusiastically at it. To our horror we then, both at the same time, recognised the ominous zeros on the wings. It was the Japanese enemy.

There had been discussions about what would happen if we had to leave Tiddim, one question being should we bury our most precious possessions in the hope of reclaiming them later? My father was adamant: 'If we do that the Chins will conclude that the British expect to lose the war.' The house would be left just as it was for our father. We would take what we could carry.

Word had come through the previous night that the Japanese forces were 50 miles away and, with the exception of Father, we were commanded to evacuate. I don't remember saying goodbye to Pa or to our pets. Things happened so quickly, and it was probably best that the interval between discussion and departure was brief. All Maeve and I knew was that we were going on an exciting journey and that we had people to look after us. We didn't realise the significance of the coming monsoon and that, at worst, the rivers would be impassable. Maeve now takes up the story:

> There were eight of us: my mother, Peter Courtenay, a British officer evacuated from Lower Burma away from the fighting on account of his malaria (he was the husband of Dodie Courtenay, Prue Bankes's friend), my seven-year-old brother Desmond, four Chin servants, three ponies, a string of mules and myself, aged nine. The date was 6 May 1942. We were leaving Tiddim where our family had lived for the past three years and were heading for the Burma/Assam border with India. There was no railway for hundreds of miles, no airstrip, no metalled road; we were expected to get out as best we could.

The village of Tiddim, HQ of the area, boasted a Baptist mission school, a hospital and a club but, beside ourselves, the only Westerners were an American missionary couple who had been evacuated months earlier. Father had already rallied the local tribes to fight a guerrilla war alongside the scattered remnants of the British forces. Armed initially with knives and ancient flintlock rifles, these Chin tribesmen, led by Father and known as the Chin Levies, helped to hold the hills against the enemy until the Allied forces could be reinforced.

But on that May dawn the monsoon was breaking as we trudged down the narrow slippery track which was to lead us westward across the frontier. The rain, which had been no more than a haze on the distant smoke-blue mountains, became a dense mist. My last memory of Tiddim is of shuddering vapour and the stark black pines dripping. At Tuibel, we crossed the fast-flowing Manipur River by a 300-foot rope suspension bridge and headed for Mualnuam (see colour map, illustration no. 27).

The day's programme was always the same: up at 6 a.m., with a breakfast usually of burnt scrambled eggs and tea made with condensed milk, drunk out of chipped enamel mugs. Then the day's march would begin. The baggage, which only included (besides food for the animals and ourselves) two small suitcases and two rolls of bedding, carried by the mules, went ahead with the servants and we followed. We usually averaged 15 to 20 miles a day, walking and riding. Clothing was simple: khaki shorts and shirts, socks and sandals. We each carried a rucksack; among other things mine held a tin of bull's-eye sweets into which rain invariably leaked. They tasted strongly of the tin.

Peter carried a quantity of treasury notes and slept with them under his pillow with a revolver. His army stories were fascinating and so was his language; he would entertain Des and me with both as we skidded down steep, glass-hard muddy roads, while black gleaming leeches crawled unnoticed up our legs. They dropped unfelt from trees and sucked blood until, too satiated to withdraw, they had to be burnt off with salt and tobacco juice. Tolerating the leeches, we travelled through green steaming jungles; crags and ravines loomed in the mist and raindrops incessantly whispered on sodden leaves. Des and I adored Peter, who shines like a beacon in our childhood.

Soon after we left Tiddim, however, Peter had another attack of malaria, so severe that he had to be carried on a litter, delirious. Mother, nearly frantic with worry, now kept the revolver herself. To make matters worse, the bamboo huts in which we camped were not ideal for a malarial patient; rain seeped in at every crack, spiders, snakes and squirrels infested them, and the weather was depressing.

The day came when we eventually waded across the Tyao River between Burma and India (see map no. 5 on p. 70), into the state of Assam (Mizoram). I remember the clear water of it, glinting with the colour of wild honey under the tropical sun. I also remember sleek black water snakes sliding among stones on the riverbed. Des recalls looking back for the last time at Burma, and thinking, 'This is where I was born; one day I will come back.'

We were now in the Lushai Hills, which were very similar to the Chin Hills, with the eternal climbs to the top of a ridge and a steep descent to a valley on the other side. We passed through Champhai, the largest village on our route. Then one day we reached an oasis in the wilderness of jungle, after eight stages and 88 miles from Champhai. Aijal (now known as Aizawl) was one of the main towns of Assam and there we stayed a day or two with the Superintendent of the Lushai Hills, Major Anthony McCall OBE, and his wife Jean. What luxury that was – to sleep on a bed and not the floor, to bathe in a tub and not in a river, to eat fresh food and to see a well-cared-for garden. With the McCalls we left some of our glass and plate – family wedding mementoes – hoping to retrieve them when the war was over. We never did.

Leaving Aijal, we set off on the last and worst part of our journey. For three days and nights we travelled northwards downstream by native boat on the Dhaleswari and Katakhal Rivers. Those boats were terrible. Shaped like long canoes, shelter was provided by a piece of bamboo matting bent over the craft like a tunnel (see photograph no. 21). Inside, it was so dark one had to grope one's way around, but so cramped there was hardly any space in which to grope. And it was so stuffy that it seemed our only hope of survival was in crawling out and sitting on the boards by the stern or bows, where the native boatmen who punted ran up and down. Their bare brown feet provided most of the view as one sat in the tunnel. So it was worth the risk of being trodden on to dangle one's hands in the river and watch the jungle slip past on banks of rubbery grey mud, and to stare at the stork-like birds wading in the shallows on their red sticks of legs.

The river was full of rapids. The most notorious were in the huge, sinister gorge called the Asmani Dhar, only a few miles from where we started; they have been the scene of many a disaster. The agony of sitting in the tunnel of matting, seeing bright sheets of water rising over the sides of the boat, towering up before us and dropping away with a sickening thud and of feeling stones grating along the bottom was almost unbearable. Then we emerged from the tunnel of matting – it was less frightening to watch what was going on – to see the sweat of concentration on the men's brows. But shooting rapids during the day was as bad as sleeping at night. Then the boatmen ate garlic and smoked rank tobacco – opium, too

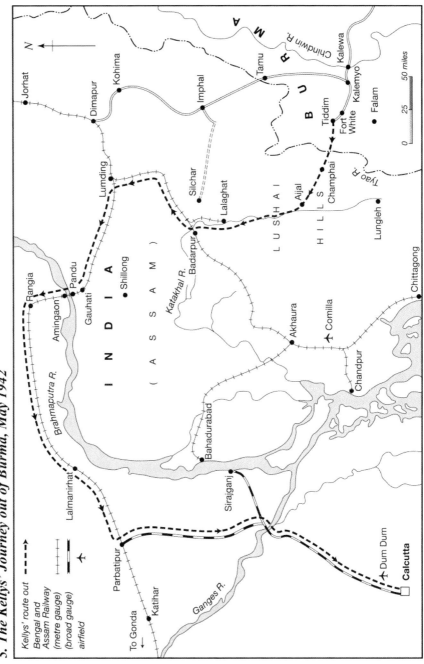

5. *The Kellys' Journey out of Burma, May 1942*

– and the fumes drifting into the blackness of the tunnel, mingling with the sweet smell of fresh bamboo, were suffocating. It was far more restful to stumble out into the clean night air away from them and listen to the waters running past us, with the ceaseless hum of cicadas in the jungle.

Then one daybreak, as light was just beginning to steal along the river, we looked out to see a dim line of grey humps above the high bank. Elephants, I thought. But I was wrong. After 19 days' travel through tropical forests we had found the first tentacle of civilisation: the railhead at Lalaghat, and the Bengal and Assam Railway. We left for Calcutta on 24 May. Odd that I didn't consider it important at the time, which may indicate how much more intense were those other memories, but my legs were covered with boils and infected insect bites, for which the only treatment was to apply salt or neat peroxide.

Sixty years on and empathising with my mother's intense anxiety, I feel nothing but admiration for her. Here she was, fleeing with strangers to an unknown future with two young and vulnerable children, possibly never to see her man again. She had much courage. The Chins, too, remembered her with affection. She had arranged for the young ladies of Tiddim to knit socks for the soldiers as part of the war effort. 'Your Mum gave them one *kyat* each and a cup of tea and cakes,' said Thang Khawin Pau, a Tiddim Chin. Of course, to Desmond and me, it was all a great adventure; pretty good training for life as well.

And so we arrived in Calcutta. Memories now of a grand hotel, with lifts – and ice cream! Of hosts of people, bazaars, and a train journey across India to the foothills of the Himalayas; lumps of ice packed in straw were loaded on at railway stations to keep the carriages cool.

Father, our home in Tiddim, pets and servants slowly became a distant memory; no hurricane lamp smoking and guttering in the wind; no pet monkey on my arm; no Siamese cat on my bed; no imaginary tiger under Desmond's; no Wendy house in the grassy garden, or mud village built with clay around puddles beneath the pines; no vistas over range after range of distant blue-green mountains and no cosmos flowers in birdsong clearings. They had all disappeared. Here instead was an American boarding school, Woodstock, in Mussoorie. But our hearts were still in Tiddim.

Only one other European family took a similar route, but they started 75 miles to the south. Lieutenant-Colonel A. C. Moore commanded the Chin Hills Battalion, stationed in Falam, and in May 1942 his wife Molly set off with her one-year-old, Patrick, and a friend, Kathleen Learmond, with her children. They were behind us, heading for India via the Lushai Hills.

Fellow Travellers

Molly Moore and her companions planned to rest when they reached Rih Lake, a delightful spot in the Chin Hills 40 miles west of Tiddim, but Peter Courtenay sent word warning them not to delay as the Japanese were advancing at an alarming rate. A little later a Japanese plane flew over, followed by a burst of machine-gun fire. They learned later that Imphal, 164 miles north of Tiddim, had been bombed. The trek took Molly and her party (including ponies, mules, Chins and a non-commissioned officer from the Chin Hills Battalion) seventeen days to cover the 175 miles from Falam to Aijal.

By now the monsoon was breaking in earnest and the river was in spate. They were in three boats, which they boarded at Sairang, near Aijal, as we did. It took them three days to reach the railhead to take them to Calcutta. As Kathleen Learmond related later:

> Our worst day was that in which we crossed the divide (Tyao River) between the Chin and the Lushai Hills. We had been given a rough description of the path – in this case it was very steep uphill for 12 miles, then steep down for 6 miles. But it said nothing of the last 2 miles (it was an 18-mile day) – it didn't mention that they were sheer up again!
>
> We had only gone a couple of miles when the rain came down so heavily that the watercourses were quite inadequate to deal with the downpour. Thus we came down the road with the tide. At several places we waded knee deep for quite 50 yards at a time. We had been soaked to the skin and it was bitterly cold. We descended to the valley to find the river in flood and our boats looked too tiny to face such a torrent.

The road from Aijal to the Dhaleswari River was a stretch of 13 miles, downhill all the way, a fall of about 3,300 feet. The country boats were very cramped; Kathleen, with her two-year-old and a baby, had less than 2 feet to lie on her wet blankets.

> That was all our space – one small mosquito net easily did duty for us all – and there we lived and pigged it for the time we were on the boat. There was no privacy at all – three boatmen, living, cooking and sleeping in the other half of the boat. I had my picnic case with a little spirit stove on it and I heated water to brew the inevitable Horlicks and Marmite.

Ian Wallace, Maeve's godfather, had been Deputy Commissioner at Pakokku on the Irrawaddy in 1933 (see map no. 3 on p. 28). His district lay between that great river and the Chin Hills. Ian, at that time, was the youngest man in the Indian Civil Service to be a Deputy Commissioner. He was in Moulmein when the Japanese invaded. Moulmein was very close to the border with Siam, and on the direct line of the Japanese advance towards Rangoon. Ian had organised its evacuation and then had quickly left himself. He had withdrawn to Monywa, on the Chindwin, until 30 April 1942, when the enemy began to mortar the town from the other side of the river (see map no. 1 on p. 2). The party he was with had left that night in a small launch travelling north up the Chindwin. At dawn they were stuck on a sandbank and could hear the Japanese guns. On 1 May Monywa was captured. At last they were able to shove themselves off the sandbank and continued upstream in the *Zobeda*, an Irrawaddy Flotilla paddle steamer, which had been used in the evacuation. They passed Kalewa and continued northwards to Mawlaik (see map no. 7 on p. 80).

After a week on the river, during which Japanese planes had flown low overhead but didn't fire on them, they reached Sittaung. Here they left the Chindwin and headed for Tamu, near the Indian border. On this part of their journey they met the major evacuation trail with huge numbers of Indians from the south of Burma fleeing for their lives. On 10 May they reached Tamu. 'We had run it rather close', Ian Wallace was to remark at the time. They managed to get an Army truck on 13 May to take them (via Imphal) the 164 miles to Dimapur, the railhead in Assam (see map. no. 5 on p. 70), where they arrived exhausted, but very relieved, on 14 May.

6. The Tiddim Road from Milestone 109, and on to Kalemyo

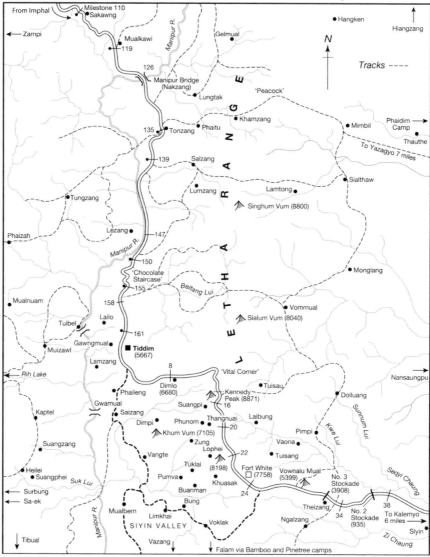

Chapter 4

LETTERS FROM TIDDIM

A Bush Warfare unit had done a tremendous job during the retreat from Burma. It was commanded by Colonel Dick Musgrave, an old Burma hand himself, who had worked with the Bombay-Burmah Trading Corporation, known as Bombine, before the war. They had been involved in rearguard action during the withdrawal and had a quantity of explosives, booby traps and, most important of all, two jeeps – the first ever to venture into the Chin Hills. Instead of going due north, as General Slim's Burma Corps had done, from Kalemyo to Tamu on their way to Imphal (the major refugee route), Musgrave's men turned due west at Kalewa and headed for the Chin Hills (see map no. 4 on p. 38). Their hope was to join forces with whoever was fighting there and return to the offensive as soon as they were rested. They had precariously navigated from Kalewa to Kalemyo, up and over Kennedy Peak and through to Tiddim. They had brought a good supply of petrol drums with them.

Norman Kelly's first letter to his wife was dated 9 May 1942, from Fort White.

Fort White
9th May 1942

Darling Mummy,

I have just received your note from Cingpikot [also called Mualnuam] with Rabbit's letter. These came by a Mualnuam coolie so I presume you had got there safely.

I am sorry I was such an idiot at parting, but it certainly has been a dreadful wrench. However, you have absolutely nothing to worry about on my account, love, for I shall take every care of myself for your dear sakes.

I am naturally very busy and have little time to write at the moment, as I am due to leave within the hour for No. 2 Stockade with Col. Musgrave who very kindly rushes me about the country in his Jeep. He and I went over to Lamzang yesterday for a conference with Haswell [see map no. 6 opposite].

Naylor has been kicked by a mule and is laid up and was unable to leave Falam. He has constituted himself the Chief Intelligence Officer attached to the Levies, but as for the organisation of the latter I am my own master under Lt. Col. Haswell's general control.

The situation here has definitely improved. We have got extra troops into Kalewa and Kalemyo and there is a brigade south of Gangaw to hold the enemy [see map no. 3 on p.28], together with Moore's [Chin Hills] Battalion. Our bombing of the enemy launches on the Chindwin has temporarily stopped their progress on that side too, so we are getting a little more time to organise things decently here.

I will try to keep up a weekly mail via Aijal and have written to McCall in this connection.

Peter Courtenay is to return from Aijal after he has safely delivered you there, and I am sending orders to this effect to him now.

Sorry I can't write more at the moment, sweetheart. Heaps of love and kisses to you all. Tell Rabbit and Tigger I will look after their pets and will tell them all the news regularly. Keep the flag flying, darling, and don't worry about me. Bysie bye.

Yours alone and ever,

Daddy

Tiddim
15th May 1942

Darling Mummy,

I met the *dak* [government] runner carrying your letter of the 9th, just at the top of Kennedy Peak when I was on my way back on the 13th. It was a tremendous thrill to get it, love, and to learn that you had got over the worst of the journey and were back to P.W.D. rest houses again. It is a relief to know that you are safely across the Tyao River and that you had had decent weather. Glad to learn, too, that the transport arrangements were working fairly smoothly.

The weather is still good here, but I suppose it won't be long before the rains set in now. Everybody has enquired how you are getting on, dearest. The house seems dreadfully lonely without you all, darling, but I am kept so busy that I don't allow myself much time for brooding. You are quite right, sweetheart, I just couldn't wait to see you disappear the morning you left. However, our separation may not be such a long one this time, and I am praying always for a speedy reunion. With your going, prayer has taken on a new meaning for me, love, and I am sure that God in His mercy will look after us all and bring us together again in His own time.

Don't worry on my account, sweetheart. For your dear sakes I shall take every care of myself, and I have no doubt that things will work out right in the end.

The Saizang Chief was very pleased to get your note of thanks, dear. I have packed the wee silver powder bowl for you, love, and will deal with the letters, photos, etc. I also hope to hang on to your sewing machine. Things are moving fairly rapidly and it may not be long before I have to leave Tiddim.

The Japanese advance was held up by the bombing of their launches on the Chindwin, but since then the Army has withdrawn completely. For some days we had a brigade in Kalemyo but they were only acting as rearguard and as soon as the other Burma brigade arrived from Gangaw, they all moved out to Tamu.

I met General Alexander at Army Headquarters at Inbaung [see map no. 4 on p. 38] the other day, and he shares the view that it would be unfair to risk bringing down reprisals on the Chins by urging the Levies actively to resist at this stage. We shall therefore go to earth and I shall try my best to collect and correlate information as to the enemy's movements and strength, which might be useful to the government in India.

The Jap intelligence system must be pretty damned good, for Inbaung had been bombed (without effect) the day I went there, although Army H.Q. had only moved in there one and a half days before. I have brought away the whole of the Kalemyo sub-treasury as the *Myook* [treasury officer] disappeared, so we shan't be too badly off for cash. All our Chins in the Burma Rifles have been disbanded and have come back to their homes, and I hope that they will strengthen our Levies considerably.

Pum Za Mang [the Tonzang chief of all Kamhau] has turned out a very broken reed, and I am having to organise his Levies entirely myself. He wants to resign and to take his family away into the jungle somewhere, and this of course is complicating the position so far as I am concerned.

The Siyins and Soktes Chins are splendid and I already have many of their sections out watching the hills to give warning of any enemy advance from No. 2, No. 3 and Dolluang. Now that Kalewa and Kalemyo are left unprotected there is nothing to prevent the Jap walking in whenever he feels like it, so we shall have to watch our step carefully. I am packing the office today before returning to Fort White again tomorrow, and I shall get most of the house stuff removed to greater safety.

The Bush Warfare people are now in Tiddim but 19 out of the 26, including Col. Musgrave, are all down with Kalemyo fever, and this doesn't make things any easier. I never wanted them here and would be only too pleased to see the last of them. I am having *dhoolies* [covered litters] made today in case they have to leave in a hurry before they are fit to walk. I am in excellent health myself, thank God.

I have got Musgrave in the house with me now, and also Lt. Hobbs, who is in charge of the wireless unit. We also have a guard on the house at night so you have no need to fear, dearest, that I shall be caught in my sleep. I am sending out some of the Nelsons' furniture to

Mualnuam, on the other side of the Manipur River, in case I have to take up my quarters out there.

It is a great pity you had to leave before the first car arrived in Tiddim. Both the Jeeps are doing regular daily runs from Fort White here, bringing rations, etc. Great excitement when they first arrived!

I hope to have letters for the children in my next mail, love, but I am sure you can understand that I have very little time these days. Everyone seems to look to me for guidance, and though I am proud that this should be so, it doesn't make things too easy for me.

I have had a letter from Robinson at Imphal and he and Sharpe [the Director of Supplies] have fixed up a weekly *dak* runner mail. By the way, Imphal was bombed the other day, so I am very thankful you took the Aijal route after all.

I'm afraid there is no hope of getting rice and salt from Manipur, but I am sending a man over to buy heavily at Champhai.

No other news at the moment, sweetheart. The situation will probably be clarified to some extent during the next few days, and I will do my best to keep in touch with you regularly.

Every scrap of my love is yours alone, darling. May God keep you all in his care.

Lots of hugs and kisses from,

Daddy

One of Norman's most important and decisive actions was the capture of the Subtreasury (bank) in Kalemyo, before it was stolen or fell into the hands of the Japanese. He needed the money to pay the Chins who had been in the Burma Rifles during the retreat and to persuade them to join his Levies. Kalemyo was in Sagaing Division and therefore outside his jurisdiction. This was the first major exploit of his Levies and he took with him Chief Thian Pum of Buanman, Ngam Thawng, Thuam Chin of Khuasak and Thuk On, all Siyins. The Subtreasury contained some cash brought back by the Burma Army, but there was no transport to take it back to India since all the Chindwin steamers had been scuttled at Kalewa. It was unguarded and they evacuated it at night via No. 2 Stockade, back to Tiddim.[1] It showed what could be done and financed the rapid build-up of the Levy movement and the purchase of food. It also demonstrated to the wavering chiefs that the British intended to make a fight of it. Chief Pum Za Mang of the Kamhau (mentioned in the letter above), who had control of 135 villages, was the most important chief, compared with the Siyins who only had 7 villages.

Another important defensive measure was to blow up the road 1 mile above No. 3 Stockade to thwart a surprise Japanese attack. Norman and Peter Bankes did this to stop the enemy driving a jeep up to Fort White.

Tiddim
22nd May 1942

Darling Mummy,

I don't know when this will reach you, love, or where, but I am sending it off nevertheless in the best of hope. Everything is so far well with me, but the last week has if anything been busier than any previous one.

A platoon of the Japs are in Kalewa, but so far they have not attempted to occupy Kalemyo although we have no troops there now. The bulk of their forces have gone up the Chindwin by launch in the Mawlaik direction (probably after the oil at Indaw) and another small force followed up our retreating army by the Tamu road and engaged them at Yazagyo [see map no. 13 on p. 284]. There is some danger that these Japs may attempt to send patrols into the hills by the roads east of the Letha [the mountain range east of Tiddim], but I have my Levies out watching. It is just possible, of course, that now that the rains have broken they will not attempt anything further after chasing us out of Burma, and will settle down for a while in the dry zone rather than risk the fevers of the Kale Valley.

Colonel Musgrave's Bush Warfare chaps have been hard hit with fever contracted at the Burmah Oil Company camp [see map no. 9 on p. 166], and they have lost three men including the Medical Officer, Major McGrath, since they arrived in Tiddim. We buried the latter last evening after I had returned from Fort White. Both the Nelsons' house and our own are full of officers at present but the crush will thin out when Dick Musgrave's unit leaves. He has given me his Jeep, which is a great help in getting about the country. The other Jeep, which is attached to the wireless unit, will also be left here when the set is moved back to Champhai. Can you imagine me running a motor service on our roads at last, love?

I took a crowd of my Levies into Kalemyo the other day with Lt. Peter Bankes without making any contact with the enemy, and for the next three days I was busy there buying more rice and peas as rations for my Levies. Everyone made a great fuss of the escapade but there was really not the slightest danger and we completed a useful job of work in buying more food, which our supply officer had abandoned as soon as the army left. We were also able to get good information regarding the enemy movements and this in itself has operated to put Daddy's name on the map among the ones that be in India.

For the next few days I shall be busy at this end and thereafter I must get back to Fort White area and thence to the eastern slopes [of the Letha] to see my units out there. I am having a meeting with the ex-Burma Rifles chaps at the end of the month and hope to raise new Levies from these trained men.

7. The Tiddim Road Going South from Imphal to Tonzang

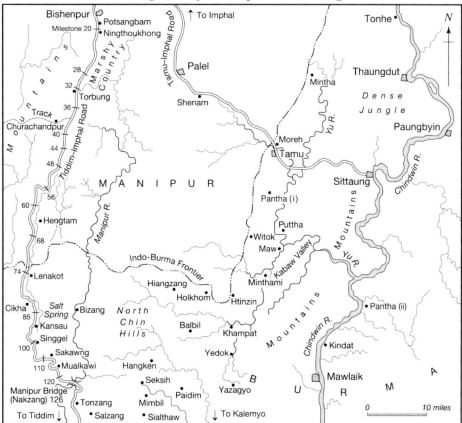

13. Betty Kelly at a garden party
held for the Commissioner of the Shan States in Taunggyi, January 1939.

14. A Haka Chin with hair tied in a topknot by Yatanabon Mg Su. (Courtesy of Ken Shaw)

Haka Chin Man
Haka Division.

Yatanabon
Mg Su.

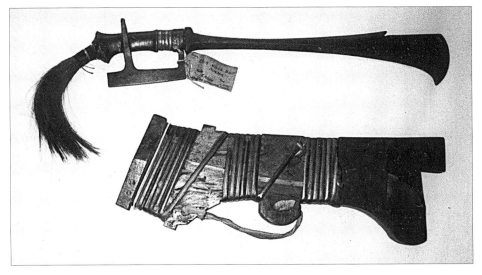

15. A Chin headhunter's sword (khin khot naam) *with scabbard, which used to be owned by Lieutenant-Colonel Noel Stevenson, OBE.* (Courtesy of Nigel Robson)

16. *A Chin girl drinking from a* zu *pot, down to the designated mark.*
(From Vumson, *Zo History*)

17. Above: *Norman on tour under canvas.*
The photographs behind the tent pole are of Maeve and Desmond.

18. Left:
The last photograph of the Kelly family together in Tiddim before the trek out of Burma.

19. *Tiddim village in the Chin Hills. It gave its name to the Tiddim Road and the Tiddim front during the Second World War.*
(Photograph courtesy of the Imperial War Museum, London)

20. *A pre-war suspension bridge over the Manipur River.*
(Photograph courtesy of Lieutenant-Colonel Patrick Cardwell Moore, MBE)

21. *A country boat on the Dhaleswari River, similar to the one we used during the trek out through the Lushai Hills.*

22. *Chin Levies, ex-Burma Rifles, at No. 2 Stockade. The bungalow in the distance is in no-man's-land, 5 miles from the Japanese HQ. This position at the base of the hill was in constant contact with the enemy.*
The Levies have .303 rifles, but there were not enough uniforms to go round.
(Drawing by Anthony Gross, courtesy of the Imperial War Museum, London)

23. *A village headman (centre) and his Levies in ceremonial dress with muzzle-loading rifles, gunpowder horns and Burmese* dahs *(knives). The headman is wearing hornbill feathers. In the distance behind him there are houses built on stilts on the side of the hill.*

(Drawing by Anthony Gross, courtesy of the Imperial War Museum, London)

24. Falam, Chin Hills.
Standing: Captain Carlyle Seppings, 5th Gurkhas (left),
Captain Kenny Fraser, 'Doc', RMO Chin Hills Battalion (right);
seated (centre): Captain Bryan Watt-Smyth, Chin Hills Battalion, with his Haka
batman in front and battalion riflemen on either side.
Carlyle Seppings knew Lieutenant-Colonel Frank Haswell, Peter Bankes, Peter
Courtenay and Tom Aplin before the war. Bryan Watt-Smyth was later killed in
Karenni State when he was parachuted in with Force 136 to help Major Hugh Seagrim
(who was awarded the George Cross posthumously).
(Photograph courtesy of Carlyle Seppings)

25. The crest of the Burma Frontier Force,
of which the Chin Hills Battalion was a
part, was a chinthe with a crown above
its head.
(Photograph courtesy of Anne Smith)

What with one thing and another, sweetheart, I'm afraid I just don't get any time to myself these days, and with so many fellows about the house, I am having to write this at your dressing table. Tell the kiddies their pets are in great form and are still well looked after. Ngin Kham is doing great work as cook here with the Nelsons' lad to help him.

I have expanded my office almost to the size of the Deputy Commissioner's as far as clerks are concerned in order to cope with the situation, but even so I seem to be in constant demand myself as the only one who knows anything about the area and can get anything done. I am afraid Tigger and Rabbit will have to wait another week before I can write to them, darling.

I am in grand health though tired, and have had a head cold for a few days which has made me feel pretty short-tempered at times. I pray as ever, sweetheart, that you are all in good health and that it will not be long before our glorious reunion once more.

All my love and kisses, dearest one.

Yours alone,

Daddy

The drive into Kalemyo with Peter Bankes was certainly not without danger, but Norman was not going to increase his wife's anxiety with the risks that he was taking. In May 1942 not only was it essential to get food from the valley back into the hills, but Norman had also made a commitment to the Chins in his speech to them on 25 April. He had spelt out the dangers to them: 'I myself will be your Levy Commander and I pledge myself to remain with you no matter what happens, and to do all I am capable of doing in your best interests.' He was going to lead from the front, because he knew that his actions must match his words.

Harold Braund, who was later to write of his experiences as a Levy officer in *Distinctly I Remember*, described Norman Kelly as

a small, tough Irishman with a bubbling sense of humour and he radiated enthusiasm for the Levy cause. He had been many years in the Chin Hills, and so much of his time had been spent on inter-village touring that he knew the Tiddim area like the back of his hand. He was widely known and trusted and was fluent in several of the local dialects. Despite that he was a civilian among Army officers, the flexibility of guerrilla operations was such that his appointment as Zone Commander, Tiddim, was as unquestioned as it was right.

Norman, in fact, was magnificent. Shortly before my arrival he had been so enraged by reports of divided loyalties in Kalemyo (notwithstanding that it lay outside his jurisdiction) that, top-hatted, in morning coat and striped trousers, with Peter Bankes and two Levy Tommy gunners behind him, he had driven 'Mrs.

Murphy' [as the Jeep was affectionately known] all the way down the hill and into Kalemyo just to show who was boss!

Ultimately Norman carried a revolver or a Tommy gun according to the task in hand, but his first love was for a massive staff that had been his self-chosen badge of office for years. Few men have enriched my life as much.

Norman was like a small boy with a new toy and I went with him on a precarious run to Fort White, which stood at the junction of the valley road from Kalemyo with the mountain road that linked Tiddim, Falam and Haka. This strategic spot had echoed to the sounds of battle on several occasions during the last half-century or more, and buried in the small military cemetery below the rest house was an early winner of the Victoria Cross.[2]

Tiddim
Chin Hills
27th May 1942

Darling Mummy,

Nawk Ngin [who had accompanied us on our trek] and party have just returned today with your letters of the 17th and 21st. I am greatly relieved to learn that you have reached Aijal safely, sweetheart, for this means the worst part of your journey finished. I am sorry at the same time to learn that Peter has had such a rotten time with his fever. The children appear to have been pretty marvellous on the journey and McCall in his letters to me is very enthusiastic about them both. I was sure he and his wife would give you a good welcome and it is grand to know that you were being well looked after.

I have had a bit of a cold this week, which I am just succeeding in shaking off, but otherwise I am in grand form. There has been no change in the situation for several days and the Japs have so far made no move to enter the hills. It appears that their headquarters are still at Shwegyin south of Kalewa, and that they are sending forces up the river to Paungbyin north of Mawlaik [see map no. 7 on p. 80]. At the same time we have to be constantly on the watch for it is impossible to say yet what they intend to do. We have so far been a party of 11 officers in all, but all the Bush Warfare fellows under Col. Musgrave are leaving for Aijal tomorrow. Thereafter I shall only have Capt. Braund here, with Bankes at Fort White. It certainly will seem lonely.

An Indian Army staff officer – Major Landon – is also here at the moment, but he too leaves the day after tomorrow by the Imphal route.

I am glad you have got your T.A.B. [typhoid] inoculations over and hope you didn't have too bad a time, love.

We had the Civil Surgeon – Yarde – over from Falam for a few days looking after the sick British troops. There have been no further deaths among them, and the mysterious disease has been diagnosed as a peculiar mass attack of blackwater fever. Musgrave is leaving his Jeep with me, and I am making arrangements to get in petrol from Imphal. This will save me a lot of time and trouble in getting about on the main road, for all my work at the moment lies between here and Fort White. It is just too bad, darling, that you were not here to realise your ambition to see a car in Tiddim.

Tell the kiddies that all their pets – Mickie and Patch particularly – are being well looked after. Mickie still comes mewing for his milk every morning, much to the annoyance of Dick Musgrave who has been occupying your bed. I have had half the fellows staying with me and the others over at the Nelsons' but we all feed together here. Ngin Kham [the cook] has been doing a grand job of work with the help of Lien Khen [the Nelsons' cook], but I am glad to get Nawk Ngin back again. They were all genuinely thrilled to see me still here I think, and I feel that I can really count on their loyalty.

We have had wonderfully fine weather for the last three days, but I have no doubt we will be in for a bad break shortly.

No other news from this end, darling. I shall try to get mails to you regularly each week, and you must not worry on my account. I hope I shall hear next week how things have turned out with you regarding Woodstock [the school at Mussoorie].

All my love and hugs, sweetheart, and God keep you all.

Yours alone and forever,

Daddy

Captain Harold Braund had arrived in Tiddim between 22 and 27 May. He had been born in Ceylon, the son of a tea taster, educated in England and posted to Rangoon in 1934 where he joined Steel Brothers, one of the great trading companies, which had been founded in 1870. He worked 'up-country', mostly in the oil fields, before joining the army in Maymyo, where he met Colonel Dick Musgrave. He spoke Burmese and on his way into the Chin Hills, from Shillong in Assam via Kohima and Imphal, he crossed the Indian border near Lenakot with some Sokte Chins. He was told by Brigadier Felix Williams that he might not be able to reach Tiddim because of Japanese activity. He and Norman were kindred spirits and he was the second British officer to join Norman. He had been told to report to Lieutenant-Colonel Jack Haswell, who was based at Falam, and who was in overall command of the Chin Levies. Unfortunately, the commandant of the Chin Hills Battalion, Lieutenant-Colonel Moore, was not in favour of the Levies and, in the words of Braund, 'Maine [Braund's pseudonym for Moore] witheld full cooperation. It was a bizarre and tragic situation.' Moore now wanted Braund to join his battalion and ordered him to do so. Braund said, 'I would be more than happy to make war with Kelly and Bankes in whatever manner opportunity offered. Haswell's response was an order to meet me at Fort White to discuss my role. The gathering at Fort White comprised Haswell and Mr. L. B. Naylor, from Falam, Norman Kelly, Peter Bankes and myself. Haswell soon made it clear that I was to come under his command.' [3]

Tiddim
3rd June 1942

Darling Mummy,

I am writing this short note tonight as I am off first thing in the morning by Jeep to meet Naylor and Haswell at Fort White. Nothing much has happened this week, love, and everything is still perfectly quiet here. No sign of any Japs yet, though we are keeping careful watch the whole time with my Levy guards on all the paths leading into the hills from the plain.

I have got a regular army under my control now, for many of our fellows are returning from the Burma Rifles and these I am forming into special Levy units [see illustration no. 22]. I have twisted Chief Pum Za Mang's tail pretty severely lately, with the result that he has got over his initial fright and now shows some sign of doing useful work in organising Levies in his tract. At the same time I do not trust him, as my private informers report that he had sent down two of his clerks to get in contact with the Japs at Kalewa and to tell them that his tract was ready to make submission without fighting.

You can imagine, dearest, that it is all a little worrying.

I have had a Capt. Braund staying with me for a few days. He has brought a company of Sokte Chins over from India and is to join Moore's Chin Hills Battalion for the time being [in the event, this did not happen]. We have also had a Major Landon through here – a staff officer from Eastern Army H.Q. in India.

The garden has freshened up a lot with the rain, darling, and there is really a fine show of colour. The dahlias are doing well and some of the gladioli are already in flower. The vegetable garden too is doing well, though there is very little stuff actually ready at the moment. I am getting a wonderful crop of tomatoes – huge ones. The hens also continue to lay fairly well so I am not doing too badly. Sorry you could not get any cigarettes in Aijal. From what Nawk Ngin tells me things were pretty short there too.

No other great news at the moment, sweetheart. Heaps of love and kisses as ever to you all. How I wish I could see our reunion in sight, love.

Yours alone, darling,

Daddy

The day before my father wrote this letter – 2 June, my birthday – we were crossing the Doon Valley in a hot airless carriage as the train chugged to Dehra Dun, the nearest railhead for Mussoorie. Then there was a twisting 15-mile bus journey up to the picturesque hill station at 6,500 feet. It was dark by the time we arrived at our destination. The next morning we were stunned by our first glimpse of the Himalayan snows to the north, and could look back at the plains of India to the south. Simla is 188 miles to the north-west and Naini Tal 200 miles to the south-east.

In India my mother was having an anxious time. We had arrived with only the things we could bring with us and finding a place to live and a school was no easy matter. June was in the middle of the school year and, for all three of us, this was our first experience of living in India.

Woodstock School, Mussoorie

Maeve and I were to start at boarding school. Our only previous formal education had been in Maymyo, the hill station for Mandalay, for a short time. I remember having my tonsils removed there, at the British Military Hospital, not without a struggle. At the first whiff from the anaesthetic mask, I was up and away. I did a runner. The odds were against me. I was soon captured, subdued and my tonsils snatched by a huge man in a green mask and gown. I awoke with a dreadful sore throat, which could only be pacified with ice cream. What joy! The little day-school there had tiny desks and it was here that I first confronted the mystery of reading and spelling. My mother was with us and we lived with friends and went to school by *gharry* (a horse-drawn carriage). One day a dog was run over and we gazed in horror out of the back window to see the lifeless body moribund in the road. Our friends had an air-raid shelter in their garden – just as well, for Maymyo was later to be bombed. There was a white line on the grass from the back door to the dugout. Pears soap, with its translucency and distinctive smell, and deep rose-coloured cotton towels, all the way from England, pampered bath time.

Mussoorie was different. At first it was a long rickshaw ride from school and although my mother taught there (and we saw her not infrequently) the pangs of homesickness were very real. I compensated by exaggerating how close the Japanese had been behind us on our trek out.

'Ridgewood' was the junior house. Mrs Joan Haskins was working as a nurse at the school. Later we were to spend happy holidays (which, in those days, were from December to March in the plains) with John and Joan Haskins and their son Brian, also at Woodstock. My memories are of pine trees and lots of American children – the school had been founded for the offspring of US missionaries. I vividly remember the 'giant stride', a metal maypole with chains and handles to hang onto; as one ran round, and as the centrifugal force increased, it was possible to be lifted completely off the ground and fly through the air with considerable velocity at 45 degrees. There was also 'kick the can', Cubs with Dr Robert Fleming, buying curry puffs from the box *wallah*, and guava cheese and peanuts for dessert. The most evocative thing to remind me of my father was the smell of wet pine needles and the mist creeping over the hills.

Mussoorie, like many of the other hill stations, had numerous schools. The well-known actor Saeed Jaffrey, the son of a doctor, went to one – Wynberg Allen – in 1941. He was later to write, 'I have for a long time believed that there has always been a strange exotic love affair between India and Britain.'[4]

Woodstock School, Mussoorie

Northward there rise snow-capped mountains,
Southward the Doon-land fills,
Westward the roads of old Mussoorie,

Eastward blue Tehri hills,
Here many happy school days were mine,
'Mid fern-oak and whispering pine.

Dr Robert Fleming

The Valley of the Doon

Is it an enchanted city drowned
In the days of long ago,
Or just my own illusion found
Within the sun's bright flow?
Howe'er it is it seems to me
As though I looked beneath the sea
And saw a country wondrous fair,
Strangely lovely, strangely bright,
Glowing with translucent light.

In the far beyond, the plain
Is girded by a mountain chain,
The sheltered vale is deep-blue green
Broad silver rivers flow between
Fair fields and forests. Dehra lies
Dreaming, peacefully at rest
Upon that rich and ample breast.

Vera Frances
Editor of the Woodstock School magazine *Whispering Pine*

While Maeve and I embarked upon our schooldays in Mussoorie, my father had more serious concerns back in Tiddim.

Tiddim
10th June 1942

Darling Mummy,

Still here, love, and no change in the situation up to date. I am still kept mighty busy dealing with the pay affairs, etc., of all the returning Burma Rifles people, but I am to get more assistance now. I am going to divide my area up into three zones and will have three British officers working under me – Major Wadhams, Lt. Bankes and Lt. Wright. Our people have had to evacuate Kanpetlet [in the far south-east of the Chin Hills – see map no. 3 on p. 28] and [John] Wadhams is making his way up from there. A couple of Americans have turned up in Haka, having crashed in their plane after bombing the Japs at Rangoon.

Haswell arrived here today and I am organising a Levy party of Burma Rifles fellows who will go out with Bankes to take up their post at Sialthaw on the eastern slopes of the Letha to watch the roads there [see map no. 6 on p. 74]. I have already sent Lt. Wright out on the northern side in a similar capacity, so I have things fairly well covered now against any surprise in the rear.

I saw Naylor at Fort White the other day. He had had a letter from his wife written the day after they reached Shillong and it appears they were to be evacuated still further to the other side of India – somewhere in Rajpatana. He has constituted himself Chief Intelligence Officer for the Levies but has no official rank. He wanted to know whether any useful purpose would be served if he showed his form and figure in Tiddim and I promptly told him no!! He took the hint and went back to Falam instead.

I have had your letter of May 22nd, darling, in which you say you were leaving for Calcutta on the 24th. As soon as you reach Mussoorie I hope you are able to wire your address to McCall to enable me to send you more funds. I will buy drafts on the Falam treasury and these will be sent by post to be cashed by you at the Mussoorie treasury.

We are having a lot of rain now, and this might lead to slight delays in the delivery of our mails at Aijal. I am sending my men off every Thursday to link up at Champhai on Sundays with the mail runners from Falam. McCall has arranged for his men to pick up the mails from there on to Aijal and I hope the system will work satisfactorily.

No other great news at the moment, love, but this letter will at least serve to let you know that I am still OK and very much alive here. May God protect you all, dearest one. With all my individual love.

Yours alone,

Daddy

Tiddim
17th June 1942

Darling Mummy,

Our mail arrangements don't seem to have sorted themselves out quite properly yet, love, for your letter of the 24th only reached me today whereas I had already had one from Mrs. McCall enclosing your wire from Calcutta saying you were leaving there for Mussoorie on the 31st. In the next mail I hope to hear from the McCalls that you have wired them your new address at Mussoorie so that I can get more funds to you as soon as possible.

I enclose two letters I have had from Mrs. McCall. They certainly are a grand couple and I can never thank them enough for the help they gave you, sweetheart. They are also doing all they can to help me and in the last mail they sent some papers, a bottle of sherry and a bottle of French Vermouth – all that was then available!!

I have been down with a touch of fever for the last few days but have got it broken now and the new doctor here – Dr. Joseph – has put me on a plasmoquin [anti-malarial] course. I am quite OK again, love, so there is no need to worry. I am taking things easy for a few days as it has left me rather groggy on my feet. Peter Bankes has pushed off to his base on the eastern slopes of the Letha so the house is very lonely at the moment, darling. I do so miss the chats we used to have over the news at night, dearest, and the place is very dull without the laughter and chatter of the kiddies.

The situation here is unchanged and so far there is no indication of the Japs attempting to enter the hills, though there are reports that they have strengthened their forces at Kalewa and have moved a force into Kyigon, which is only 6 miles from Kalemyo [see map no. 4 on p. 38].

Moore is having a lot of trouble with his men deserting on him, and some of these deserters are said to have made contact with the Japs and gone over to the enemy. Moore was always well hated by the troops and his overbearing manner is complicating things considerably now. He has quarrelled finally with Naylor (though this was not to be wondered at) and now he is failing to co-operate at all with Haswell on the Levy side. I wouldn't be a bit surprised if he gets a shot in the back one of these days.

My own show is going well and I feel much more satisfied now that I have organised patrols out, formed of seasoned Burma Rifles troops. Can you imagine Daddy in full military command of more than 1,000 men with a full-blown Major as one of his subordinates!! Doesn't it all seem just too funny.

My own supply situation is still not too grim, but I am on to my last tin of kerosene with no hope of further supplies. I am not too badly off for stores but local supplies – chickens, eggs, etc. – have all soared in price and there are very few villagers coming in to sell things these days.

The servants too are finding it difficult to get food with rice selling at only 8 *kwets* to the rupee whereas it used to be 40 to 50. In order to keep them with me I am helping them out with rice and dried peas issued from the Levy rations stocks.

Tell the kiddies that all their domestic pets, Mickie, Patch, etc., are well. I was delighted to get their last letters written from Aijal and I am hoping that once they get settled in school at Mussoorie they will have lots of adventures and experiences to tell me about.

I have had a serious casualty in that the small wireless set is out of order. One of the valves has burnt out, and though I am trying to replace it from the Army at Imphal I have little hope for the time being. The big set, however, is still OK so things are not too bad when I am in HQ.

Father Blivet comes in to see me regularly and has given me his bicycle to replace Pau Za Kam's [the headman of Tiddim] which is on its last legs.

No other news at the moment, sweetheart. All my love to you as ever. Yours alone,

Daddy

Fort White
23rd June 1942

My darling,

I am writing this now so that it will reach Tiddim in time to be despatched on Thursday morning to link up with the Falam mails to Aijal which leave Champhai every Sunday.

There has been no excitement at all here this week though we are still keeping up our vigilant patrols on the lookout for the enemy. So far he hasn't moved further than 6 miles west of Kalewa and it seems very doubtful indeed whether he will attempt anything further during the rains at least. My Jeep is lying here out of order at the moment so on this occasion I had to come over from Tiddim by the time-honoured method of horse and bicycle!! I think there is something wrong with the dynamo and I am having difficulty in finding a mechanic who knows sufficient to put the trouble right.

I am picking up a Siyin platoon from the Burma Rifles, which I am taking across to Dolluang. They will be based there for patrol duty on the paths leading up from the plains. The other regular platoons are already in place at Hiangzang and Sialthaw on the eastern slopes [of the Letha Range – see map no. 6 on p. 74]. Apart from these precautions and the difficulty of obtaining supplies, you would little dream that times were other than normal here. At the same time the strain is a bit wearing for one gets such varied rumours from the plains. A few days ago rumour had it that the Kalemyo traders had made their submission to the Japs and that the latter had a force of 300 men only 4 miles from the town. Subsequent reports have denied this, but it is very difficult to sift out the truth and to know exactly where one stands.

Dacoity [banditry], committed by the Burmans who armed themselves from our retreating army, is the greatest menace we have to face at the moment, for it means that peaceful cultivators are afraid to return to their villages from the jungle and are making no attempt to start the planting of their fields. This will mean that next harvest will be negligible in the plain and our Chins will have a harder time than ever in supplementing their own crops. So far our crop prospect is good, but it is too early to speak with confidence yet.

The great news of the week is that one of our planes has dropped certain essential medical supplies over Falam. I haven't learnt the full details yet, but we knew some time ago that this was to be attempted, and that if we saw a plane which fired a green Verey light we were to lay out two white strips as a guide.

Considering the rain and mist we have been having I think this was a grand effort. At Tiddim I heard a plane go over very low one morning but it was entirely cut off by low mist. It was flying in the Falam direction, but returned after ten minutes presumably having given up the attempt. The next day this plane got through successfully.

It is grand to know that we are not entirely forgotten by the outside world, dear, and I am hoping we may get some supplies into Tiddim before long by the same means. It won't be for want of trying on my part, for I have been at every staff officer I have met on this very point. I have had the large trees at the bazaar end of the football ground cut down for this very reason. Isn't it amazing to think of the developments which it has taken a war to bring to the Chin Hills?

I have entirely thrown off the spot of fever I had last week, love, and am feeling as fit as a flea again. All in Tiddim enquire after you and the children and are frequently asking for news.

The hens have not been laying so well in this wet spell, but the garden is thriving well. I have given the *mali* [gardener] a week's leave but the others are all still with me – now employed at the expense of the Levy!

I am sure you will be annoyed to know that we spoiled the badminton ground at the north side of the house by digging a slit trench as an air raid precaution. We have had our threats of bombing over the Tokio radio so I got the town traders to dig trenches for their own protection. I hope they will never be put to use.

You probably have little idea, sweetheart, of the thousand and one ways I miss you at home. Did you know, for instance, that you went off with all the wool in the house and that I was left with nothing for the darning of my stockings? So far I haven't needed to do anything about it but it looks as though I will have to unravel an old pair and get one of the women from your old war knitting class to do the darning!! A case of war charity beginning very close at home!

I'm afraid I am not making any great use of the raspberries this year as there is still lots of jam in the storeroom. The grapevine promises well again and the fig is bearing heavily. Also the peaches. The Indian corn will soon be ready and should be excellent. The strawberries really didn't come to very much. They grew into enormous plants with lots of flowers, but the fruit did not develop on any great scale before the rains arrived and finished them. Mickie and Patch are still with me and Nawk Ngin and the *mali* report well on Patch's pups – now both lanky hounds.

I have managed to confiscate a number of government mules which returning soldiers had picked up and brought home with them, so now I have all the transport I could ever want. Isn't this just the irony of fate when you are not here, darling, to tour with me in comfort? Naylor rang me up the other day to say he had great hopes of getting me a spare valve for the little wireless from Aijal, so I am living in hopes. I have no set here with me this time, but at my request he is wiring me the news every night. Our post offices at Tiddim, Falam and Haka are still functioning and I have a telephone installed at No. 3 Stockade, which I pinched out of Kalemyo before it was sacked, and another one in the bungalow here which I removed from Tom Atkinson's place in Kalewa on one of my early visits there.

So you see, dearest, we are a very self-contained little world of our own now.

All my love as ever, sweetheart, and here's hoping for another letter from you soon.

Yours alone,

Daddy

Just received yours from Calcutta, Mussoorie (3/6) but have no time to reply for this mail, love. Thank God you are at journey's end for a while. Norman.

Fort White
24th June 1942

My own darling,

I had no sooner handed my letter to you over to the policeman last night when your letters written from Calcutta and Mussoorie were delivered to me from Falam. I was only able to get it back to re-address it to the Imperial Bank, Mussoorie and had no time to reply further then, love.

What a terrific month of travelling you have had, dearest! I am sure you must have arrived at Mussoorie absolutely deadbeat with the worry of it all, but I think you have done marvellously, sweetheart, to get through as you have with the children. I have been very worried throughout lest any of you should fall ill en route as a result of such strenuous moving and, in your case, love, of such incessant worry as I know you must have suffered on the kiddies' account. We have much for which to thank God, indeed.

I thought your letter from the Calcutta hotel was a little excitable in its plea to me to get out from here, but that is easily understood in view of all the people you were then meeting and all the stories you were hearing from Burma.

You will realise by now, dearest, if you are getting my letters, that there can be no question of my getting out at the moment. I have got no civilian orders from India, but as the Officer Commanding Tiddim I can't move now as we are under the orders of 4 Corps Imphal. However, you have no need to worry on my account, sweetheart, for I do not intend to hang on if things become too hot here in the future. If India wants to retain the Chin Hills as an eventual buffer from a Japanese-occupied Burma, it is up to them to defend the area adequately, and we cannot be expected to do that job for them with a handful of villagers if we come up against a strong and well-equipped enemy force. In such a case I know that I shan't be long in skipping over the border and making my way to you, love.

Fancy meeting Griffiths and the Bazetts in the hotel on your arrival. I'm sure they all had a great deal to say.

Sorry to hear that P. C. Fogarty [ICS] had died after an air crash at Kunming. I could rather have hoped he had been killed outright. The rumour regarding [Lieutenant-Colonel A. C.] Moore's death must have made it awkward for you with Molly [his wife] staying in the hotel at the time. You will since have learnt from my letters that he never even did the fighting he was expected to do in the Gangaw Valley, but moved up to the hills from Sihaung to Webula on the Falam Road even before the Army left. He is still there, and apparently having a pretty lean time with wholesale desertions from his command.

It must have been a comfort to you, love, to meet Moya at Mussoorie as one reliable friend. I wonder what nonsense J. C. [Poulton, BFrS] had got up to when she left that he had to be placed under suspension. Has anything been heard of him yet, or of [John] Leyden?

The journey from Aijal to Calcutta must have been very trying for you, darling, with so many changes and such varied modes of travel.

Glad Grindlays were helpful. I am drawing an advance of three months' pay which I shall send over in a draft to you, sweetheart. I think I may as well draw all I can while the going is still good. This should carry you on for a while and give you a little capital on which to draw in addition to the monthly remittances which I will also be sending from my pay. The latter will of course be reduced by deductions of the advance, but you must let me know if you find that the provision I make is proving or likely to prove insufficient for your needs, love.

Peter Courtenay doesn't seem to have been very helpful once you reached Calcutta and you were lucky to get your train bookings arranged so promptly through the hotel staff. I am sure Prue Bankes must have been in an awful state about her husband, and will be powerfully relieved to learn the truth. You certainly must have met a lot of Burma people in Calcutta. Sam Cope was a great friend of Bankes and was expected to join us in this part of the world. Some of his clothes are still lying here in Peter's care.

Your letter seems to be full of news, dear, but I suppose that it is really only a fraction of what you will hear by degrees. Keep me posted, love, with any other news you get of people known to us both. What about the Leitches, Plunketts, Eccles, Bullens and the rest? And the Baylys and Macdonalds from Loilem?

I am trying to fix up with Sharpe [William Sharpe, Director of Supply for Burma] about your boxes which we sent there. As soon as I heard that communications at the Imphal railhead were congested, I sent him word to return them to me if he had not already tried to despatch them. I do hope they turn up OK, dear.

The heat in Calcutta and in the train – particularly in the blackout – must have been very trying and it is marvellous that the children were so good. What an hour of the night to arrive at Mussoorie! And what a birthday for poor old Tigger. I hope we are all together and able to make up for it next year, sweetheart.

Woodstock seems a long way from where you were staying – 1½ hours by rickshaw – and I am sorry you were not able to tell me that you had got the children fixed up definitely there. I do hope all will be well and that the school can take them. Cannot the Nelsons and Gates use any influence they have in the matter?

I am worried too to learn from your letter that the woman at Connaught Castle, Mussoorie, could only have you until the 6th June.

I do hope that in next week's letter I shall learn that you are finally settled. Give my love to Moya and tell her I expect her to stick by you all, until we meet again.

All my love as ever, sweetheart,

Yours alone,

    Daddy

Thank the kiddies for their letters. It is nice to think that Rabbit remembers me in her prayers. N.

The East has captivated generations of British people, as it did my father. Burma itself was a province of India until 1937, and my father had been recruited into the Burma Frontier Service, selection for which was by interview. In the opinion of Sir Leslie Glass of the Indian Civil Service, it was renowned for containing 'a wide variety of eccentrics, mostly passionately devoted to their tribesmen'.[5] The Burma Frontier Service had been created because the British appreciated that the hill tribes were so different in origin, religion and temperament in comparison with the Buddhist Burmans who lived in the plains. The

Chins, Shans, Karens and Kachins were often regarded as second-class citizens by the Burmans, and these hill races had many dialects and customs. For this reason, they needed a cadre of competent linguists, physically fit, self-sufficient men who could withstand the long periods of isolation – quite different qualities than those required by the mainstream Indian Civil Service.[6] It was the mutual respect that the majority of Chins had for the majority of British officers that was the key to success in the Chin Hills campaign. The Burmans offered very little resistance during the Japanese invasion whereas the Chins were a natural hunter/warrior race. It was this quality which was to play such an important part in the unfolding drama of the Chin Hills campaign.

The British officers had great respect for the Chins, in some cases akin to the relationship between the British Indian Army and their Gurkha troops. Although they came from entirely different backgrounds, they shared the same conditions and in wartime bonds are very strong. Here men are at their most basic and vulnerable. Often short of food and sleep, wet and cold, exhausted and afraid, their very lives are in the hands of their comrades. Kenny Fraser and another Levy officer were both struck by the loyalty of the Chins to the British government. As one of them told me, 'During the brief time I was in the front line they could have easily betrayed me and thereby gained kudos with the Japanese.' Mutual respect was the catalyst that held them together, for they were fighting each with their individual national pride.

Chapter 5

WAITING AND WATCHING

The monsoon had forced a lull of sorts, not unwelcome to the British. They had been badly bruised in their retreat, the longest in British military history, and now needed time to consolidate. Although major moves were in abeyance, there was much skirmishing and harassing of enemy lines. Kalemyo was being reinforced by the Japanese, and so the Chin Levies were busy.

Jack Oats was known as 'Wild Oats' to his friends to distinguish him from 'Tame Lieutenant-Colonel "Titus" Oatts', who was later to command the Levies from Falam. Jack Oats was a Cornishman, a tough teak *wallah* who, like Peter Bankes, had also worked for the Bombay-Burmah Trading Corporation where they knew each other from before the war. He commanded the Chin Hills Battalion's Mounted Infantry Company. Harold Braund had never seen him in a flap: 'He had a laugh that was always fun, and the self-reliance and jungle craft of a man who was completely at home in a forest. His men trusted him completely and he had a contempt for paperwork.'[1]

On 29 June 1942 Jack described the situation at No. 2 Stockade:

The Japs were threatening Fort White by a concentration at Kalemyo and were collecting pack transport there as though for a move into the hills. Blocking the road was Peter with 60 or 70 villagers and ex-Burma riflemen, poorly clothed and armed, and a company of my Battalion under an Indian officer. The Siyin Chiefs wanted to surrender. I was sent with a troop of 75 Mounted Infantry from near Falam to reinforce this job and to personally command our infantry company there. I got to Fort White in 48 hours and left my mounted infantry there [see map no. 8 on p. 96].

At Fort White I met Kelly, Haswell and Barton and learned that Peter was at No. 3 Stockade – 10 miles east. Next day Colonel Haswell and I went down to No. 3 and were greeted by Peter. He said 'Hello, Jack. Pyinmana – hot weather over two years ago.'

Peter had some 80 to 100 Levies, some ex-Burma Rifles and some villagers and I had one company of Chin Hills Battalion at No. 3 and one troop at Fort White in reserve. Some of Peter's men were armed with muzzle-loading flintlocks (exactly the same as you see

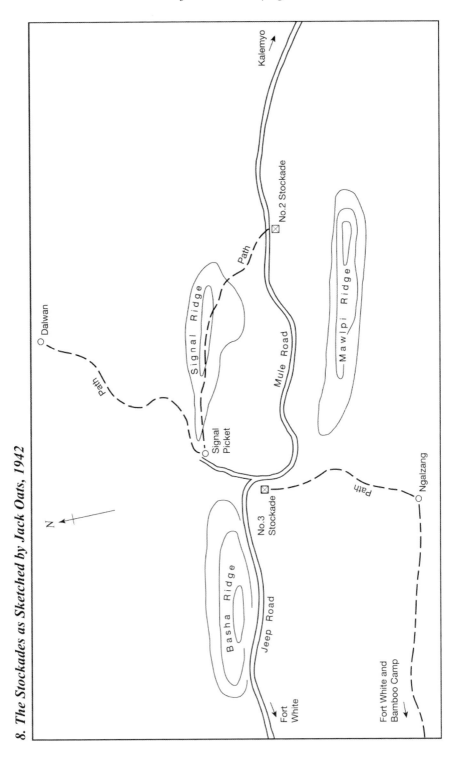

8. The Stockades as Sketched by Jack Oats, 1942

on the timbered walls of old hotels here and used at Waterloo). Morale was poor and weather misty and damp. Lovely views of Myittha Valley when clouds lifted at dawn and dusk.

We were quite comfortable in the *dak* bungalow and Peter, as always, had a reasonable cook and was making the most of available food. As a matter of fact we were not too badly off at that time for Peter and Kelly had collected a lot of tinned stuff left behind by Burmah Oil Company refugees. Wherever Peter was, there was always an abundance of plain loaves of bread and I always appreciated this as when alone with troops I always stuck to *chapatis* [Indian bread].

That evening Peter and I and Haswell were sitting round a table talking, with a hurricane lantern on the table and no blackout, when a single rifle shot crashed close to us. I put the light out and Haswell flapped like hell, sending patrols here and there, but Peter and I guessed it was just a *sepoy* [Indian soldier] loosing off an accidental round.

In the morning Haswell pushed off and Peter showed me round the area. We walked six miles forward to No. 2 stockade where he had a precarious picket and we also looked at Mawlpi Ridge (which we were later to come to know intimately). On the way back we first heard bombing in the Plains (probably Kalemyo, eleven miles away) and then a big bump quite near. Then on the way up we saw a big burnt patch on a hillside and a few minutes later we were met by my *sowar* [mounted orderly] and two ponies and the information that a plane had crashed – hence the burnt patch. It was a Blenheim and we found the crew of three in our H.Q. Navigator badly hurt in the back – pilot very shaken – both Canadian – rear gunner unhurt. He was a cocky little north-countryman who had been lucky to force his way out of the burning plane. The gunner gave us some English tobacco – our first for sometime. The navigator was very cold and we wrapped him in blankets and parachutes. Next day we pushed them all off to Tiddim via Fort White with escorts, pilot and navigator on stretchers and gunner on jungle pony.

Also that day and the next we got in several escaped prisoners, some wounded, and did a lot of first aid. Later Kelly sent us a Chin medical student who did some good jobs. Although we were well off in many respects, compared to later times, we were short of many things – notably cigarettes and tobacco. We smoked cigarettes made from chopped-up tobacco leaf. Peter had a queer contrivance of board and cloth to roll them with and seemed to spend a lot of time on this job. It was an interesting time for we were probably, during that period, getting more news about the Jap occupation than anyone else.

A few days later Harold Braund arrived and took over Peter's job and we started a long partnership. Peter went up north, some 60 very rough miles, about four days' march, and was there before and after his 1942 leave, for a long spell. His job was similar there, collecting information and guarding some of the minor tracks into the hills from the Kabaw Valley. I knew the area between us but never went into his sector and do not know the country. We communicated irregularly by runner and, later, by helio [a method of signalling at night by flashing lights from one hilltop to another] and signal lamps.[2]

These individual officers were civilians in peacetime and it mattered little to them that they were under different chains of command – the Levy cause or the Chin Hills Battalion. If there was a job to be done, they got on with the task of winning the war. Their friendship meant everything.

The Chin Hills Battalion in 1942

The battalion officers Captains West, Oats and Peebles had carried out a great deal of good work during the months of May, June and July, were tireless on patrol and a splendid example to their men. In July 1942, the information that the battalion had was that there were 300 Japanese in Kalemyo with an estimated 2,000 more in support at Kalewa. Gurkha patrols from Webula said that the Japanese had light mountain artillery and pack ponies. They had been joined by some Siyin deserters from the battalion. The Japanese commandant in Kalemyo sent a letter to Lieutenant-Colonel Moore 'commanding retreating armies of the British' and calling for all Chins to rise against British rule and join the Japanese. Bombings and reprisals against the villages were threatened if they failed to act in accordance with these orders. Rewards of 2,000 rupees were placed on the heads of Moore and Captain West. At that time the battalion and the Chin Levies were defending a 300-mile front against a well-organised, fully trained Japanese army that had yet to lose a battle in Burma.

The Sokte and Siyin chiefs had petitioned Norman Kelly and Haswell for the removal of Levies and the battalion detachment from No. 3 Stockade and the Tiddim area generally. Their feeling was that, in the event of armed resistance to a now widely expected Japanese attack, they feared reprisals against their villages and were prepared to submit without a struggle. They undertook to provide every British officer with a personal escort to see him safely out to India. Norman Kelly and Haswell met with the wavering chiefs and they were persuaded to remain loyal to the British cause.

The problem of the warring Moore and Naylor had to be addressed. Brigadier Felix Williams was sent over from India to Tiddim and on 17 July 1942 summoned Moore and Naylor to appear before him.

Lieutenant-Colonel Moore was to return to India on sick leave, because he was suffering from steatorrhoea (tropical sprue), a bowel complaint. He told Jack Oats – and to use his own words – that he was 'being sacked'. This must have been a personal tragedy, since he never returned to the Chin Hills. He was highly regarded by many of his British officers, and had been nine years with the battalion. Following his departure, morale improved, and at once there was more cooperation between the Chin Levies and the battalion. Lieutenant-Colonel Duguid took over as commandant, in the short term, before he was succeeded by Lieutenant-Colonel Roddie Russell on 1 September 1942. The senior officers in the battalion were Major Tommy West, Captains Percy Smart, Jack Oats, Syd Hyde, Bobby Peebles and David Milligan. On the Levy side, Haswell was promoted to Brigadier, and Colonel Frank Ford of the Burma Rifles took over his Levy role. Naylor remained, but was to be replaced later as Deputy Commissioner.

When Lieutenant-Colonel Moore reached India he had interviews with General Irwin, commanding the Eastern Army, as well as General Wavell, Commander-in-Chief India, who stated that the battalion had done very well in the defence of the Chin Hills; his remarks were conveyed to all ranks. Moore also met His Excellency The Governor of Burma.[3]

On 5 August Norman wrote again to his wife from Tiddim.

Tiddim
5th August 1942

Darling,

I have just received a message that the Japs have again returned to Kalemyo so I'm leaving at once to join Capt. Braund & Capt. Oats at No. 3 Stockade. I don't imagine for one moment that they intend any attack on the Hills as they only appear to number about 120, but we will have to stand by again all the same.

I'm afraid this will have to be only a short note for the mules are ordered for 2 p.m. which means we shall only get to Fort White somewhere about 10 p.m. tonight.

Don't worry, darling, they haven't caught us out yet and the knowledge that we can rely on the RAF assistance is great comfort.

The last mail brought the ten tins of cigarettes you so thoughtfully sent me, love. For a long time we have been reduced to smoking Chin tobacco as cigarettes so you can imagine what a joy it was to get a decent smoke again. I gave one tin each to Bankes & Capt. Carey who are with me. The latter will accompany me tonight but Bankes has had a good deal of trouble with a septic foot and is only waiting here until it is sufficiently healed to enable him to proceed on six weeks' leave to India. I envy him greatly, but I'm afraid there is little chance that I can get away at present. Although I have all these other officers to help me now, there is none who really knows my Tiddim Chins and could take over full control in my absence. However, I am still praying that it may be possible soon for me to get over to see you, sweetheart, if only for a few days. It would of course be expensive, but don't you think well worth it, love? Although time has been so fully occupied with alarums and excursions, it still seems ages since you left and I would give all to be with you again, darling, if even for a brief glimpse.

I will be sending money by Bankes which he will find some means of sending to you.

No more at the moment, dearest. My mind is so occupied with this latest development that I don't seem to be able to concentrate.

All my love, sweetheart, and may God keep you all in his care.

Yours alone,

Daddy

Rupert Carey, mentioned in Norman's letter above, formerly of the Burmah Oil Company, was described thus by Harold Braund: 'His father had been the first Administrator of the Chin Hills after their pacification and Rupert, ever the comedian, had cast himself in the role of a one-man flag march through ancient domains. If not being greeted precisely with "palms and scattered garments", he was at least enjoying himself and would be an asset to the rest of us.' [4] His father, Bertram S. Carey, was the co-author, with H. N. Tuck, of *The Chin Hills: A History of the People, our Dealings with Them, their Customs and Manners, and a Gazetteer of their Country*, published in 1896 and the most authoritative book on the Chin Hills.

No. 3 Stockade, the forward HQ, with a semi-furnished government rest house, was about halfway up the climb into the Chin Hills from the Kalemyo plain to Fort White. Situated at about 4,000 feet, it had a magnificent view of the Kabaw Valley to the north and Kale Valley to the south, with Kalemyo in the centre. With a telescope on Basha Hill, west of No.3, people could be seen moving around on the streets (see photograph no. 43). From the stockade two spurs ran down to the valley below on each of which was a standing picket post. No. 2 was at the foot of the ascent (see illustration no. 22). Beneath it there was a semi-furnished rest house in no-man's-land, 5 miles from the Japanese HQ.

On 11 August Norman wrote to his wife from No. 3 Stockade. Obviously the situation in Burma was of paramount importance to him, but he also had domestic concerns; his next batch of letters betray his loneliness without his family and his worries for them in the increasingly disturbing world of war.

No. 3 Stockade
11th August 1942

Darling,

I'm having to send this off today in order that it will reach Tiddim in time for inclusion in the mail which leaves for Aijal on Thursday morning.

The Japs didn't risk staying in Kalemyo this time and have all returned again to Kalewa. We have just returned from a patrol down to the plain – to some of the villages between No. 2 and Kalemyo, and on the 13th I think we shall be going down again to visit Kalemyo itself in the hope of buying some more rice, etc., there for the Levies. It appears the Japs have ordered the people not to supply us but to send all their rice, peas, etc., to them at Kalewa. They have also expressed their intention of returning again shortly and say they will require 50 coolies. It looks as though I shall be here the best part of another week and if everything remains quiet I shall then return to Tiddim.

I have got your letter of July 15th darling, which has been sent on to me here from Tiddim together with Aunt Nellie's letter.

Don't worry about the things from Imphal, love. Sharpe hopes to send them back to me in a week or two, but transport appears to present some difficulty. When I get them I shall find some means of getting them through to you, dear, as quickly as possible. Peter Bankes has left Tiddim for Aijal and is carrying Rs 2000 for you. It doesn't appear so easy to get drafts through – Philip Barton (Burma Frontier Service) who is attached to me – has had one returned uncashed from India. Incidentally, he is being sent back to India, having given Brigadier Williams the impression that he is a defeatist [he was later to be awarded the MBE, for the utmost devotion to duty, in 1944].

Delighted to hear that Desmond has got into his class at last and I trust he will work hard. I do hope Rabbit will settle down well in her boarding school. You must have been thrilled, darling, to see her acting on her own in her class. I wish I could have been present.

If you are not satisfied with the games at Ridgewood, by all means try to get Tigger into another school even if it entails extra cost.

Thanks for the news of Burma friends. J. C. Poulton seems to have broken up badly. I understand John Kennedy got through but was very ill with dysentery and malaria. I believe Paddy Eccles [my godfather] has fallen into Jap hands after getting as far as Monywa. J. R. K. Wallace [not to be confused with Ian Wallace] was also caught at Lashio.

I do hope you have been getting my letters more regularly recently, love, for I am making a point of writing every week.

Two British planes have just passed over us and have been in bombing Kalewa. Yesterday they went in, and after bombing Kalewa, came back and machine-gunned Kalemyo. The previous day Kalemyo was bombed. There is no doubt the RAF are giving us valuable assistance in keeping the Jap on the move. I also hear from Tiddim that another plane has been in dropping supplies there. So far they have dropped us about 6,000 lbs. of rice, the same of *atta* [flour], some 600 tins of bully beef, a lot of tinned milk, tea, sugar, etc., No luck, however, with kerosene oil, cigarettes or spirits, which are very short with us.

The McCalls very kindly continue to send me papers regularly, love. I do hope the troubles in India are not going to come close to you. It is indeed a disturbed world.

I will send on to you, darling, the remains of the roll of white silk when I get back, also the tartan blouse and black skirt. There is also your brown morning frock with the pink piping – 'garments' that have caused me many a heart wrench because they are hanging idle.

No more now, sweetheart. Let us finish this job thoroughly and what a reunion we will have. I have given Bankes your address and asked him if possible to arrange a meeting. If you have the kiddies happily settled in school by then perhaps you would think of coming back here to help me – in perhaps other little ways than the typing and Hindustani! Peter is very anxious for his wife to come back with him, too.

All my love as ever to you, sweetheart mio, and to the kiddies.

Yours alone for ever,

Daddy

Tiddim
26th August 1942

Darling Mummy,

The mails at this end are disappointingly irregular these days. Last week, instead of coming in on Wednesday night or Thursday, only arrived late on Saturday – and then it contained letters from the children but not a single scrape of the pen from you, love.

The Jap seems to have decided to leave the Kalemyo area alone again for a while, so I am back in Tiddim for a spell of rest from some very strenuous patrolling in the valley between No. 3 Stockade and various villages in as close as 3 miles from Kalemyo. These patrols entail 28 to 32 or 34 miles a day and are no joke, and I can say I am only too glad to lie off for a little and to leave the work to Braund and Oats who work with me at No. 3 Stockade. This week I have got reinforcements for Tiddim in the shape of three platoons of the Falam Battalion under the Naib Pau Chin. Oats is under me with three more battalion platoons at No. 3 and Braund has one platoon of the returned Burma Rifle Levies with him there. Carey, a son of Sir Bertram Carey who conducted the operations civilly at the annexation, is with me at Tiddim in charge of the Burma Rifle Levy Training Platoon and soon will have one village Levy-training platoon also from the Kamhau tract. From the Siyin and Sokte country I have some 500 village Levies employed on various patrol duties, etc., so you will realise, dear, to what a size my Tiddim Zone Command has grown. Unfortunately the rationing responsibilities grow with it and hence my personal visits to the plains to buy more and more rice. It makes it all rather a cat-and-mouse game when the old Jap is trying to do the same thing, and I only hope we never try to do the same thing at the same time.

My latest rival in the enemy camp at Kalemyo was a fellow who signed himself in a Burmese manifesto as Colonel O'Hara (though to the Nippon this might have been 'Ha Ya'). Nevertheless I sent a useful counterblast into his camp signing myself as Mother Reilly so I hope he has a sense of humour. At any rate he hasn't made any attack on my virginity yet!! From which I hope you will see, darling, that we are still in good heart here.

I've even been informed that we are likely to get a whiskey ration issued from Falam though the smell of the cork hasn't been wafted from Fort White yet.

This week I have had two other visitors in the shape of one Capt. Parsons, who is looking further into the question of getting supplies in to us, and a Lt. Godsell who was in charge of a Royal Engineer recce party exploring the possibilities of making both the Tiddim–Imphal and the Falam–Aijal roads 'Jeepable' for the cold weather.

The weather has been poor and consequently we have had no further spectacular droppings of food by air over Tiddim. Our greatest shortages are still cigarettes and kerosene oil and it is no fun trying to type by candlelight – I haven't even the large candles to fit the candle lamps we used to have in the P.W.D. bungalows.

But here again, dear, this is all about myself and must cease. Has Bankes got in touch with you with the Rs 2000 I sent? At long last Naylor has got a wireless from India – from [Bernard] Binns [ICS] who is now supposedly our Commissioner under the Acting Governor [John] Wise – to the effect that Treasury Drafts from Falam will be cashed by the Reserve Bank in India provided Naylor is satisfied that the amounts are reasonable!! Did you ever hear of such red tape, love, that India should refuse to pay out on drafts issued from Falam when we have been working here steadily throughout when the rest of the b—rs who have imposed these restrictions were comfortably away in Delhi and elsewhere. Doesn't it give one to wonder sometimes? Nevertheless, darling, as we have often said at this very fireplace, the Empire is not to be so easily beaten. On the new arrangement I shall have a large draft through to you, dearest, before long. These bloody worries keep me long awake at night in my lonely bed, and it makes things worse to think that at your end you, too, are probably lying awake wondering what is happening here and where the next cash is coming from.

Don't let a week go by, love, without sending me at least a few lines. Things are difficult enough, but unless I hear from you in every mail or unless you come back to me with Peter Bankes, the job would just be unbearable.

I was thrilled with the kiddies' letters received last week, and as I am likely to be here on Sunday I intend to take some time off to write to them both individually and at length.

I'm afraid that in the force of circumstance, sweetheart, thoughts are now very much divided between yourselves and this job of dealing with the enemy, but I know that *you*, darling, know that this heart beats still, only for the three of you who in absence are going through equal hell.

May God continue his blessings on us all.

By the way, Father Blivet visits me occasionally, usually for a morning meal, and has promised some rather special French stamps for Tigger. Unfortunately he forgot to bring them in with him the last time he came. I find his visits are always refreshing and a source of greater fortitude. May you sleep well, my Loves.

Ever yours alone, darling,

Daddy

Tiddim
2nd September 1942

Darling Mummiekins,

It was marvellous to get your letter of the 6th August, which turned up here on Friday together with all the letters from the kiddies. Rabbit certainly does write a newsy letter and Tigger, too, is very good to write to Daddy as he is doing. It is a great relief to learn that they are both settling down to school life so well, but I was worried to hear about Desmond's eyes. I am glad, however, you have had them attended to, dearest, for the chances are that later on he will be able to discard his glasses. I had the same trouble at school, but was able to drop them later.

I haven't been getting any news at all from Falam about the Frontier Service, so yours was doubly welcome, sweetheart. Was interested to hear that Leedham was on his way and I am wondering whether A. K. Thompson [Norman's predecessor in Tiddim in 1939] will really come after all. What is wrong with Roy Ogden? Is he supposed to be seriously ill, or is he just avoiding a return to these parts?

You mention that you were sending me some cigarettes, darning wool and three pairs of stockings, dear. Only the stockings have arrived and it looks as though the cigarettes have gone astray. The parcel of stockings, too, was in a very battered condition and [Edgar] Hyde, who is McCall's assistant at Aijal, wrote to say the parcel had reached there already opened, and had been repacked by him. This mail service is certainly not satisfactory, though God knows it is better than nothing so long as it enables us to keep in touch, darling.

I should have liked to have met Fitzherbert of whom you speak in your letter, love. Perhaps someday I shall. I travelled down on a train from Lashio on one occasion with Po Saw, who was then in the A.G's [Accountant General] office, and thought him a very decent fellow. Don't get too swelled up with pride, love, for I am sure I am no second Lawrence of Arabia. You must have met Peter Bankes by now and learnt from him at first hand something of what we are doing here. We are hoping to get steadily increasing support from India in the near future, and I have just had a Capt. Parsons through who is returning to India to buy supplies for us.

I am worried about your clothes which were sent to Imphal, as I can't get any letters out of Sharpe [the Supply Officer]. It is ages ago since he wrote saying he hoped to be able to send the boxes back to me by coolie within a week or two, but since then nothing has happened. I have now decided, however, that it will be worth while to pay Sein Twe privately to go to Imphal to bring them back himself, and I will get them on to you via Aijal as soon as I can, love. I can't bear to think of you short of suitable clothes and feeling the damp and the cold. The other things you left in the house I am sending through to Aijal for despatch to you, dearest, and I trust the parcel reaches you safely and includes all you wanted.

Some time ago I had the misfortune to lose my best pair of field boots and my best pair of slippers in a kit bag which was lost from one of my mules on the march. After much enquiry Awn Ngin [Norman's interpreter and one of his right-hand men] has just discovered the Mualbem chief wearing the boots with the tops cut off! It appears he bought them from a Buan villager for Rs 6/8 so I have sent out to arrest the culprit. The boots themselves are still in good condition so it is good to get them back, for I am getting pretty hard up for footwear and had asked Bankes to bring me back a couple of pairs from India. Incidentally, I had sacked Chin Dam for having been careless enough to lose them from the mule, but have had to take him back for the simple reason that he is our only cobbler here, as you know, love.

I have little other news, dearest, but this will at least serve to let you know that I am still in good form, though I had to have my foot lanced a few days ago to get pus out of a deep-rooted blister.

All my love and devotion to you all, as ever.

Yours alone,

Daddy

Camp
Fort White
7th September 1942

Darling,

I am here with Naylor, so you will know what that means! Can't get any of my own work done on account of his constant egotistical interference, and I fear that this will be nothing more than a mere note to assure you that I am in good form.

I have got your letter of the 12th, darling, and am worried to hear about your tonsils. I do hope they have fully subsided, and that they will cause you no further trouble until such time as this specialist arrives in Mussoorie. You must then see him at once and get his advice as to whether they should be cut again or not.

At Tiddim I was laid out for a day with a typhoid inoculation. I had not had time to have it before, but things were forced on me this time, as [Jack] Oats of the Burma Frontier Force went sick at No. 3 Stockade and had to be brought in to Tiddim where his case was immediately diagnosed as typhoid. I had him removed at once from the house to the hospital, but the doctor thought it advisable that I should have my inoculation at once. Fortunately I had this one tube of my own for none is available at Falam at all.

Tomorrow we are going down to No. 3 where Naylor wants to see my Levy dispositions there and to show his face to the people. Thereafter he proposed to come over and sit at Tiddim for ten days for the same purpose, so I've no doubt I shall be fit to be tied by the time he leaves. He tells me he is to get Frank George I.C.S. [Indian Civil Service] as his Assistant Deputy Commissioner and that I am to get an Assistant Superintendent to help me at Tiddim. In addition, we are to get five more Levy officers, plus a party of six Army officers who are expected to do propaganda work. I can see who will have to do most of their work since they won't know a damned thing about the language. Another party of six Army people are due at Lenakot on the 13th, coming in to settle up the accounts of the returned Burma Riflemen. This will probably take them some time, so Tiddim looks like being crowded out entirely unless the Jap drops a few bombs on us. One or two were dropped harmlessly near a village just west of Haka a few days ago and more fell near Lungleh on the Haka/Lushai border.

You will have to excuse me tonight, love – it is now 7.10 and even in writing this in the privacy of my own bedroom, I have been interrupted by his Nibs as usual. And I've still to get my bath and be ready for dinner in reasonable time since he likes his meal at 7.30 p.m. He has just had the cheek to say he is going to feed with me for a few days at Tiddim as he intends to give his cook a few days' leave, while the latter is in the vicinity of his home!

Roy [his son], he tells me, has joined the Merchant Service and is now a cadet in the B.I. [British India Steamship Company] on his way to somewhere in the Middle East.

Heaps of love, and God bless you all, darling.

Yours alone,

    Daddy

Tiddim

18th September 1942

Darling Mummy,

No letter from you for a fortnight now, but I think this may be due to the fact that from this month our local post offices have been linked up with the Indian postal service. This means that in future we must post letters in the ordinary way via Falam to India. It remains to be seen whether this will prove more successful than our own runner service between Tiddim and Aijal.

I am in the middle of a long spell of Naylor's company and Haswell has now joined him here today. I met Naylor at Fort White and then took him down to No. 3. From there I took him on patrol to the plain to within 4 miles of Kalemyo and he was darned quick in taking cover from a Jap reconnaissance plane which passed over us. We got back here on the 11th and since then my time has simply not been my own. Usual result – I can get nothing done. He is in every evening, and with Capt. Carey & Lt. Wright (in from my Hiangzang outpost) also in the house, I just didn't get a moment to write last week, love.

Bankes is due back at the end of the month and we are now planning dispositions for the open season when it is expected that the Jap will attempt penetration of the Hills. The Fort White–Tiddim area is regarded by India as strategically the focal point from the defence of the whole hills so I am facing heavy responsibilities. It is realised that if this area should fall, all falls.

I am to have a second Assistant Superintendent to assist in the civil work as soon as one is available, but Govt. seems damned slow in sending them over here. Turnbull has arrived in Falam to relieve de Glanville, who is being sent on leave in view of his defeatist attitude.

The package of de Reske cigarettes which reached me without any letter was a Godsend, darling.

I am taking the tonics religiously though I am in good form and hardly require them. I am, however, a bit tired and it is just as well to build up for the cold weather when we might have hard times and short rations ahead of us.

I am writing this in our bedroom, love, and by the increased noise in the sitting room, it is clear that Naylor and Haswell have arrived.

The former has had the cheek to tell me that he will be annoyed if he doesn't get a CBE out of this show! He thinks Poo Nyo [Assistant Superintendent, Haka] should have an OBE but that my case is difficult since I have already got mine '…and they don't give a bar to the same and could not very well give me the same as he should get as Deputy Commissioner'! Can you beat that, sweetheart?

All my devoted love as ever, sweetheart mio. Don't know Haswell's dates yet but I am due to go down to No. 3 Stockade with him. Naylor leaves only on the 22nd after earning his full T.A. [travel allowance], eating our rations and having his fifteen mules fed free!

Yours alone, darling,

Daddy

Others had found Naylor difficult. His superior in India, T. L. Hughes CBE, Secretary to the Governor of Burma, in his fortnightly report to Sir John Walton, Undersecretary of State for Burma, had this to say: 'Although Naylor is over 55 years of age he has done a very good job of work in keeping the administration going in the Chin Hills, but he is now a very tired and rather a cranky old man.'[5]

In August 1942 there were only nine administrative officers in the Chin Hills, with responsibility for an area larger than the size of Wales. All of them were in the Burma Frontier Service except for Frank George, who was in the Indian Civil Service. In Falam the Deputy Commissioner was L. B. Naylor, the Additional Deputy Commissioner was Frank George, the Headquarters Assistant was Stephen de Glanville, the Treasury Officer was Gilbert Turnbull, the Assistant Superintendent was Robbie Sayer and the Second Assistant Superintendent was R. Tuang Hmung. In Tiddim the Assistant Superintendent was Norman Kelly and 'attached to the Levies' was Philip Barton. In Haka the Assistant Superintendent was Joshua Poo Nyo. Later John Franklin, Toby Leitch and David Simpson, all Burma Frontier Service men, were sent in. Norman was responsible for defending 120 miles of the front line from Kalemyo in the south to the border with Manipur State (in India) in the north – facing the formidable Japanese 33rd Division.

September was a really stressful month for Norman. Jack Oats became ill with typhoid and there was the risk of this spreading. The military had also clearly indicated to Norman that his fiefdom was critical to the whole defence of the Chin Hills. He was overworked and understaffed but the last straw was his boss Naylor, who increased his workload and irritation.

Chapter 6

A CONFLICT OF LOYALTY

My father desperately hoped that that my mother would pay him a visit with Prue, Peter Bankes's wife. It had been a long, worrying time since he had last seen her but he was too indispensable to go on leave himself. If they could get to the Lushai Hills at least a brief meeting would be possible. The separation and the responsibility of the campaign were beginning to put a strain on their marriage, a Japanese attack was an ever-present threat, feeding the Chin population was becoming increasingly difficult and, in addition to all this, he had been asked to make a motorable road from Tiddim to Lenakot, near the Indian border.

No. 3 Stockade
28th September 1942

My own darling,

   This week the mail has brought your letters of September 3rd and 5th, and your telegram of the 9th which had reached Aijal on the 13th. While Naylor was with me (as usual), I hardly had time to call my soul my own, love, but now that he has gone at last I have time to reply. I am glad you got the draft for Rs 2000/– safely through Peter Bankes. It still seems difficult to get Burma money through to India as the Reserve Bank there are suspicious that attempts might be made by Jap agents to get money through which they have seized from Burma treasuries. After August 31st, India would accept no Burma notes unless certified by a responsible Chin Hills officer that they have been honestly come by and are reasonable in amount!

   You must have been very worried, darling, by the delayed arrival of my letters. Yours, though sometimes delayed, appear to be getting through fairly regularly, but I know how I feel when a week goes by with no word from you, sweetheart.

   I'm furious that you are not to be allowed to come even as far as Aijal. In present circumstances I agree that it would be highly dangerous for you to return to Tiddim but it appears that no outsiders are even allowed beyond Lalaghat to Aijal owing to lack of accommodation there. As soon as Naylor learnt of your intention he wirelessed the Transport Officer at Lalaghat to send you and Mrs. Bankes back to avoid useless expense and I perforce have had to send a special message to Tony

McCall asking him to wire you at Mussoorie in the hope of catching you before you would leave as you would only have a fruitless journey. I am dreadfully disappointed, dearest, and this has knocked the heart out of me completely for I know how keenly you will feel it, too, love. It doesn't help to hear of all those bloody slackers finding jobs for themselves in India while we hold the line here. I'm afraid I have no hope of getting out on short leave now as the cold weather will soon be on us and there are already signs that things are likely to hot up here. It makes me furious to think of Leyden as a Deputy Commissioner – the bloody creep.

Frank George is due any time as additional Deputy Commissioner and Naylor is scared stiff that he has been sent as a spy with the intention of ousting him before he can collect a decoration! Gilbert Turnbull [BFrS] has arrived in Falam and was delayed, as he had to take his Shan wife back to Calcutta from Lalaghat. John Franklin [BFrS] is to come to Tiddim as my assistant, but I don't know when he is due.

The Japs have been active in the Kale valley trying to stop us from getting rice and paddy supplies from there. A certain amount of supplies are being dropped in Tiddim, Falam and Haka by plane but these are nothing like sufficient to keep the people going, and it appears that neither Aijal nor Imphal can arrange sufficient coolie labour to get us supplies through by road. We have 500 tons of rice and 200 tons of salt lying at Sairang but no coolies to move it forward. I do think that McCall's Levies would be better employed at the moment as a Labour Corps to move this stuff than waiting in their villages. If we have to abandon the Chin Hills for want of supplies I'm damned sure the Lushai Hills will stand a pretty poor chance of survival.

A big party of officers has been expected for some time from Imphal bringing with them 410 coolie-loads of stuff for us, but it appears they are held up at Shuganu [due east of Churachandpur – see map no. 7 on p. 80] indefinitely as the Army sappers pinched all the coolies for road work. I understand from Capt. Mackay, who brought a Mahratta patrol through to Tiddim, that the Army is working on roads furiously on that side and there is every indication that we intend to make a push back into Burma in the cold weather. I have been ordered to make my road from Lenakot to Tiddim motorable, and also to make a new motorable road west of the Manipur from my northern border. I have represented that priority of labour must go to ration-carrying, but the Chief Engineer, Operations – some Brigadier or other – is to get in direct touch with me on this matter. I shall have no hesitation in saying he'll have to send in his own Labour Corps for the roadwork – and arrange their rations.

The Japs are threatening a bombing campaign here as soon as the weather permits and all pro-Jap Burmans in the plain have been advised to move to Kalewa to avoid the results of such attacks. The RAF are keeping up their attacks on Kalewa, Mingin, and Monywa, etc., and hardly a day passes – even in rain and mist – but we hear our planes going over into the valley [see map no. 1 on p. 2]. I haven't the slightest doubt, however, that Tiddim, Fort White and Falam will be bombed soon. The Japs have been working furiously to prepare an aerodrome at Monywa, so we can look out for trouble. At Tiddim and at all our other posts we have our air-raid trenches ready and I trust casualties and damage will not be high.

We have special fighter squadrons now standing by in India to come to our aid in response to an air-raid warning which – by telegraph and wireless – will reach Dum Dum [Calcutta] and Tezpur [on the Brahmaputra] aerodromes within 15 minutes of despatch from Tiddim. We have had several successful test warnings and the line should work well in our support when the real thing hits us. What changes since last year, love! Your garden is cut up with air-raid trenches – near the kiddies' sandpit and among the orange trees. I have had all the trees cut on the ridge between the Lailo and Tonzang roads and this is where air supplies are dropped. Can you imagine big transport planes zooming in low over the pines at our compound gate (office side) and banking steeply between the roof of the house and the flagstaff in their circle to drop bags of supplies? It gives me a good idea of what I could expect if they were Jap planes bombing and machine-gunning.

[Roddie] Russell, the new Battalion Commander, has reached Tiddim in my absence and was met by Tommy West – now a Major. (I am still retaining my civil rank, though offered a Majority by Brig. Felix Williams, since it leaves me free to tell any of the military from the GOC [General Officer Commanding] downwards to go to hell!)

Naylor and I came over to Fort White on the 25th and met Haswell there. The latter had been inspecting our defences at No. 3 Stockade. He and Naylor pushed off to Falam on the 26th and I came down here. Tomorrow I will take Russell and West down to the plain on patrol to show the former the lie of the land, and to counteract for my own part Jap threats in order to get further supplies of rice moving to No. 2 Stockade. Yacub Ali [a rice merchant in Kalemyo] – who has been sitting very much on the fence – appears to have stopped co-operation with me on account of Jap threats of reprisal, so I must find some other contractor to arrange cartage to No. 2.

Darling, I must have bored you beyond measure with so much shop talk. Everything so far is well with me, dearest, and I trust God will continue to help you all safely in his care.

All my love and kisses, as ever, sweetheart to your dear self, Rabbit and Tigger.

Yours alone,

Daddy

Tiddim
5th October 1942

My own darling,

I have had a wireless message to the effect that Peter Bankes has reached Aijal, so I fear that my message to stop your journey couldn't have been received before you were already en route to Aijal with him. I feel dreadfully sorry that we should be frustrated in this way, but I'm afraid we must just steel ourselves to face further separation, love.

In my last trip down to the plains with the new Chin Hills Battalion Commandant – Russell – I managed to pick up a beastly influenza cold which even your Rhino-Antipeol has not cured. This has made me feel a bit under the weather, but otherwise I am in good form still, darling.

I was thrilled to get the Woodstock school magazine and to see the Rabbit's poem therein. I think it was an excellent effort on her part and I feel quite proud of her. The cigarettes have not arrived yet, love, but many thanks for the three pairs of stockings. They seem very good value, though I preferred the khaki ones you sent earlier.

Since Sharpe didn't appear to be doing anything about the return of your boxes, I have sent off my own party to Imphal to bring them back. I understand there is so much pilfering on the railway line that it is unsafe to send anything unattended, so it looks as though I shall have to send someone through to Mussoorie with your things, dear. It will be worth the extra expense to have them safely delivered.

Did I tell you that I am now living rent-free? This, together with my fixed T.A. [travel allowance] is a great help, and I can live quite well on my allowances. I have also put some of the servants on the Levy pay roll and will not be slow to claim any other perks that are going. I had to pay Rs 52 for a tin of kerosene from Aijal, so I have put that down, too, to the Levy account. I am also doing myself fairly well in the matter of free rations, but local supplies have soared in price and chickens and eggs are now very scarce.

A number of new officers have arrived during the last week from Imphal. Capt. [David] Milligan is an additional officer for the Chin Hills Battalion, and will be stationed at No. 3. Stockade. [Sam] Cope has also arrived, but is being sent on to Haka. He tells me he was greatly impressed by the children when he met you, dearest. Two other fellows, Major Mackay and Capt. Cousins, have come in to settle the pay claims of the Burma Riflemen who have returned.

No sign yet of [John] Franklin who is to come as my assistant here.

Tiddim is now stripped for action, so to speak, and you would hardly know the place. I have moved all the townspeople out into jungle huts in case of bombing, and we have air-raid trenches all over the place. I have also organised Air Raid Precaution fire-fighting parties, and in short have taken all the precautions I can think of to ensure the safety of the people and the troops.

There are signs that the monsoon is breaking up, and the cold weather will be upon us shortly.

Am trying to arrange the despatch of a draft to you, love, through Falam to your bank, but there seems to be a hell of a lot of red tape in this connection. If we had anybody else going through to India, I would much prefer to send it by them, but I fear we are out of luck at the moment.

No more news at the moment, dearest, and as I have Milligan [see photograph no. 42], Cousins and Cope coming in to dinner, I must get my bath.

All my love and kisses as ever, darling, go with this letter.

Yours alone,

Daddy

Tiddim
19th October 1942

Darling Mummiekins,

Naylor turned up unexpectedly on the 11th after a three-day dash from Falam, and as I had to go off to Tonzang with him on the 12th I only had time to get a telegram off to Aijal for you, dearest, before I left, and had no time to write you a letter.

My wire was in reply to your two letters dated the 17th and 18th of Sept. in which you told me of your visit to Simla and your meeting with Sandy and [Sir Raibeart] MacDougall. It was grand of you, love, to take things into your own hands in the hope of obtaining leave for me, and I hope you won't be too annoyed at the reply I have sent you. I am sure you must see that, provided my health holds, *it would be impossible for me to leave my Chins at the moment when they are relying on me so much for help and guidance.* With the advent of the cold weather, the Japs might make an advance at any time, and we must all be at our posts. If, however, nothing has happened by the end of January, I shall certainly take steps to get a few weeks' leave.

The whole incident appears to have been very confused, looking at it from this end. Frank George [Indian Civil Service], whom I have not yet met, brought in your letter dated the 31st August (not even enclosed in an envelope), and also one from Sandy, dated Aug. 27th. He said he had heard from you and that you had asked him about the possibility of my getting some leave. He says he told you the answer was 'No' as I was too valuable where I am at the moment, and they were unable to relieve me.

Then came your letters of Sept. 17th and 18th, from which it appears that the powers that be had some hope of relieving me for a short spell. Following on your visit to Simla, it appears Naylor was informed by wireless that it was the intention of government that every officer in the

Chin Hills should be given a recess of six weeks out of the hills. He was told that I was first on turn and was to proceed on leave, immediately being relieved by [Stephen] de Glanville [BFrS]. I was then to be re-posted to the Hills. Neither Naylor nor Haswell let me know anything about this message, and they simply replied without my knowledge that I could not be spared for leave at the moment. This I only learnt when Naylor arrived on the 11th. Meanwhile de Glanville had left for India, as Naylor wouldn't have him in the District, as he was too much of a defeatist. Franklin, who is being sent in as my assistant, is ill and cannot come yet, and it is now the intention to send [Toby] Leitch back.

However, there is still more intrigue at the back of all this. Naylor himself received a letter from MacDougall (brought in by Frank George) in which he was informed that whereas Govt. fully appreciated his services, it was hoped that they could relieve him about the end of October, as this was a young man's war and likely to become more so! Naylor was livid about this as he saw his long-cherished hopes of a decoration fast disappearing.

I have since learnt that the intention was that I should get my leave in quickly so that I could come back as Deputy Commissioner in Naylor's place. Now you can see, darling, how the blighter has queered my pitch by replying that I couldn't be spared to go on leave at the moment. In this way he has so far saved his own bacon. I have no doubt, however, that his time is nearly up and he will soon be shifted if Moore [the former battalion commandant] gets his way in India. It doesn't seem to be clear yet who is to be Deputy Commissioner here, but Frank George as Additional D.C. knows nothing of the Hills, and Joshua Poo Nyo [a Karen, Norman's opposite number in Haka] is likely to be overlooked as his nerves have recently gone to pieces with neuritis which is troubling him greatly.

It thus appears that my chances are still pretty good, provided I could carry on without leave for a while. Personally, I should like to get the District for your sake, love, but on the other hand I would be loath to leave my Chins at this particular juncture.

It is all very complicated and disturbing, but one thing at least is pretty certain, and that is that my stock is standing somewhat higher with the powers that be than that of many others in the Service. I at least have the satisfaction of knowing that I have throughout done my job conscientiously and have had no part in Naylor's intrigues. I am damned annoyed with Moore for suggesting in India that I was quarrelling with L.B. [Naylor]. I have had no official quarrel with him though I have little respect for him since his treatment of you at Tiddim. He himself has throughout recognised my loyal service and has given me excellent reports to India.

It is no good worrying further about things at the moment, darling, and we must just wait and see what comes of it all. Perhaps it won't be long anyway before we are all going out to India, for the Army seems incapable of giving us the support we so badly need in the matter of men and arms, and trouble is already brewing with the Jap. I have just got a report in from Haka by wire today, that the Levies there were attacked on the 17th by a Jap party on the road from Kan to Haka [see map no. 3 on p. 28]. We wounded five Japs and suffered no casualties ourselves, but had to fall back. Another report says that Poo Nyo's party was also attacked on the 18th and no details are yet known beyond the fact that his party had to disperse. On the strength of this, [Gilbert] Turnbull, who is also at Haka, has wired in to Naylor for instructions regarding the evacuation of Haka. It seems as though he has very soon got the wind up.

I have also had your letters of Sept. 25th, 26th and 30th, sweetheart. It is bad luck that in those you seem much less hopeful of our early reunion. Don't despair, darling; with God's help all will come right in the end.

We have got urgent orders to build a motor road from Tiddim to Tonzang and this is what brought Naylor over here so hurriedly. He knew that I could not attend to everything at once, so he is taking over the supervision of this work and is at present down at Tualmului. *I returned to Tiddim from Tonzang on the 14th after having organised the labour for the roadwork. Tools have been dropped in by plane and work has commenced today* [19 October 1942]. I was no sooner back on the 14th than Lt. Col. Duguid got me on the phone wanting me to go over at once for a patrol into the plains with him. Consequently I went off to meet him at Fort White on the 15th and only got back yesterday.

So you see, I have had no time for writing during the past ten days. In fact, every day seems more rushed than ever, and I am getting little leisure at present. However, the main point is that I am in good health and have much to be thankful for on that account, love. I do not know how long Naylor will be in the vicinity, but he is coming up here again tomorrow. In view of the Haka developments, I have no doubt he will want to run back to Falam, in which case I shall have to get on with the road as best I can in addition to my other Levy duties. I am due to meet a Royal Engineer officer at Tuitum in this connection on the 26th – Japs permitting. Reports indicate that about 1,000 Japs are expected in Kalemyo from Gangaw within a day or two and it remains to be seen whether this is the prelude to their attack on the hills in this area.

No other news at the moment, dearest. All my undying love you, sweetest, and to the kiddies.

Yours alone,

Daddy

The background to what was happening as regards staffing in the Chin Hills is contained in official correspondence. On 22 September a telegram had been sent by Ralph Wilkie, Commissioner, Frontier

Division of Burma, to L. B. Naylor in Falam. It was his duty to provide liaison with the Assam Government and 4 Corps. He was based in Burma Defence (Burdef) HQ at Jorhat and had been DC of Mandalay before the war. The message read:

CONSIDERED DESIRABLE GIVE RECESS* IN TURN TO CIVIL OFFICERS STOP KELLY MUST COME OUT NOW STOP PERIOD OF ABSENCE HILLS NOT MORE THAN 6 WEEKS STOP SUGGEST SEND DE GLANVILLE AND TURNBULL TO TIDDIM TO RELIEVE KELLY IMMEDIATELY STOP SUGGEST KELLY RETURN AS ADDITIONAL DEPUTY COMMISSIONER WITH** GEORGE AS DEPUTY COMMISSIONER STOP NAYLOR TO RETIRE STOP PLEASE DISCUSS WITH 4 CORPS, ISSUE ORDERS URGENTLY FOR KELLY'S RECESS TO DEPUTY COMMISSIONER FALAM AND REPORT [1]

Naylor replied on 29 September:

HASWELL NOR SELF CAN AGREE KELLY RECESSING NOW AS SITUATION DOES NOT PERMIT STOP TURNBULL AVAILABLE AS HE MUST GO HAKA AS POO NYO SICK STOP DE GLANVILLE ALREADY LEFT DISTRICT STOP BOTH HASWELL AND SELF WITH FULL KNOWLEDGE AND RESPONSIBILITY CONSIDER DE GLANVILLE UNSUITED EMPLOYMENT HERE STOP KELLY DOING MAGNIFICENT WORK STOP NEXT FEW MONTHS VITAL AND FORESEE DEBACLE IF KELLY CHANGED, ESPECIALLY FOR DE GLANVILLE STOP PLEASE ACCEPT WORD OF TWO SENIOR OFFICERS ON SPOT FULL REASONS BY LETTER FOLLOWS [2]

The military emphasised the necessity for an energetic officer at Tiddim to provide the labour for the new Tiddim Road. Frank George, now in Falam, had sent a telegram to Ralph Wilkie on 16 October:

CONCERN IS FELT BY NAYLOR ABOUT MOORE'S MISINFORMATION IN SIMLA STOP MY OPINION IS THAT NAYLOR AND KELLY ARE ABSOLUTELY KEY MEN FOR DEFENCE OF THE CHIN HILLS AND THAT TO RECALL EITHER OF THEM WOULD BE A MISTAKE STOP HASWELL SUPORTS THIS VIEW STOP IT WOULD DO GOOD IF ASSURANCES COULD BE GIVEN THAT THEY WILL NOT BE RECALLED. [3]

On 17 October, two days before Norman's letter to his wife above, Wilkie had replied:

---

* leave
** Frank

MOORE SAID NOTHING TO ME AGAINST KELLY STOP ARE YOU
CERTAIN THAT KELLY WILL NOT HAVE A BREAKDOWN If HE HAS
TO CONTINUE ON DUTY WITHOUT A REST STOP LEITCH* HAS
STARTED FOR THE CHIN HILLS [4]

On 20 October George wired Wilkie to say:

ALL HERE AGREE THAT KELLY IS FIT. ENEMY ACTIVITY MAKES
SITUATION IN HAKA SERIOUS [5]

Wilkie reported on 22 October that Naylor had spent twelve days with
Kelly who was quite fit. Haswell wired a special request:

NO CHANGE IN OFFICERS IN VIEW OF OPERATIONS NOW
PROCEEDING. PRESUMABLY REFERS TO JAP THREAT HAKA STOP
MAY NOT BE POSSIBLE TO RELIEVE KELLY NOW [6]

Meanwhile, on 19 October, the Governor of Burma's Secretary, Thomas
Hughes, ICS, CBE, wrote to Sir John Walton in London:

> De Glanville is already out, and it is hoped that Kelly who has done
> a magnificent job in the key post of Assistant Superintendent,
> Tiddim, will come out next.
> Naylor, the present Deputy Commissioner, has reached retiring
> age, and the present proposal is that, as soon as Kelly has had his
> rest, George, I.C.S. who has gone into the Chin Hills as Additional
> Deputy Commissioner should take over from Naylor and that Kelly
> should go back as Additional D.C. to provide the local knowledge.[7]

Joshua Poo Nyo had become Assistant Superintendent of Haka on 27
March 1942, and was Norman Kelly's opposite number there. The
danger of going into the plains is well illustrated by his experience.
Unfortunately, in mid-October he had let people know that he was
about to purchase rice in Tintha. The Japanese were lying in wait for
him. He was told of this and turned back, but they gave chase. After
putting what he thought was a safe distance between them he halted,
but the Japanese did not. His party was surprised and had to bolt;
fortunately, there were no casualties. Poo Nyo then sent back word to
evacuate the civil population of Haka because the road was open. Gilbert
Turnbull (Burma Frontier Service), who was in Haka, had already
sought orders and had been instructed by Frank George that all officers
should remain at their posts and that the small amount of money in the
treasury should be moved to a place of safety, on the Falam–Champhai
road.
  Poo Nyo was somewhat shaken by this close encounter with the
Japanese; they had intended to capture him. Later he learned that Pe

* Toby Leitch, Burma Frontier Service

Tha, a close friend of his who was looking after his wife and family, had been shot. He, like Norman Kelly, in addition to his civilian duties, had to organise the Levies, the Burma Rifles and be responsible for gathering intelligence.

Norman wrote again to his wife on 26 October, telling her of the plans for the motor road and what was happening in Tiddim with the ever-present threat of Japanese bombing and attack.

Tiddim
26th October 1942

Darling Mummiekins,

Your last letter received was dated Oct. 5th, which speaks well for the new mail service, but I understand from Bankes that parcel mail is being held up badly and I have had no cigarettes from you for ages now, love. Am now back to Chin tobacco again, but the position with regard to other supplies is not too bad. The army has sent in some kerosene oil from Imphal and we get tinned milk, bully beef, flour, *atta* and rice dropped by plane periodically.

During the last week I have been having road tools dropped by air for the Tiddim–Tonzang motor road where I now have 1,500 coolies a day working. These heavy droppings have naturally cut up our old football ground a bit, but in any case no one ever thinks of playing on it these days and it is solely a parade and training ground.

No Jap attack has developed yet in this area, but on the Haka side our forces have had two brushes with the enemy, accounting for 55 killed on the Jap side with no losses to ourselves. Five hundred Japs apparently advanced in close formation on the road from Kan and were ambushed about 51 miles from Haka. Our people did good work with hand grenades and with the automatic Bren gun, which fires very rapidly. Results have been very encouraging so far, but we had temporarily to fall back to positions some 36 miles from Haka, expecting further Jap advances. These have so far failed to materialise and it would look as though he has withdrawn at least temporarily. The situation, however, is still pretty tense and is likely to flare up at any moment and at any point. Naylor rushed back to Falam on receipt of the news, and on my advice, though I am sure he would have liked to remain here while the fighting was approaching Falam. The treasury at Falam has been moved back to Surbung as a precaution.

Owing to the risk of bombing I have ordered the evacuation of Tiddim during the daylight hours and everybody, including the troops, is housed in jungle huts well covered from the air. The only parties remaining are A.R.P. fire-fighting parties, which I have organised. Pau Za Kam is the section leader of the bazaar party, and I have other parties from the Burma Frontier Force, the civil police and the Burma Rifles.

Franklin was expected at Champhai today and should be here by the end of the month. Other officers due to arrive shortly are Mullen, Rae and Shircore of the Burma Police coming from Imphal, a Royal Engineer road recce party coming in from the trans-Manipur to see me about the motor road, and an air force recce party, also from Imphal. Major Mackay will also arrive in a few days from Falam to settle up the pay claims of the Burma Riflemen. It looks as though the place will be pretty full, and most of them I am putting into the Mission house; here Franklin will take up his permanent quarters. It will help me a lot to have him as an assistant, and I shall take damned good care he doesn't have a slack time either!

I have shaken off my cold and am in great form. The cold weather has come in suddenly and the days are really marvellous. If only you could all be here with me, sweetheart, as in the old days.

I am off in the morning down to No. 3 but this will only be a hurried visit as I must get back to go to Tonzang to see how the work is going there. Kyan Sone is helping me there and I have a dozen temporary overseers supervising the work. Have roped in all sorts of people including Kai Kho Lian and Khai Kho Thang for this work. Also Sein Twe.

I am worried, love, by your remark that you are unable to put on weight. Are you perfectly well in health, or is your throat causing trouble? With me not there to look after you, darling, you must call in the best medical attendant for yourself. Will be sending you another cash draft in November, love.

Your boxes have not turned up yet from Imphal, so if the weather is cold at Mussoorie you must buy warm clothing no matter what the cost. Your health and that of the kiddies must come above all else, without care for our financial position for the future.

Are you getting my mails any more regularly now? I am writing once a week from here, and never seem to be able to do more. At the same time I am squeezing time every week for a letter of some sort, even if they are sometimes short, as I know how worried you would be if you were not hearing regularly in the present circumstances. I can only hope they are reaching you safely to keep your mind at rest on my account. Would it not be grand if only we could send private wireless messages, love?

No more news at the moment. Look after yourself well, darling. Hugs for the kiddies, and to you, cara mio, my undying love as ever.

Daddy

On 30 October, replying to letters from his wife, Norman sent the following telegram. Evidently the strain of their separation was having an effect on Betty.

INDIAN POSTS AND TELEGRAPHS DEPARTMENT

TELEGRAM FROM AIJAL

30TH OCTOBER 1942

MRS KELLY CARE WOODSTOCK SCHOOL, MUSSOORIE

YOUR LETTER OF SEPT 17, 18 NO SUGGESTION OF LEAVE STOP
NOR HAS YOUR WORK THROUGH SANDY MATERIALISED STOP COULD
ONLY LEAVE NOW BY ABANDONMENT MY OWN CHOICE AND
CONSEQUENT SACRIFICE OUR HONOUR STOP PENDING JENKINS
ARRIVAL AND TRAINING AS MY ASSISTANT, CANNOT
CONTEMPLATE MUTUAL DESERTION STOP SO PLEASE HANG ON,
LIKE SELF, AND KEEP FLAG FLYING

WITH LOVE NORMAN

Betty Kelly felt that Norman should take some leave, and Norman's next two letters reveal the strain they were under as a couple in this wartime situation. Norman was determined, as he said, to 'see this thing through'.

Tiddim
7th November 1942

My Dearest One,

I really don't know how to reply to your letter of Oct. 14th, which has worried me greatly during a week which has been full enough of worries as it is. I am just back from a visit to No. 3 Stockade where we had a pretty anxious time for a few days wondering what move the Jap was going to make next. A few days ago he made a surprise raid with some 500 men on Tahan village and captured all my friendly ration contractors. This has not only put an end to my hopes of obtaining further supplies from the plains, but has also probably resulted in the enemy getting much valuable information regarding our present positions, etc. Present information shows that my men have been taken to Kalewa and I have reports that two of them have already been shot by the Japs – Chin Lang and Kham Theo. I feel pretty rotten about it since I had persuaded them into working on our side, and when it came to a showdown, was not on hand to help them in any way.

However, darling, these local worries, which can be of no interest to you, pale against the domestic worries which your letter arouses.

I have been praying to God to give you an understanding of my point of view over the question of this leave which I AM NOT GOING TO TAKE UNTIL I HAVE SEEN THIS THING THROUGH. You seem to have got the idea that I am both mentally and physically a sick man. Nothing could be further from the truth. Admittedly these are wearing days, but I am as fit as a fiddle and thrive well on the mental alertness required to cope with this cat-and-mouse game of grabbing supplies of rice out of the plain without precipitating a direct showdown with the Jap. It need not worry you to know that they have now placed a price of Rs 5000 on my head – the same value as they gave Maj. Moore some time ago. Rest assured I am not going to lose the old head or fall into their bag if I can avoid it, but it is essential in my view that we should work to get supplies out of the plain to the maximum limit while the going is good. It appears the Jap is trying to do the same, and he is getting some supplies back to Kalewa by the river route, which you know.

I know full well you are thinking that my letters are too impersonal, and possibly that has given you the idea that I have ceased to care. Please, darling, put any such thought out of your mind. *My only object in remaining here is to keep my honour among the Chins* you *knew and to be able to let Desmond know hereafter the importance of sticking to a task once you have put your hand to the plough.* The Tigger boy is *OUR* child, darling, and so far has been lacking in tenacity – tenacity of purpose in his studies. It is a weakness that I fear has come from me, and for that reason I want him to realise from my present example that he in turn will be called on sometime and somewhere to stick it out.

Darling, you bring up my father's argument that a man's first duty is to his wife and family. That view I am keeping steadfastly in front of me and at times my love for you, sweetheart, has even overpowered my call to official duty. Please don't make things more difficult than they already are. You seem to hint (pretty obviously) in your letter, that I might go 'off the rails' sexually. For God's sake get that out of your mind, love. Days are too tense for such considerations to be uppermost in one's mind, and you can rest assured, sweetheart, that I have no desire to be sleeping in other arms than yours. It all sounds very cold in print, I know, but the time is coming, love, when I will prove the truth of my words. No matter what calumnies you may hear against me, you and I are *ONE* and will remain so. I do not know what your sources of information may be, but on the sexual count anyway I shall meet you, darling, with a clear conscience. I am happy in my job, fit in body and mind, and am only living for the day when we will once more be re-united as a family.

I know this is a very inadequate answer to your letter, darling, and for that reason I am returning yours because I feel that, when you wrote it, we were not in the complete harmony without which my task here loses all purpose. Should you still be of the same mind when you reply again, sweetheart, then I am going to throw in my hand and we shall return to Ireland together.

Yours alone,

Daddy

Tiddim
14th November 1942

Darling,

Can you possibly have in store for me any greater shocks than the one that reached me in your note of Oct. 20th, on the eve of your operation [Betty Kelly was to have her tonsils removed]. The mail has also brought yours of the 19th, in which you made no mention of the imminence of the event, and I was dreadfully upset on opening the other note to learn its contents. The days of waiting for your next letter, darling, are well nigh unbearable, but I am continuing to pray that all is well, and assuring myself that no news is good news. I feel a cad that I was not with you, dearest one, at such a time, for I know that only to be beside you might perhaps have eased the terrible mental worry through which I am sure you must have been passing. Was it on that account you were so anxious to get me on leave, darling? If so, it makes it worse for me to know that I was having to oppose you on what I thought a point of honour in staying put here.

It is dreadful that nothing ever seems to go right with us, darling, during these separations, and I am feeling awful about it all. I had sent off a bank draft for Rs 2000 before I got your letters, dear, so I trust you will at least have no financial worries to add to your others.

I think you really must get out of Mussoorie for the winter, darling, for the place will be deadly dull and the cold I understand is very severe indeed there. Unfortunately I cannot advise you as to which would be the best place to move to, as I know nothing of India. John Franklin suggests you might get in touch with his wife whose address is c/o Mrs. Gatmell, Srinagar, Kashmir. Otherwise I would suggest Shillong, but then every place will be very crowded and you can't just arrive at a place on speck when you might not be able to get a roof over your dear head. Don't spare the cost however, love, in making yourself and the kiddies as comfortable as may be in the circumstance wherever you feel you would like to go. How I only wish you could come back somewhere nearer here, sweetheart.

For the future I am going to register all my letters, for I have a shrewd suspicion that several of them have been tampered with at Falam. Yours to me enclosing Aunt Carrie's letter had been opened and stuck down again with a strip of paper, and your last one was wide open, though this appeared to be more due to the wearing of the edges of the poor-quality envelope. The latest cigarettes with the stockings and tonics arrived safely. Did I tell you that the previous consignment of cigarettes was ruined entirely. They were flat tins of de Reskes and though the cellophane was intact, when opened out all the cigs. were black and unusable. It almost looked as though the tins had been salvaged from the sea. Don't send me more stockings, love, as I am well supplied, but *do* keep up the regular supply of cigarettes.

The boxes from Imphal have gone off to you in charge of Col. Duguid [former Commandant, Chin Hills Battalion] who will forward them from Calcutta. He left here in a hurry while I was down the road at No. 3 so Franklin handed them over to him. I do hope they arrive safely. The one containing your fur coat it appears had been tampered with. John says it was open when brought from Imphal and was only half full, though your coat was safe. He tells me he sealed it up before handing it over to Duguid, as he had no keys for it in my absence. He says there were no shoes of mine in it, though I could swear this was the box in which I had placed my suede shoes and the other new walking pair. Please let me know what is missing on arrival your end, dear.

You ask about extra pay, dear. I have given you all these details in earlier letters and told you how well off we are. Also my reasons for refusing military rank as a Major, in which I should get considerably less pay than I now draw. I told you I no longer have to pay house rent, and draw an additional Rs 125 fixed Travel Allowance in addition to the old Rs 140 Cost of Living Allowance. From Nov. 1st, I also get another 150 from the Levies in lieu of bungalow fees, cost of fresh meat, etc., and since I am supplied with free rations as far as the scale can be achieved, I am not doing too badly.

There is a proposal that we should get an allowance of Rs 500 which is presumably the one you referred to in connection with Leyden [John Leyden, BFrS]. In any case we are better off than we have ever been before, for my expenses are very low. I think I shall have to get rid of Tuam Zel the *mali*, for he has recently been doing very little about your flower garden though he keeps the vegetable patch in fair order and I get a sufficiency of green stuff. Tomorrow I shall try to write you another letter, dearest, giving details of the garden.

Have been very busy this week arranging new platoons of the Burma Rifles to reinforce our outposts. There are also indications that we shall shortly be getting reinforcements from India. Indeed, only problems of rationing, arming and equipping the men prevent me from mustering what would be almost a full battalion of the returned Burma Rifles from the Tiddim area in addition to my 600-odd village Levies. In any case now that I have raised my extra platoons, I feel much happier and am sure we will be able to give the enemy a nasty crack if he attempts to venture into our hills.

After his surprise raid at the end of last month, of which I spoke in my last letter, there have been no further developments of any note in the Kalemyo area, though he has not released my ration contractors whom he arrested at that time. Information shows that the Japs have taken them back to Kalewa. This has rather broken up my chances of renewing any further contracts for rice, paddy and peas from the plain, but in any case our supply position is sound, and I am thankful now for having paid so much attention to this side of the business ever since May, when I realised that our ability to keep men in the field would be strictly limited by our capacity to feed them. On the Haka side, no rations have hitherto been available for the men, and the position at Falam is pretty strained, indeed so much so that we are having to help from here to some extent. I was inclined to resent these extra demands on our resources at first, since we had won the food out of the valley by the labours of our own villagers, but after all it is all in the same cause and it would be a fatal mistake to be parochial in one's views at this time.

Planes continue to drop us a certain amount of supplies. The great thrill this week has been the dropping of one *lakh* of rupees [1 *lakh* = 100,000 rupees][8] required for payments on the motor road from Tiddim to Tonzang. This was just as bad as any bombing for the plane came in at tremendous speed and the bags of cash were simply flung out all over the countryside. I had sentries out all over the vicinity, but I couldn't cope with bags dropping so far afield as Gawngmual village, and the net result was that we have lost Rs 13,550 of the total amount. I was out with my officers trying to count the bags as they left the plane, and narrowly escaped decapitation from a bag which fell and bounced off like a rocket just over my head. Thereafter I went to ground!! Two of the barracks were damaged by flying bags, and one went right through the roof of our store godown [warehouse].

You wouldn't know the Tiddim–Tonzang Road now, love – widened to 12 ft. with sweeping curves instead of sharp corners, to allow 3-ton lorries to pass. What developments since you were with me, love!

No more news now, dearest. All my love as ever goes with this letter. Never for one instant think, sweetheart, that I could even be inconstant to you in present circumstances. You and the kiddies are my only life, and as I have told you before – you and my job are my only preoccupations. In these stirring days my sex urges are entirely sublimated and subordinated to the calls on my physical stamina necessitated by the present task in hand, so you need have no fears on this account, dear.

Yours alone,

Daddy

The dropping zone at Tiddim that Norman talked about was on a long, narrow piece of land, lying north and south across a flattish spur. In the past, all the RAF planes had approached it from the north and so had the length of the target before them. Unfortunately, the aircraft with the money attempted to unload their cargo across the area, coming in from the east on the first day and the west on the second.

Lockheeds were used instead of the usual Dakotas. They flew much faster and higher and their pilots were unfamiliar with the Tiddim dropping zone. As a consequence one parcel of 1 rupee notes, worth Rs 20,000, was never found, and some bags landed miles away in the jungle. At that time it would take a mule a whole month to get 4,000 rupees to Tiddim from India. Lessons were learned and, later, money for the Tiddim Road was packed in sawdust, placed in two bags and put in a box in a sack. In this way, coins were prevented from flying all over the countryside like shrapnel.

In May, June and July 1942, when the Chins normally supplemented their grain from the Kale and Gangaw Valleys, the supply was gradually drying up due to Japanese activity. Meanwhile, coolie labour was desperately needed to bring food into the hills and simultaneously to construct the Tiddim–Tuitum part of the road. The people in the Lushai Hills, who were being protected by the Chin campaign, said they could not help. Government servants were rationed to one bag of rice (or rice and peas) and one pound of salt per month. Frequently they did not even get that.

By 17 November the villagers of the Tiddim and Falam subdivisions had given 196,375 coolie days for transport alone since 1 April. This is equal to eleven days' work for *every house* in these two subdivisions. Besides this, the labour on the Tiddim Road had run into 200,000 coolie days. Ralph Wilkie in Jorhat said: 'It is not possible to supply full rations to the Chin Hills Battalion, or even half rations to all the Levies.'[9] But L. B. Naylor wrote back: 'If the Chins had not responded so magnificently the military would have been forced to leave the area through sheer want of supplies.' [10]

The scale of the supply problem can best be appreciated when it is realised that the Chin population alone needed 1,000 tons of rice and 100 tons of salt annually. It was feared that unless the Chins were able to obtain something approaching their usual import of rice in 1942 famine threatened in May, June and July 1943. [11]

The good news in November 1942 was that Kenny Fraser arrived in Falam as Medical Officer of the Chin Hills Battalion. Dr Yarde was the civilian surgeon in Falam. Cholera was expected to break out in March and smallpox would also be imported from the plains by coolies, and vaccination programmes were urgently needed.

Tiddim
19th November 1942

Darling Mummiekins,

You can have little idea, love, what a relief it has been to me to get your letter of Oct. 27th and to learn that you were safely through your operation. I am sure you will feel much better for the removal of the old tonsils, but you must build yourself up, sweetheart. For some time now I have suspected that you have been worried about your health, dearest, and since I am not with you to look after you myself, I want you to promise not to stint yourself in anything you require to build yourself up again. Sorry to hear you were still finding the throat very painful after six days and were having to dull it with aspirin, but I am sure I will hear in your next letter that this has disappeared and that you are feeling more normal again, dear.

The weather here is perfectly delightful now and I am feeling absolutely on top of the world but for the fact that you and the kiddies are not with me, darling. Still no sign of any enemy attack in this direction, but one of my patrols from No. 3 had a skirmish with a party of *Thakins* [Burmese Nationalists] on the road to Kalemyo. After an exchange of shots the enemy retired and we have taken three prisoners with no loss to ourselves. Stout work.

More regular troops are being sent in here and I am expecting them shortly. This will relieve the situation greatly. The RAF has been successfully bombing Kalemyo and surrounding unfriendly villages during the week. I personally think the Jap forces are pretty weak in the Monywa–Kalewa area, and that they are relying mainly on the *Thakin* party to do their dirty work for them. They have been supplying arms to the latter.

We are now getting good supplies of rations dropped by plane nearly every day on the football ground here. I also had a *lakh* of rupees dropped by air to make payments in connection with the new motor road. We are getting ahead well with this work and Pum Za Mang has done a very good job of work in arranging the coolie labour for it. In all we have a force of some 4,500 hard at work so you can imagine the cost of the project. Wouldn't the kiddies just love to be here to see the ration planes roaring over the compound!

I am also to get a wireless-transmitting station at Cingpikot [Mualnuam] which we will keep in touch with from here by helio. It is meant of course for purely military messages, but I have no doubt that in case of need I could get urgent messages through to you, dear. If you have anything urgent for me, love, you might try to get it through by addressing the message to the Oriental Mission, Calcutta, and asking them to transmit it to me by wireless.

Franklin is a considerable help to me and has relieved me of the treasury work. Leitch has arrived but is being posted to Falam. He is hating the prospect of going there for reasons you will not find hard to guess.

In future all our letters are to be censored at some Army Base Post Office so I may not be able to tell you freely all that is going on here. Latterly some of your letters have been opened by the censor too, darling. Isn't it just hateful? It makes me wild to think of some stranger conning over the terms of endearment I might use to my own lady-wife.

Leitch tells me that Duguid has let me down by abandoning your boxes halfway to Aijal. Toby, however, made arrangements to get them forwarded to [John] Wadhams at Aijal, who is the Burma Govt. forwarding agent, so I trust they will eventually reach you at long last. I had a short note from Sharpe of apology. He says that someone looted his house and among other things one of our boxes was looted. This will be the one which Franklin told me was broken open and only half full.

No more news at the moment, darling. What about some more cigarettes?

All my love as ever, sweetheart, and hugs for Rabbit and Tigger.

Yours alone,

Daddy

When do you intend to get out of Mussoorie into a more congenial climate?

Eileen Leitch is up at Darjeeling with some other Burma people, and Margaret Franklin is in Srinagar.

Norman's life in Tiddim was preoccupied with the enemy, the new motor road that he was involved with and the problem of supplies, along with the personalities and rivalries of his colleagues. Domestically, the activities of the censor were an irritation and he was constantly worried about his wife and family far away in India; communication was erratic and difficult. In his next letter he thought that it was a possibility that he could take some leave in the following January 'without sacrifice of honour'.

Tiddim
26th November 1942

My darling,

I am very worried at having no letter from you this week, and I do hope you have had no relapse after your operation. Last week's letter was dated the 27th Oct. and I was hoping to learn this week that the pain had disappeared finally from your throat, dear. But, most mysterious of all is a helio message I received last Sunday the 22nd which I am enclosing. You see, sweetheart, it gives your address as Aijal and I could hardly believe it was true. So much so in fact that I sent a helio message back addressed to you at Aijal saying the news seemed almost too good to be true and asking if you had the kiddies with you. I have been in an agony of impatience all week for a reply to this but nothing has come in though I have had other helio messages from Aijal on official matters. You see I have a helio in Tiddim connecting with another one which I have placed on the top of the ridge above Mualnuam and which connects with Champhai. I have now sent a message to our supply officer Wadhams at Aijal asking if it is correct that you are there, but here again I have had no reply in three days. In these circumstances I do not know what to think, so I am sending this letter as usual to Mussoorie. If you are really at Aijal and I hear from you in a day or two, I can easily get in touch with you by helio and so keep in touch. If I hear nothing within the next week, I am going to send a wireless message to Mussoorie.

I have the Oriental Mission wireless set in the area now, and the corporal in charge – in return for small kindnesses such as the loan of some crockery, etc. – has offered on the Q.T. [quiet] to put through any private messages I wish to send to their agency at Calcutta whence he could arrange with a friend of his there to have them sent on by telegraph. This will assure us of prompt communication at any time in future, sweetheart, and is most comforting to me.

We will need to be discreet, however, in the use of this service lest other people we know of put their spoke in the wheel. Incidentally, please let me know if my letters to you are opened by the censor. We have been ordered to send all letters now through the Levy Office Falam to be forwarded to some Base Post Office for censorship in India. To evade this I am registering mine, as I understand Falam does not include registered letters in the parcel for the censor's office. I don't know how far this is true, and would like to hear in what form you receive my letters, darling.

There has still been no sign of any enemy advance in this direction this week, but there are ample indications, which I cannot divulge, that help is on hand for us from your side – not before time! Various officers from the India Staff have been through here this week and Haswell only left this morning after meeting one of them here. He is now a full Colonel and this little corner of the world is likely to become increasingly important to our cause in the very near future.

I am enclosing a draft for Rs 2000. I mentioned having sent this some time ago but there has been a mistake at Falam. When I drew my pay here at the beginning of the month, I re-credited the amount to Tiddim Treasury and asked Falam to issue the draft and to forward it direct to you c/o Imperial Bank. Actually the Falam treasury has been moved elsewhere for safety and it takes some days to get to them. They appear to have issued it on the 16th but instead of forwarding it via Aijal have returned it to me to send on to you. This has led to a whole month's delay nearly and is most annoying, but I hope it reaches you, love, before you begin to feel the pinch for funds. Everyone I meet tells me of the terrifically high cost of living in India. Leitch has passed through here and has been sent on to Falam where he is to act as cipher officer. He is frightfully fed up as he thought he was to relieve me here. As I have told you already, darling, I would like to stick on until the end of Jan. next and if nothing has blown up by then, I fully intend to press for my leave as I feel I could do so then without sacrifice of honour.

No other great news at the moment, love. I do hope the mystery of your 'Aijal' wire will be cleared up soon. It will be just too good if you are there for I would then take steps to get you back here, sweetheart. After all, you could always move back if that became necessary, but I feel sure we would both be happier to be together again to face whatever may be coming our way.

All my love as ever, darling Mummiekins, to yourself, Rabbit and Tigger. I am sure they must be delighted that school term has ended.

Sealed with a loving kiss,

Yours alone,

Daddy

As Christmas 1942 approached the question of leave became more pressing. Tiddim still had not fallen, the school term had ended and, among Norman's domestic worries, there was the constant problem of money.

Tiddim
4th December 1942

My darling,

What a relief it has been to get your letters of the 14th and 16th Nov. Your last was of Oct. 27th and I had begun to wonder what had happened when I got your wire. Had you been ill in the meantime, love? And if so, why couldn't you let me know?

Please believe me, dearest, when I say that I have never written anything to Sandy which has entailed a loss of face on your part. On the other hand, in my letter to him which he has no doubt shown to MacDougall, I made perfectly clear my keen appreciation of your grand loyalty in undertaking on your own to get me out for a few weeks' leave. Maybe I have been pigheaded in the matter but at least, darling, our honour is not besmirched, and I can still look forward to looking you in the eye, sweetheart. And that's a thing I couldn't have done had I slunk out on leave in September. It is admittedly galling to hear your news of Leedham [John Leedham, BFrS] and Chartrand, etc. but even so, I would rather have my conscience than theirs. It must be nice for Moya [Poulton] to have such dreams of J. C's future! Judging from his immediate past she has all my sympathy and I think we can let it go at that!!

I can see, darling, that you have had a perfectly bloody time at Woodstock and I am wiring to you on this matter. I think you should move to Simla, and I have also wired Sandy to help you in the matter of getting accommodation and also to see if he can help in the matter of fixing up the kiddies in a school there for the new term. Without being with you, dearest, you cannot know how closely I agree with your decision that nothing but the best is good enough for the darling Rabbit and the Tigger, and I trust you to follow your own bent on their account, without further reference to me. It is damnable that this separation prevents us from talking over the matter together, sweetheart, but with a clear mind I know you will take, alone, the responsibility which we would otherwise share, and will make a thoroughly good job of it in their interests.

As to the question of funds. I hope my draft reaches you in time for Christmas, dearest. What the hell are Scotts doing? As soon as you get the balance of cash out of them, love, close your account with them at once and stick to the Imperial Bank in conjunction with Grindlays. The first thing is to get out of Mussoorie if you are being coerced into assisting at the school. This is no job for you, love, and I'm damned if you are going to be beholden to a lot of bloody Americans in any way. I don't like the sound either of the school report from Ridgewood. Stricter discipline is necessary I think, and that alone is sufficient reason for seeking some other school for our two bundles of love. Don't worry about the funds. As I told you in an earlier letter, I am able to live on my fixed Travel Allowance of Rs 125 plus an allowance of Rs 150 which I get from 'V' Force [Assam Rifles and Naga villagers with British officers] and my free rations, so that all my pay is yours. Incidentally, we were due an increment on the 7th Nov. last and I am claiming this. You need therefore have no worry on the kiddies' account, dearest, and I trust you will make full use of the funds I am able to send you without stinting yourself in anything.

I hope Sandy will be able to help in the matter of getting the kiddies into a school at Simla.

Everything is quiet here this week, and I am more quietly confident than ever that Tiddim is not going to fall. It won't be long now until the period of suspense is past and I shall be coming out, darling, to meet you with a broader grin than ever on the old face-piece.

All my love, as ever, sweetheart, to you all.

Yours alone,

    Daddy

Awn Ngin (Norman's interpreter in Tiddim) sent a letter to Betty Kelly on 12 December together with a Christmas gift:

From: Awn Ngin, Esq.
c/o N.W. Kelly, Esq., O.B.E.,
Asst. Supdt., Tiddim
Chin Hills

Tiddim
Chin Hills
British Burma
Dated Tiddim, the 12th December 1942

Dear Madam,

I am very very pleased to be able to inform you that my Chief the Assistant Superintendent and myself are still working together without any trouble as you were here. And that on account of his sole help we all the Tiddim Chins and myself have not met with any anxieties. All

Chiefs and other influential people are also doing their duties for Government very willingly under him on account of his fair and able leadership.

I fervently hope that the day is not far distant when I will meet you in good health and hope also that you and your children are keeping excellent health as their father does here.

In token of wishing you a Very Happy Xmas, I send you one Siyin Chin cloth under registered parcel.

With best wishes from,
Yours sincerely,

Awn Ngin

Mrs. N.W. Kelly
c/o Woodstock School
Mussoorie, U.P., India.

On 17 December 1942, Mr Hughes, secretary to the Governor of Burma, reported to the Undersecretary of State for Burma in London: 'Civil officers and body military have steadily maintained morale against constant Japanese propaganda directed at the civil population.'[12]

Back in Mussoorie, school term had ended for Maeve and myself and we had a long holiday ahead.

The school break

During the school 'break' (long holiday) from December 1942 to March 1943, we stayed with Brian Haskins' parents, John and Joan, in Benares (Varanasi). Many of the boarding schools were in hill stations to escape the hot weather of the plains. To get there could take two or three days' journey by train. John, a chartered civil engineer from Trinity College, Dublin, had worked with the Oudh & Tirhout Railway when he first went out to India in the mid-1920s. It was the successor of the Oudh & Rurikhund Railway, whose chief claim to fame was that in 1892 it introduced lavatories in third-class carriages. These holes in the floor measured a mere 5 inches. Apparently, the designer had taken a first-class closet as his standard, and decided that the diameter of the orifice should be in proportion to the fare!

John Haskins was Chief Engineer of the O&T (affectionately known as the 'Old and Tired Railway'), which was metre gauge, running through Bihar and Bengal. One of the problems with the Indian railway network was that the width between the tracks was sometimes dependent upon the terrain. Lines into the hills had a smaller gauge than those in the plains, where space was not an issue and the cuttings were not so narrow.

The Haskins' house, a railway property, was extensive, standing within a large compound, as befitted John's senior status. It was situated on the outskirts of Benares near the main line from Lucknow, which went through the town to the Dufferin Bridge, and crossed the vast expanse of the Ganges. Our most memorable adventure, unknown to our parents, was when Brian, Maeve and I climbed up onto the track as it passed over the Dufferin Bridge. It was originally constructed in 1887 out of huge girders, with seven spans, 3,518 feet in length on concrete pillars, sunk into the bed of the Ganges, to carry the Grand Trunk Road to Calcutta. How we managed to go undetected I shall never know because there was a blockhouse at the Kashi station (Benares) end of the famous landmark. But there we were, under the track, when a passenger train roared overhead, creating a deafening sound in the latticework of steel. I can vouch for the holes in the floor of the passenger compartments, but whether they were first, second or third class, I shall never know. There would have been dire consequences if Brian's father had heard of our escapade.

John had his own splendid railway inspection saloon, with a veranda on the back, which could be hitched onto the rear of other carriages. We were occasionally very privileged, if we behaved ourselves, to be allowed to accompany him on his tours to check on his handiwork. He also had a small four-wheeled trolley, pushed by trailer-*wallahs*, who would run along the rails in their bare feet. The contraption could be dismounted, so that when a train came along the four men would haul it off the track until the train had gone by.

We recognised the marshalling yards by turntables, steam trains shunting, shouting and whistling, punctuated by the metallic clang as carriages slammed together. We sang ditties to the accompaniment of the clatter of wheels over the rail joints: *'che-che paisa chel Calcutta!'* ('Six, six pennies to go to Calcutta!'). We went to sleep and awoke to these sounds as the sun set and then rose the next day across the great open Indian plain. The sound of the iron monsters belching smoke and steam as they rushed through the night was haunting. They had huge lamps to illuminate the track and save stray cattle from being hit by the 'cow catchers', which prevented the cattle going under the wheels and derailing the train.

The four *malis* doubled as trolley men, and would also draw water from the brick-lined well. The water table was 20 feet down and brought to the surface in buffalo-skin bags, by means of a crude mechanism, usually man-powered but occasionally buffalo-powered. One of these lugubrious beasts would be brought to the house each day to be milked. Joan Haskins, a trained nurse and a staff member at Woodstock, would supervise the washing of hands, teats and anything else likely to have germs, and would then ensure the milk was brought to the boil at least three times before it was covered and left to cool. A later luxury was a paraffin-powered fridge.

Joan was attentive and humorous but never intrusive. In her efficient way she would arrange social evenings for some British troops, mostly 'other ranks', who were stationed nearby on their way to or from the

Burma campaign. We would play games such as cards or mah-jong. The ivory bricks of this fascinating Chinese pastime had different suits engraved in bright colours on them, for instance 'winds' (north, south, east and west), 'bamboo', 'characters', 'dragons' and 'circles'. The chink of the pieces as they struck each other made a characteristic sound. There was also 'pick-up sticks'; which made a deep impression on ten-year-old Brian. Those going into Burma had steady hands, 'those on their way out trembled' – their nerves had clearly been affected by experiences of war.

There were other memories for us – among the last children of the Raj – of mosquito nets, hurricane lamps, scorpions and snakes, wild *pi* dogs scavenging on rubbish dumps, crows, vultures, flying squirrels, beautiful birds and leaping langur monkeys that would jump from the treetops onto metal-roofed houses. Memories, too, of the sound of the monsoon rain rat-tat-tatting like machine-gun fire on the corrugated iron above our heads and the fun we had sliding down the hillsides on pine needles.

Chapter 7

THE LIFELINE WITH INDIA

High Command appreciated that if the Chin Hills were to be defended there needed to be a reliable supply route from Imphal to Tiddim. Previously there had been only a mule track, which was also used by coolies. It would have to be converted into a mud road, 164 miles long and, after Milestone 73 at the Indo-Burmese border, it would have to be dug out with basket and spade only through to the Chin Hills.

Building the Tiddim Road

Lieutenant-Colonel Towers described how the road was made in an article called 'The Tiddim Track', published in the *Journal* of the United Service Institution of India: 'In September 1942, the "Great Ones" decided there should be a road between Imphal and Tiddim, and in the manner of the "Great Ones" someone took a rule, drew a line on the map between the two places, and said: "Let there be a road."' Towers continued:

> We established camp at Bishenpur (Mile 17). My instructions were to convert the Imphal–Torbung (Mile 33) section into an all-weather road, single track with by-pass points, and make a Jeep road from Torbung to Tiddim, to be converted later into a motor transport road behind forward units [see map no. 7 on p. 80].
>
> One of the finest engineering feats of the war has been the construction of great mountain roads into Burma. Thousands of troops who will traverse them know little of the difficulties of the builders. Here is the story of one of them. It is published as a tribute to the men who sweated and toiled in lonely places, away from the limelight, and without whose courage and toughness our future reoccupation of Burma would not have been possible...
>
> At our next stop – Kansau – we decided that the Hengtam–Kansau route was of no use, so we pushed on to Tonzang, where we met the party headed by Major Hellicar and also Mr. N. Kelly, A.P.S., Chin Hills. The only means of communication in these hills has always been by mule path, which used to be kept in good repair, and the grades of which seldom exceeded one in six or one in seven. As time was limited, we had to keep to these mule paths to view the country and seek possible alignments for a road.

At Tonzang lives a Chief named Pum Za Mang, head of all the Kamhau Chins. He had played a great part in supplying all the Chin labour for the Tiddim–Burma border road, and, in fact, the whole of the Tiddim–Manipur River road was cut by Chins from villages under his authority. He rather fancied himself as an engineer, and I remember him making two classic remarks *à propos* engineering. There are numerous suspension bridges all over the Chin Hills, nearly all of them built by Pum Za Mang or his father. The one over the Manipur River is a particularly large one, with a span of 300 feet and, incidentally, one rope is two inches and the other 1½ inches.

On being asked how he knew what size of rope to use on any given bridge, he airily replied: 'Oh! it just depends on how much money I have got to spend.' On further questioning as to how he knew what weight the bridge would take when it was erected, he explained: 'We send one mule across, and if it seems all right we then send two mules across; and then three, and then four. If it looks dangerous with four we declare it to be a three-mule bridge.' We said that it seemed a little extravagant on mules if the bridge collapsed, to which he replied in a rather horrified voice: 'Good heavens! They're the Deputy Commissioner's mules, not mine.'

The country in which we were operating was not a road-builder's paradise. The Manipur River is fast-flowing and some 300 feet wide, with mountains rising sheer on both sides, that on the west bank rising to 7,000 feet, while the mule path rises from river level to between 50 feet to 100 feet, continues along the bank for about five miles, rising to 500 to 600 feet at the mouth of the Kaphi Lui, and running north-ward along the side of the hills some 600 feet above the Kaphi Valley, through Mualkawi, in and out of the long re-entrants that add miles to the road until it reaches the junction of the Kaphi Lui and a stream from Khuabem [see colour map no. 28].

General Irwin, the commander of 4 Corps, who was senior to General Slim, was adamant that there should be a fair-weather road as far as Tiddim. Towers wrote, 'It was accepted that road construction took priority over everything, even over battle.' He continued:

What was the object of the road? The main objects were two, first, to maintain a force in the Chin Hills and, secondly, to get in supplies to feed the civil population. So much labour had been utilised in the construction of the Tiddim–Manipur River section and for portering supplies that little or no cultivation had been done. Thus unless supplies could be got through before the rains broke on May 1, the civil population faced famine.

By mid-March 1943 we were over the Singgel Ridge and starting on the downward journey to the Kaphi Lui. My unit was then ordered on to beyond Tonzang to make a trace over the Letha Range to Fort White.

At the end of his article Towers gave tribute:

> My officers and Staff Sergeants must not be omitted. In tiny camps in the depths of the jungle, their sole companions Chin coolies, they pushed their way on through impenetrable jungle. And, finally, a word of praise to stout-hearted Norman Kelly, Political Superintendent at Tiddim, who put his heart and soul into the construction of his portion of the road.[1]

The effort put into building the road was also commented upon in an article by *The Statesman*, which mentioned the 'Chocolate Staircase', part of the road that climbed up the steep face of a mountain:

> The importance of this work was recognised by the army command who sent out regular personnel and a few experienced officers to stiffen and organise the Chin forces. It is not only for war that they have organised the hillmen. When this place was still more than 100 miles beyond the army's most advanced base, two of the officers started to build a road which would link them with the military forces. Neither man had the smallest experience in roadmaking or surveying. The country they had to cut through was bush-covered and precipitous. In one of the villages they found a Sino-Burman who knew a little about engineering. His was the only expert aid they had. They recruited 5,000 Chins as labourers and set to work. In five months, though continuously interrupted by rains, they had built 30 miles of motorable road and joined the sappers working from other parts. One section of their work, now widened and improved, remains a striking landmark. It is a stretch of road zigzagging up the almost sheer face of a 4,000-ft. mountainside [up to Tiddim]. Our troops call it 'the chocolate staircase' from the colour of the soil; perhaps there is a touch of wistfulness in the name, for a bar of chocolate here is as rare as a lemon in England.
>
> Though sappers have now taken over from the amateur pioneers there are still thousands of Chins working on roads. Sometimes they work as individuals, sometimes as families. Sometimes a chief contracts to level a certain stretch or cut away a given length of hillside. Then his whole village – men, women and children – turns out to speed up the job. The women are valiant labourers. As they shovel and dig they draw at hubblebubble pipes slung round their necks so as to leave both hands free. Chin women not only work for their men but smoke for them too. The men are generally non-smokers, but after hard labour they solace themselves by sipping the nicotine which collects in a little trap at the base of their wives' pipes.

These sturdy hill people are important to us now as fighters, scouts and labourers. They may be much more important as re-conquest approaches. For, though only one among Burma's races, they provide a link with the land to be freed, an assurance that when we advance further into these hills we shall find friends to help us. That help will be valuable whether we have to fight our way mile by mile or whether, as a consequence of victories elsewhere, we march at last unopposed into territory from which the enemy is in flight.

Chief Pum Za Mang was awarded the coveted King's Service Medal for his part in the construction of the Tiddim Road through the Chin Hills. He celebrated his award with a feast and lavish party at his royal house in Tonzang. All the high-ranking officials were invited and the drinking, eating and dancing went on all night until the following morning.

The Chin Levies

Just as the Tiddim Road was essential for troop movement and supplies, so the formation of the Chin Levies was to prove essential for the defence of the area around Tiddim. An Indian newspaper described how they came to be formed:

The formation of Chin Levies was largely due to the courage, foresight and influence of one man, Mr. N. W. Kelly, a Deputy Commissioner [he was, in fact, an Assistant Superintendent at this time]. When the Burma Government and British Forces withdrew into India in 1942, Kelly remained at his post. The wave of invasion stopped short before reaching his area of the Chin Hills. Presently hill men, who had fought with the Burma Rifles during the campaign, began to drift back to their homes. Kelly rallied them, kept them in military trim, recruited others from the villages, equipped them as best he could and paid them out of his civil funds. They formed an irregular frontier force spying out the enemy's movements and harrying him whenever possible.

Khen Za Moong was one of the original Chin Levies, and later wrote an account of the campaign in *Lest We Forget*. He pointed out that the Chin Levies were later, in 1943, known as the Western Chin Levies, to distinguish them from the Kachin Levies of North Burma. It was his father, Tong Za Kai, a subedar major pensioner, who was recalled into service during the war and was the Tiddim police chief. The Tiddim headman, Pau Za Kam, was also in the Chin Levies.

The Chins knew every footpath and hillock and there was little chance of the Japanese remaining undetected once they had entered the Chin Hills. To ambush the enemy, they dug concealed pits and surrounded the site with sharpened bamboo spikes, *panjis*, with poisoned tips. When the firing started the Japanese would throw themselves off the path into the jungle and get impaled. Because many of the Chin guns were antiquated muzzle-loading flintlocks, after the first rank had fired, as at Waterloo, the second rank would fire while they were reloading.

The Chin Levies often wore a cock's feather in their caps, or that of a jungle bird – the racket-tailed drongo – so that they could be distinguished from the enemy. Some wore a life-preserving charm, a small tuft of feathers from a string around the neck. Many were barefoot and had been called by the Indian press 'hawk-eyed, soft-footed men of the frontier'; they were used to stalking animals and birds for the pot. They had been headhunters before the arrival of the British, who had outlawed their blades of sharp steel known as *khin khot naam* (see photograph no. 15). Many of these had been hidden but reappeared during the campaign, and a number of Japanese were to lose their heads. A Chin who killed his first Japanese was given a small patch of red cloth to attach to his shirt by a safety pin.

Supply problems for these guerrillas were formidable. Some units were fifteen days' mule journey from Tiddim. This meant that every third mule in a column had to carry fodder (Tiddim to Tonzang was about 25 miles). In the other direction Fort White was 25 miles distant, and it was 50 miles from there to Kalemyo. The Western Chin Levies were also based at Falam. The ex-Burma Rifles Chins had been trained as professional soldiers and were armed, in the main, with .303 rifles.

General Slim and 4 Corps realised that the Chin Levies and the Chin Battalion needed to be strengthened. To gain practical experience of jungle warfare, groups of military formations from India were sent into the hills to gain experience, bolster the Levies and reduce their feeling of isolation. Because the Tiddim Road, linking Tiddim with Imphal, was far from completed by December 1942, it was decided to send a detachment of the 17th Indian Division to Tiddim, which at that time was being supplied by air. A company of the 2/5th Royal Gurkhas was therefore despatched to Tiddim. In December 1942 there was increased Japanese activity around Kalewa, and on 26 December the Japanese advanced from Kalemyo and occupied No. 2 Stockade. The Gurkha company moved down from Fort White to No. 3 Stockade, a position about 3,000 feet higher than No. 2 Stockade, to block their path.

Harold Braund and Jack Oats, who were with the Levies, decided to make a pre-emptive strike against the enemy at Tahan, a village 6 miles from No. 2 Stockade on the road to Kalemyo (see map no. 4 on p. 38). There were about twenty to thirty Japanese in full view in the main street. They shot the sentry who was on guard up a tree, and he fell. They next inflicted a number of casualties as the Japanese ran for cover and the Levies opened fire from balconies and upper-storey windows of the street-side shops. Braund and Oats then pulled out and made for the hills. As they did so, they were machine-gunned by an RAF Lysander, mistaking them for Japanese. The BBC mentioned this microscopic action in its news bulletins of 26 December 1942. It was the first time the

Japanese had been attacked – as distinct from resisted – at ground level since the retreat from Burma. The twelve dead were taken back to Kalemyo by bullock cart to be cremated, and the rest of the force withdrew from Tahan the same day.

Peter Bankes did even better. While patrolling from his eyrie on the Suanglangsu Vum, he attacked a party of 60 Japanese, who had occupied the small Burmese village of Nansaungpu, north of Kalemyo – the villagers had abandoned their homes. At night, an armed party of Levies raced between the two rows of houses, setting fire to the roofs as they went. The Japanese were shot up as they fled.

When the first news of Bankes' raid on Nansaungpu came through, Braund said, 'That's worth an M.C.' Little did he know the full story. Peter – described as the 'Chin Express' by an Indian newspaper because, with his enormous legs, he was the fastest climber in the hills – confided to Jack Oats, who recalled:

> He told me that before going down to raid the Burmese village in revenge for their attack on a Chin village he explained his plan the evening before. A few hours later he got news that there were many more Japs in the village than he had known of. He let his plan stand. His men – a very undisciplined crowd – said they wouldn't come. Peter said: 'Well, I'm leaving in the morning on this job with or without you.' And in the morning while it was still dark, they followed him.[2]

A 'Lone Outpost of the Empire'

The 'lone outpost of the Empire', as General Slim called Tiddim, was about to experience the gradual but steady build-up of the celebrated 17th Indian Division, known for its 'Black Cat' sign, which had been conferred on it in June 1942. It had fought the Japanese 33rd Division during the retreat from Burma, notably at Shwegyin on the Chindwin. Now, as a Light Division, it had two brigades, 48 and 63. Norman Kelly was Senior Civil Affairs Liaison Officer to the Commanding Officer, General 'Punch' Cowan. On 15 February 1943 he was commissioned as a Major in the Army Burma Reserve Officers (ABRO).

The Chin Hills Battalion at last got the long-awaited medical officer, whom Colonel Moore had wanted so badly in April 1942. He was Lieutenant Kenny Fraser, Royal Army Medical Corps (RAMC), who joined the battalion on 4 December 1942 (see photograph no. 24). A graduate of Aberdeen University, he had arrived, against all the odds, via the Aijal route, after he had received the following order: 'Secret. You will proceed forthwith and report to the Commanding Officer, Chin Hills Battalion, Burma Frontier Force, Falam.' As far as Movement Control in India was concerned, there was no such place.

He later described his adventures in his book, *'Don't Believe a Word of It!'*

The reason for confidentiality became apparent as soon as our new friend ushered us into his office. It was a huge map-room, for he worked in military intelligence, and on one wall was a great map of the Assam–Burma region, showing locations of our forces and arranged, as it seemed to me, with the border between those countries parallel to and near the roof. The search began again, from the top of the ladder this time.

Twenty minutes later, 'You know, you're right, but the order must be wrong.'

'Why?'

'Because it isn't in India. It's in Burma, and we are not in Burma: the Japanese are.'

'What is the nearest Indian place where we have troops?' I asked.

'Aijal, in Assam.'

'Good, I'll get a railway warrant to there and enquire.'

'Can't be done. Aijal has no railway.'

'Where's the nearest railway station?'

'Silchar.'

'Then I'll go there and "proceed forthwith" by road.'

'You won't. There's no road to Aijal.'[3]

This was not an auspicious start for Kenny Fraser.

Next morning I reported my arrival in to the local Army Commander, a lieutenant-colonel, at headquarters in Aijal and tried to explain about 'proceeding forthwith' to Falam. My reception was unexpected and somewhat harsh: 'No British officer travels in India without a servant; no British officer in India walks, he rides. You will consider yourself under arrest until further notice, when your disposal will be arranged.[4]

After four or five days' internment in Aijal, he was allowed to go on his way. By dint of considerable ingenuity he finally arrived in Falam, where he found his battalion. All the officers, except the Commanding Officer, were amateur soldiers.

His introduction to Norman Kelly came later and is worth recounting:

You will see from it the admirable nature of Mr. Norman Kelly, whose outstanding relationship with the folk of the Chin Hills I shall tell you about. The second party, unlike the first, just grew. There were no invitations but, judging by the number of civilian officers there, and by the superior quality and amount of the drams provided, I guessed that a contingent of Levy officers had come in and brought their 'comforts' with them. The bottles had been smelled from afar. The Area Commander and the Battalion Commander were not present...

We had a consoling round of nectar – I never discovered who donated it – and a more boisterous entertainment was devised. What furniture we had was arranged as leaps in a circular racecourse, tables and benches right way up, one old sofa up-ended. There was no betting on winners – at least, not in money – and somersaults got extra points.

There are those that maintain that odour is the most evocative of our senses but, after all these years since 1942, it is colour, a beautiful, glowing, deep claret that brings back to me the fun, the noise and the introduction to a new acquaintance at that party. Racing commenced. Winners suffered most, the prize being another potation. At the seventh – or was it the seventeenth? – came an end.

Our encounter was not so much of moment as of momentum. Perhaps my ignorance of horse-racing accounted for it, or perhaps I had won a prize or two too many, but somehow I mistook directions and collided with a stranger, well dressed in civilian attire, and brought both of us down. My right elbow not only caused his nose to bleed, but also altered its alignment so much that it pointed one way while he walked in another. My first surgical task after arrival was to repair an injury, which I myself had caused.

At that time we had no anaesthetic except the potable spirit that we had broached but, braced with a generous measure or two of it, the victim allowed himself to be held firm by enthusiastic helpers whilst I pulled all straight. It looked good. We showed him the result in a metal shaving mirror.

'Thank you, doctor', he said politely, then pulled out a navy-blue silk handkerchief, blew his choked nose and put it squint again. And there was that glorious colour, deeper and finer and glowing more than any claret held before a lighted candle. I do not claim that anybody's blood and all shades of blue would produce it, but his blood and his handkerchief did – or is a little alcohol needed somewhere in the mix? But there was work still to be done. Five times was the same sequence of events repeated, each accompanied by no more than 'Thank you, doctor', and an occasional 'Hell's bells', his favourite expletive. I never heard him say anything stronger than that. Finally, he gave up, being tired of it, and I gave up, having missed my first chance of creating a favourable medical impression.

Such was my introduction to Norman Kelly, a peacetime Assistant Deputy Commissioner in the Chin Hills, who had stayed on in war-time to help the Chin people to resist the Japanese. By the time I got there he had already organised a sort of home guard of lightly armed Levies.

Norman Kelly never once referred to this unfortunate start to our acquaintance, and that characterised his equable, warm and friendly temperament. Officially we had nothing to do with each other, and our meetings, always a pleasure, happened mostly when excursions were made into empty villages in the Myittha valley and in which great baskets of un-milled rice could be found.

The nearest that Norman Kelly and I came to be on official terms was a consequence of my appointment as Senior Area Medical Officer, which made me, in effect, MO to the Chin Levies. Extra confirmation of my good regard for Norman Kelly came when I began to travel between positions occupied by the Battalion, passing through villages in which the people were at a loss to see a quack doctor, without troops, descend on them and would hold back their welcome. I soon learned to say 'Kelly *Boi-pa na thei maw?'* which is 'Do you know Kelly, sahib?', and all turned to smiles and friendship. It never failed. He was known everywhere in the Chin Hills, from Falam to Tiddim and far beyond.[5]

With the increasing militarisation of the Chin Hills in January 1943 Haswell decided that Norman Kelly should hand over his command of the Tiddim Levies to Braund; likewise Poo Nyo, Assistant Superintendent in Falam, passed his Levy responsibilities to Rupert Carey. Peter Bankes was in charge of the Fort White and No. 3 Stockade sector.

Chapter 8

'THERE'S A BOY COMING HOME ON LEAVE'

By 1943 Tiddim was recognised as more important than Falam, the capital of the Chin Hills, because of its strategic importance. Norman was at last able to apply for some much-needed leave; as the Japanese threat increased, the censor was becoming more eagle-eyed. L. B. Naylor summarised the situation in this letter to Ralph Wilkie, the Commissioner, in India. Wilkie had joined the Indian Civil Service in 1921 and was Naylor's superior (later given the rank of brigadier).

Office of the Deputy Commissioner
Chin Hills, Falam
3rd January 1943

To: Burma Commissioner
Jorhat, India

Dear Mr. Wilkie,

Last month I visited Tiddim and spent a long time on the road and also some days in Tiddim itself.

Kelly is being worried by his wife to come out and he thinks he ought to go, but he is extremely keen to be on the spot if 'anything is doing'. Finally he himself stated that he would like to remain until mid-February, by which time he thinks things will either have happened or won't be happening at all. I have therefore provisionally agreed to allow him to recess from the middle of February. If you agree and should he still desire to go I propose putting Franklin in charge of the Subdivision. I have been favourably impressed by Franklin and although he knows but little of the Subdivision, still I think he will be able to carry on provided it is not a time of great activity. I understand Kelly's feelings. On the one side he is being pressed by his wife, who is worried about schooling of the two children. On the other hand Kelly wants to be in at the local 'kill'. With the Japs sitting close up to the foothills we are no longer able to get up rations from no-man's land and so this very important work for which Kelly, with his special knowledge of the locality and people, was especially fitted, has ceased.

Chief Pum Za Mang, who in July seemed to be sitting on the fence, and whom I had to call to Fort White to receive some plain talking, now seems to have made up his mind that he had better be loyal to us. Anyway he is now giving us wholehearted support and doing excellent work in arranging coolie labour both for the road and for transport from Lenacot. There is a tremendous amount of work still to be done on the Imphal–Tiddim Road by way of improvements, correct banking of corners and the widening of them, etc., etc. Besides this a better alignment should be sought for, if the road is to be kept open in the rains [May to October].

I have wired Kelly to consult Chapman [Public Works Department] about the road but will not get his reply for a couple of days as he is down at No. 3 meeting Haswell.

The Civil Govt. Servants' rations have now slightly improved as I have succeeded in getting a small ration of tea, sugar and milk issued to them. It is not always fully realised that if the Civil Administration was to break down, the whole of the transport system would go 'phut' also.

And that is also a reason why I must keep on stressing the necessity of having salt for the Chins. Frank George [Assistant Deputy Commissioner] and I, but mainly George, have managed to get a few bullocks onto the Aijal–Champhai road bringing in salt and today I have just been able to make a first distribution of 131 boxes of 40lbs each for the Falam Subdivision. It is not much but it will help. George leaves on the 4th to meet Wadhams at Champhai when he will pay for our mule camp there and discuss with Wadhams what further transport, etc., can be arranged. He will also enquire into what amount of paddy and or rice is available at Champhai. McCall has impounded the whole of the crop there at a fixed price for Govt. use and the Chin Hills will get most of it. I have tackled Haswell about the Chins having a share but the armed forces are so badly off for this necessity that although Haswell fully realises the necessity of feeding the Chin, if he is going to work as a transport coolie, still we were unable to fix a proportionate division until we know the amount available. Even if I do get some, the amount will be relatively so small that it will NOT affect my request for 1000 tons.

Sharpe is arranging to send in 250 tons of rice through Demagiri and Lungleh [see map no. 3 on p. 28]. Although this is much further south than I wanted it, I shall be able to use it for the southern half of Falam Subdivision. The two areas which require rice are Tiddim and Falam Subdivisions. Haka can manage to support itself. So the problem of getting rice into Tiddim and the northern half of Falam still remains. I hope that Sharpe will succeed in either getting the use of local labour between Taipuimukh and Haichin or importing labour for the route.

I have also written you separately about the Civil Surgeon and my fears of a bad outbreak of cholera in the hot weather. When the Battalion Doctor, Fraser, comes back from tour I will have a discussion with him on this subject. But in conversation with Russell, who commands the Battalion, he was unable to hold out any hopes of Fraser being able to

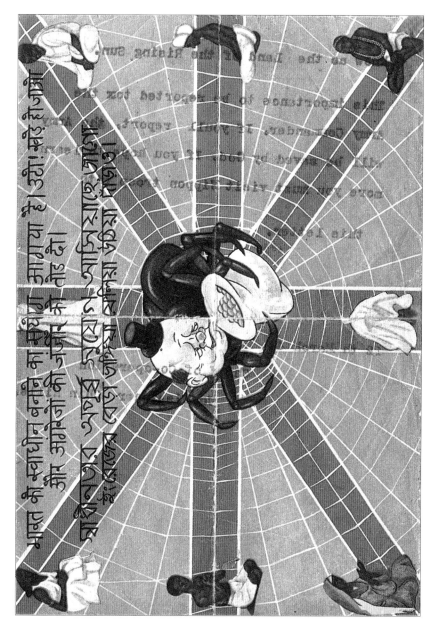

26. *Japanese propaganda cartoon printed on the back of a letter to Norman Kelly dated 12 March 1944 from the Chief Japanese Commissioner, Chin Hills. Winston Churchill, the black spider with a bag of gold, is set against a Union Jack and is exploiting Indians at the edge of his web.*

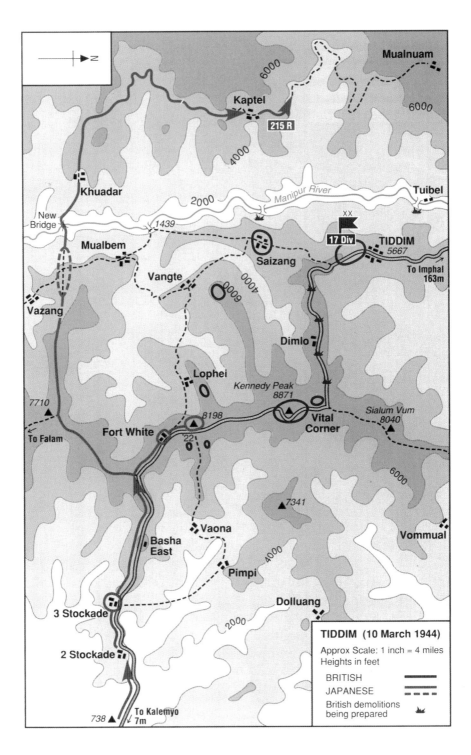

27. *Tiddim front contour map, 10 March 1944, showing the Japanese advance from Kalemyo by the 215 Regiment of the 33rd Division. Note that north is to the right.*
(Courtesy of Major-General Ian Lyall Grant, MC)

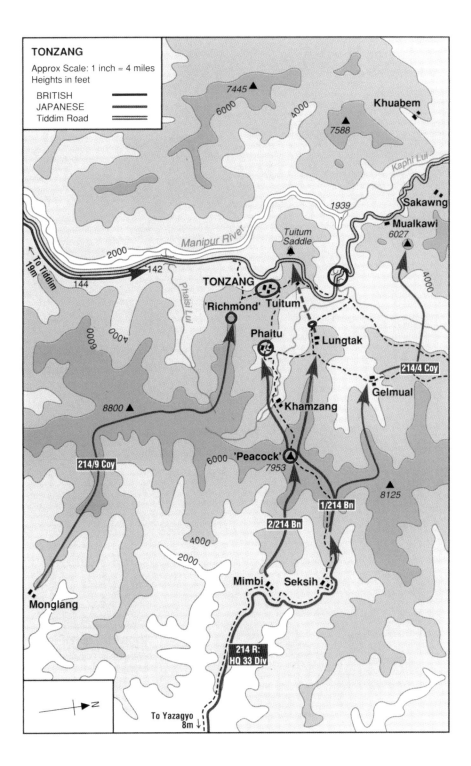

28. Contour map of the Tonzang area: the Battle of Tonzang, 8–26 March 1944. Note that north is to the right. (Courtesy of Major-General Ian Lyall Grant, MC)

29. The view from the top of Kennedy Peak (8,871 feet), looking east towards the Kalemyo plain. (Author)

30. The Manipur River, at low water, in November 1999, long after the monsoon rains. (Author)

31. Naini Tal Lake from the Talli Tal end, looking towards Cheena Peak (8,568 feet), scarred by the massive landslide of 1880, and 'The Flats' which it then formed. Brookhill House and the Hallett War School were on the right-hand hillside. From near the school the Himalayas could also be seen.
(Photograph courtesy of Ernest Yeo)

32. Pandaw I on its maiden voyage up the Chindwin in 1998 to Kalewa. It was here that the British Army crossed the river during the retreat of May 1942.
(Photograph courtesy of Barbara Adshead)

33. The centre of Tiddim in 1999 with the post-war clock tower. (Author)

34

35

36

34, 35 and 36. The 'Sing Spiration' produced by the Tiddim (now Tedim) Theological College students in 1999: Tiddim Chin dance (top); the Chai-hpa-rau (centre) by Haka students – the men have a bamboo pole in each hand and bring them together in time with the music while the girls dance gracefully in and out of the fleeting space available; and (below) the author with a Chin student in Tiddim national costume.
(Photographs courtesy of Leo Deng Hau)

37. The Nakzang Manipur River Bridge; 100 yards downstream is where the 17th and 5th Indian Divisions constructed their bridges. (Author)

38. The author at Fort White. Taingen is where the Chin memorial stone was erected (see photograph no. 62). Akluai points toward the strategic Siyin Valley.

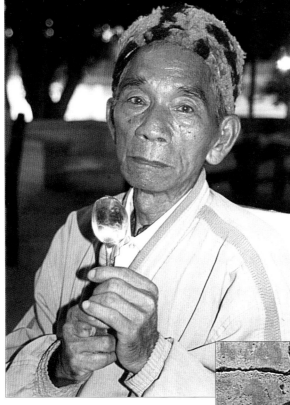

39. *T. H. Go Khan Pau, Norman Kelly's table boy, with the spoon that Norman gave him when they parted for the last time, just before Tiddim was evacuated in March 1944.* (Author)

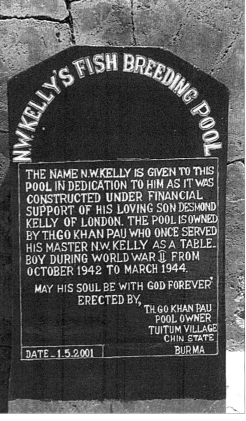

40. *The memorial to Norman Kelly constructed by T. H. Go Khan Pau in May 2001.*
(Photograph courtesy of T. H. Go Khan Pau)

give the time required to organise a campaign of prevention or to assist us if an outbreak occurred.

As you will have seen from the situation reports we have had a further couple of clashes with the Japs and inflicted punishment without suffering loss ourselves. We have been extremely lucky so far and all these clashes have put the tails of our men and of the Chins generally well up. The myth of the invincible Jap is exploded.

If it is not too late may I send my best wishes for the New Year.

Yours sincerely,

L. B. N. [1]

Tiddim
9th January 1943

Darling Mummiekins,

Owing to local activities here I have missed the last two mails and you must be wondering what is the matter. To make up for this I tried to send you a wireless message for the New Year, darling, but I have just heard that the charging engine for the wireless has been out of order and that all messages have consequently been held up. I do not know if it is in working order again or not. It is almost impossible to get in spare parts for anything mechanical and my own motor transport is still lying at Fort White out of order. It is damned bad luck, for it would be so much more pleasant to use it during this glorious weather than it was during the rains. Did I tell you that the little wireless set had also broken down? I have sent this off to Calcutta for repair in charge of a wireless chap who was passing through.

There has been a hell of a row and a consequent tightening up of the censorship with regard to letters being sent by officers from this area. I am told that one of my officers from No. 3 and myself are among the offenders though, God knows, I can't remember anything I have said in my letters that might be calculated to give information away if the letters got into wrong hands. I hate to think of my letters to you, darling, being read by other eyes.

There is little news I can give you, dearest. We have had a certain amount of local excitement and have been kept very busy all round for the last three weeks – all starting just before Xmas – but things are quieter again now. I have been out of H.Q. most of the time and got back this morning only to leave for the North on the 11th to meet some other parties. We are getting much more support now and the influx of 'strangers' raises many problems with the local people. An increasing number of 'big noises' also require tactful handling. Indeed, Tiddim is now becoming more important than Falam owing to the present circumstances, and L. B. Naylor talks of making this his H.Q. as he thinks he could carry more weight with such gentlemen!!

I feel sure that I can safely come out for a while at the end of Feb., sweetheart, without any risk of letting my show down. I shall plan to move from here on March 1st and this should set me up and give me time to get back before the break of the next rains – it looks, after all, that we shall be here for another rains.

John Franklin has been having a good deal of low fever lately, but is being a great help and enables me to get round to my stations more regularly. Hope to be visiting Peter Bankes later this month. His wife very kindly sent me 500 cigarettes (arrived late for Xmas) in appreciation of kindnesses shown to her husband!! Wasn't it damned amazing about your Army & Navy parcel, dear? It hasn't turned up, and all the A&N offer is a letter of apology which I enclose. No suggestion of defraying the extra postage.

John Franklin tells me that Freda was torpedoed on the way here but that she and the twins were safe at St. Helena. Bill Bayly is at Dimapur and Nancy has gone home as their youngest daughter had had meningitis and was paralysed. Too awful, isn't it?

I *do* trust and pray that you and the kiddies are keeping in good health, love. I have finished up all your tonics and am feeling fighting fit still. In fact, the thought of being with you again, sweetheart, is the greatest tonic of all and I'm looking forward to that day. Possibly we can make a show of St. Patrick's night. I think we should spend most of the time in Simla where I want to bombard government with my own case arising out of the reports that Leyden is enjoying the rank, pay and allowances of a D.C. I have not let the grass grow under my feet and have represented the matter officially, but these things are so easily shelved if one is not on the spot to prosecute one's own case.

I hope you have had my letters about the new school, and that you have got the kiddies entered. You haven't acknowledged the last draft yet (Rs 2000/–) which was enclosed in one of my letters, dearest. To make sure you have funds enough I shall send another in a few days – haven't drawn my Dec. pay yet. No more at the moment, darling. All my love, kisses and hugs as ever.

Yours alone,

Daddy

From: N. W. Kelly, O.B.E., Assistant Superintendent, Tiddim
To: The Deputy Commissioner, Chin Hills District, Falam

Dated at Tiddim the 18th January 1943

Sir,

1. I have the honour to invite a reference to an earlier letter from the Government of Burma, the number and date of which are unknown to me, in which I believe it was expressed as the

intention of Government that all civil officers serving at present in the Chin Hills should enjoy a recess as opportunity permitted, and that I was to be the first to be relieved under this scheme.

2. In view of this, I have the honour to make application to avail myself of this recess with effect from the forenoon of March 1st 1943, on which date I would propose to leave my Headquarters at Tiddim. I understand the recess would actually take effect from the date of my arrival at railhead – i.e. either Lalaghat or Dimapur depending on the route taken.

3. As you are aware, Sir, it has been my privilege and good fortune to have been able to raise a sizeable Levy in this subdivision, which I trust will play its full part if necessary in the defence of the Hills. The organisation of that force has been completed and it is now functioning to a large extent under military officers. I feel, therefore, that my primary duty in this respect has been discharged, and that though I remain Zone Commander of the area within the Levy organisation, the strategical implications of that command have been largely met, with the result that it becomes increasingly possible for me to efface myself before the military outpost officers whose duty it will be to make the required tactical dispositions to deal with the local situation as it develops.

4. I am also confident that if the present threat to the Hills from this region does not eventuate before the end of February, the enemy will have lost the initiative and will be in no position to deliver a blow which would in any way shake the present morale of the people locally.

5. It would therefore appear that March 1st would be a good date from which to avail myself of a few weeks recess, with your approval. This would allow me to return to Tiddim and resume charge of my duties both as Civil and Levy Officer before the break of the next rains. In view of a promise I gave to my people when forming the Levy, that they would never be subjected to entire military control, I would suggest that in my temporary absence, the subdivision should remain in the charge of Mr. Franklin, who has been of the greatest assistance to me in the past few weeks and has already acquired a good understanding of the problems involved, both from a military and civil point of view.

I have the honour to be, Sir,

Your most obedient servant,

N. W. Kelly

Tiddim
5th February 1943

Darling,

I have sent off your birthday message and trust it will reach you in time. I understand that the wireless was broken down and that my New Year message was badly delayed. Better luck this time I hope, love.

I am in the greatest excitement now as my recess has been sanctioned. I have also sent you a message giving my probable date of departure from here and asking you for proposals as to where we meet. I should like you to make Calcutta, darling, but that might be a bit risky in view of the possibility of bombings. I can hardly believe it is true that we shall be together again at last, and though my recess will only be a short one, we will make the most of it, sweetheart, and I know that thereafter we shall both be happier in mind.

I am up to the neck in preparing handing-over notes and as usual snowed under with visitors who take up a large part of my time. I have already started to hand over my Levy duties and later in the month will be handing over the civil side as well. In view of the censorship I cannot tell you much about it, love, but I can tell you I am quite ready to go fairly skipping down the road to Aijal.

Recently we have had severe brushes in this area and have been very successful indeed. I think for the future all will be well here but it looks as though next rains will be much like the last as far as affairs here are concerned.

The parcels mails appear to have been long delayed, and all yours have arrived in a bunch. I want to hug you for them all, dearest. The mincemeat and plum puddings have been thoroughly appreciated although the festive season was so far past. The pullover, handkerchiefs, slippers, etc., were all most thoughtful gifts and are in full use.

The weather is still bitterly cold here and we have had a few showers of rain this week. Snow has been reported from Fort White, and the local opinion is that this has been the coldest winter for many years.

I am afraid I have no decent shoes in which to arrive back in civilisation and this will have to be our first purchase. At the moment I am reduced to ammunition boots which are right enough for marching about these hills, but not so hot for re-appearing in populated surroundings. I will be bringing along your various cosmetics and other garments which I have not liked to risk sending earlier in view of all the difficulties we have had over the Imphal boxes. I do hope they have arrived with their contents complete – your last letter tells me that the railway people had reported that they were improperly locked. One of them was unlocked but it was sealed when it was sent from here, dear, and I trust all is well.

I am longing to see how the kiddies have developed and how they will settle down in their new surroundings at Naini Tal.

It just strikes me that it will be damned hot in India when I arrive, and as you know I have nothing presentable in light suitings. I suppose I shall just have to swelter until I can get something made up on arrival.

Poor old Franklin had bad luck with his Xmas parcels as his plum puddings, mince pies, etc., were all thoroughly bad on arrival.

I am wiring you to address letters to me at Aijal up to about Feb. 24th. Thereafter it will be useless to write, darling, as I shall be on my way. At long last 'there's a boy coming home on leave'.

Nothing further now, love, other than all my love, hugs and kisses as ever.

Yours alone,

Daddy

In early February Norman Kelly's Chin Levies had a skirmish with the Japanese east of Fort White at No. 2 Stockade. In the words of L. B. Naylor, 'Apparently they put up a fine show and caused the Japs 40 casualties at a minimum. They, the Levies, had three men wounded and three are missing, I fear wounded and captured.'[2]

In February 1943, the leading Gurkha company was reinforced in Tiddim by a second one. At that time the Tiddim Road was only motorable to Milestone 82 from Imphal and, from there, mules had to carry all the supplies forward for 80 miles to Tiddim and a further 30 miles, over the Letha Range, to No. 3 Stockade. The land route was supplemented by airdrops begun in September on the Tiddim football field. At first Hudsons were used, but these came in at too high a speed, which meant the contents could explode like anti-personnel bombs. Later, the slower RAF Dakotas proved to be much more satisfactory. Finding the target in the hills must have been a nightmare for the pilots, with mist, low cloud and Kennedy Peak rising to nearly 9,000 feet.

The Skirmish at the Stockades

Here is Jack Oats' account of the build-up to what happened, after he returned from sick leave in India:

> I reached Tiddim again on December 20th via Aijal and learned that Peter [Bankes] was still in his old sector. I sent him a bag of woollen socks and balaclavas for his troops and the boots and parcels I had brought in from Prue, his wife. I went back to No. 3 Stockade and found Braund still there, with Milligan in my place. One of my platoons was temporarily lent to Peter, but soon after my arrival our area was hotting up and I had to recall it. In January 1943 the spearhead of the 17th Division, a company of 2/5 Gurkhas, came to us at No. 2 as well as some British commandos. We now had

149

almost a complete battalion and line of communication open behind us – big change from June 1942.

With the platoon recalled from Peter I had four platoons and a big mortar in forward positions at No. 2 and Mawlpi Ridge [see map no. 8 on p. 96].

On February 3rd Braund was ordered to Tiddim as big noise Major and [for] liaison with Levies and the 17 Division. Peter came back to No. 3. I was delighted at this as I would then be working in with Peter again, especially as Braund had been showing the strain a lot and was taking things even more seriously than usual. Peter and I were always a bit on the irresponsible side.

I was camped 4 miles in front of No. 3 where Peter had his H.Q. with the 17 Division people. Peter and Braund came back from Mawlpi one afternoon through my camp and had tea. Also I went sometimes to No. 3 for conference, square meal or bath. Then Braund went.

At that time Capt. James Crombie of 2/5 Gurkhas was in overall command, Peter with two or three platoons of Levies did most of the intelligence work and interrogation of spies, although I also had some of this to do. I was holding advanced positions and patrolling into the Plains many days and nights. We had just got two-inch mortars dropped by air and took occasional mornings at firing these and training crews.

Peter also had some and we used to combine firing practices. I had an Anglo-Burman (Tommy Aplin) as my company officer – a decent little fellow with his head screwed on.

On 8th February in the morning, Peter and I and Neesen, a Gurkha officer, were firing big and little mortars near No. 3. I also had a party out fishing with grenades in the creek. I got back to my camp at five and had some tea while Peter and Neesen had gone back to No. 3. Then I heard firing start on Mawlpi Ridge – fighting went on till about eight with mortar and machine gun. In the end, I found myself pushed far back on Mawlpi Ridge with one platoon. We were on an open hillside with no dug positions. Japs brought to a temporary halt with heavy casualties. A scratch on my knee had stiffened and I could not walk much. Sent back a note to No. 3 for ammo and gave news. About 1 a.m. Peter arrived alone with a tommy-gun and offered to take my place. We lay out with fixed bayonets and fingers on triggers. My platoon were very windy and showed it – not a good platoon (a pity as the rest were excellent). About 3 a.m. the Japs started shelling us – fairly accurate but no one hurt. Two sections suddenly panicked and ran back towards No. 3. Peter said: 'Your men have all gone. What are you going to do?' I spoke to the platoon commander and confirmed this, so we all pushed back towards No. 3 – Peter assisting me initially, then he stayed behind with the next position – a platoon of 2/5 Gurkhas. I collected my remaining platoon, put them in another position and then went up to explain how things stood to Crombie. Got my leg dressed at the casualty clearing station and then got my big 3-inch mortars into a good position. Peter joined us again after dawn and Crombie went to his forward Gurkha platoon. We were a hundred yards uphill with mortars. Japs shelled again and opened machine-gun fire from our night halting place. We opened with our big mortar and silenced their machine gun.

On 10th February Crombie refused to counter-attack all that day. I got my platoons together, fed and into new positions. In the night all quiet but many Jap Verey lights. Crombie missed big opportunity that day as Japs were in complete confusion – so were we but we had reserves.

In the morning counter-attacked, Peter and Parry (intelligence bloke) with two of my platoons, towards No. 2; Crombie with two platoons [of] 2/5 Gurkhas and two of mine along the ridge.

Remaining Japs ran and all our positions reoccupied.

10th February to 8th March: During this period Peter and I were on the same job. My camp was moved (as the Japs had the old one taped) on to the bare and waterless Mawlpi Ridge and made into a strong well-dug fort, in helio and morse lamp communication with Peter's HQ at No. 3. Sometimes Peter came down and we had tea and lunch in my dog kennel with swarms of flies and dirt. Other times I went up to Peter's for baths, better meal, meeting Gurkha officers and looking after my own administrative side.

On March 7th, Gurkha Battalion moved its Battalion H.Q. forward and a company relieved me on Mawlpi. Had a final night at No. 3 with Peter, many other officers and some local *zu* and then marched south to rejoin my own Battalion near Falam.[3]

It was at this time that one of the Chin servants who had worked for Betty Kelly before the war wrote to her from Tiddim. He had accompanied Norman as far as Aijal when he went out on leave.

Tiddim
Chin Hills
Date: 7–3–43

Mrs. Kelly,
India

Dear Madam,

I beg to take leave to write to you just a few lines. I am glad to have a chance to inform you that Mr. Kelly and I have been keeping fit since we parted at Aijal.

And I am proud to say that I have been trying hard in all my undertakings under Mr. Kelly whom I daresay I satisfied and to whom I acknowledge my indebtedness and gratitude for what had been done for me and to me.

Could my earnest wish were materialised I would have come with Mr. Kelly and would have met you also; and I am hungry for the presents you used to give me especially those of clothes which is no longer obtainable here.

I should say the condition here is much changed from what it had been during your stay – especially in matters regarding commodities. But I am proud to insert here about the peace and tranquillity that we still enjoy through the unremitting efforts of our patron Mr. Kelly whose providential helps safe-guarding us shall not and never fade out from the memory of our community, the Chins.

And I am glad to think that you will also learn from him all what had been going on and what is now being.

Hoping and praying to meet you again.

Your respectfully servant,

      Khual Khan Tual

From: L. B. Naylor, Esquire, B.Fr.S., Deputy Commissioner, Chin Hills, Burma

Dated: Falam, the 20th April 1943

To: The Commissioner, Frontier Division, Burma, c/o HQ, 4 Corps.

Sir,

I wish to bring the names of the following officers and Chiefs to the notice of Government.

1. N. W. Kelly, Esq., O.B.E., Frontier Service:
   The work of this officer was of a very high order. He threw his whole heart into the raising of Levies and obtaining the maximum amount of grain from the Kale Valley from under the noses of the enemy. Nothing was too arduous and by his energy and devotion to duty he materially contributed to our being able to hold these Hills.

2. J. Poo Nyo, Esq., Frontier Service:
   This officer raised the Haka Levies. Throughout he showed great enthusiasm and energy. His work was of a very high order. The Haka Levies were the first to meet and resist the enemy.

3. Chief Pum Za Mang, A.T.M., Kamhau Tribal Area:
   For the last nine months this Chief has wholeheartedly co-operated to the utmost of his power. His Tribal Area has been called upon to supply a very large number of porters for the carriage of rations and coolies for cutting the M/T road between Tuitum and Tiddim. Without the Chief's co-operation and power of organising, labour sufficient for these tasks would not have been forthcoming.

4. <u>Thuam Za Mang, Chief of the Soktes, Mualbem:</u>
   This Chief is the second most influential Chief in the Tiddim Subdivision. Besides efficiently administering his Tribal Area he has organised large numbers of porters and also led his Tribesmen in the field as the Sokte Levy Leader.

5. <u>Thawng Za Khup, Chief of Saizang</u> has taken the field as Levy Leader of his Tribesmen besides keeping close supervision over his Tribal Area. He has rendered loyal and devoted service.

6. <u>Thang Tin Lian, A.T.M., Chief of the Zahau Tribal Area and Hlur Hmon, A.T.M., I.D.S.M., Chief of Lomban Tribal Area</u>
   Have shown throughout the trying circumstances of the last year their loyalty by assisting the administration of the Hills in every possible way. Their devotion and loyalty have considerably influenced other Chiefs of the Falam Subdivision.

7. <u>Kio Mang, Chief of Mi Er Tribal Area, Haka:</u>
   The Japs have repeatedly attempted to seduce this Chief from his loyalty to the British Rule. The Chief, however, immediately brought these attempts to the notice of the Assistant Superintendent. He was appointed Chief in 1931 and has administered his Area with conspicuous ability.

8. <u>Mang Poom, Headman of Voklak, Siyin Tribal Area, Tiddim</u>
   In 1917 this Headman accompanied the Tiddim Labour Corps to France as a Havildar. On his return he served as a Havildar in the Auxiliaries (Levies) in the Kuki Rebellion 1917/1918. He was awarded a Silver mounted *Dah* and Certificate. In 1925 he was appointed Headman of Voklak and has efficiently filled that post which he still holds. In May 1942 he was appointed Platoon Commander in the Siyin Levies. His loyalty and devotion to duty has been conspicuous.

9. I have already brought to notice the loyal behaviour of the Chins as a whole. Besides the few names mentioned here there are many others who have rendered equally loyal and devoted service but at this stage a list of all their names is not called for. A roll of honour might possibly be prepared at a later date.

I have the honour to be,

Sir,

Your most obedient servant,

Deputy Commissioner, Chins Hills District [4]

Norman Kelly was at last on his way to Naini Tal to see his wife and family.

Naini Tal

In December 1942 we had left Woodstock in Mussoorie at the end of the academic year and had spent the long holiday from December to March, known as the 'break', with the Haskins family in Benares. Now we were in Naini Tal and at a new school. The Hallett War School in Naini (Tal means lake) was situated on the rim of a bowl of mountains 900 feet above the lake amid rhododendron and pine (see photograph no. 31). It was named after Lady Hallett, wife of the governor of the United Provinces of India. It was opened in 1941 mainly for children who could not get back to England because of the war. The buildings had previously been used by Philander Smith College, who had moved out after being told that the hillside might slip into the lake! There had been a dramatic and disastrous landslide from Cheena Peak, a mountain of 8,568 feet, in 1880:

> The rain commenced to fall steadily and without cessation from Thursday 16th September, 1880 until Sunday, the 19th. During Friday and Saturday, 33 inches of rain fell, of which 20 to 25 inches had fallen in the 40 hours preceding Saturday evening…This was followed by an earthquake – a common occurrence in those hills…A rumbling noise, similar to that occasioned by the falling of large masses of earth was heard by many in the station…A large portion of the hill behind the hotel from the Upper Mall, disunited and descended with enormous velocity and violence and completely buried the hotel…A portion of the public rooms was hurled into the lake.[5]

The dead and missing numbered 151.

Talli Tal was at the south end of the lake where we had arrived, by bus, from Kathgodam, the railhead. At the north-west end were 'The Flats', where the landslide had run into the lake. It was now an extensive piece of level ground, where polo had once been played. Prior to the landslide there had been a temple, in the place where the Boat House Club stood in 1942. The bandstand and Capitol cinema were also on 'The Flats', on the lake shore. Naini Tal was a magical setting for a school. From Snow View on Cheena Hill there was the magnificent spectacle of the Himalayas, touched rose-pink by the setting sun, with Nanda Devi – over 25,600 feet– the fifth highest peak in the world.

'Naini Tal'

> From old Kathgodam on the O and T line,
> You'll motor through forests of oak and of pine.
> The shiny tarred road with a twist and a turn,
> First skirting a valley, then crossing a burn.

Away from the plains with the heat and the flies.
Seeking the azure blue Naini Tal skies,
Where air is so fresh, full of health giving joy,
No fear of mosquitoes up there to annoy!

To watch the prim yachts sailing up and then down,
On the clear sapphire lake amid dear Naini town.
See hotels and shanties aglow in the night,
All mirrored on water. A beautiful sight!

Stately old Cheena towers high, Oh so high!
Mid six vassal hills rising up to the sky,
Rugged but verdant. A chilly wind blows
From those snow-capped pavilions, the Gharwali snows.

Oh Naini Tal! Naini Tal! Queen of them all
With coolies and bearers to beck and to call.
No need to work but, just live at your ease,
Order a *dandy* – "Oh carry me please?"

But when you go back to that sweltering plain,
And fix your mosquito net up once again.
You'll not forget Naini, her lake and the Mall,
Or the blue skies and green hills of old Naini Tal.

> Attributed to Sheenagh Urquhart and a master
> at St Joseph's College, Naini Tal

When my father was in Naini he stayed at Brookhill House, a guest house run by Topsy Bailey, at the Malli Tal (Flats) end of the lake. The Malli Tal bazaar was linked to Talli Tal by the Mall Road, which ran beside the lake. It was an odd feeling meeting my father again in May 1943, after nearly a year. The separation had fractured our relationship; at first he seemed a stranger. Because it was term-time we did not see that much of each other except at weekends, and going back to school on a Sunday evening was a painful separation after the warmth and gaiety of the weekend. There were other parents and their children at Brookhill House and servicemen on leave. My father did not want to talk about the war, but instead he tried to explain the game of rugby football, which is incredibly difficult to do if the listener has never seen it played; soccer and hockey are so much more logical. He gave me a balsa-wood kit to make up a Flying Fortress and a Spitfire, and helped me with the difficult parts. The smell of balsa-wood cement will be forever linked for me with Naini in 1943.

The Hallett War School was tough. The Reverend Robert Llewelyn, known to the boys and girls as 'Chief', was a young headmaster in his early thirties. Tall, with dark centrally parted hair, he wore a black gown and a white clerical collar. He was a compassionate, committed Christian but at the same time he was no stranger to caning, a common punishment in that era. A visit to the headmaster's study invariably had one ending: 'Bend over that chair. I am going to give you four of the best.' It certainly hurt! We would compare our weals across the backside in the dormitory afterwards. He wrote in one of my reports: 'This boy has a guilty conscience. I only asked to see him in my study and he bent over!' But there was another side to this. Patrick Gibson was an older boy who recounted:

> On one occasion Paul was caught twiddling his toes at the end of the bed after lights were out at nine o'clock and was caned, but not before he was held down by two prefects. As was the custom with the Rev. Llewelyn, he held out his hand to shake after the caning, but Paul, who was an excellent pugilist, simply smacked it away and challenged him to a boxing match. The Rev. Llewelyn surprisingly accepted. So a few days later they met in the ring. The match lasted less than two rounds with the Rev. Llewelyn receiving a bloody nose and a very swollen eye; he had thrown in the towel to cheers from all the boys.[6]

I enjoyed the Hallett much more than Woodstock. The teachers were kindly and I don't remember any bullying; we had a lot of fun and there were huge merits in a co-ed school. Looking back now, most pupils thought it was an excellent school. Maeve takes up the story now. She was good at hockey, and remembers:

> the dreaded Mrs Armstrong, a good-looking but fearsome Irish international. She imposed her will with a gym shoe on the girls' bare bottoms! Terrified though we were of her, she totally disarmed me once by remarking: 'You'll never be pretty – but you may be attractive.' When I blushed and fumbled, she snapped, 'For heaven's sake don't be so wet – learn to accept a compliment.' I still have difficulty with compliments, but that was the training for girls in those days. Being meek and gentle was the female conditioning in the pre-war era of childhood. And besides, Mother had brought me up by a book fashionable in the 1930s. 'Feed the child every four hours', the author advocated, 'No picking up in between, no matter how much it cries', 'No cuddles or getting into the parents' bed, certainly not!'
>
> But along with some emotional confusion came an adult ability to endure. I've certainly had cause in life since to thank our parents for such an upbringing. Corporal punishment from them was completely absent. They were, in fact, naturally generous, warm-hearted, fiery but loving Irish people. As role models they were magnificent and, as always, most appreciated when they were dead and gone. An Oriental childhood was no passport to an easy life – though we had servants – and we also had the benefit of learning Burmese from our gentle *ayah* along with English. Our parents, I feel, gave us a wonderful start in life.

My father must have found Naini a welcome relief after the strain and overwork in Tiddim. There were the long, arduous marches down to Stockade No. 3, never knowing when the Japanese might make their next incursion into the hills as well as attacks of malaria, worries about getting enough food for the Chins to keep the Levies in the field and the strain of command. In Naini he was safe and with my mother again. Their relationship was critical to him and his letters eloquently describe how much she meant to him, but he was also only too aware of the stress that their separation put on her. She was now a matron and also teaching at the Hallett War School (in 1944 she was to become my form mistress), and had needed to take some major decisions about our education; in addition, her own health was far from good. Now he could relax, play some tennis and bridge, go to the cinema at the Capitol or Roxy, or go dancing at the Boat House Club. Topsy Bailey, who ran Brookhill House, also loved a party. There were many servicemen on leave in Naini on 'R & R' (rest and recreation), away from the fighting, although the overall number of troops in Burma was tiny. The RAF and US Air Force were doing a magnificent job flying in supplies for them.

During April my father visited Simla where the exiled government of Burma had its headquarters. It was in regular communication with the Secretary of State for Burma in the Burma Office, London. Mr Hughes in Simla wrote regular fortnightly letters to Sir John Walton KCIE, CBE, MC, the Assistant Undersecretary in London. In one of these, dated 26 March 1943, paragraph (e), he stated: 'Kelly has now arrived in India on recess. He has been in the Chin Hills for several years and put up a very fine show during the events of the past year. He badly needs a rest.' On 16 April 1943 Mr Hughes reported further: 'Kelly has recently been in Simla and is in good heart. He returns to Falam at the end of this month as Additional Deputy Commissioner, relieving George of the I.C.S. [Indian Civil Service]'

In order to integrate the military and civilian administration of the frontier areas of Burma still in British hands, the Civil Affairs Service had been set up on 1 April 1943. The Commander-in-Chief India now had a Chief Civil Affairs Officer (CCAO), Burma, with the rank of Major-General; C. F. B. Pearce, ICS, formerly Commissioner of the Shan States, was appointed to this post. He became an officer on the staff of the Commander-in-Chief India and the service of the Civil Affairs Officers (CAOs) under him became a military service. Members of the Burma Frontier Service still in Burma were given military rank. Ralph Wilkie had responsibility for the Chin Hills and L. B. Naylor, who was still DC in Falam, reported directly to him. My father was to return to the Chin Hills with the rank of Major.

While my father was on leave in India our house in Tiddim was burnt down and we lost everything in it. By 27 April my father knew he would have to leave his family once again and return to the uncertainty of war. We did not know if we would ever see him again.

Grand Hotel
Calcutta
2nd May 1943

Darling Mummiekins,

I do hope the wire I sent you en route has proved some bit of a comfort to you, dearest, for if you are feeling the same way about it as I am, this new separation must be hitting you equally hard. I think, however, that you were frightfully brave seeing me off at the Talli Tal bus, sweetheart, and, after all, we must be thankful for the wonderful weeks we have had together and for the fact that you have the children on hand to be some comfort to you.

We made the journey OK but the heat down here is terrific and it is likely to be two or three more days before I shall leave. The Haskins were unable to meet me at Benares, but I enclose the letter she sent to meet me at the train.

On arrival here – train 3 hours late – I got my reservation at the hotel but am having to share the room with two other officers so that there is very little privacy. It was too late on Friday evening to do more than report arrival to the military authorities – the S.S.O.[Senior Service Officer] & A.P.M. [Army Paymaster] (I'm very much in the Army now!!)

On Saturday I reported to Ewing who is now a Brigadier and he is fixing me up for a new military identity card for which I have had to have new photos taken. It will be 2 or 3 days before this is issued by Army H.Q. and he has told me not to leave until I get it.

I have also been to Sharpe [the Supply Officer] but as Saturday was a half-holiday he couldn't do anything for me until Monday. I shall write again then, love, to let you know what he can provide in the way of bed linen, and at what prices. He wants me to take in 100 cases of stores for sale to civil officers at cost prices – things like cheese, flour, sauces, fish, fruit, jams, etc., to supplement the rations. I couldn't manage to get a typewriter out of him as he says they have already been supplied to the Falam office.

On Saturday morning the first people I ran into were Doris and Bob Cook. Bob has something wrong with his arm and is having electrical treatment for it – arthritis or something. He is also having all his teeth out!

No other exciting news at the moment, love, but I shall write again on Monday evening by which time I should know more of my movements. Sandy had written to me c/o Sharpe giving details of the fire. He also has sent me the official notification posting me as A.D.C. [Additional Deputy Commissioner] at Falam.

Look after yourself well, dear, and let me know how you get on at Suffolk Hall. I am thinking of you, darling, having the kiddies with you today.

All my fondest love, as ever sweetheart,
Yours alone,

Daddy

Harold Braund wrote an account of the fire in our Tiddim home in his book *Distinctly I Remember*, which gives a vivid – though slightly inaccurate – description of what happened while we were away in India:

> During my absence from Tiddim I had had myself built a stilted hut under a clump of pines at the extremity of Norman's extensive garden. Though I continued to mess with Norman and Philip (Barton), I had grown wary of living in recognisable targets, and in any case wanted the peace and quiet necessary to the enjoyment of a portable gramophone and records I had just had sent through to me from India. Perhaps instinct played a part also, because I woke one night to the roar of flames and, running down my steps saw Norman's bungalow ablaze and Philip, as he leapt from his bedroom window at the precise moment, demonstrating convincingly that it was his habit to sleep in the nude! In very truth he got away with nothing! Norman had got clear on the other side of the house and within minutes the fire had got such a hold that there was nothing we could do but watch the blaze against a background of detonations from the arsenal of ammunition and explosives that Norman harboured in his bedroom.[7]

In fact, Harold Braund was wrong about my father being there – he was still in India at the time.

Camp
Manipur River
16th May 1943

My own darling Mummiekins,

Here is half the month gone and I haven't even reached Tiddim yet. I can't give you all the details of the long journey and the interminable delays en route, love, but you can judge for yourself. I didn't get time to write again from Calcutta, as after my conference with Sharpe on the Sunday I was hustled off on Monday by goods train in charge of 124 cases of govt. stores (all amenity commodities to supplement the rations on payment). There have been so many losses on the railway that I had blithely undertaken to look after this consignment personally. I little dreamt what I was letting myself in for!! You can imagine what the heat was like stewed up in a guards' van, with long and seemingly unnecessary halts on the line. It took me eight days to reach Rail Head [Dimapur] and I would never do it again for a fortune. Even then, with the closest personal supervision I have managed to lose one case, but every one seems to think this is an excellent result. I was again delayed at Rail Head which you know is a dreadfully hot place.

Macdonald [Burma Frontier Service] has been replaced there as our supply officer by a fellow called Edwards (Frosts) [Frosts was the name of a firm in Burma] who looked after me well and was very helpful. All transport, however, is controlled and I had to wait my turn to get lorries. Fortunately I met another fellow there who was travelling my way so he took me on the next stage in his journey – the kit, stores and boys following in the lorries. I do not know what I would have done without Nawk Ngin [one of Norman's most valued servants] and Tun Khai [another servant]. En route I called in at Kohima to see Irvine (now a full Col.) and we had a great chat. He is running a fine show there but suffers as badly as ever from halitosis!! Once more I missed seeing old Tarmac [Dr MacAdam]. At Imphal – Willie and Rossington as off-hand as ever – I was again pushed into the barn known as Burma House, where I collected the camp kit I have left there. Steve Sutherland helped over my transport, but saddled me with a lot more govt. stuff – bicycles, etc. From there I had to travel in a lorry without a windscreen and I eventually reached a point 20 miles from here covered from head to foot with thick red dust [he had travelled down the Tiddim Road from Imphal].

There I was again held up until I could get sufficient transport to proceed to the river [where the road crossed the Manipur]. Even so I have had to leave a lot of the govt. stuff behind to follow on. I shall be livid if it goes astray now after all the trouble I have taken with it.

Noel Stevenson [the new DC] was here when I arrived and I have been with him four days now with no time to call my own.

The place is a tremendous hive of activity on a large scale and we are working from 5 a.m. to 8 and 9 p.m. daily checking the rice and stuff which is now being poured in for the civil population. Naturally I can't say much about it all in a letter, dear. Stevenson has run into Imphal on some business so I am holding the fort here. Leitch and Franklin are both down here, but with so many bigwigs about one or other of the DCs has to be here to make decisions re. priorities, etc. However, now that my precious leave is at an end, love, I am glad to be back to work and am as happy as a sand-boy but for memories of our great days – and nights – at Naini. I have not had any letter from you yet, darling, and am anxious to know how things are with you. I asked Rossington to send you the bulk of Rs 600 by telegraphic money order.

Stevenson talks of taking a short leave before the end of the rains, and I am not going to be backward in demanding another after six months or so. I can see the pressure of work is going to be increasingly great and I feel we will require frequent and regular relief from the strain. [Philip] Barton and [Robbie] Sayer are the next two for recess, then [Gilbert] Turnbull and [John] Franklin, followed by [Toby] Leitch.[8] If Stephenson returns today I hope to get up to Tiddim tomorrow and will wait for him there a day or two before going on together to Falam. I have had a great welcome here already from the local people and Pum Za Mang and the Saizang chief came down specially to see me when the news got round that I had arrived here. Their simple faith is all rather touching and appears greatly to have impressed Stevenson and the rest. I think Leitch will in time be popular, but I am not so sure of Franklin's manner. Freda has at last got safely home with the twins. There is some suspicion of sabotage about the burning of our house, but not sufficient proof. The suspect is an old PWD contractor whom you will remember, dear, and whom Franklin had sacked. I find it hard, however, to believe that this can be true and I doubt if we shall ever really get to the bottom of the matter.

The Chiefs, Thaing Chin Maung, Awn Ngin, etc., all made anxious enquiry as to how you and the kiddies are. John [Franklin] tells me Patch has had another litter of pups – well-bred terriers this time apparently. I'm sure the kiddies will be interested.

The heat and the flies in the camp are dreadful and it is almost unbearable under canvas, more particularly as I have contracted one of my filthy nasal colds. I shall be glad indeed to get up to Tiddim. Isn't it amusing, darling, to think that I can now run up there through Tonzang [on the Tiddim Road] in two hours!

No other news at the moment, love. Isn't the completion of the Tunisian campaign grand news? Will be writing again from Tiddim where this will be posted.

All my love and kisses, sweetheart mio, as ever. Look after yourself well, love, and keep smiling. We'll soon get our correspondence straightened out when I reach Falam and things won't be so bad when we are hearing from each other regularly. Have you packed away the nifty nighties against my next arrival, lovekins?

I suppose Sam Gardiner will have arrived by now. Don't forget to give me all the lurid details of the boyfriends you pick up for yourself!! I'm as jealous as hell, but there's safety in numbers you know!!

Yours alone, darling,

Daddy

Camp
Tiddim
21st May 1943

My darling,

At long last I have got as far as here, and I must say I have had a terrific welcome back. Half the headmen in the area seem to have heard I was on my way and had assembled to meet me. Office staff, school staffs, Government Commissioned Officers, etc., all seemed to appear from nowhere when I drove up, and the spontaneity of their welcome was most heartening and made me feel that I am more popular than I had really thought. I only wish, sweetheart, that you had been with me to share the honours, for one and all of them are asking about you and the kiddies.

It is grand to be back among them, but you would weep, love, to see the bare ruins of the house in which we have spent such happy times as a family. I have heard at first hand from Barton and Braund the full details, and the whole thing is still entirely inexplicable.

It certainly appears, however, that the ventilator arches below the floors had helped to fan the flames which spread rapidly over the dry ceilings and rafters which collapsed quickly and prevented any entry to the rooms. Philip Barton shed his Shan pants in leaping through the bedroom window on the north side, and had to run round to call the servants in his bare pelt!! I had forgotten that I had left a box of incendiary flares in our bedroom ready for the destruction of office papers if such a course became necessary owing to enemy action, and these of course would add greatly to the conflagration. Everyone is most sympathetic, but I'm afraid that doesn't carry one very far. However, it is little good crying over spilt milk, dear. Looking over the ruins it has struck me that perhaps I can pin the blame on the P.W.D. for faulty construction, for you may remember that there was no brick or cement hearth, and that the floorboards ran right up to the grate and had to be protected by a sheet of zinc.

I drove myself up, yesterday afternoon, and I must say that the road is excellent. It is remarkable that the rains have not broken yet but whereas this favours continued motor transport for the carriage of food, it is disastrous for the villagers whose crops are suffering badly.

I handed over the eye ointment to Mrs. Ohn Pe who was most grateful for your thoughtfulness, darling. Dr. Ramji Das was one of the first to beard me in the Rest House – moaning as usual over having to share a house and about the deficiency of food values in his rations. I am afraid he is not the type to remain here in the present circumstances and I shall not hesitate to get rid of him. Everyone seems delighted at my promotion to Falam. Barton and Braund were most genuine in their welcome and insist on my mealing with them so long as I am here. This is likely to be two or three days yet as Stevenson is remaining at the river until all motor transport is brought to a stop by the rains, when we will go on together to Falam. I phoned Frank George last evening, and he seems to be in no hurry to get to India. Barton and Braund are both going on leave shortly, the former before the end of this month. We have agreed that Leitch should then come into Tiddim with Franklin to assist him. Franklin and Turnbull will be the next pair on turn for recess, and Stephenson himself will go out for a short spell towards the end of the rains. It is quite likely that in due course he will move elsewhere and that I shall then remain in charge.

Naylor [the retiring Deputy Commissioner] went out by Aijal, but I shall give you more information of him in another letter. Barton is going out on leave tomorrow so I shall send a letter with him by hand as he is spending his recess at Naini. I have told him to get in touch with you.

Your note dated April 30th was delivered to me, dearest, when I arrived here yesterday. It had missed me at Imphal. I also got two consignments of bacon – both despatched in March by Keventers – in good condition. Other earlier ones had turned up irregularly and had been eaten by the other chaps.

It was marvellous to have your letter, love, though it was so short. Glad you got my wire from Lucknow – I thought it might help you just a little, sweetheart. Of course I knew what a fight you were putting up when we parted, darling. I was putting the same restraint on myself and dared not let myself go, and I too, felt that to outsiders it might appear that we did not seem to care. However, we know each other, dearest, and that is everything. I am sure you must have been very depressed when you wrote your note, dear, but I trust you have cheered up since.

I am still feeling pretty heavy and dull with this head cold, but it will have run its course in a few days. I took some M & B [M & B 693, the first sulphonamide antibiotic to be available in the Chin Hills] last night and that seems to have cleared the sinuses somewhat. Otherwise I am in grand form.

I have been interrupted in the finishing of this letter by a deputation of the local ladies of your old war-knitting circle who came round with Pau Za Kam [the Tiddim headman] to express their sorrow that you have not returned with me, love, and to ask that I should let you know how much they look forward to your ultimate return to the Hills. Don't you think this was rather sweet of them, darling? It would be nice I think if you could write to Mrs. Ohn Pe telling her that I have conveyed their message to you and thanking them.

Nothing more at the moment, sweetheart. With all my fondest love as ever,

Your vagabond lover,

Daddy

L. B. Naylor, who was fifty-six and could have retired, decided to accept the post as Brigadier Ralph Wilkie's assistant in Imphal. He had local knowledge of the Chin Hills, which Wilkie did not have. Noel Stevenson was appointed as the new Deputy Commissioner in Falam. He was a good choice, for he had served in the Chin Hills before the war and, of equal importance, had been with the Kachin Levies in North Burma.

The Tiddim Road

While Norman Kelly had been on leave, the road from Imphal to Tiddim had made good progress. There had been a mule track to Milestone 109; by February 1943 the Sappers, with their angledozers, had cut a road south up the valleys of the Khuga and Tuivai Rivers, then back over the Watershed Range, where it climbed 3,000 feet to Milestone 100 and then headed down the valley of the Kaphi Lui to Milestone 109 (see colour map no. 28). Here water was available and there was a flattish area. They were now faced with an impasse; large quantities of explosives were needed to blast away the steep rocky slopes of the Kaphi Lui gorge, and this had to be done by hand labour.[9]

It had always been planned that the 17th Indian Division should advance along this route when the road was made. Now the imaginative decision was taken that in 'Exercise Navvy' the 17th Indian Division should itself cut the first stage of the road for the vital 17 miles through the gorge to the Manipur River at Milestone 126.[10] Using 4,500 soldiers as 'navvies', carrying only personal arms and equipment to Milestone 128, the work began in mid-March. This tactic greatly increased the speed of construction. For the division it made a welcome break. The weather had improved, the countryside looked attractive, they were back in Burma with orchids growing on many trees and the wild magnolias were in full bloom. The troops were in good humour, and the infantry and gunner units, who were each allotted their own stretch, dug and blasted the road out of the mountainside. The Gurkha battalions, familiar with similar problems in their own country, and the 1st West Yorkshire Regiment, did particularly well.[11] The operation as a whole was not easy, however. The Tiddim Road to Milestone 100 was a 'mountain cut' with some horrifying gradients and a mud surface. To save time, every form of vehicle was impressed to carry the navvies in a shuttle service. To complicate the problem there came a sharp and long spell of early rain, turning the mud road into a skating rink. Only the best drivers could be used and they worked night and day. [12]

By the end of April 1943 jeeps were being ferried across the Manipur River on a pontoon raft. 'The Deputy Commissioner, Tiddim [Norman Kelly] had already completed the 40 miles of road between the river and Tiddim on a "jeep basis".'[13] The 17th Division then sent one battalion up to Tiddim to guard the parties improving the road east of the Manipur River. The battalion at Tiddim could now be maintained by jeep, but the work of widening the road and repairing it after the landslides caused by the coming monsoon would go on until the dramatic events of March 1944. The road was not only for military aid, but also to feed the population, especially during the periods when visibility for airdrops was non-existent. The rest of the division was moved to Shillong in Assam for the rains – for a rest, out of the forward area, and for reorganising, proper equipping and further intensive training.

Chapter 9

THE STORM BREAKS

In April and early May 1943 a party of Japanese had entered the Chin Hills near Dolluang, due east of Tiddim. The Chin Levies fell back, not wishing to be engaged in hand-to-hand fighting. They were not equipped with bayonets or *kukris* but were best in an ambush situation where muzzle-loading flintlocks were at less of a disadvantage. B Company of the 2/5th Royal Gurkha Rifles was sent to drive back the enemy; they found that the Japanese had already withdrawn to establish themselves at Dolluang. The HQ Battalion and D Company were at Tiddim, while A and C Companies were at No. 3 Stockade with Peter Bankes' piquets and Levies at No. 2 Stockade. In May 1943 Captain Anthony Gross, official war artist, and his party visited Tiddim, Fort White, Falam, No. 2 and No. 3 Stockades, and said, 'The Levies were conceived and organised by some remarkably adventurous Englishmen.'[1]

Norman Kelly found, on his return to Tiddim, that the 17th Indian Division was increasingly taking over operations from the Levies, who were now under the command of Lieutenant-Colonel Oatts. Unfortunately, his predecessor, Lieutenant-Colonel Frank Ford, known as 'The Assassin', had been posted at short notice to command the Kachin Levies. They were operating in the Fort Hertz/Sumprabum area of North Burma (see map no. 1 on p. 2). Lieutenant-Colonel Oatts was an indigo planter's son, later known as 'Titus', and had been an officer in the Highland Light Infantry but volunteered for service with the Burma Frontier Force in the Chin Hills in 1938. His first assignment in 1940 was in the Naga Hills where the local inhabitants were renowned for being wild, naked headhunters – an excellent education for the Chin Hills campaign.

Noel Stevenson was the replacement for Naylor as Deputy Commissioner in Falam. Also known by his initials, H. N. C., he would get very angry if anybody inadvertently spelt his name with a 'p'. 'I'm V for Victory', he would shout, 'not P for Phoney!' He had joined the Burma Frontier Service in 1926, a year before Norman Kelly. Before the war he had been Assistant Superintendent in Falam from 1934 to 1936. There he had carried out anthropological research and written about many aspects of Chin culture.[2] He knew and understood the Chins. He

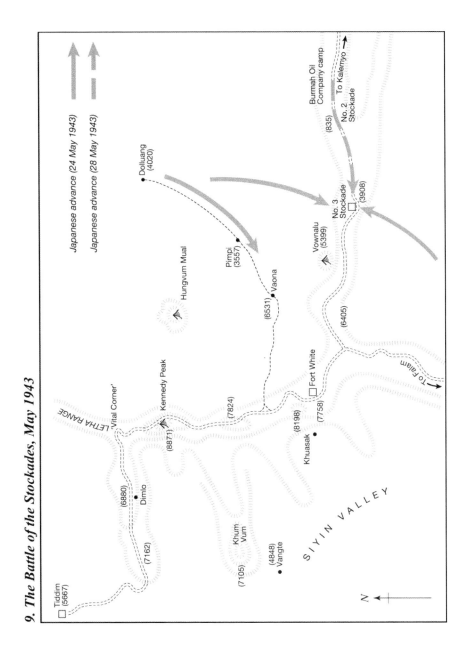

9. *The Battle of the Stockades, May 1943*

had said in his book, *The Hill Peoples of Burma*, 'When God created the world, he forgot to put the other finishing touches to the Chin Hills.'

Stevenson had operated with the Karen Levies and Captain Seagrim in the Shan States and Salween area in January 1942, and had arrived as an Army captain in Assam in August 1942. He then made his way to Fort Hertz in the far north of Burma because this was not occupied by the Japanese. From there he flew out to see General Wavell in India but on the return flight the plane crashed and he was injured. After treatment in hospital he reached Falam on 23 February 1943 where Brigadier Jack Haswell and Lieutenant-Colonel 'Titus' Oatts, who were both professional soldiers, were running the Levies. They were sometimes called the Western Chin Levies to distinguish them from the Karen Levies on the eastern side of Burma. Stevenson did not take over from Naylor until April 1943; this was to enable Naylor to brief him thoroughly with the up-to-date situation in the Chin Hills. One of his first reports (8 April) to Major-General C. F. B. Pearce, CBE, Chief Civil Affairs Officer (Burma), GHQ New Delhi, stated:

> The lack of serious co-operation with the Assam people is troubling us a great deal. Our hillmen do not much grudge us their labour, but they do object to being the 'slaves' of Government. They [the Lushais] are not doing one-tenth of what the Chins are doing. Never was so little done by so many for so few...
>
> The District is remarkably quiet and orderly for a place on the fringes of the Japanese-occupied territory, and I think Naylor had done a very good job indeed and so have the Chins. The trouble here has been that there has been nobody at either 4 Corps, Eastern Army or G.H.Q. who understands the local position and who, when speed is everything, can advise on what should be done.[3]

It was a very positive step that L. B. Naylor was now to be moved to Imphal in order to assist Wilkie at 4 Corps HQ.

The Battle of the Stockades

On 23 May 1943 the Japanese attacked the piquets at No. 2 Stockade and the following night attacked No. 3 Stockade. A long ridge ran down from Fort White to No. 3, a distance of 9 miles (see colour map no. 27). The ridge, which started at Kennedy Peak, was covered on its upper half by wet jungle; then it changed to stunted trees with very little undergrowth. The whole length of the spur had precipitous slopes on the north and south sides, and it was only possible to manoeuvre troops on the crest of the spur itself. Basha Hill was knife-edged, just west of No. 3, and dominated it to the extent that it had to be taken before any advance could be made on the stockades from the west.

On 23 May Norman Kelly was in Tiddim when No. 3 Stockade was attacked. No. 3 Stockade was a large bamboo camp in the jungle, above No. 2, with a perimeter of sharpened bamboo stakes, foxholes and booby traps around it. The 2/5th Royal Gurkha Rifles fought bravely but their main position was overrun by the enemy's greater strength, and they had to fall back on the Fort White–Kennedy Peak area. From 24 to 29 May Norman was at Fort White. The six-day battle for Basha Hill had begun. During that time of hand-to-hand fighting it was estimated that the Japanese suffered heavy casualties. The Japanese had attacked with over 1,000 men just before dawn in an attempt to reach Tiddim. The Gurkhas had 71 casualties but only 7 were killed.

In the first surge the enemy ran into nests of booby traps set by the Chins. Once clear of these they came on in waves. A Gurkha mortar team fired on them until the crew was killed; a Gurkha havildar, in charge of the post, fired his revolver eighteen times at short range and is believed to have killed ten Japanese by this means alone. Early in the clash, the Japanese battalion commander, Major Horikawa, who was leading the attack, was killed with several other officers.

Heavy artillery fire from the Kalemyo Valley below sent shells crashing into the jungle-covered hills and the Siyin Chin village. The Japanese were using two-pounder infantry guns, which they had dragged up the jungle trails, and heavy mortars. After giving the stockade a severe strafing, they attacked in large numbers through the jungle. They were met by machine-gun and rifle fire from the Gurkhas, taking a heavy toll as the successive hordes were mown down. The Gurkhas then withdrew to prevent being cut off. When the order to retreat was received, a major and a Parsi doctor manhandled two mortars and all the equipment through 9 miles of dense, hilly jungle until they thought they were safe. They then hid them in the jungle and rejoined their unit, which had fallen back towards Kennedy Peak.

After a day's lull the troops, who had been reinforced by two companies of 1/4th Gurkhas for the main battles, were ordered to counter-attack Basha Hill, which overlooked No. 3 Stockade. Two attacks by Gurkhas were made in twenty-four hours. The first was only partially successful, owing to heavy Japanese machine-gun and mortar fire, as well as from snipers in trees. Then the second assault went in. The Gurkhas were magnificently led by a British officer, the son of a general, and stormed Basha Hill, using 'blitz' tactics – firing bren guns, Tommy guns and rifles from the hip as they raced forward.

It was during the assault on Basha East Hill, the key to the Japanese position, that a Gurkha platoon commander, Gaje Ghale, won his Victoria Cross for conspicuous gallantry on 27 May 1943. His citation read:

> Havildar Gaje Ghale had never been under fire before and the platoon consisted of young soldiers.
>
> The approach for this platoon to their objective was along a narrow knife-edge with precipitous sides and bare of jungle, whereas the enemy positions were well concealed. In places, the

approach was no more than five yards wide and was covered by a dozen machine-guns besides being subjected to artillery and mortar fire from the reverse slope of the hill.

While preparing for the attack the platoon came under heavy mortar fire but Havildar Gaje Ghale rallied them and led them forward.

Approaching to close range of the well-entrenched enemy, the platoon came under withering fire and this N.C.O. was wounded in the arm, chest and leg by an enemy hand grenade.

Without pausing to attend to his serious wounds and with no heed to the intensive fire from all sides, Havildar Gaje Ghale closed his men and led them to close grips with the enemy when a bitter hand to hand struggle ensued. He dominated the fight by his outstanding example of dauntless courage and superb leadership. Hurling hand grenades, covered in blood from his own neglected wounds, he led assault after assault encouraging his platoon by shouting the Gurkha's battle cry ['*Ayo-Gurkhali*'– the Gurkhas are upon you].

Spurred on by the irresistible will of their leader to win, the platoon stormed and carried the hill by a magnificent effort and inflicted very heavy casualties on the Japanese.'[4]

On 27 May 1943 Norman Kelly's field diary simply recorded: 'Action at No. 3'.

For days after the battle, scores of bullock carts and hundreds of coolies were requisitioned by the Japanese to carry their wounded back to hospitals in the Burma plains. A prisoner, who escaped from the enemy, described the great ceremony that the Japanese held for their dead battalion commander. Tied to a tree, this prisoner watched the Japanese bringing Horikawa's body into the centre of their camp and lay it down. All round the body the Japanese placed sharpened bamboo spikes and blazing pine torches. The soldiers, detachment by detachment, filed past where the body lay in a jungle clearing. Each man bowed three times towards the body. After this the Japanese soldiers carried the body, by night, down steep jungle tracks back to their main base in the plains for burial. There they ordered seven days of mourning for the dead major with special military parades in his honour. His body was cremated and the ashes sent home to his relatives in Japan. The Japanese now call Basha East Hill by the name of Mount Horikawa (see colour map no. 27).[5]

Jack Oats and the Defence of the Stockades

In his book *Distinctly I Remember* Harold Braund wrote about the defence of No. 2 Stockade and the part Jack Oats of the Chin Hills Battalion played in it:

Jack Oats had won an immediate M.C. for a spirited repulse of a Jap attack at No. 2 Stockade just before the last Allied forces disappeared through the passes to India [in 1942]. We probably owe it to this 'bloody nose' that the Japs thereafter seemed to overrate the strength of the opposition we could offer in the Hills.[6]

Jack Oats himself vividly described his cooperation with the Levy officer Peter Bankes, and their mutual understanding. Oats also recounted the part played by the 17th Indian Division together with the role of Lieutenant-Colonel 'Titus' Oatts, Peter's commanding officer. (Rather confusingly, Jack Oats and 'Titus' Oatts have the same surname, although spelt differently.)

About April 18th 1943
Peter still at No. 3 with the 2/5 Royal Gurkha Rifles. Japs advanced towards Dalwan north of Peter [see map no. 8 on p. 96]. I was, at that time, on my way back to No. 3 with troops to take over again, as the 17th Division and 2/5 RGR were moving out for the monsoon in Shillong. This push altered things and 2/5 stayed. I came under the command of 2/5, and was four weeks in reserve for No. 3 and other areas at Fort White. Soon after arrival I took a patrol via No. 3 to Dalwan and had lunch with Peter at No. 3. He wasn't liking it very much, as under 2/5 his old freedom and responsibility were gone.

Later a 4 Corps Intelligence colonel arrived by jeep at Fort White from Tiddim. He wanted to go to No. 3 so I went with him. The road was all right until about a mile above No. 3 where it had been destroyed in May 1942 – by Peter and Kelly. He was there now with one Gurkha officer and dozens of Chins and Gurkhas all stripped to the waist repairing the home-made landslide to take through traffic again. This was really quite historic, for it was one of the first through links forged between India and the Burma plains. It was very hot and dry although not as bad as the Plains, but at three o'clock in the hot weather even at 3,000 feet it was pretty warm.

There was then a big discussion between Peter and Major [Philip] Townsend (2nd in command, 2/5 RGR) versus Colonel Holbrook, the Corps bloke. Corps bloke said that there were not more than 50 Japs in the whole Myittha Valley. Peter's information said five to eight thousand. Holbrook laughed, said his sources must be right and went off back to Imphal. What happened in the next few days showed that Peter was right.

May 15th
48th Brigade of the 17th Division were definitely to stay for the rains so I was again relieved and moved south to my own battalion. I reached Falam on May 17th and on May 22nd the big attack on No. 3 started and No. 3 fell to the Japs on 24th May. I was pushing

along the Falam/Fort White road to block it, when Fort White fell. Although we did not then realise it, this was the first move in the Jap attack on India via Imphal and Kohima.

Halfway to Fort White I got a message to come under command of the 48th Brigade again (with my Company and mortar) and move to Ngalzang on the ridge just south of No. 3. I got my troops on the move as we had some 30 miles to do and myself galloped to Fort White and saw the Brigadier. He wanted me to guard his southern flank and if possible make a diversion there when ordered. Brigade had failed in a counter-attack that day and there was a general air of despondency. At the same time Colonel Oatts – Peter's wretched new C.O. – told me that Peter might be at Ngalzang. If so, he was to operate under my command. This did not mean much for we always cooperated without either commanding. I reached Ngalzang just before dusk. All down the ridge we were in full view of the battle on No. 3/Fort White Road and could see their guns and bursts and our mortars – the whole layout about 3,000 yards away – but over a deep ravine.

Down at Ngalzang I met my men and arranged camp and pickets and food, and then found Peter below the village in a tiny camp with a handful of men watching the road from No. 3 to Ngalzang. Night passed quietly as Japs had taken a bigger knock than we then knew and had suffered heavy casualties the day before. Next day was unpleasantly quiet. We got into defensive positions but were ready to go forward when Brigade started attacking on the main ridge. However, they didn't. I was afraid that Brigade, who were much weakened, would pull out without letting us know and we didn't trust Lt. Col. Oatts to let us know.

During this day Peter gave me some account of the final battle at No. 3. Peter with his Levies was in position at the base of Signal Ridge near No. 2 stockade. It was a good position at the junction of two creeks. After a lot of shelling apparently Major Townsend decided to pull in his horns and only defend the top of Signal Ridge. Peter was then back at No. 3. in Townsend's H.Q. Signal Ridge and station was taken by storm with bayonet after being held nearly all night by a Gurkha platoon. Townsend sent Peter in to counter-attack and they attempted this, although Townsend had no right to use Levies and irregulars for such a tough job. They were beaten off and Japs used either tracer or explosive bullets.

Another Levy officer confirmed that these were not ordinary bullets. These, he said, 'besides the crack of their arrival, went off pop when they hit the trees. The effect was very uncanny and disturbed the Siyins.'[7] Jack Oats continued:

(I never heard Townsend's account but it seemed to me that his use of reserves, etc., in this battle was not good. He had two Gurkha companies but one of them never seemed to get into action at all.)

At sunset I left Peter with one of my platoons in dug positions and put myself above with the other two for Peter to fall back on. Early in the morning I went into Fort White and my fears were justified for Brigade were pulling out that day at noon and no word had been sent to us. I got my orders, including Peter's. I heard from Brigade that they were reduced to three hundred fighting soldiers. I stayed to put up some sort of defence of Fort White, while Brigade dug in on Kennedy Peak – eight miles north and was then to withdraw south on my own unit. Meanwhile Peter was to send one section to make a diversion that evening below and to the south of No. 3 and then fall back to Bamboo Camp (twelve miles south of Fort White) and wait for me. I sent Peter a written message with definite orders that he was not himself to go with this section as I thought it a damn silly scheme and was not going to risk him on such a useless undertaking.

Two days later I staggered into Bamboo, to a hidden camp with a few men but found no signs of Peter. I found out that he had been there but Falam had ordered him to a position three miles further back. I was damned annoyed with such H.Q. interference and next day got my own Colonel's sanction and moved forward again to Bamboo. I slept like the dead that night and found Peter in the morning. He was busy digging in with my troops and not too happy, for they were Hindustani-speaking and were being a bit difficult. They didn't like the Burmese and objected, I think, to getting orders in Burmese. Also, they were always a bit touchy with a new British officer until they got to know him. I had had to learn Hindustani and then learnt Chin voluntarily, but Peter – dealing with different men – throughout refused to learn anything but Burmese. One thing was that he kept his Burmese a lot better than ours since ours deteriorated through overlaying other languages.

Next day my Colonel, Roddie Russell of the Chin Hills Battalion, came forward from his new H.Q. about eight miles from Bamboo and took Peter away. Peter then took twelve of our Battalion Gurkhas on a long commando raid to the road between Kalemyo and No. 2. I was a bit anxious for he had to cross a biggish mountain river – the Zi *Chaung* – and re-cross it afterwards. It was a creek that could rise six feet after an hour's rain. However, he got to the road but saw nothing in twelve hours except a couple of carts and let them go by to await a better target. He got back OK and inferred that Japs were only using this road for occasional escorted convoys to feed their forward troops and thus it was very difficult to ambush. You cannot wait in a concealed ambush for more than twelve or twenty-four hours in the rains before your men start coughing and spitting and making a noise.

Peter then went back to his own Levies for orders and was sent off to organise resistance in some villages further east but had little success as they were a mean lot. Meanwhile Colonel Oatts from the north had been sending me repeated foolish orders which I ignored as I came under my Battalion orders and not his. He was frantic to get Peter back to Tiddim, whereas Falam were using him from their end. He was eventually located and moved back to Ngalzang near No. 3. From here he was recalled to take over Braund's administrative job in Tiddim whilst Braund went on leave. On his way Ngalzang/Tiddim I went from Bamboo and saw him at Fort White road junction. Not too pleased by his move and still wearing Lieutenant's pips although now a major. I can't remember much about this meeting but I fancy we had a quick brew of tea at the roadside.[8]

Noel Stevenson, the Deputy Commissioner, had based himself at Tiddim from 24 May where he felt he could exert maximum influence on the 17th Indian Division.

Fort White in Grave Danger

Colonel Headley visited Stevenson at midnight to tell him that, following the loss of No. 3 Stockade, he had been ordered by Area to concentrate his forces for a counter-attack and that this concentration on his part involved the evacuation of Fort White. Stevenson told him that this would have a very serious effect on local morale, as the Chins regarded the Letha Range as their final bastion and that in the past they had rarely put up much of a show after the mountain chain had been taken. Headley added that he could do nothing aggressive without reinforcements in view of the enemy strength. On 26 May Brigadier Cameron, who was directing the battle, and Stevenson joined Norman Kelly at Fort White.

The Japanese threat continued and Norman Kelly was touring the Chin villages from Fort White, where he had been from 24 to 29 May. On the 29th, because of casualties and a very high sickness rate, Brigadier Cameron of the 17th Indian Division had decided to evacuate Fort White again. To keep the enemy guessing Norman visited Khuasak with the Siyins on 29 and 30 May. On 31 May he reoccupied Fort White with three sections of his Levies and moved some rations to greater safety at Tuklai. Noel Stevenson reported this action to Brigadier Ralph Wilkie:

The move back from Fort White had the expected bad effect but the people and the Levies rallied quickly under Kelly's inspiration and succeeded in removing about 100 bags of rations, left behind on the 29th through lack of coolies, after the first Jap patrol had been and gone back again.[9]

On 1 June, when 'all quiet', Norman Kelly sent a Levy company back to Fort White. On 2 June the Levy HQ was moved from Tuklai to Khuasak, and Lieutenant-Colonel Oatts left for Tiddim. Norman visited Fort White on the 3rd and found his Levies there with Robertson. On 4 June orders were received to move HQ to Dolluang. On the same day a telegram was sent from the Governor of Burma to the Secretary of State for Burma, Burma Office, London:

(B) CHIN HILLS. JAPANESE ADVANCING IN SOME STRENGTH TOWARDS TIDDIM. OBJECT SEEMS TO BE TO CUT SUPPLY ROUTE TO FALAM. CHIN LEVIES RESISTING HEROICALLY. YOU MAY DEEM OF SUFFICIENT IMPORTANCE TO REPORT TO WAR CABINET[10]

Following the six-day battle for the stockades, it seemed prudent to keep the enemy in the dark as to the whereabouts of the Levies. The defensive screen was centred on Dolluang, which was near a stream, the Sunnum Lui, running down to near No. 2. Stockade (see map no. 6 on p. 74). Another stream, the Kwe Lui, flowed in the same direction from Pimpi. There were no letters from Norman Kelly during this nervous period but his diary often indicated where he was. There were also technical problems: the wireless transmitter was out of order while he was at the HQ in Dolluang on 7 June but he met up with Braund and Mitchell on 9 June. He moved to Pimpi that day and remained there until 12 June, when there was a false alarm at 11 a.m. and the Levies fled. The Gurkha Rifles arrived shortly afterwards. There was a second alarm at Pimpi when a Japanese patrol with two officers came within a mile of the village at 8 a.m. the following day.

Langdon's Gurkhas then arrived. On 14 June the Gurkhas left, leaving behind the Levies at half-strength, but they had three British officers (Ted Wright, 'Stiffy' Johnstone – both Anglo-Burmans – and Frank O'Donel) to be followed by Harold Braund on the 15th. After discussions with them, Norman Kelly left for Dolluang on 16 June where he met the Deputy Commissioner, Noel Stevenson, and three Gurkha officers, Langdon, Gribble and Clarke. They were joined by Lieutenant-Colonel 'Titus' Oatts on the 17 June. It was decided to move out of the village into a jungle camp on 21 June, where they received news of the Japanese in Phaitu. Stevenson, in his letter of 8 June to Brigadier Wilkie in Jorhat, reported:

Kelly, Leitch and Franklin have all worked very hard and are still doing so. I am afraid I shall have to keep Frank George at Falam until such time as I can get back there. Kelly cannot yet take my place at the local military headquarters, Tiddim, because his influence is so badly needed in the exposed Siyin Valley. If only we could get some clear weather which would enable the RAF to get into action in a big way, I feel confident we can kick the Japanese out again pretty soon… The Japanese have treated all their subject people with the utmost brutality and I cannot imagine that any degree of inexpedience, short of impossibility, can justify our relinquishing our protective hold over these Hills.

Dysentery is appearing in many villages and we are taking active steps to keep it under control. So far we have nothing worse, thank God. Many of the coolies who worked with us at the Manipur River Bridge have been down with fever and there have been several deaths. It seems that we must continue to bring one calamity after another on the Chins in our efforts to help them. Could you possibly drop me a supply of Cinchona Febrifuge or Quinine to issue to these poor people.[11]

The military build-up, centred on Tiddim, was dependent upon the long lines of supply back to Imphal along the Tiddim Road. By June 1943 this was jeepable to the Manipur River, where sappers had constructed an improvised bridge with eight local wooden boats and a petrol-drum raft. The monsoon had begun, and with it the Logtak Lake, south of Imphal, began to fill (see map no. 3 on p. 28). It emptied into the Manipur River, which started rising dangerously. The current increased dramatically and the bridge was kept open to jeeps only with difficulty.

On the night of 10/11 June, which was pitch black, a further surge occurred, which broke four of the six cables holding the bridge. In spite of the darkness, Jemedar Dharam Singh of 70 Field Company, who was in charge, decided that the only way to save the boats was to dismantle the bridge. During this hazardous operation four sappers were washed downstream on a raft, but eventually got ashore. Two flying ferries were constructed, with the recovered boats, so that jeeps could continue to make the crossing. This earned Dharam Singh the gratitude of General Cowan, Commanding Officer of the 17th Indian Division.[12]

The flying ferries were made by initially passing the main cable across the river. The raft to carry the jeeps was attached to this by extension cables through a pulley, which allowed the raft to swing and be moved by the flow of water. By manipulating the extension cables the raft swung from one bank of the river to the other. The current of the Manipur was very swift – even in the summer, when the level was low, a straight swim across was impossible.

In support of the Battle of the Stockades, HQ of 17th Indian Division and 63 Brigade had been moved from Shillong to Milestone 109 on the Tiddim Road, and 63 Brigade was now sent to take over the defence of Fort White from 48 Brigade, which returned to Shillong at the beginning of July. A small HQ was left behind at Milestone 100 to manage the difficult line of communication to Tiddim – 80 miles of track kept open with only one small break throughout the monsoon rains. General Slim observed, 'The making of this road was hardly a more wonderful feat than keeping it open against the spates, subsidences and the great landslides of the monsoon.' He fully understood the terrain of the Chin Hills. 'The wild country is a chaos of jungle matted knife-edge ridges, running up to peaks of over eight thousand feet, split by precipitous valleys and pieced from the Indian side only by a fantastic mountain road from Imphal that the troops themselves had built.'[13]

At the end of the six-day battle the Japanese casualties were so large that they were unable to advance further. Instead of conquering the Chin Hills, as they had repeatedly threatened to do in their radio broadcasts, they had to bide their time. Meanwhile, the 17th Indian Division was being reinforced from India.

The 'flag marches', as they were called, which Norman Kelly and the other Levy officers were engaged in, were essential to keep up morale amongst the Chins. They were exhausting, and involved moving from village to village, living under canvas. They would climb along steep footpaths, only to reach the top of a ridge and have to plunge down to a stream miles below. The track was about wide enough to accommodate a mule with its pack. There were even steeper shortcuts along the route which cut off hairpin corners, and consisted of an uphill scramble, marked out by the feet of porters, who for generations had found it worthwhile to clamber up in this way.

During the construction of the new motor road from Imphal, military supplies were being brought in by coolies and, later, by army mules from India. There were two kinds of rations – BT (British Troops) and IT (Indian Troops). Besides these, there were ammunition and explosives, and various military stores such as clothing, equipment and other essentials for the front line. The Khasi coolies would carry their loads on their backs as far as the supply dump established at Nakzang at Milestone 126, below the village of Tuitum at the Manipur suspension bridge near Tonzang (see colour map no. 28). At the dump, repacking took place of the bags, tins and cardboard boxes prior to distribution. Along the way a percentage went missing due to pilfering. When the Tiddim Road conditions improved, mules replaced coolies, and eventually jeep convoys arrived. These could not use the suspension bridge, and later the flying ferries were replaced by a Bailey bridge. The Army had a Supply Corps to manage their provisions and organise the supply dump. The Levies had to make their own arrangements and provide security to prevent precious food and equipment from going missing from their storage area.

Norman Kelly was also the Levy Paymaster for the Tiddim Zone. His field diary records that he was given a voucher (no. 244) of Rs 2,000 on 1 May 1943 and a further sum of Rs 13,000 on 1 June. The total paid out to seven Levy personnel for May was Rs 7,507. These payments were made on 2 June, depending on rank and status. Meat and supplies had to be paid for out of Levy funds. Certain village headmen were rewarded for good deeds or information about the enemy. Everything had to be accounted for.

Laurie O'Hara did a masterful job as the Tiddim Levy Quartermaster, and was a great help to Norman. He had originally been assigned to the Chin Hills Battalion, but when he reached Tiddim from India, Norman expressed disappointment that he had not been given extra supplies of food and clothing to bring into the area. His store was a spacious building, which had been the American missionaries' Mission House previously. Laurie O'Hara later described his predicament to me:

> The local produce was grossly insufficient for the many mouths to be fed. Everybody was on 'half-rations', a term that over-simplified the problem. Rations were constantly adjusted to meet the situation of the moment. All the survival skills known were brought into play, including some of doubtful legality. Explosives left behind during the retreat could be used to procure fish from pools. The supply officer sent by 4 Corps HQ in India, Neville Coutts, was surprised to learn how we had survived.[When the air-drops began, matters improved considerably.]
>
> I had the occasional 'sundowner' with my boss Norman Kelly. On one occasion he became quite sentimental and told me how he missed his wife and children.
>
> In my opinion the Chins played a vital role in the eventual defeat of the Japanese and your father deserves some of the credit. I could see that the Chin men had responded well to defend their land. Your father was a respected leader of the Chin Levies. Together with the Chin Hills Battalion they formed a 'screening force' over a large area. In their outposts they were able to trap and resist several Jap probing patrols of various strengths until the all-out Jap assault on India. Even at that time they gave the Indian Army time to organise an effective resistance.[14]

Laurie O'Hara had met Captain Jack Oats, and had been at school with Tom Aplin before the war in Maymyo. It was Tom who looked after the outpost near No. 3 Stockade while Jack Oats was away. Jack Oats had been involved in an earlier battle for Stockade No. 3. He was subsequently wounded, but on returning to the Chin Hills after he got back from hospital, he reported to his Commanding Officer, Major Tommy West of the Chin Hills Battalion, in the presence of the battalion Medical Officer Kenny Fraser, 'Now Tommy, don't expect that I shall be able to do this over again [referring to his defence of the stockades]. I might not be able to stand it. Two days on our own fighting for no certain purpose and not knowing whether support was coming or even whether there was any available, is a terrific strain.' Kenny Fraser was shocked at the time; however, later he commented '...but he, like a school-mate of mine who got three immaculate Military Crosses in the 7th Indian Division, was *a thinking soldier*, as I learned to understand later.'[15]

In 1943 Ken Shaw became a Sector Commander of the Western Chin Levies. He was born in Burma, of distinguished lineage. His grandfather, Sir O. W. Shaw, had been knighted in 1913, in the year that he was Acting Lieutenant Governor of Burma, and had married the daughter of the senior official in King Thibaw's court. Ken's father had been their eldest son and was co-editor of the *Rangoon Gazette*. He was at the College of Engineering when war broke out and, after officer training in Maymyo, was posted to the 10th Burma Rifles. He operated in the Tiddim, Falam and Haka areas and used Chin Hills operational maps. He and his fellow Levy officers marked them with English names so that they could speak to each other on 'open' radio links without the Japanese understanding what they were talking about.

In June, July and August, with monsoon rains teeming down, leeches, heavy mist and at times a biting cold, it must have taken enormous stamina to keep going mile after mile with the ever-present risk of stumbling into a Japanese patrol. Often the distance travelled on foot on these steep mule tracks could be from 24 to 31 miles in a day. Norman Kelly walked these tracks which he had come to know so well. What a relief it would have been to see at last the poles of a village boundary – sometimes adorned with skulls – or a stone platform. And there might be a headman nursing a bottle of *zu-riel*, an inferior brew, to be shared with the weary traveller. Often Norman would be taken to the headman's house, relieved of his hot, wet boots and socks, and given an opportunity to burn off the leeches with a lighted cigarette. These would fall through the cracks in the floor to the pigs in the space below the house. There would also be a chance to get rid of some of the ticks and sit in a tub of warm water – what bliss! – and then put on his trousers again before heading for the *zu* pot followed by sharing the family meal: rice, chicken if lucky – pork would be a real treat, without too much thought for the habitat upon which it had been reared.

Noel Stevenson had a conference with the Divisional Commander in Tiddim on 14 June 1943. He was told that the High Command had agreed to defend the Tiddim area in strength. Stevenson commented,'This will entail, in turn, maintenance of a large number of Levies at full strength and all the maintenance and porterage problems will be increased proportionately. As soon as possible Kelly will be relieved of Levy work.' [16] This was to enable him to have more time to carry out his duties as Additional Deputy Commissioner of the Chin Hills. Stevenson wrote to Brigadier Wilkie on 26 June on the issue of 'Labour and Morale in the Tiddim Subdivision':

The Chins wish passionately to keep the Japanese out of their country and to that end he has already submitted to labour requisitioning on a scale unheard of in the neighbouring areas in Assam and Manipur. Should the military situation demand it he is prepared to go even further to keep the Japanese out, but this can only be done at serious risk to his crops. Approximately 50% of the adult labour force, instead of working in their fields during the cultivation season, are involved in the war effort. The Chins are perfectly aware of the scale of requisitioning over the border and the disparity in effort gives them acute displeasure.

One question I am asked continuously in this connection is 'Where are the 300,000,000 peoples of India one hears so much about?' They add 'If we can build with a labour force of less than 5,000, a road for jeeps 35 miles long, why cannot the millions in India make motor roads into the hills sufficient to cope with our military needs?'

There is no answer to this. Local labour is requisitioned to the tune of one person per house per day or very near it.

There are about 8,300 households in the Tiddim subdivision, of which about 800 belong to widows. These are spread over some 3,000 square miles of territory with no good communication other than the Tiddim Road. The balance contains an average of two adults and three children per house. Since somebody must remain to look after the children we cannot normally count on more than one adult per household for labour purposes. But of this total of houses 3,000 have already supplied one person to Government in the form of Civil and Frontier Force personnel, Levies, Chiefs, Headmen and Elders. From the total number of houses therefore we can only draw upon approximately 4,500 for coolie work. Of this number some 600 houses are on the Eastern Slopes of the Letha range and are therefore in constant use as ration coolies for forward posts, as guides, as sentries on roads to supplement the Levies, and so on.

As to morale, I feel no one can honestly cavil at the morale of a people who can still produce coolies to work in front of the troops, who form their guard, who still produce good information and whose irregular fighters have done at least as well as their trained commando comrades in attacks upon the Japanese line of communication. Far too much has been made of every little failure on their part, and far too little said about their great achievements of the past year on our behalf.

Everybody here is very proud of the way our troops fought at No. 3 Stockade and pleased at the potent blow they gave the enemy in strength. But the fact remains that owing to our failure to produce and maintain an adequate means of supply, each battle between our troops and the Japanese has led to a withdrawal of our main force, first to Fort White and secondly to the present position on the ridges. It is no use blaming the Chin for noticing this fact and drawing his own conclusion from it.

The use of harassing tactics against the Japanese lines of communication has strengthened morale considerably in the areas behind the Letha Range, but has not noticeably reassured the villagers east of the Range, who watch our main forces, and who fear that further reduction or withdrawal for supply reasons may expose them to reprisals for the acts of regular and irregular commando parties. The Chins themselves know this, and fear that if the enemy is allowed a foothold in the hills he will gain with it, in the form of occupied villages, the key to further infiltrations. For this reason the local feeling is unanimous that the Japanese must not be allowed to settle on Chin soil.

The Levies have produced good results in both gaining information and in assisting and carrying out raids against the enemy. What faults there were in the past with the Levies were largely our own – failure to provide adequate numbers of good officers, failure to find the all-important wireless equipment, failure to deal with malcontents from the Burma Rifles and so on. Where good officers and G.C.O's have been with them, as at the first battle of No. 3 Stockade, the Burma Rifles and Levies behaved very well and inflicted casualties on the enemy in proportion to their own strength, which are comparable with what we have achieved later with first class troops. [17]

Norman had so many matters to take care of, but what would have been an impossible burden was relieved by first-class support and loyalty from Thawng Chin Thang and the other Levy organisers. They were all working flat out for each other in an environment of high morale. Betty Kelly had written to Thawng Chin Thang, the Inspector of Schools in the Chin Hills, who was also Levy Assistant to Norman Kelly, and he replied to her on 4 July 1943 (which also happened to be Norman's thirty-ninth birthday).

Tiddim
4–7–43

Dear Madam,

It is a tremendous gratitude for me to receive your letter dated 8–5–43. It was sent out to me in the jungle towards the end of June, and I am actually writing this reply in the jungle still now.

Desmond has really been very kind to us. The pocket diaries are very useful.

It is very pleasing indeed to learn that Desmond has done so brilliantly in his arithmetic. I presume Patricia [Maeve] is doing equally well.

Major Kelly has not yet gone to Falam. He has been confining his activities in the Tiddim zone since his arrival. Likewise, the DC, Col. Stevenson, has been in this area for the last three months. Their presence amongst us is a great inspiration. Everybody is putting forth the best effort towards our common cause, so there is a rare chance for one to meet another as conveniently and frequently as before.

The rains this year has been rather late and not heavy. This is good for the wet highlands but offered some difficulty to the low dry areas like Saizang. Crop prospect in the wetlands is good but the same cannot be said of it in the dry areas.

Providence guiding, I am looking forward to seeing the children and you in the Chin Hills in a short time.

Yours respectfully,

Thawng Chin Thang

Tiddim
Chin Hills
2–8–43

Dear Madam,

I feel most grateful to you for your letter of July 2, together with its enclosure. It is a stimulus to an enhanced enthusiasm on the part of people like ourselves to learn that what we are doing is being known and gaining the appreciation of those who are looking after our interests in these difficult times which are not yet over.

I am hoping that with all the facilities made available now, the Chins have a stronger mind than in the very initial stages and are resolute to stand firmly themselves till the hour comes for final victory which is well within our grasp.

I am taking steps to have the articles translated into Chin for distribution to all notable persons and I am sure everybody will, like myself, be deeply interested in them.

Please convey my best wishes to Patricia and Desmond. I am delighted to hear of the excellent work they are doing at school and am looking forward to the time when I shall hear that they are doing best in their respective classes.

It might interest you to hear that the Kamhau chief received the award of King's Service Medal and my brother, the Saizang chief, the A.T.M. [Burmese Good Service Medal] in the Birthday Honours list.

Owing to the rain falling somewhat late and somewhat less than usual, millet crop in the hotlands is not very good. Indian corn will be good, but all *taungyas* are not receiving the adequate attention they ought to for the simple reason that we are subordinating every other sphere of activity to work of the most urgent and important nature connected with the present emergency.

I have temporarily returned to the Headquarters from jungle owing to my suffering from a run of slight dysentery, which is subsiding now.

With all my best wishes, I remain,

Yours most respectfully,

Thawng Chin Thang

The Last Meeting of Jack Oats and Peter Bankes

Jack Oats described meeting Peter Bankes for the last time in August 1943. The strain of command and fatigue from constant marching was taking its toll on relationships.

> I was by now second in command of my Battalion and so we met both as Acting Majors. I went through to Tiddim to see Peter and get his sanction to recruit some Siyins from his Levies for the Chin Hills Battalion to bring our Siyin Company up to strength. I travelled from Lungngo straight to Tiddim, i.e. Lungngo/Haka a hundred miles, Haka/Tiddim ninety-three miles, on foot except for about seventeen miles in a jeep. Found Peter in a pokey little office – just room for a table and two chairs – off the main office of Kelly and his local administration. Peter was fed up with the administrative work and his C.O. worrying him all the time for returns, etc., and 48 Brigade, on his doorstep, wanting things repeatedly. Spent the night with Peter in the burnt-out ruins of Kelly's house. Peter was very worried about a daft letter from Col. Oatts about many things Peter was alleged to have done wrong. Oatts had completely the wrong end of the story. Peter had seen Brigadier Cumming of 63 Brigade and I advised him to demand a Court of Enquiry.
>
> Next morning, Peter said his usual 'Fare thee well' and we parted for the last time. I left by jeep on my return journey and, unknown to Peter, called to see Brigadier Cumming and told him what I thought of Oatts and his letter etc. If it had been 'Punch' Cowan or Brigadier Cameron something would have been done but Cumming although agreeing said he couldn't do much as Oatts and Peter were not under his command. I thought he would have written an account anyway for 4 Corps H.Q., but I gather he did nothing. Col. Oatts anyhow was greatly shaken by Peter's reply and apologised and shortly after that sent Peter on leave.[18]

Peter Bankes was awarded the Military Cross for 'Gallant and Distinguished Services' in the Chin Hills from 21 May to 20 June 1943. This included his brilliant raid from Suanglangsu Vum on the Japanese-occupied Burmese village Nansuangpu. Peter Bankes, Jack Oats and Harold Braund were known as the 'Three Musketeers' of No. 3 Stockade.

Others had also found Lieutenant-Colonel 'Titus' Oatts difficult. Harold Braund even described a Lieutenant-Colonel Hayes (I assume he is actually Oatts) in his book *Distinctly I Remember*. He only deliberately changed the name of one other officer. He talks about their first meeting:

> I watched Hayes go with a nameless apprehension that was fulfilled on his return. During a carefully modulated summary of his impression thus far, Hayes reproved me, having officer status,

for manhandling stores with my Levies, and then said that he was not at all impressed with Bankes as a Levy Officer!

We had been sent the wrong man. Obviously our affairs were no longer in the hands of such men as Brigadier Felix Williams and Lt. Col. Critchley.

He had the deplorable habit of referring to the Anglo-Burmans amongst us as half-castes. He never remotely understood the Chins, or they him. Personally I got on with him well – indeed I was the only one of his officers whom he habitually addressed by his Christian name. Hayes never lacked the loyalty of his officers in the months that followed.

In fairness I should add that Hayes was awarded a D.S.O. at the conclusion of the Chin Hills Campaign, so there is that much at least to support a contrary assessment. [19]

Norman must have been aware of the personality clashes among the British officers. They were all strong, independent characters – one of their great strengths.

Another diary that Betty Kelly had sent was inscribed 'To Awn Ngin, from Desmond', and had become Norman's field diary for 1943. It lists the essential dates and places for June to August of that year, when the Japanese seemed to be closing in. Fort White and the Siyin Valley were critical and the enemy was fully aware of this (see map no. 6 on p. 74).

28 June	Halt Fort White
	Sent telegram
29 June	Fort White to Ngalzang with Brochrich – Peters
30 June	Ngalzang – Suangphei
1 July	Suangphei – Bamboo Camp
2 July	Bamboo Camp – Fort White
3 July	Halt Fort White
4 July	Fort White – Khuasak
5 July	Khuasak – Tuklai on evacuation
6 July	Halt Tuklai
7 July	Tuklai – meetings (see below)
8 July	Tuklai – Tiddim
9 July	Halt Tiddim
10 July	Tiddim – Tuklai
11 July	Halt Tuklai
12 July	Halt Tuklai
	Evacuation arranged Pimpi, Vaona, Ngalzang, Suangphei. Oaths taken
13 July	Halt Tuklai
	NHC [Stevenson] arrives

14 July	Halt Tuklai
15 July	Tuklai – Tiddim, where we remained until
21 July	Tiddim – Tonzang
22 July	Tonzang – Tiddim
23 July –	
5th August	Tiddim
6 August	Tiddim – Fort White
7 August	Fort White – Tiddim. Action at No. 3

On 1 August 1943 Noel Stevenson, now back in Falam (leaving Norman with the Tiddim subdivision) wrote to Brigadier Ralph Wilkie, Deputy Chief Civil Affairs Officer at HQ of 4 Corps (Imphal) about the situation in the Chin Hills:

> Office of the Deputy Commissioner, Chin Hills
> Falam
> 1st August 1943

My dear Wilkie,

This rather long letter will give you a survey of the present position in the Chin Hills. On my way back from Tiddim I met Kelly at Tuklai where I also saw the Siyin elders [7 July]. I gave them a pretty straight talk on their position, pointing out that it was not a question of them defending us but of defending themselves. I think they now realise that there is much more to be lost by taking a weak line against the Japanese. I asked Kelly to arrange for the evacuation of women and children from a few of the eastern slope villages, such as Pimpi and Vaona, Ngalzang and Suangphei, which were under immediate threat from the Japanese. I have not yet received his report on progress in this direction. I understand that many more Tuisang villagers have fled to our protection. These refugees said they were able to get away because the new Japanese troops who have been recently moved in to No. 3 ran and left them, under air bombardment, and the villagers took their chance to bolt. Only a few who misguidedly tried to save their property were captured. The refugees also report that the Japanese are having considerable difficulty over transport and are now using only elephants, of which three were shot by Buanman Levies recently, with two mahouts. In addition to the Levies, I have ordered the creation of a Home Guard of the remaining men for whom we can find arms. Those will remain as normal villagers until called up to face a crisis. They will then draw A Levy pay and rations for the duration of the threat to their area. I hope we shall never need to use them. The good response both in Tiddim and Falam to this call indicates good morale.

Crops: On my way down I travelled through the Sokte, Siyin and Ngawn areas lying between the Fort White road and the Manipur River. With the exception of crops growing in the gardens in the villages, most of the crops are poor and very late. In normal years the millet is ripe by the second half of July and maize showing cobs. This year I saw only one field of ripening millet at Hmunpi and much of it has not even seeded yet.

Propaganda: I found in all the villages a very keen desire to know what was going on in the world in general and in particular in the neighbourhood of No. 3. I explained at length the reasons why the army has left No. 3 alone for the time being. Everybody can see that the Japanese are losing far more men and transport by remaining at No. 3 and trying to maintain it than they would if they had retired to their last rains headquarters on the [Chindwin] River. The existence of the Japanese outpost at No. 3 has given the Levies an excellent training opportunity to polish up their wrecking attacks against an enemy line of communication.

The people need the personal contact of the civil officers very badly, and it is a difficult job reconciling this important duty with the army's insistent demands, both in Tiddim and Falam, to have the civil officers close at hand. The people are used to turning to civil officers for help and guidance and the Levy officers cannot satisfy their needs for reassurance from time to time, as most of them cannot speak the local language and some cannot even speak Burmese.

Rice and salt supplies: I have decided to make a further issue of rice to the civil population – a tin of rice per household, a very small amount in all conscience. The remainder of our salt stocks will rapidly disappear.

Trade goods: No one who has not been here can realise what it means to see rows of shops without a single article for sale in them. There is a chronic lack of trade goods such as iron for hoes, which are essential to the people's life and cotton for clothing.

Noel Stevenson

Deputy Commissioner, Falam[20]

A few weeks later, on 20 August, Stevenson wrote to GHQ in New Delhi, with copies to 4 Corps, Imphal:

SECRET

I do not know whether or not the High Command [New Delhi] intends to reconquer Burma in the cold weather of 1943/44, *but one thing is certain – if this does not happen and communications are not improved to the extent that adequate supplies of food and other essentials can be brought in for the people, this area will be forced into the hands of the Japanese.*

The Chins have now suffered requisitioned labour, call it forced labour if you will, on the grand scale for nearly eighteen months. They have stood this under conditions of which the complete cessation of imports of essential goods such as iron for hoes, cotton and clothes, oil for lights etc., is but a small part. They have lived in partial starvation during much of the period, and they have lived under constant threat of the enemy throughout. They have constructed some fifty miles of excellent jeep road in the Tiddim area and maintained it so far throughout this rains: they have carried ration loads by the tens of thousands during both this rains and last rains: they have borne a large direct share of the defence of their land (and thereby the defence of India) and acted as guides, porters and stretcher-bearers to regular troops operating both in front of and behind the enemy's lines: they have taken part, both men and women, and sometimes in groups more than a thousand strong, in ration raids many miles into enemy-occupied Burma to snatch desperately needed rations for our troops and Levies from under the very noses of the Japanese, protected only by relatively small bodies of our garrison troops.

It will be realised that there is a limit to human endurance, especially when the people upon whom the strain is imposed are ignorant of world affairs and unable to grasp why it is that a country of 300,000,000 people just behind them cannot spare the time and trouble to open routes into the Chin Hills and give to the Chins the much needed material help for which they cry out.

It will also be realised that with the best will in the world local officers cannot get the people to live indefinitely on propaganda alone. There are only seven Civil Officers at the moment in an area of some 10,000 square miles of country almost completely devoid of fast communications. Half of these officers are tied to their H.Q. to meet the needs of the military organisations, and the few remaining are hard put to tour sufficiently to keep up the people's spirits. That they have succeeded so far is a great tribute to the Chin people's staunchness. *But it can't go on forever.*

The water supply problem is difficult. Efforts have been made for years to improve it, as it is inadequate even for the existing population. In view of supply difficulties I recommend the construction of a pine aqueduct to bring the water in from Lungpi, and of two cisterns each 3200 sq. ft. in area and 5 feet in depth. This water could be used for watering animals, for transport, for washing and bathing and for vegetable gardens, while the existing piped water supply would be reserved strictly for drinking[21]

On 10 September Noel Stevenson again reminded Wilkie: 'No civil rice = no labour = no rations for troops and Levies = loss of Chin Hills'.

In May, June and July 1943 the expected large-scale attacks on the Tiddim subdivision had materialised. Because of these, the urgency to complete the Tiddim Road during the monsoon weather before September had increased and troops from the 17th Indian Division were used to work on the road and then open it. A brigade of regulars and a considerably enlarged Levy force were required in the Tiddim subdivision to face the Japanese, who had increased their garrisons in the Kalemyo Valley from March 1943 onwards. This made it foolhardy to attempt further large-scale raids to get rice back into the hills from that source. So the pressure to create, feed and maintain a large labour force of coolies fell very heavily on the Tiddim subdivision, where 1,500 on average were employed on the road to Imphal. The army wanted a jeep road to Fort White as well as the transport of loads from the Manipur Bridge on the Tiddim Road. Now the priority was to feed the coolies with 600 tons of 'civil rice' to cope with the extra work which the crisis in September demanded. To add to these problems, the late rains had also resulted in a delayed and very poor harvest in the Chin Hills. The *History of 17 Indian Division* records:

> At the beginning of August, 63 Brigade carried out an operation to discover the enemy's strength and dispositions and to harass them so severely that they might have to pull back. 1/10 Gurkha Rifles attacked Basha Hill but failed to capture it because of machine-gun fire from three strong bunkers covering the narrow ridge, only a few feet wide, along which the attacking troops had to approach. At the same time a party of 1/3 Gurkha Rifles raided Theizang but although they did not capture the village they created considerable damage with mortars. Another party of 1/3 Gurkha Regiment with sappers, after a difficult cross-country march down the *Zi Chaung* and up along the main road, from the foothills to No. 2 Stockade, attempted to blow the bridge, just east of the Stockade itself. This party never reached its objective but shot up a party of Japs met on the road and caused much confusion and casualties in base camps in the area. Yet another party from Dolluang succeeded in crossing the swollen Segyi *Chaung* and took enemy parties on the road west of Slyin completely by surprise.[22]

During the first eight months of 1943 the Chin Hills Battalion had been operating out of Falam and protecting the Haka subdivision. Action consisted of preventing Japanese infiltration into the hills, and of ambushing Japanese and raiding supplies collected by them in villages in the plains. A typical 'show' of this nature had been that of a patrol of Whelngo Chins under Lance Naik (Corporal) Za Khuai beyond Webula on 16 July (see map no. 3 on p. 28). They had seen new bullock cart tracks at the Ngapai road junction and, pushing on, had heard men talking. Za Khuai, on a personal recce, found some forty Japanese about to bathe. He ordered his section to fix bayonets, fire a volley, and charge. The Japanese fled, leaving nine dead and six rifles. While searching the bodies the section was counter-attacked under machine-gun and, later, mortar-covering fire and they were chased up into the hills, where they cut their way back to Webula, through trackless jungle, carrying the Japanese rifles. Their casualties were nil. The CO reported, 'An excellent show of initiative on the part of the Section Commander'. [23]

During the month of August Norman Kelly was in Tiddim but also visited Fort White, Mualbem, Tonzang (24 miles), Bualkhau, Vazang (24 miles), Lumbang and Falam. One journey between Lumbang and Falam and then to Bualkhau and back to Falam was 31 miles. On 29 August

Noel Stevenson left for Haka. Both these officers had to tour their territory to keep up the morale of the Chins.

By late August the Gurkha Company of the Chin Hills Battalion was under the command of Captain Frank O'Donel, an Anglo-Burman of great dependability. It had one three-inch mortar when it took over protection of Haka subdivision from the Siyins and Khongsais. They had, cooperating with them, about 1,000 Haka Levies under half-a-dozen officers. In September Japanese forces moved into the Haka subdivision from Gangaw but, finding the Gurkha Company and Haka Levies on the alert, halted operations there and pushed in strength further north against the main battalion area. The first contact with these was on 26 September. A patrol of six Kumaoni sections and one Haka section, under Captain Dare, pushing out from Pamun *chaung* (stream) towards Natchaung through Haka (b)[24] (clear of the enemy on 20 September) found Japanese in strong defensive positions there with heavy fire power. Battalion casualties were two killed and three wounded, and the Japanese probably suffered slightly more.

In September 1943 Robbie Sayer, who had a Chin wife, was the Assistant Superintendent for Haka. Every day his office was besieged by swarms of villagers, mostly the families of soldiers, asking for food. Unfortunately their requests could not be met. In the subdivision, where *zo los* plots were cut for maize every year the yield was fair, but in the *lai los*, or more permanent *taungyas*, which were the people's main standby for food, they were in a very bad condition.

Norman Kelly, Acting Deputy Commissioner

Noel Stevenson was due to go on leave in September 1943. Norman Kelly, as Additional Deputy Commissioner, would act as DC in his place. The Post Office, in spite of hostilities, was still operating in Falam.

One piece of good news was the surrender of Italy. This information was passed rapidly through the Chin Hills to help reassure the population that, in spite of all the threats and privations, eventual victory in the East was not only possible but anticipated. Some ex-Burma Rifles Chins, called up for Levy service, either did not come or had various excuses, and there was an undercurrent of dissatisfaction especially in the western parts of the district bordering the Lushai Hills. A Chin Levy shot another man for saying he hoped the Japanese would win their way into the Chin Hills because then the people would get more trade goods. Certain chiefs and headmen were keeping back their ponies for the Pony Levy/Corps. Many had been overworked and those sent in – one was required from each village – were often unfit for work. Norman Kelly was trying to arrange for ponies to be given rest periods for a percentage of time instead of working them, on very little food, until they died.

The fall of Italy gave an opportunity to gather chiefs and headmen together to bring them up to date with the war and prepare them for tactics to use when the Japanese attacked again. They would have to evacuate everything from their villages including food, grain and livestock; they would also have to destroy bridges and roads, set up traps and ambushes and hinder the enemy advance in every way they could think of. They were told to ignore the Japanese propaganda. What the Japanese had promised bore no resemblance to what they actually did to the villagers on the eastern slopes of the Tiddim subdivision. The chiefs and headmen were told that, once evacuated, their villages would be bombed and shelled by our troops. They had asked for better guns, but in the meantime they should use those that they did have as well as axes, or whatever came to hand. At one such meeting 28 chiefs and headmen attended, with about 55 elders. The DC sanctioned the expenditure of Rs 200, with which two cows and pots of *zu* were bought for their entertainment.

During September 1943 much troop movement was reported by Levy scouts and the enemy began to reinforce the whole area. At the same time rumours were current of an impending attack on the Chin Hills. Enemy patrols became more active in the Fort White area and there were several clashes on Pimpi Ridge and Vownalu Mountain. On 4 October the Chin Levies, under the command of Thian Pum, chief of the Buanman tracts of the Siyin area, were engaged in a fierce frontal assault upon the Japanese at Ngalzang, near No. 2 Stockade. The chief was wounded in the attack and had to be carried by his men, through jungle paths, back to Tiddim Hospital.

It was soon apparent that large Japanese forces were concentrating at Gangaw. Some moved north, and then struck off west along the Manipur River towards Falam, while others were striking west along the Kalemyo–Natchaung–Webula–Falam road. One battalion of 214 Regiment of the Japanese crack 33rd Division, 'The White Tigers', was heading towards Falam, while another battalion of the same regiment was moving against Webula.

The Battle of Webula

In the first week of October 1943 advanced elements of the Chin Hills Battalion, who were covering Webula, came under heavy machine-gun and 4-inch mortar fire from the Japanese 214 Regiment; two platoons covering Mualzawl were affected. Lieutenant-Colonel Tommy West, CO of the battalion, and Captain Dare, with one platoon of Hakas, came up to support them. In the fighting for Mualzawl, under heavy 4-inch mortar fire, Tommy West was wounded. The Japanese were in strength (estimated as one battalion) and Mualzawl had to be evacuated, while Captain Dare and the Haka platoon carried out rearguard duties. The two platoons got back to Webula. Captain Dare, who was also wounded, and his platoon were cut off but managed to rejoin the battalion with difficulty later. The Japanese, however, did not advance beyond Webula and then withdrew. This was probably a feint attack, so they then concentrated on the advance via the Manipur River on Falam.

Tommy West had been Assistant Commandant as a Major, under Lieutenant-Colonel A.C. Moore, from June 1940 to August 1942. His CO wrote that he was

> a very reliable, conscientious and hardworking officer, of exemplary character and very popular with all ranks. He was a good linguist speaking three Chin dialects and the difficult Burmese language fluently.
>
> A product of Glasgow High School, he had been Captain of the school, his house, the 1st XV rugby team and Company Sergeant Major of the school's Officer Training Corps. He was an outstanding sportsman, heavyweight boxer and tennis player. He had worked in Rangoon and was the manager of the Mandalay branch of his firm before he took up his commission with the Chin Hills Battalion, where his powers of command and leadership were quickly recognised. With little to eat, less to wear and seldom dry, day in and day out, his personal example was magnificent and did much to reassure those under him. The popularity of this officer with the Burmese villagers was such that it greatly facilitated the local purchase of supplies, on which his unit then depended. [25]

When Tommy West was wounded it was fortunate that Kenny Fraser, the battalion Medical Officer, was present. His recollection was that 'a chunk of his shoulder was blown out – probably by machine-gun fire, not a rifle nor a mortar bomb'. Kenny Fraser dressed his wound and bound it up. He was then carried on a stretcher back to Tiddim Hospital, which took three days. 'I got Lt. Col. West on a stretcher and, with some walking wounded, took him up a subsidiary track to the Tiddim Road that I had used before. All this time I had no notion that Lt. Col. West had been without a company commander or any other officer other than commissioned native officers.' [26]

Noel Stevenson had flown from Calcutta to Delhi on 1 October. On the 10th he was recalled from his leave in Simla and arrived in Delhi on the 12th. He saw various people in GHQ and flew on to Calcutta on the 13th. He then visited Eastern HQ to get the latest news from the Chin Hills and arrived in Dimapur on the 16th. There he met Colonel Holmes and saw Mr Pawsey, Deputy Commissioner of the Naga Hills, and found that 'our civil effort in the Chin Hills is at least 50% better than even that of the Nagas'. [27] On 17 October Stevenson was in Imphal where he saw Ralph Wilkie and the 4 Corps Commander. He learned, with great satisfaction, that Wilkie, the Deputy Chief Civil Affairs Officer (DCCAO), had secured 200 tons of rice in Imphal and he promised to find out if Milestone 82 on the Tiddim Road could receive it at once. The following day he drove to Milestone 100 with Lieutenant-Colonel Roddie

Russell and John Franklin. On 19 October he arrived back at Tiddim, and noted:

> The road throughout is in remarkably good condition and it should not be long before three-tonners can get to mile 109. Under existing arrangements, we hope to complete the section from Tuitum [Manipur] Bridge to Tiddim as a 15 cwt. road by 15th December and in the meantime work on progressively improving the jeep road from Tiddim onwards. [28]

The Battle of Falam

On 25 October Noel Stevenson wrote: 'In the evening received a message from Norman Kelly to say that the Japs were across the Pao Va [River].' Stevenson arrived in Falam two days later, on 27 October, where he was debriefed by Norman in a conference with Brigadier Haswell and Manning of the Levies (see map no. 10 on p. 192).

The Tashon chief's son had failed in his duty – his father was known to be pro-Japanese. Subedar Tai Kual was put in charge of the B Levies instead. The Japanese were now less than a day's march from Falam. With Stevenson's return there, Norman Kelly moved to Haka, which was very much under threat, on 29 October. At this point Stevenson had decided to turn all the civilian officers into Levy officers and put 'our whole organisation into the fight'. The military crisis on top of the bad harvest had ruined all the carefully laid supply plans.

The food situation for coolies in Falam and Haka was now critical and a wireless request was sent for one plane-load to be dropped between the two places. Even this only allowed for a partial ration of one pound of rice per day. The coolies were required to help in the evacuation of the wireless sets, ammunition and other essentials should the enemy threaten to overrun Falam. Confidential papers had already left for Roshi as well as the non-Chin civilians, who were moved to places 10 or 20 miles further west.

The Kumaoni Company of the battalion was the one doubtful element. They were dispirited, which was not surprising. They had been in Falam without a break and without adequate rest and relief for eighteen months. No regular battalion would normally be subjected to such treatment. On 30 October Stevenson commented:

> True, the Chins and Gurkhas have done the same, but they are of tougher material. The Haka Levies are putting up a most inspiring show, and have killed 100 Japs since the fighting began. The Falam Levies and Home Guard have also done their stuff well and if we had but an extra company or two of fresh regulars here the Japs would be out again in double-quick time. [29]

A few days earlier, on 26 October, the Chin Hills Battalion, under the command of Lieutenant-Colonel Roddie Russell, moved across to cover

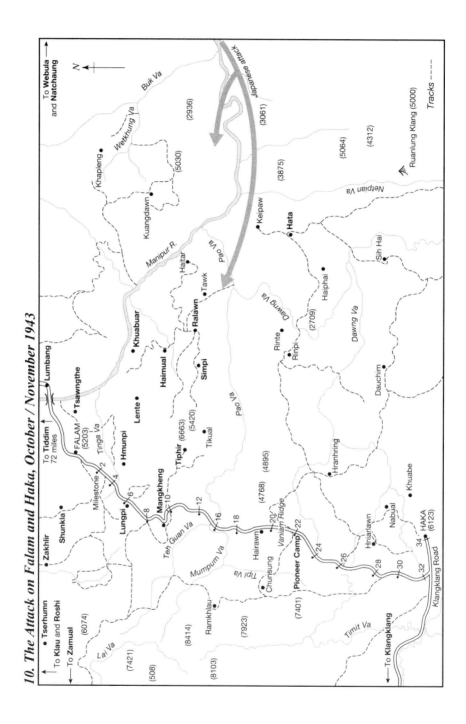

10. The Attack on Falam and Haka, October / November 1943

Falam from the Japanese advance and took up a position 10 miles south-east of Falam at Simpi, Ralawn and Haimual. There was a small party of Haka Levies, the Kumaoni Company, Siyin Company and a Haka Company. The Whelngo, a Haka tribe, and Khongsai Companies were in Falam while the Gurkha Company had detached and was in Haka subdivision. The enemy, two companies forward, with others moving up, were facing them.

During that evening, one Japanese company, with mortar support, attacked the Siyin Company but was repulsed with the loss of at least twenty men; there were no losses on the Allied side. This was followed by a heavy attack on the Haka Levies' position at Haimual – a bad position, but there was not a better one available. The Kumaonis on the right were in a very bad state of morale. On the principle of delaying actions, but not risking annihilation by fighting it out (the principle laid down for the unit by High Command), the battalion withdrew back on to the Lente Ridge, 4 miles south-east of Falam. This had been ordered on 27 October and was completed by 0500 hours on 28 October. There were no entrenching tools, but the troops dug in with *kukris* and mess tins. The enemy failed to realise the change of position, and continued their mortar bombardment on the old one for two hours, much to the amusement of the troops. The Haka Company was well forward on the left flank at Khuabuar.

By 31 October the remaining platoon of the Siyin Company came up, with the Whelngo Company, which relieved the Kumaonis on the right, the latter being withdrawn to rest. The Japanese in the meantime had made no further advance, so supplies and ammunition were brought up from Falam, and operation orders issued for an advance of all companies on 3 November to drive back the 214 Regiment. On that day the Siyins advanced in the centre and reoccupied their old positions near Simpi, south of Haimual.

It appears that the Japanese had selected the day later as their 'D-Day' for advance. On 4 November the enemy attacked the Siyin position, supported by mortar and battalion gunfire. Repulsed at first, they took the position at 0030, the Siyins dropping back onto the Lente Ridge. On the left, the Haka Company repelled attacks but, being so far forward, was withdrawn a few miles to the general line. The Khongsai Company came up in reserve at Hmunpi, behind the Whelngos on the right.

It became apparent on 6 November that the enemy was moving round on the right. At 1100 hours a Whelngo fighting patrol, under Jemedar Thang Ling, contacted them moving into Hmunpi. The patrol shot up the Japanese advance, killing six and wounding several more, but had to retire with one wounded, before the main body's heavy machine-gun and mortar fire. At 2130 the Japanese attacked the Whelngo position, and were brought under very heavy fire in close order at 50 yards. They rushed up to the platoon positions but were shot down with heavy casualties. Further on the right, at about the same time, the Levies ambushed a force of some 60 Japanese on the Tiphir–Mangkheng Road. At 2300 the enemy made a noisy attack on the Siyins in the centre, and at midnight on the Hakas, who drove them back. A Kumaoni mortar detachment won a duel with a Japanese infantry gun.

In the morning a further attack on the Whelngos was fought off but, with Japanese infiltration in the centre, the position could not be held, and on the evening of 7 November, a withdrawal onto the Lungpi–Falam Ridge was ordered. During the day and evening all supplies and ammunition which could be moved out of Falam were evacuated and the rest destroyed.

The men had been cheerful and morale was high on 6 November, but on the 7th the noise of demolitions in Falam brought the realisation that, although all the actions of the battalion and Levies had resulted in heavy losses to the Japanese, the Allies were in retreat and about to leave Falam. The Chins became fidgety and anxious.[30]

The battalion withdrew on the night of 7/8 November to the Lungpi–Falam Ridge, with the Whelngos at Lungpi, the Siyins in the centre and the Hakas at Falam. The Khongsais were sent further right to encounter two Japanese companies, reported by Levies as approaching Mangkheng. They seized this village just in time and fought the Japanese all day, until driven out at 1700 hours on 8 November. The company commander, Captain Milligan, was killed. Jack Haswell, the senior Levy commander, then withdrew from Falam, with the Zahows under Manning and Gammel, and joined the battalion on the Lungpi–Falam Ridge.

At 2300 hours on 8 November the battalion retired some 3 miles north-west to the Zakhlir–Shunkla Ridge, the Khongsais and Whelngos retired to Zakhlir, and the Hakas and Siyins to Shunkla. The Whelngos and Khongsais were distinctly jumpy. The Japanese attacked the Whelngos at 2030 hrs on 9 November; after a few shots they broke and fled. They were rallied at about 0900 hours on the 10th, taking post with the Khongsais, some 5 miles to the rear at Klau.

The way in which they had panicked after so many days of exemplary action was extraordinary. The CO felt it was due to exhaustion and battle fatigue and that they had become stupefied at the thought of the battalion headquarters in Falam, which they had fought so bravely to defend, being evacuated so near to their homes.[31] In Chin culture, Falam was the key from a military point of view and was also the administrative capital. It had last been captured when the British had come to the hills in 1892. For the British, knowing that they were up against the 214 Regiment of the 33rd Division, it was a strategic withdrawal. Fighting to defend Falam at all costs would have been futile.

The Siyins came into the Klau position on 16 November, leaving the Hakas on the left flank. It was then decided, in view of the news that the Japanese were moving from Falam to cut off and surround the Gurkha

Company in Haka, to counter-attack the Lungpi–Falam Ridge to relieve the tension. On 18 November the Siyins moved south along the ridge, some 7 miles to Zamual, the Whelngos moving west to Tserhmun. The Japanese were heard approaching and the troops were ordered into ambush positions. But the Whelngos were so jittery that they could not be organised to take action and the company commander had to withdraw them to Klau, and put them into reserve. On 19 November the enemy attacked the Khongsais at Klau and drove them out of position. The battalion then withdrew 15 miles north to Roshi.

Where was Norman Kelly during the battle for Falam? Lieutenant-Colonel Oatts had asked for 'increased civil assistance', so Norman had already left Falam very early in the morning and had arrived in Haka on 29 October to help plan the response to the impending Japanese attack.

The Evacuation of Falam

On 2 November the civilian refugees had left Falam on the Champhai road, heading for the Assam border. The Zahau chief, Thang Tin Lian, had supplied them with coolies. On 3 November Stevenson sent Philip Barton to cross over the Manipur River to organise a Home Guard in the east Tashon tract. Some 500 to 600 coolies were moving civil and military stores out of Falam to Klangkhua on the Aijal road.

On 4 November 4 Corps had approved the evacuation plan. On the following night the Japanese were occupying positions within sight of Falam and were only an easy day's march away. On the evening of the 6th the medical and engineers staff had left for Zakhlir, accompanied by a heavy cannonade as the battle approached the last ridge below Falam. All military stores and rice were destroyed. Meanwhile, Haswell, who had already had one British officer killed and another missing, was preparing to evacuate. Everybody was short of British officers. Stevenson and his Chin partisans ('Chinwags') were the last to leave Falam (on 7 November); he blew the suspension bridge over the Manipur River at 1700 hours and continued eastwards.

The Tashon chief, Van Hmung, had held since 1942 an implicit belief in a Japanese victory. Stevenson commented, 'I must note here shortly the effect of the pusillanimous conduct of the Tashon, Laizo and Zahow [Zahau] Chiefs.' In Stevenson's view they had had an adverse effect on the morale of the Falam subdivision since the beginning of the Chin Hills campaign. The Tashon chief disobeyed orders to remain with Barton east of the Manipur and the other two chiefs failed to stay, as ordered, with the Assistant Superintendent, Falam. All the Tashon chief's family remained at his house until he and his sons met the Japanese at Tsawngthe on the morning of 8 November. They gave the enemy a peace offering of a considerable number of *mithun* and pigs and, in return, the Japanese promised that he would be the paramount chief in the Falam area. The chief's daughter, Than Thuai, who had been a nurse in Falam Hospital, failed to obey the civil surgeon and accompany the hospital to Surbung while the chief's son, Shiah Luai, Assistant Inspector of Schools, also defected. Stevenson noted:

> The Zahau Chief went into Falam also to meet the Japanese and accompanied a party of them back to his village in Klau. His attitude resulted in several acts of treachery by his tribesmen against the British forces protecting the Champhai road. The Laizo Chief had simply given in and handed over his people to be the beasts of burden of the enemy troops in the Falam area.
>
> I would like to bring to the notice of Government the exceptionally steady behaviour of all ranks in all departments of the Civil Staffs in Falam during the days before its fall. Everybody stuck to their jobs until the very last minute and left in a quiet and orderly manner. I must say I felt proud of them. [32]

At Haka 'Titus' Oatts was in command of the Chin Levies. It was clear to him that once Falam was captured, it would be impossible to hold Haka for longer than a week or so. Oatts was worried that, if the Levies knew this, they would lose heart and probably return to their homes. He therefore prepared to move west along the road to Klangklang, 20 miles away. Norman Kelly, who was with him, was responsible for building up a dump of supplies and ammunition in Klangklang. In his position as the Civil Affairs Officer and Additional Deputy Commissioner, he was able to do this without attracting particular attention.

The Battle of Haka

Oatts then chose a site for a jungle camp about 2 miles along the Haka–Klangklang road. This also overlooked the Haka–Falam road to the north, down which the Japanese were expected to come. It was well concealed and in an admirable position. The northern perimeter of it was manned by a platoon of Burma Rifle Hakas, who were unaware that the Gurkhas were constructing other defences, facing Klangklang, to the west. The quartermaster was instructed to arrange for the next airdrop to be into the jungle, from where it could be collected by mules for the new, hidden and well-defended camp. In this way the Haka Chins were not aware that this was a fallback position for when Haka was attacked. [33]

To the east of Haka, on the Ruanlung Klang mountain at nearly 5,000 feet, Dick Reese's Hakas had the Japanese surrounded on all sides in a tight pocket and were slaughtering parties of walking wounded trying to get back to the Gangaw Valley (see map no. 10 on p. 192). They were also raiding the enemy's supply trains, so the Japanese were short of food and medical aid. Dick Reese was Welsh and had been a physical training instructor before the war. He was a man of tremendous physical strength, who had joined the Chin Levies straight from England; he fulfilled the role of a Levy officer magnificently.

To the north of Pioneer Camp, on the Vaniam Ridge, there was a Burma Rifle platoon positioned astride the road leading from Falam, which was in a perfect spot to cover that approach for about a mile. Anybody on it would have 'hell knocked out of them'. Oatts calculated that from the time the Japanese reached the Pioneer rest house, it would take them five hours to arrive at Haka. A man on horseback, riding flat out, could cover the distance in half an hour, which would give time for the Levies get back into Haka before the Japanese arrived. Unfortunately, Oatts did not have a British officer to take charge of this strategic platoon until he was sent a new subaltern by Jack Haswell. This officer rode off to take up his assignment, but to Oatts' astonishment was followed by a driver with three mules to carry his kit! The next day, when Oatts went to inspect the position, he found the new officer asleep in a basket chair in the middle of the compound of the rest house, and his men sitting and lying about at the back of the bungalow. He could see with his field glasses a party of Japanese on the road, marching towards Falam. Oatts was speechless with rage, but after positioning the men, he galloped back to Haka to warn Haswell that the Japanese were heading his way.

The situation in Falam was untenable, so Brigadier Jack Haswell, Area Commander, was going to withdraw the Chin Hills Battalion across the Manipur River to the east bank and blow the suspension bridge at the bottom of the valley, about 12 miles from Falam. He intended to do this the following evening at 6 p.m., and make a run for it. In the event, Stevenson blew the bridge.

Since the fall of Falam was imminent, Oatts told his British Levy officer, Pat Rathbone, to fall back on Haka with his Zahows. Harold Braund was also warned of the situation but Joe Byrne, an Anglo-Shan, and Jimmy Carpenter, an Anglo-Burman from Steel's Forest Department, could not be contacted, so had to be left to their own devices. The Hakas were fighting harder than ever, but Oatts knew that as soon as he started a retrograde movement, morale would collapse. The next evening a dense column of smoke arose over Falam, which must have been visible over the whole of the northern Chin Hills. Haswell was burning his stores and ration godowns (storage buildings) in preparation for his departure. On 6 November Norman Kelly was in Haka when Falam was abandoned and on 8 November he moved to the camp on the Klangklang road, where he remained on the night of 9 November.

For several days the Japanese made no offensive against Haka. After being reinforced they had broken out of the laager on the Ruanlung Klang, but Harold Braund and Dick Reese, with their Levies, held them on the Dawng Va River in the most gallant manner. Pat Rathbone arrived with his Zahows to join the Hakas in the northern defensive positions. Although the territory of the Zahows had been occupied by the enemy they showed no sign of leaving the field of battle and, with the Hakas, attacked the Japanese lines of communications.

Rathbone eventually sent word that the Japanese had concentrated at Mangkheng, on the road from Falam, a day's march north of Pioneer Camp. At this point, Oatts felt obliged to tell Norman Kelly to warn the Chins in Haka to get out. Word soon came through from Rathbone that the Japanese were on the march from Mangkheng, so riders were sent out to bring in the Levies, evacuate Haka and move to the jungle camp on the way to Klangklang. The Japanese dropped leaflets on the inhabitants of Haka in Gurkhali so were obviously under the impression that, in the main, they were fighting Gurkhas rather than Chins. The officer from Pioneer Camp arrived in the middle of the night on 9 November to say that the Burma Rifles had run at the first shot and the Japanese were hard on their heels. This was bad news for Oatts because the Levies had not yet come in, and if the Japanese reached Haka before them, they would be cut off, and their British officers would be lucky to escape with their lives.

Oatts planned to ambush the Japanese as they came down the road from Pioneer Camp. To conserve his supplies and ammunition he had mules loaded and sent to Klangklang with an escort of Gurkhas, under the new British officer who had been asleep at his post on two occasions. To the astonishment of Oatts he still had his three mules, laden with his kit. Oatts commented, 'This made it at once apparent that, whether his platoon had run or not, he must have been a long way ahead of it.' Oatts had his kit unloaded and replaced with stores and ammunition, in spite of his protests. When the Jemedar of the Burma Rifles platoon arrived, with his men at half-strength and the worse for wear, he told Oatts that the Japanese had been seen at dusk on the march, and had immediately sent down word to the Sahib, who was asleep in the rest house. The Jemedar told him, 'The Sahib had immediately had his mules loaded and left without giving any orders.' [34] The platoon had engaged the Japanese and ambushed them on the road on two or three occasions. Eight of his men had been killed and one of his section was missing. The Jemedar and several of his men were wounded.

Rathbone and Ian Hillis (a young Scot from a Glasgow shipping office and another first-class officer) ran into the head of the Japanese column as it approached within a few hundred yards of the jungle camp on the Klangklang road. Braund came in alone. His Levies had left him as soon as he reached Haka, saying that they would have to go and see to the safety of their families. The Hakas with Hillis had put up a spirited attack against the Japanese, but departed after the action to return to their villages. Rathbone had thirty Zahows with him when he arrived and, meanwhile, Oatts was waiting for Reese to rejoin him. Reese was held in great respect by his Hakas for his valour in action, and it was hoped that they might stay with him.

On 11 November the Japanese arrived in Haka just before dusk. They had been knocked about by the Zahows and Hakas under Rathbone and

Hillis, and had left the road and made a wide detour, thus bypassing the Gurkhas at the road junction. When they reached Haka, their discipline broke; they could be heard singing and shouting and wandering about as if they were all drunk.

Just after nightfall, Dick Reese came over the hill with 100 Levies and walked straight in amongst them. He did not realise that Haka was in enemy hands. The Japanese received another 'bloody nose'. Some were having a party and singsong round the piano in the rest house when the Levies caught up with them; they were all killed to a man. Unfortunately, the Hakas soon realised the situation and gradually pulled out and went home, leaving Reese alone. He joined Oatts at daybreak when the Gurkhas went into action at the road junction as the Japanese came down the Klangklang road.[35]

11. On the Run after the Fall of Falam and Haka, 1943

Chapter 10

ON THE RUN

Norman Kelly was with Lieutenant-Colonel Oatts as they headed for the narrow mountain stream that ran across open country about 6 miles from Klangklang. The wounded had been sent on ahead on mules and ponies as the rearguard action raged along the road. The Japanese were in an ugly mood and everybody was rapidly approaching exhaustion, while the walking wounded slowed the withdrawal. Norman spent the night of 11 November at Nengrang, a small village near the Cwal Va stream (see map no. 11 opposite). The following day he and Oatts rode on to Klangklang to try to get their supplies moved to Salen, the next village to the south, before the Japanese caught up with them. There were only the Gurkhas and Zahows left, all told about 100 men, but it was hoped that later the Hakas could be persuaded to rejoin.

Klangklang was a very large village, which could not be defended. It lay in the middle of an open plain bordered by hills on all sides. The chief was away; he had not offered any assistance to the British since the start of the campaign and his men had not joined the Levies. Norman went off to find porters for moving the supplies while Oatts went looking for the headman, who was found in his garden making *zu*. He gave Oatts a glass but would not speak and made emphatic gestures to ensure that the lieutenant-colonel should not speak either. All the women and children had left the village and the men were fighting drunk. Pandemonium broke out in the village as the Hakas began looting the supply dump; they were swarming all over it like ants. Norman, while endeavouring to persuade the elders to provide porters, had also been plied with *zu*, as was the Chin custom, and by this time was himself the worse for wear!

The wounded were in a small hospital on the outskirts of the village under the care of an Indian doctor and a nurse. Oatts was approaching the ridge to watch the road from Haka, when he heard heavy mortar fire coming from that direction. Braund had been involved in the rearguard action. Just as he reached the top of the ridge the other Indian doctor, who had been with Braund, came marching along in great haste. He said the Japanese had rushed Braund's bivouac and killed everybody, including Braund. If true, this would have been devastating news. The doctor was sent off to join his colleague with the wounded. Oatts hid his horse in the jungle and sat down to watch the road.

The first to appear was a large wounded Gurkha, hobbling along with the help of two sticks. He was covered in blood and wounds, and was in a very bad temper. He said they had bivouacked in a rotten position and been overrun in the dark while they were asleep. Although some of his comrades had been killed while still asleep the others, when properly awake, had soon got the Japanese on the run. Oatts' orderly then arrived, to say that the new officer was nowhere to be found. The section that he was supposed to be in charge of had not seen him since it had left Haka. More wounded arrived and then the whole party, with Braund looking very much in the position of honour, in the rear. He had been obliged to halt because of exhaustion and the sick and wounded.

Braund had put six sentries out around the bivouac the night before but the Japanese had found them in the dark because the ill-trained native troops had the habit of clearing their throats, as many sentries did, to while away the hours of darkness. Fortunately, the Japanese put in a set-piece attack, after a mortar bombardment, which woke up everybody. The Gurkhas were waiting for them with their *kukris* out. The Japanese lost thirty men in this encounter, all chopped by *kukris*. The Zahows were unwilling to go south to Salen, so they were sent to escort the badly wounded and the most critically ill across the Indian frontier into the Lushai Hills.

On 13 November Norman went to Thlualam, where there was a rest house near the village, and tried to get porters to help move the stores from Klangklang to Salen. The following day he marched south to Vambai, crossing the Sipi Va stream on the way. He was not as well known in these parts as he was in the Tiddim and Falam areas. The hostile Klangklang chief, who had not joined the Levy cause, made it imperative to keep on the move. It only took one informer in a village to tell the Japanese of his whereabouts. On the night of 14/15 November the enemy had entered Klangklang, and on 15 November Norman arrived at Salen.

In the interim Lieutenant-Colonel Oatts had met up with a 'cloak-and-dagger boy', the term used for 'The Johnnies', later to be described by Lieutenant-General Sir Geoffrey Evans in his book of the same name. They were part of Z Force, whose job it was to live in enemy territory and send back information by powerful radio transmitters to 4 Corps in India. The most famous of them was Major Sammy Newland, who had been born in Haka in 1900, the son of a Chin mother and Surgeon-Captain Arthur Newland, formerly of the Indian Medical Service, who had served in the Chin Hills in 1891–92 and written *The Image of War or Service on the Chin Hills* (1894). His grandfather had been Chun Kai, a well-known Chin chief. Sammy was the only son. In *The Johnnies* Evans wrote:

Arthur Newland was the most loved and respected Englishman ever to have been in the Chin Hills, and in return he loved and respected its people. This affection and respect was also enjoyed by his son as he grew up, and was amply demonstrated when he was hunted by the Japanese forty-two years later.[1]

Sammy Newland had left Calcutta with Captain D. W. Rae in the first week of August 1943 and had arrived in Haka some time later.

It was poetic justice that Newland should appear out of the jungle, to the great surprise of Lieutenant-Colonel Oatts, and he handed Oatts a sheaf of signals from 4 Corps. The Levy wireless set had been out of action for some days, because one of the three mules carrying it had fallen over a cliff. Since 4 Corps could not contact Oatts they had tried the cloak-and-dagger network. The signal read: 'Imperative you report the military situation immediately'. Oatts recalled that he

> was now without a horse to do a bunk on, having had to put one of the wounded on him, and so hesitated for a moment before sitting down to compose a situation report with nothing between me and the Japs a mile away. However, I did not like to ignore so urgent a signal and accordingly wrote out a reply in haste. Reading it through made me realise the scrape I was in and so added a request for an air strike along the Klangklang/Haka road, and also an airdrop of ammunition, food and medical supplies at Salen.
>
> The 'cloak-and-dagger boy' encoded it and sent it off in a highly efficient and speedy manner, after which we hastily set out for Salen.
>
> Scarcely had we marched an hour from Klangklang, than with shattering roars a large number of aircraft appeared and swept low up the Haka road, dropping bombs and shooting off cannon. It impressed both the Chins and the Japs, and certainly saved my bacon.[2]

The result of the airdrop at Salen was not so happy. The supplies of rations were most welcome but, although strips had been put out on a small open space outside the village and with great skill the pilot had placed the drop upon it, unfortunately, as Oatts said: 'Nevertheless, I had made a mistake in asking for a drop, for the aircraft gave away our position to the Japs. Worse than that, it clearly indicated my intention of soldiering on from further south.' [3]

Salen was deserted; all the villagers had taken to the jungle. Just after Oatts arrived he received a message from 'Jamie' James with a report that the Zokhua Hakas were leaving the battle and that the villagers had looted his dump and made off. 'Jamie' James, formerly of the Bombay-Burmah Trading Corporation (Bombine), had been involved earlier in 1943 when the Japanese had advanced from Kan in the Gangaw Valley into the Chin Hills towards Haka, in his zone. Initially they had a screen of press-ganged villagers. He withdrew with his Levies to Shimpi, the village immediately to his rear, when the Japanese opened up with mortars (see map no. 3 on p. 28). Here he was attacked again, but withdrew to 40 miles from Haka, to a strong defensive position. Once again the enemy attacked, but sustained some 50 casualties. Both Oatts and Kelly must have realised that it was impossible to carry on guerrilla warfare without the help of the local inhabitants. The 'Jamie' James messenger had reported that all the villages along his route were deserted.

Salen was situated on high ground and surrounded by dense forest, through which the road from Klangklang wound up the hill. It was not a good place in which to be attacked, even if the Chin Levies had remained in the field. There were just about 60 Gurkhas who were fit and approximately 20 sick and wounded. They could only move slowly and many needed assistance. Pat Rathbone was the most seriously ill. He was now a stretcher case, with double pneumonia. The nights were bitterly cold and Captain Bryan Watt-Smyth had phlebitis (see photograph no. 24).

Everybody was too exhausted to leave on 15 November, so they had to stay the night. There was a half-moon riding high up in a clear sky – just the sort of night for the Japanese to be on the march. From the rest house, every leaf on the upper branches of the huge trees surrounding it was plainly visible. Beneath was a pattern of shade and light, across which led numerous jungle paths and the narrow road from Klangklang. It was a foreboding sight. Oatts went to inspect the sentries, knowing full well that the enemy might arrive at any moment. There was an unusually large proportion of British officers, most of whom had been fighting on their own for weeks under a very considerable strain. Danger did not worry them; they had lived with it for so long. The men were now a small body, under the personal command of Oatts.

At dawn a dozen Levies came in. They had been with Dick Reese and were from Haka. They were ashamed of leaving him but said they would stand by the British from then on. They reported that the Japanese were in Klangklang and so plans were made to leave at once. The airdrop was loaded up on to the mules and what could not be carried was hidden. While this was going on, a messenger from 'Jamie' James appeared to report that the Japanese had arrived in his area and that most of his men had left to look after their families.

The plan was to make for the Indian border. There was only one direction to go, and that was south, to avoid the enemy. The Boinu River ran along the frontier with the Lushai Hills, but along the Chin side of it was a belt of impenetrable jungle. There was only one path through it to the river, from Zephai, and that was many days' march ahead. The party was in a tricky and dangerous situation. Reese and Ian Hillis were left behind in Salen, with orders to keep a day's march behind, and to inform on the enemy's movements to the rear. They had only their orderlies with them, so that they would not get involved in a fight.

The new officer, who had been asleep at Pioneer Camp rest house instead of watching the road to Klangklang, needed to be got rid of. He was sent with a section of Gurkhas to block one of the flank approaches from Zokhua. The Gurkha Naik (corporal) would fight to the bitter end, even if the new officer did a bunk – the very sight of this officer infuriated Oatts.

On 16 November the first day's march finished at Vamkua, after the Vakhawng Va stream had been crossed. It was a very anxious time, for the country they were passing through was rough and mountainous. The sick and wounded could only move slowly and with difficulty. Bad news came from Reese and Hillis – that the Japanese were following up. The next night was spent camping by the La-aw Va stream. In order to shake off the pursuing Japanese the next day's march was over 30 miles, with only a few short halts. Pat Rathbone was still being carried on an improvised stretcher, which the British officers took their turn to bear. He was being treated with sulphonamide tablets, prescribed by the Indian doctor.

'What will happen if you stop the M & B?

'Why then, of course, sah,' the doctor replied blandly, 'he die of the disease.'[4]

Fortunately, Rathbone had no intention of making a rapid exit. His spirit was remarkable, and he fully intended to wed his lady and live happily ever after. 'Once or twice one of the stretcher-bearers stumbled and he was flung out of the stretcher down the mountain-side. Physically quite helpless, he was unable on these occasions to do anything but swear, which he did in the most hearty and fluent manner.'[5]

At last Vuangtu was reached on 18 November. The village was deserted, but while the mules were being unloaded, mortar bombs began to rain down. Oatts ran across the empty square shouting orders, feeling that this was indeed the end, when he caught sight of Rathbone lying on the veranda of a house. Oblivious of the Japanese, mortar bombs and double pneumonia, he was reading a paperback with the title *Death Tolls the Gong*. His powers of detachment were indeed astonishing!

The expected attack never came. There must have been a patrol of the enemy from as far afield as Zokhua or Shurkhua who were too few in number to press home their advantage (see map no. 3 on p. 28). Sammy Newland and his detachment were still there, and would appear mysteriously with wireless signals, one being congratulations for the stout defence of Haka, which had greatly helped military operations. Instructions were given to keep the Superintendent of the southern Lushai Hills informed of the situation. Norman Kelly knew that his colleague to the north at Aijal, Major Anthony McCall, who had planned the defence of the Lushai Hills, must have known that Norman was with the party, and had sent word to Betty in Naini Tal.

Another airdrop was called for but in the dense forest it was not possible to put out dropping strips. A Dakota constantly followed them, but was unable to effect a drop, and the height of the mountains through which the jungle track passed increased the pilot's problems. The shortage of food was disagreeable, and was compounded because the plane also gave away their position. It was bitterly cold at night and the few blankets that were available were given to the casualties. One night Oatts discovered he was marked out for preferential treatment. He awoke to find the fierce, savage face of a Haka kneeling beside him, as he softly tucked a blanket round his shoulders. It was gone in the morning, before he awoke, in case Oatts should object.

They passed the flank road from the east, up which the new officer had been sent to lay an ambush for the Japanese. As Oatts half expected, when he went to call him in, he was not there. He eventually caught up with him at Hriphi, which was the first inhabited village, cooking himself a chicken! He was put under arrest and was later sent packing with a report on his behaviour. The Gurkha section, which had been under his command, had remained at their post on the road, and were in the ambush position. They had not seen any Japanese.

On 19 November Zephai was reached. The quartermaster and Norman Kelly had been sent on ahead and had managed to attract the attention of the pilot of the Dakota, who made a drop near the village. His note read: 'Please put out dropping strips next time, good luck.' Little did he know that the dropping strips had been left behind in Salen. Unfortunately the enemy had seen the drop in progress, and during an enormous meal on the veranda of the rest house, Braund rushed up to say that Reese and Hillis had just arrived, half a jump ahead of the Japanese. This was a very serious situation. Everybody was exhausted, but if it ended in a shoot-out they would not be able to get the sick and wounded out of Zephai. The Gurkhas were sent out to cover the withdrawal while the mules were being loaded.

The headman provided guides to the track through the jungle to the Boinu River, which had not been used for many years and was overgrown. It began about a mile from the village, and was covered in undergrowth and fallen trees. Oatts went back to call in the Gurkhas, who had not seen any Japanese. Zephai was empty; the villagers had decamped. When he returned to the head of the column, he found to his dismay that the guides had also disappeared. By now it was pitch dark inside the forest and impossible to distinguish the track. There was no option but to continue, and with the aid of a torch they began to cut their own path. During the night Oatts got lost and passed out with exhaustion. He was revived by two Chin women, with a gourd, who splashed water on his face and with great care poured it from a ladle into his mouth. He then went off to sleep, and when he awoke dawn was breaking.

Oatts went down the path to find that the Gurkhas had cleared a way through the thick bamboo with their *kukris*, and found himself on the banks of the Boinu River. The whole column was swimming about in it, men, mules and horses. It was about 75 yards across and fordable at this point – beyond lay the Lushai Hills and a well-defined path. While the column was making its way slowly up the steep trail into the Lushai Hills, Oatts took a swim. At the same time as the Indian doctor was painfully removing ticks from Oatts' naked body with tweezers, there was a devastating roar as Japanese planes climbed in a steep bank over their heads. They had dropped their bombs into the jungle on the Chin side of the river.

Oatts then came under fire from the enemy in the jungle on the opposite bank. He froze for a moment, then grabbed his trousers and sprinted for cover. Although he avoided the bullets, as he reached the undergrowth he was stung on the back of the neck by a hornet. He thought he had been hit as it felt like a red-hot poker – the sting was an inch long. The Japanese did not follow after chasing the party into India.

On 21 November the British and Gurkhas, fit and wounded, were in Alnak, and the next day in the village of Tuisih, 16 miles away. They arrived at Tuipang to a civic reception on the 23rd. A red banner was stretched across the entrance to the village, proclaiming 'Welcome dear Colonel'. The headman and elders had organised two girls to bestow a garland round Oatts' neck, along with much giggling. More girls were drawn up as a guard of honour, which he duly inspected. The headman made a speech in English. The Lushais, he said, had watched with the greatest admiration the gallant fight that the Chins were putting up against the Japanese and to which they, the Lushais, owed their safety.

The Lushais in Tuipang were very well informed about the plight of Lieutenant-Colonel Oatts' party. Edgar Hyde (ICS), the Superintendent of the southern Lushai Hills in Lungleh, who had heard the news from 4 Corps via Newland, had sent out Lushai scouts to patrol the marches. There they met the first party of wounded, sent from Klangklang, and took them to Lungleh (see map no. 3 on p. 28). Hence McCall also had a very clear picture of what was going on and what to expect. He knew Oatts' name and must have also known that Norman Kelly was still with him. According to Norman's diary the party were in Tuipang from 23 November to 1 December. It must have been a great relief to reach safety and the support of the Lushai Hills civil administration after the ordeal of jungle marches and attacks by the Japanese. They were all in very poor shape, with torn and bedraggled uniforms, arms and equipment, possessing nothing but what they stood up in.

The sick and wounded were taken care of by the mission. After all those days of danger, and at times near-starvation, to have regular meals and the security of a safe bed must have been enormously welcome. The mission itself was set in a clearing in the forest. It looked like a piece of old England, with lawns and clipped hedges, an adjoining home farm and cattle. The missionary was unable to leave his bed and was dying of old age, but his spirit was indomitable. He was still working on a Lushai dictionary, hoping to complete it before he passed away. He had the enterprise to have obtained a printing press from England, on which he produced Bibles for sale at a nominal figure. He had to put up the price because he could not keep up with the demand. He was delighted, until he discovered that the Lushais were using them to make cigarettes with! 'The rogues were smoking 'em!' he roared, with a twinkle in his eye. He had come to this remote spot of the British Empire 50 years previously when the Lushais, like the Chins, were pagan headhunters. Now he lived with his wife, daughter, son-in-law and granddaughter. He had only been back to England once in all that time, for his daughter's wedding. His son-in-law would take over after he died.

There was no place for an airdrop in the dense jungle surrounding the village of Tuipang: because of the mountain-tops, there was no room for a Dakota to circle, and no dropping strips to guide the pilot. After an apologetic signal had been sent, a plane appeared, the pilot of which put in an astounding performance. After a preliminary look he disappeared out of sight and then made a long run in at a height of what appeared to be only a few feet and put down the drop so neatly that, when complete, it appeared as if it had been stacked by hand. There were complete sets of kit for the officers and many 'comforts', such as hand-knitted pullovers and so on. The luxury of a bath, shave and clean clothes must have done wonders for morale.[6] Then 'Jamie' James arrived with his 30 Zokhua Hakas to report that the Japanese were still on the Boinu as well as all over the Haka area, where all the villagers had fled into the jungle.

The casualties were making good progress, especially Pat Rathbone, and were now ready to take to the road again. On 1 December Oatts set out with his column for Lungleh to the north. They were divided into small groups so as not to overstrain the accommodation facilities in the intermediate villages. Norman Kelly was with them, but his destination was different. He wanted to make his way back to Tiddim, but dared not recross the Boinu, back into the Chin Hills, until he got to the north of the Japanese.

Oatts and Kelly headed off together on the first leg of the journey and by 5 December had reached Sangau, marching about 14 miles a day. They rested for a day there, before parting company. When Oatts reached Lungleh, he and Rathbone stayed with Hyde, before Rathbone was sent out on sick leave to India and Oatts later returned to the Chin Hills to join Jack Haswell. Norman Kelly crossed the Boinu River on 7 December on his way to Bungklang back in the Chin Hills. He continued to head north-east, until he was at Lungding, due west of Falam, on 11 December. When he eventually got back to Tiddim it was to find that

41. Major Peter Bankes MC.
(Photograph courtesy of
Prue Brewis, formerly Bankes)

42. Major David Milligan
(Photograph courtesy of his
sister, Alison Anne Whiting)

43. *Gurkha commandos overlooking Japanese territory from Basha Hill above No. 3 Stockade; they could see the enemy's movements in Kalemyo. It was on this hill that Gaje Ghale won his VC a few days after the artist's visit in May 1943.*
(Drawing by Anthony Gross, courtesy of the Imperial War Museum, London)

44. *Milestone 26 on the Tiddim–Kalemyo Road, where the road had collapsed beneath a tank of C Squadron, 3rd Carabiniers (Prince of Wales's Dragoon Guards) on 11 November 1944, and Trooper Eric ('Dickie') Bird had been killed. The sepoy was on guard to ensure that the following tank did not fall over the cliff with its 1,000-foot drop.*
(Photograph courtesy of Bernard Bird, Eric's brother)

45. Panoramic drawing showing Tiddim, the Imphal plain, Tamu in the Kabaw Valley and, in the north, Kohima and the railhead at Dimapur. (Courtesy of Dr Trevor Williams, son of 'Elephant Bill')

46. Above: *Two bombs fall away from under the wings of a Hurribomber as it attacks a bridge on the Tiddim Road, already hit by a previous Hurribomber (an adapted Hurricane MkII).*
(Photograph courtesy of the Imperial War Museum, London)

47. Opposite above:
The Kelly family reunited on the steps of Brookhill House, Naini Tal, in September 1944. Maeve and Desmond were pupils at the Hallett War School, where their mother Betty was teaching. Lieutenant-Colonel Norman Kelly of the Burma Frontier Service was on one of his rare short leaves from his very successful subversive activities behind Japanese lines in Burma.

48. Opposite below:
Maeve and Desmond with Norman, and Naini Tal Lake in the background.

47

48

49. *Supply train mules were liable to panic at the sight of the fast-flowing Manipur River, so here they are crossing on a specially camouflaged ferry.* (Photograph courtesy of the Imperial War Museum, London)

50. *Indian troops crossing the Manipur River in pontoon ferries. The bridge was blown by the Japanese as they retreated further into Burma before the advance of the 5th Indian Division.* (Photograph courtesy of the Imperial War Museum, London)

51. *Jeeps of the 5th Indian Division bringing essential supplies through the thick mud of the Tiddim Road.*
(Photograph courtesy of the Imperial War Museum, London)

52. *A view of the 'Chocolate Staircase' on a dry day, showing some of its thirty-eight hairpin bends as it climbs 3,000 feet in 4 miles before it drops down to Tiddim.*
(Photograph courtesy of the Imperial War Museum, London)

53. *Indian sappers clearing the road to Tiddim of mines. The one on the left is starting to remove a mine.* (Photograph courtesy of the Imperial War Museum, London)

54. *A captured Japanese bunker in the hills overlooking Tiddim.* (Photograph courtesy of the Imperial War Museum, London)

Fort White was occupied by the Japanese, and that the whole of the 17th Indian Division was in the Tiddim zone. They had brought their field artillery with them up the Tiddim Road. Tiddim had been bombed by the Japanese on 28 November. The headman, Pau Za Kam, and postmaster, Ohn Pe, stayed behind but the wives and children were evacuated to the nearby village of Gawngmual. The 17th Indian Division had set up headquarters several miles away from Tiddim to avoid it being bombed.

Norman had to come to terms with the fact that Peter Bankes had been killed on 28 November on the forward slopes of the Suanglangsu Vum near Lamtong (see map no. 6 on p. 74). He had been the first Levy officer to work with Norman, joining him on 18 April 1942. Both Norman and General 'Punch' Cowan held him in the highest regard. Peter did not live long enough to see his son. Nor did Peter know that his brilliant raid on Nansaungpu (see map 4 on p. 38) had won him the Military Cross 'For Gallant and Distinguished Services in Burma and on the Eastern Frontier of India 21 May 1942 to 20 June 1943'. Jack Oats had also had a tragic accident while on leave in Shillong. He was at a party to celebrate the Gurkha's fifth VC. He wanted to drive the jeep home himself, but was overruled. On the way the driver lost control on a bend, the vehicle went down the mountainside and landed on Jack's back, damaging his spinal cord. He lost the use of his legs for the rest of his life.

Stevenson in Trouble and General Slim's Involvement

Norman Kelly was unaware that the 4 Corps Commander, General G. A. P. Scoones, was so incensed by a report sent to him by Stevenson on 9 November 1943 that he wanted Stevenson replaced. The Deputy Chief Civil Affairs Officer, Ralph Wilkie, wrote to his boss Major-General Pearce, CBE, Chief Civil Affairs Officer, Burma, at GHQ New Delhi, explaining the situation on 19 November 1943.

OFFICE OF THE D.C.C.A.O. (B) 14TH ARMY
12 Dalhousie Square East
CALCUTTA

SECRET
Reg. No. 526...Date 19th November 1943
No. F/43-3270

My dear General,

I wrote privately by Mackay about Stevenson. Yesterday morning I was given the file with a note that the Army Commander [Slim] wished me 'to have a successor found for Mr. Stevenson to report to 4 Corps'.

The main complaint of the Corps Commander was a signal sent by Stevenson on the 9th November 1943 addressed to 4 Corps, repeated [to] 63 Brigade in which the following sentences occurred.

'Pt. I. Your view of situation NOT mine. Jap move against Falam was designed to empty area of troops. It succeeded. Next move was to swing round bottom of 63 Brigade positions and up West Bank of Manipur River relying on your tenacious determination not to move south. That looks like succeeding.

Pt. II. Even Chins realize your position and pray for originality and bold support of forward screens.

Pt. III. Only 2 platoons of [Chin Hills] battalion any use now. I insist you put one regular company 32 Chins [in] this area volunteer every weapon in field for offensive effort.

The Corps Commander said he saw no object in sending a strong rebuke and the signals he sent disregarded the rude tone of this one. They merely contained instructions, suggestions and views. His whole reply was, I must say very reasonable. He had sent Naylor up to see how things were going and he wrote 'The removal of Stevenson at this juncture would probably do more harm than good' and in any case he wanted to wait for Naylor's return before reaching a decision on the immediate issue. He ended up 'I must however request that a relief for Mr. Stevenson should be found and that he should be sent forward to Corps H.Q. to relieve Stevenson when the situation permits and relief is deemed necessary.'

Apparently a minor complaint was that Stevenson had 'assumed military command of the forces west of the Manipur River'. No stress has been laid on this and I fancy it must have been because no other officer was available. Stevenson is still in mufti of course [i.e. not a professional soldier].

After reading the files I went to see General Slim. I told him there were no officers not already in the Hills who knew the District and that if Stevenson comes out Kelly must take over and that he is out in the blue somewhere with the Levies.

He said he did not want to bring Stevenson out now, that by all accounts including reports from General Scoones Stevenson was doing excellent work rallying the Chins and keeping things going (incidentally it looks as if once more our Civil W/T [wireless] sets are the only or almost only means of communication).

I said that Stevenson was in his element in such circumstances, had a great hold on the people and was full of guts and go. He said that so he gathered and it was a pity to have to take such people away and he hoped I would – as he was sure I had – impressed on our officers that nothing was to be gained by sending rude signals and that even if we did so in peacetime now that we [civilians] are all mixed up with the Army we should try and conform to their ways and rules.

Finally he asked me to write personally to Stevenson and suggest that he should write and apologize to General Scoones about the signals saying he appreciated that General Scoones had to take other factors into consideration; whilst he himself asked General Scoones to go tenderly with Stevenson for a bit. When things have settled down Stevenson should come out to have a rest and if wanted elsewhere – (I mentioned he was earmarked for the other side [of Burma] eventually) – that could be arranged. In the meantime leave things as they are. I have written to Stevenson accordingly and hope he will produce a decently repentant letter to mollify General Scoones.

Please let me know if you agree that if or when Stevenson eventually comes out Kelly should take over. I cannot think of anybody else at all. If an Additional Deputy Commissioner is required [as Norman Kelly's replacement] then Franklin is quite fit for it. I am sure that Naylor would agree with both points but I have not written to him about it yet as General Slim asked me to write Stevenson a personal letter.

Yours sincerely,

R. S. Wilkie

P.S. I attach a copy of the note which I have placed in the Army H.Q. File on the subject.

When I showed this to the senior staff officer – G.1.(O) – he said would I please make sure from you that Kelly is earmarked as Stevenson's eventual successor.

I saw the Army Commander about this and he asked me to write to Mr. Stevenson. I am doing so. I am also writing to the C.C.A.O. The obvious successor to Mr. Stevenson eventually when things are quiet and he can be relieved, is Major Kelly who is already Additional Deputy Commissioner and believed to be out somewhere with the Haka or Falam Levies in the southern part of the District. [7]

On 19 November, when the above was written, Norman Kelly was at Zephai. Naylor agreed that Kelly was 'the obvious successor to Stevenson'. A signal marked 'Secret', dated 23 November 1943, was sent to the Deputy Chief Civil Affairs Officer, Fourteenth Army, by Major-General C. F. B. Pearce, Chief Civil Affairs Officer:

My dear Wilkie,

I confirm your proposal that Kelly should take over the Chin Hills if Stevenson comes out.

I hope your letter to Stevenson will bear fruit, but I am not sure of it. The terms of Stevenson's signal to the Corps Commander however were obviously improper and, what is worse, most unlikely to achieve the effect desired.

Yours sincerely,

Major-General C. F. B. Pearce [8]

The Replacement of Stevenson by Kelly

Major Norman Kelly met General 'Punch' Cowan, Commanding Officer, 17th Indian Division, at Tiddim on 20 December 1943;

Lieutenant-Colonel Stevenson, DC, Chin Hills, was present and the organisation of the Tiddim Levies and guerrilla activities were discussed. Tiddim was the headquarters of the 17th Division at that time, and the meeting was called by General Scoones, the 4 Corps Commander. He directed that the existing Levy force in the Tiddim zone should be reduced from 600 to 500 picked men. They would be used in a true guerrilla role under selected leaders. Major Kelly was directed to put up recommendations on these lines to General Cowan for his approval. The arms in the possession of Levies who would be 'stood down' under this system would be withdrawn and form a reserve in the area for arming other guerrilla parties as and when required. General Scoones pointed out 'that orders had been received for Major Kelly to relieve Lt. Col. Stevenson and that the latter was to proceed on recess for health reasons. Both Lt. Col. Stevenson and Major Kelly stressed the importance of Lt. Col. Stevenson remaining to carry out those duties in the Lumbang–Falam area, as he was the only officer who was known in this area in whom the local people had real confidence.' [9] But Stevenson's plans were fraught with danger. Brigadier L. B. Naylor had written a confidential letter to 4 Corps on 17 December 1943, recommending that guerrilla activity around Lumbang should be 'damped down until both Fort White and Bamboo Camp are reoccupied by us. Such activity, prior to the reoccupation of the places mentioned, will probably lead to the burning of villages and other reprisals by the enemy which we are not in a position to prevent.' [10]

Stevenson appealed to the Commander of 4 Corps to be allowed to carry on with his plans for a month. 'Much as I value Lt. Col. Stevenson's work in this particular field, I am unable to grant this request without a satisfactory medical report', Scoones continued. (This was to be carried out on 20 December.) 'If that is not satisfactory, he must be relieved at once and we must be satisfied with a less ambitious programme.' [11]

Lieutenant-Colonel Stevenson was far from fit. He was suffering from stomach trouble and insomnia. L. B. Naylor reported on 17 December: 'I consider that in his present condition the strain imposed by his present work will lead to a breakdown and that therefore he should come out on leave.' In the same letter he said Major Kelly 'should make his H.Q. at Tiddim and co-ordinate such activities as the situation permits. It is proposed that he will remain in the Chin Hills as Deputy Commissioner after the Army has moved forward.' [12]

The attack on Falam and Haka was the subject of an informative report by Captain Rae. He was a junior Forest Officer, recruited by Sammy Newland to be his partner in Z Force, the intelligence-gathering organisation. Their task was to organise an intelligence network in the Gangaw Valley, south of Kalemyo. They had left Calcutta in the first week of August 1943 and arrived at Haka towards the end of September, having been delayed in the Lushai Hills because of lack of coolies.

MOST SECRET

The Japanese advance and its effect on the Chin population of Haka and Falam
by Captain D. W. Rae

The Advance

The Japanese plan was to push through to Falam and hence to drive a wedge between the Tiddim and Haka areas [see map no. 10 on p. 192]. When the attack on Falam began, the Japanese had a force of about 500 men with mortars and a mountain gun. These weapons were carried by Japs with coolies carrying rations. This force crossed the Pao Va in two columns, one heading for Tawk. Our positions at Tawk and Haitar were overrun. It was here that the enemy used his mountain gun 'with devastating effect on the morale of the defenders'. Near Lente the gun was again brought into action. With the occupation of the Lente Ridge by the enemy, the evacuation of Falam commenced.

Falam was occupied by about 10th November, the enemy having taken a month to reach his objective. This delay was due to: a) difficult terrain; b) supply and transport problems; c) attacks by the RAF; and d) the harassing of their lines of communication.

Haka

On 12th November, a large force of enemy entered Haka in two columns, one through the village of Hniarlawn and the other along the main Falam road. The enemy then occupied the ridge east of Klangklang and dug in on either side of the pass.

The Japanese expected to find large quantities of supplies in Haka. These had been given away to the local villagers and the Chins were intimidated into returning what the Japanese called the 'reward of the victors'. A fair amount of rice was found.

Up to the last the Hakas were confident of the Government's ability to defend the Hills. Even after the Japanese occupation the average Chin was loyal to the Government that 'had ruled him for 50 years, but he was not prepared to risk his life to help it'.

The hurried withdrawal of our forces from the South Chin Hills and the consequent collapse of the Administration, left most of the Chin Chiefs in a state of complete bewilderment and inclined to panic. The less courageous and those close to the town decided to go to Haka and pay allegiance to the invader in the interests of their villagers. To most of them it was merely lip service as Major Newland, who is well-known and respected in this area, used to receive letters containing full accounts of what they saw in Haka and what supplies the Japanese were receiving and from where.

There were a few exceptions, notably Kar Khoom of Haka and Ma Thio of Klangklang, who went over completely to the Japs.

By mid-December, the Hakas, most of whom had left their villages and were living in camps in the nearby jungle, were completely disgusted with the Jap and his oppressive measures. A considerable number started to move west in small groups, partly to evade the Japanese press gangs, and partly to save what little grain they had left from falling into enemy hands. This movement continued to grow and by the end of January all those, who were able to evacuate, had done so. Clerks and other Government servants joined the civil officers, and a large number of Levies, both ex-Burma Riflemen and 'A Levies' (villagers) reported for duty. Captain Cozens, the Levy officer in the Naring–Lungngo area further south, had collected sufficient food for 2½ months [see map no. 3 on p. 28]. This force kept law and order, passed back valuable intelligence and maintained the prestige of Government.[13]

A secret report was sent to 4 Corps by Major John Franklin, now the Civil Affairs Officer of the 17th Division:

Falam

In Falam, Van Hmung, the Tashon Chief, was appointed 'Commissioner' with his son Sai Luai to assist him, while Shiah Luai, the late Assistant Inspector of Schools, appears to have been given command of the Levies being raised by the Japs. Van Hmung appears to have taken over the Lumbang tract on January 25th. He has been having a house registration made. He has been trying to collect the arms previously held by the old Home Guards: without success as those that did not come in to Tiddim have hidden them, though he collected some Chin flint-locks. The Lumbang tract has been ordered to provide 35 men for the new Levies as well as coolies.

Feelings against the Tashons are running very high among the Lumbangs though it is unlikely to develop on account of the savage practices of Van Hmung and his Jap Masters. Persons who did not readily obey him were beaten and those denounced by him to the Japs, killed. Five people are reported as having been put to death at Falam including ex-Subedar Major That Dun, whose end was particularly brutal. Three of the others reported are from Tlortang and a fifth, a Haka sepoy named Hra Kung.

One of Van Hmung's daughters is said to be 'stenographer' to the senior Jap officer in Falam. [14]

David Milligan

While Norman had been on the run from the Japanese, David Milligan (whom he had first met in Tiddim on 5 October 1942) had been playing a most important role as second-in-command with the Chin Hills Battalion during the defence of Falam. He had been educated at Oxford where he had studied forestry and Burmese, and then joined the Burma Forestry Service before the war. He met Harold Braund at the Officer Cadet Training Unit in Maymyo. Norman had invited him to dinner when he first arrived in Tiddim before he was posted to No. 3 Stockade. Shortly after this he wrote to his girlfriend, Rachel Murray Kerr, in Kirkaldy, describing his route into the hills (which was similar to the one my mother, sister and I had taken out in May 1942). In his letters the loneliness and misery of the retreat, the awesome responsibility of command and his empathy with the Chins are clearly revealed. He also vividly described what it was like fighting the Japanese in the Chin Hills.

13th October 1942

c/o A. Scott & Co.
c/o Grindlays P.O. Box 93
Bombay

Dear Rachel

The fighting, if one can call it so, was not much fun, but it was not too bad. One was frightened and hungry, over-fed and cheerful almost alternatively. I was alone for most of the time with a lot of troops under me and the strain, not only of being responsible for them, their deaths, and their troubles with their wives and families hundreds of miles away, but also of fighting for them, with brigadiers and divisional staffs, made one long at times for one companion.

They were so incredibly innocent of war. Not that I knew much, but films and books had given one a fairly good idea of everything except the feeling of being frightened to death. But these poor little beggars had not even that much warning. The first casualties I had were from bombs, and to see men, who were only children, looking for their dead brothers, brought the war home for the first time to them and to me. You must have had a lot of it now, but to me real fear, fear of being hurt or blown to bits, was the only new emotion that the war had to bring. Fear and perhaps hate, but with hate second. Everything else, even pity, one had felt before in some way. I suppose one owes that to the easy, kind way one had been brought up. It seems a pity that fear and hate had to be brought into oneself at all. If only they could be entirely excluded for one generation it might mean so much to human understanding and forgiveness. One got very fed up with marching and counter-marching, fed up with the heat, the lack of water, the no washing, the sleeping with one's boots on, and finally the marching and marching and marching and then the rain, cold, dysentery and malaria. It was all unpleasant, but nothing like as unpleasant as one can make it seem on paper. Just tiresome and boring. In a sense it was an adventure, but of the poorest sort. It was something new to be so tired that one simply lay down on the rock hard ground, unwashed, unblanketed, and slept like a log. It was no fun at all to be woken four hours later and to be told to get the men fallen in to march at once...

I had a short time in hospital in India. Feeling pretty grim I went off the train into hospital with a temperature of 105, the usual malaria start.

After a lot of incredible delays, mainly in Calcutta, which wasn't too bad, we got up into the hills, and had another wait. From then on things have been very enjoyable. Four delightful days drifting down a river [on the way to Aijal] in long, thin wooden boats, guided by dirty villagers, who hummed as they paddled. Nights camped under the stars looking up into the moon, from one's pillow listening to the ripple of the water. Days, lying in the bottom of the boat, one's hat tilted to keep out the hot sun, or playing casual chess between one's dozes. The river became too fast and rough for boats so we took to the hills. That meant waiting for coolies and four days of marching through driving rain, up one mountain side and down the next, through rivers and over them, slipping and falling on slippery paths and finally spending the night in some village, but cooking ones meal over a fire laid on the wooden floor while the smoke swirled into one's eyes and the rain beating hard on the roof overhead. But after four days that changed. The skies cleared, the sun blazed and one saw what beautiful country one was going through. In 13 days walking we only slept once below 5,000 feet and the last day but one the road crossed a peak [Kennedy] just below 9,000 feet, and we slept that night just below 8,000 feet. And the villagers have a charming habit of building great wide seats of flat grey stone slabs, where there were clearings in the pines. There was nothing pleasanter than to sit on these in the evening with a soft breeze whispering the needles, watching the sun set over the incredibly blue and vast mountains through which we had come.

So here I am. In a small grass, leaf and wood hut, a hurricane lantern on the table, one man asleep on either side of me, their white mosquito nets tucked around them. Two rifles leaning against the wall. The hill jungle outside full of night insects chittering, backed by the sound of the river still in flood down in the valley 4,000 feet below. It is just twelve o'clock, midnight. There is a chance that a runner might get in still with letters. But I don't think anybody knows where I am yet. It will be your birthday in a month. I haven't a present to send you. Only my love. Here it is.

      Love from David

            15th January 1943, somewhere in Burma

                        c/o A. Scott & Co.
                Gresham Assurance House
                    Mint Road, Bombay

Dear Rachel

I am a Lieutenant, but have been acting Captain for over a year. January is such a damnable month at home and here it is so lovely. At home it is after Christmas, and going back to school. Here, it is after the rains, no clouds in the sky, cool and sunny, fruit blossom and flowers! I wrote to you from a place 40 miles north from here, an hour's flight if a crow, two day's mountain walking if me…

I haven't got a camera but this picture torn from 'Victory' somebody sent me will show you what the country round here looks like. View from Chakrata, 'over the hills and far away'. Isn't it lovely! You must imagine that the trees are pine trees and that underneath are growing wild rhododendron bushes. They are covered with a mass of brilliant red flowers glowing in the afternoon sunshine. Far down in the valley below are bright green patches of fields, and beside them, the roofs throwing black shadows on the hard earth streets, are the brown thatched houses of the village. When the moon comes up tonight, as it glides serenely into the clear cold sky between the clouds, you will see the moonlight reflected on the mountain river as its icy water falls from pool to pool. If you hush your breathing you can hear the sound of its roar, 4,000 feet below. And as you focus your glasses on the moonlit village, you hope that the Japanese troops are not slipping in, to be waiting, hidden, when you go down on patrol in the morning.

It is a marvellous country. Behind that range of mountains lies range after range for a hundred miles. Each time you patrol into new country and each time you turn a new corner, each time your pony plunges onto a new crest, you get a thrill. I would keep on travelling round the world if I could follow mountains like these.

The sun is just sinking below the blue crest. I am in the shadow but the clouds resting on the peaks are lit to a golden pink. Lathum Gam, my orderly, has just lit my pinewood fire and the chill of 5,000 feet is making my hand stiff.

Good night and return me, Rachel, love for love,

> David

Camp
8th June 1943

My dear Rachel

How charming of you! You have sent me two airgraphs in the last fortnight. They have arrived here I mean like that. One today which I read drooling along the path on my pony. The pony likes you writing too. I can't read and whip him at the same time.

We are having a good deal of excitement here at the minute. The monsoon rains have really started, but the Jap is no gentleman and seems to enjoy fighting in a bathing suit. I spend most of my time – when not brooding rather bitterly on the infrequency of your letters – scrambling up and falling down precipices. You have no idea how exhausting. Then tottering home to bed, in what we call a *'chapper'*, a collection of sticks with some leaves on top and if you are a lucky chap, a tarpaulin to keep out the rain.

Keep yourself safe.
Very much love,

> David

On 30 October, David wrote another letter to Rachel, which was to prove his last.

30th October, 1943

Dear Rachel,

We are having rather a hectic, not to say tedious, time up here just now, thrashing and churning all over the place. Our C.O. got hit the other day (not too badly though) and I have got up to second in command temporarily...

> Love David
> Temporary Major
> Chin Hills Battalion[15]

Ten days after his last letter, David Milligan had been leading a company of the Chin Hills Battalion defending Falam when he was killed on 9 November near Mangkheng, a village 10 miles south-west of Falam. He was coming round a corner when he was hit in the chest with a burst of machine-gun fire. Kenny Fraser, the battalion Medical Officer, who described him as a very brave man, was there at the time. The Japanese buried him in a shallow grave. Later the Chins, who must also have had great respect for him, buried him beneath a memorial stone. He was only twenty-six.

Peter Bankes

Peter had not long returned from leave in October 1943 and in India had discussed with his wife Prue what would happen if he were killed. They were a devoted couple and were both serving in uniform. Peter was very friendly with Jack Oats and Sam Cope, who had dinner with Norman and David Milligan on 5 October 1942. Harold Braund thought Peter was an outstanding Levy officer.

Some of the Chins, who had been captured by the enemy during the retreat from Burma while serving with the Burma Rifles, were very well treated and indoctrinated before they were encouraged to return to their villages in the hills. A number of them were fairly loyal to the Allied cause but Jack Oats described others as treacherous and mutinous. Peter was on patrol with a group of Chins who were much less reliable than the loyal ones he was leading before his recess. Because of his good work and high reputation the Japanese had placed a price of 2000 rupees on his head – a very considerable sum in the Chin Hills in 1943. On 28 November Peter had found a man asleep on guard duty at night for the second time and was furious; he was taking him off to further reprimand him when the Chin shot him in the back of the head. Peter was buried above the village of Lamtong; the traitor returned to the Japanese to collect his reward. Jack Oats wrote to Prue from the British Military Hospital in Shillong on 17 December 1943:

c/o B.M.H.
Shillong
17/12/43

Dear Prue,

It is difficult to say anything to comfort you in your tragic loss of Peter. You will not be alone in your thought that the finest fellow on the frontier has gone. I think so and I know many officers in the 5 Royal Gurkhas who had worked with Peter who thought the world of him.

I met Peter during the past 18 months in some curious places (of which he must have told you something). I have memories of our various meetings and partings: Peter stripped to the waist in the hot weather blasting a road: Peter alone and coolness itself carrying a Tommy-gun and striding calmly forward to assist me in a battle: and again back from some patrol or other sitting down to great slabs of bread and jam or piles of rice and curry.

I am asking Mrs. Taylor to forward this. I wonder if there is any chance of you coming up here for a spell. I may leave here any time after mid-January for Poona and home probably by March or April. If I don't see you here we must meet in England.

Yours aye,

Jack Oats

An English newspaper printed the following tribute:

All who knew Peter Bankes found in him a wonderful character. One friend said in a letter, 'Peter was to my way of thinking one of the finest young men I have ever met both in mind and body. He is the sort that can so ill be spared; we need character like his so badly for the post-war world.

He was only 30 years of age when he was killed and it is sad to think that so useful a life and such a charming personality has been cut off in its prime. His young widow has been working with a mobile canteen [WAS(B)] for the troops in Assam since the fall of Burma.

Lieutenant-Colonel J. H. Williams, the author of *Elephant Bill*, also wrote to Prue:

c/o 4 Corps Headquarters
No.6 Advance Base Post Office
6th January 1944

Dear Prue,

I know Prue what you have lost my dear – everybody does – who knew Peter – and if it were ever true that war takes the flower of England's men – then it was never truer than when it took him. I share a tremendous pride in having been one of his friends, and one day we shall know that tragic as it all now seems, his death was not in vain. He capped that lovely docile nature of kindness to everybody and everything, by deeds of valour in his M.C., against the enemy of us all, and by God you can be proud of him as his son will be.

Yours,

Billy[16]

Peter's son (also called Peter) was born after his father's death. It was Prue Bankes who received Peter's posthumous Military Cross from King George VI in 1946. Over 50 years after her husband's death, on 19 August 1995, during the VJ 50th Anniversary march past down The Mall in London, Prue represented the Women's Auxiliary Service, Burma, and was a guest in the Royal Box outside Buckingham Palace. The Burma veterans of the Fourteenth Army were at last able to salute their monarch. Peter would have been deeply proud of her.

David Milligan and Peter Bankes epitomised so many young men who lost their lives in the Burma campaign. They were men of idealism, integrity, great courage and an empathy with the Chins, who would not have been able to give of their best had it not been for their outstanding leadership. They died for their country and what they believed in. The epitaph in the cemetery on Garrison Hill in Kohima sums up the tragic loss of life in its succinct and moving words:

> When you go home,
> Tell them of us and say,
> For your tomorrow,
> We gave our today.

Chapter 11

THE JAPANESE ADVANCE ON TIDDIM

> Sticking it out in Tiddim
> Living on biscuits and beef
> But how are the boys down in Delhi
> Still living up to their beliefs?
>
> Sticking it out at Kennedy
> Eight thousand up at the peak
> But what of the boys down in Poonah?
> It is said that their bath tubs now leak.

From *S.E.A.C.*, the Fourteenth Army newspaper

When South-East Asia Command (SEAC) was formed on 16 November 1943, the Central Front, which contained the Chin and Lushai Hills, was defended by 4 Corps with its headquarters at Imphal. It was commanded by General G. A. P. Scoones. The Chin Hills Battalion and the Chin Levies now became the responsibility of 4 Corps. General Slim was G.O.C.-in C. Fourteenth Army while General George Giffard commanded the Eleventh Army Group. In the winter of 1943–44 the 17th Indian Division had not succeeded in its plan of closing in around Kalemyo and displacing the invaders.

From November 1943 to February 1944 the Allies were making plans for a major offensive in the spring before the monsoon. One of the objectives was to clear the Chin Hills of the Japanese as far as the foothills south-east of Tiddim, but the Japanese attacked before the British could start to advance. Falam, 75 miles south of Tiddim by road, was captured on 7 November 1943. Webula, further south, had been occupied by another battalion of the 214th Regiment, which linked up with the Japanese garrison in Falam. Haka was entered by the Japanese on 11 November after they had captured Pioneer Camp 10 miles to the north.

Fort White

Soon after Falam and Haka fell, the Japanese 33rd Division increased its activity around Vownalu, Pimpi and Dolluang (see colour map no. 27). On the night of 12/13 November 1943 they attacked Point 6531 in the Vaona area as a diversion to their main objective, which was Fort White, not in itself defensible. It was dominated to both north and south by high ground – especially Point 8198. This overlooked Milestone 22 on the Tiddim–Kalemyo road, 4 miles south of Kennedy Peak and 2 miles north of Fort White. The Japanese knew that if they could capture this important feature they would control the tracks east, south and west of Fort White, including the Siyin Valley.[1] To achieve this objective they moved four 105mm guns (firing 33lb shells) and one 155mm gun (firing 80lb shells) up to No. 3 Stockade. The 1/10th Gurkha Rifles were on Kennedy Peak and the battalion of 1/16th Punjab Regiment, from 23rd Indian Infantry Division, were holding Point 8198. When Japanese guns opened up on the Punjabis on the night of 24/25 November, the colonel and three other British officers were killed by shellfire. The enemy then launched a two-battalion attack from both north and south. After several hours of desperate fighting, this attack succeeded and the survivors made their way back to Kennedy Peak via Laibung. The Japanese quickly made Point 8198 into an impregnable fortress, which they called 'Golden Peak'.[2] They had achieved their objective of finding a way over the Letha Range and down into the Manipur River valley via Fort White. These operations in the Chin Hills were in preparation for the offensive against Imphal, orders for which were given, by the Japanese, in January 1944. Originally, only the 63rd Infantry Brigade of the 17th Indian Division was operating in the Tiddim area. It was under the command of Brigadier A. E. Cumming VC, OBE, MC. Later the rest of the 17th Indian Division arrived as well as some of the 23rd Indian Infantry Division.

When Norman Kelly got back to Tiddim in December 1943 a number of major changes had occurred, and he was to replace Noel Stevenson as Deputy Commissioner. Stevenson had been very impatient with the inactivity of 4 Corps in general and the 17th Indian Division in particular. He was forthright in expressing his views and was frequently tactless. Oatts was later to write:

> When Falam was evacuated, however, he crossed the suspension bridge with half a dozen Zahows, removed the heads from half a dozen Japs and sent them with his compliments to the G.O.C., sealed up in kerosene-oil drums. This gesture was meant to be a gentle hint to the soldiery that it was time they got a move on. The gesture was ill received. Stevenson speedily found himself in front of a panel of psychiatrists, which unanimously decided that the only thing for him was a long sea voyage; and he was packed off to the United Kingdom accordingly.
>
> Looked at in cold blood, this exploit of Stevenson's may well be considered to have been in lamentable taste and in fact disgusting. It must be appreciated, therefore, that it was not carried out in cold blood but in close action. The courage and resolution which Stevenson required for his lone adventure were more than sufficient under different circumstances to earn a man the V.C.

The atmosphere prevailing at Falam at the time of its evacuation was very far from providing a stimulus to heroic endeavour, and to have crossed the suspension bridge just before it was blown and set off in the middle of the advancing Japs, with only six natives [the Chinwags] at his back, was no light matter. Listening to the story, I was filled with admiration and enraged at its sequel, especially as Stevenson was one of the very few men who knew and understood the Chins.[3]

Norman Kelly was joined in Tiddim by Oatts, who had visited Imphal to sort out the command of the Chin Levies. He now made his new headquarters in Tiddim. He found that a brigadier of 17th Indian Division had been put in command of the Levies in the absence of Kelly, Oatts, Stevenson and Haswell, during November and December. Rupert Carey, who had been in charge of the Siyins, had been sacked and Pat Rathbone, after his recovery, had been shanghaied onto the divisional staff.

The Siyin Levies appeared to have been broken up, were scattered all over the place, feeling very depressed, and had been made to work on road building. The 17th Indian Division did not understand the Chins and probably did not know of Norman Kelly's undertaking to them in April 1942 that they would not be put under direct military command. Worse still, on 23 January 1944, all the Siyin Chiefs and Levy commanders in Tiddim presented a petition to Norman Kelly. The last straw was that shells fired by British troops had killed some women and children, who had been hidden in the jungle for their safety. They had been left to fend for themselves because all their able-bodied menfolk had been withdrawn to Tiddim, and the 17th Division had not known they were there. They not unreasonably wanted Siyins in future to accompany the British forces defending their highly strategic valley so that they could indicate where their families were hidden (see map no. 9 on p. 166). It took Norman and his second-in-command, Thawng Chin Thang, three days at Vangte to settle the dispute. On the first day he saw the Chins, on the second the military and, on the final day, both together. His speech, summarised later by a Chin, T. H. Go Khan Pau, went something like this:

'I am pleased to say that the Lord God blesses us, the British people, because we are here in Chinland to save the tribal people and ourselves from the enemy. I ask the Chin Levy men and their families to forgive what has happened. I would ask the British soldiers to forgive the Chins, who are not educated like us, if they make mistakes. They are our people and we must love the land and the inhabitants as we love ourselves. To be gentle and polite is our English policy, especially in wartime. We regard you, the Chins, as ourselves, and we sacrifice to save you all and the land you are living on from capture by the Japanese. United we stand, divided we fall is our motto.'

On the third morning the Siyin Levy leaders nodded their heads, as did the British military officers, smiled at each other and dispersed with thanks to one another. [4]

The increased militarisation of the Tiddim area was inevitable and, indeed, highly desirable. The divisional headquarters had been set up on a hillside about a mile or more from Tiddim on the road to Fort White. It was an elaborate affair, clustered around a village green with numerous well-built *bashas* (huts made of bamboo). There were scale models of the area around the stockades, and a Japanese bunker. Jimmy Carpenter was in a village near Fort White with 80 Zahow Levies, only a few miles of undefended jungle track separating him from the Japanese. Cuthbert Burne was with his Zahows on a hilltop surrounded with barbed wire.

At the beginning of January Dick Reese, with about thirty Levies, had crossed back into the Chin Hills and was based at Hriangkhan, midway between Klangklang and the Indian border (see map no. 11 on p. 200). From there he could report on the Japanese in Haka. Harold Braund and Joe Byrne were operating to his north, near Thlualam. Joe was an Anglo-Shan, a tough little warrior and an orphan, who would rapidly break into song after a session of *zu*!

David Cozens had been with the Burmah Oil Company before the war. His HQ was near Lungngo, and his Levies revered him as the only *bawi-pa* (British officer) who had stayed with his men during the fall of Falam and Haka. He must have been a man of tremendous self-containment to have retained his sanity in such stark loneliness in a remote jungle, and he had sent back invaluable intelligence. He loved what he was doing and his ambition was to join the Burma Frontier Service after the war.

The Japanese left Haka in mid-January in search of David Cozens, who was operating on his own in the most southerly part of the Chin Hills. He had been warned of the approaching enemy. He ambushed a patrol of about ten Japanese and one Chin as they were wading across the Boinu River. The Levies killed one officer and eight others, and wounded the Chin interpreter near Phaipha Khuathar. They captured one machine gun, one mortar with bombs, one revolver, seven rifles, plus grenades and ammo papers. This was Levy warfare at its best, and did wonders for morale. Braund was ordered to send the arms and identification tags to Divisional HQ at Tiddim, where the delivery coincided with the arrival of Lord Louis Mountbatten, the Allied Supreme Commander, South-East Asia, on 11 February 1944. Harold Braund later commented:

Lord Louis witnessed a demonstration under firing conditions of the machine-gun and the mortar included in the haul, but I was told later that no credit was given to the Levies for their capture. Here was a minor example of the professional self-seeking that seemed so often to scar the business of winning the war. [5]

The commander of the Eleventh Army Group, General Giffard, accompanied by Cecil Beaton, a friend of Lord Mountbatten, also visited Tiddim to photograph and publicise the Burma campaign. The Supremo at divisional headquarters 'felt really proud pinning the ribbon of the DSO on to that gallant and famous fighter General 'Punch' Cowan, in front of all his staff'. [6] No longer was the Fourteenth Army forgotten. Mountbatten commented on the very high spirits of the units he met who 'have been fighting solidly in Burma ever since the Japanese invaded two years ago'. During the short but impressive ceremony at Lawibual, near Tiddim. Chief Lian Thawng of Khuasak was awarded the ATM, among other Chins, for his excellent work as a Levy officer. [7] As Deputy Commissioner and Senior Civil Affairs Officer to General Cowan, it is likely that Norman Kelly was presented to Lord Mountbatten; Vum Ko Hau, his chief clerk and stenographer, certainly was.

Lord Mountbatten enjoyed his trip and noted that 'the scenery is incredibly beautiful and although it takes an average ten solid hours of driving to get from Imphal to Tiddim every moment of it was really thrilling'. He recorded that 'the views from Kennedy Peak beggars description' and was amazed to see Kalemyo, 37 miles away.

The Chin Hills Battalion in 1943

After Falam was abandoned on 7 November 1943, Jack Haswell had taken the Chin Hills Battalion to a ridge further west, near Roshi. The Japanese had not followed him further than this point. The Zahow Levies were now under the command of Manning and Gemmell, and Jack Haswell had sent out a proclamation recalling all the Levies to duty. 'Jamie' James reported that the Hakas were beginning to rejoin him. On 21 January 1944 one Zahow and two Haka platoons of the Chin Hills Battalion raided Klau, 15 miles south of Roshi (see map no. 10 on p. 192). They surprised the Japanese troops in the school and outbuildings with mortar and Bren fire. Not only were the enemy's casualties heavy but the Chins captured the Japanese Deputy Commissioner Designate. On 24 January Captain Tom Aplin, with the 8th platoon of C Company, ambushed a Japanese advanced guard platoon, eighteen strong, from Bualzawl and drove back the main body. The enemy lost ten killed and about five wounded.

The strain on the Chin Hills Battalion was immense. The cat-and-mouse skirmishes with the Japanese and the abandonment of their depot Falam had demoralised the Siyin Company. The battalion had been on active service for two years without relief or respite when, on 29 January 1944, a most regrettable incident occurred – the mutiny of the Siyin Company: [8]

12. *The Japanese Advance on Tiddim, Imphal and Kohima, March 1944*

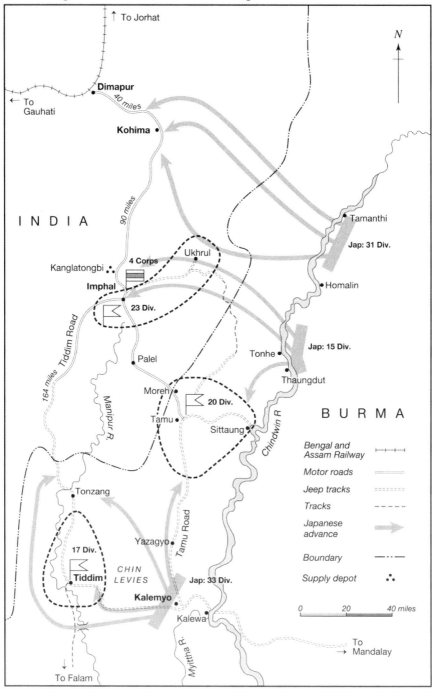

The Commanding Officer [Lieutenant-Colonel Roddie Russell] received a letter signed by 84 Siyins to the effect that the Company intended to march back to Tiddim and ask the General if it was the custom for a battalion to be left two years in the firing line without relief. Shortly after, having collected the *Naib* Commandant [the most senior Governor's Commissioned Officer] and three Siyin GCOs, he found 70 men under four *Naiks* [corporals] marching past Battalion Headquarters. They refused to return to their positions and the *Naib* Commandant had his wrist broken by a rifle butt trying to stop them. No *Havildars* [sergeants] had taken part in the mutiny. [9]

The battalion, less the Gurkha Company, was relieved by the 7/14th Punjab Regiment in February 1944. A and D Companies reached Imphal in the same month, but HQ and C Company remained in Tiddim until March 1944. Major Syd Hyde, a senior member of the battalion, was there when Lord Louis Mountbatten visited Tiddim, before the 'balloon went up' in March 1944. In February Major Rupert Carey left the Chin Hills with 884 Tiddim Chins, most of whom had previously served with the Burma Rifles, for their camp in Hoshiarpur.

The Withdrawal from Tiddim

On 29 February 1944 General Scoones realised that, although 4 Corps had as many ground troops as the Japanese, their lines of communication were lengthy and vulnerable. Dimapur to Imphal, and then to Tiddim, was a distance of 300 miles, 167 of which were on unmetalled road. The Japanese had a much shorter supply chain, and great mobility. Their favourite tactic was to infiltrate through the front and sit on the Allies' supply route.

When General Scoones at 4 Corps HQ in Imphal became aware that, as well as the 33rd Division, two other Japanese divisions (the 15th and the 31st) were assembling across the Chindwin, he realised that an entirely new situation had developed. Instead of preparing to launch an offensive himself he had to first defeat a Japanese attack. [10] The plan was to concentrate his forces and fight the battle on the perimeter of the Imphal plain with its airfields (see photograph no. 45 and map no. 12 opposite). The British had achieved air superiority at the end of 1943, and this area was nearer the railhead at Dimapur.

On 7 March Scoones discussed his plan with General Slim in Imphal. Slim agreed to it but made the proviso that permission to withdraw the 17th and 20th Divisions to the Imphal plain should be given to divisional commanders personally by Scoones, only when he was satisfied beyond all reasonable doubt that a major offensive had begun. [11] It was imperative that this should not be done prematurely.

On the night of 7/8 March 1944, the 17th Indian Division learned that a party of 50 Japanese had crossed over to the west bank of the Manipur

River 12 miles south of Tiddim, near Vazang. The Japanese had built their own bridge south of Mualbem and crossed on 8 March. A mixed force of Japanese and Chins went through Kaptel on 10 March and reached Mualnuam in the early hours of the following morning (see colour map no. 27). The local villagers reported that a force of about 1,000 men, with mountain guns, were operating west of the Manipur River. In response, Indian patrols were sent west across the Manipur from Tonzang. The Japanese had reached Tuibel by the suspension bridge on 12 and 13 March.

The Chin Hills Battalion Medical Officer, Kenny Fraser, had also found his way to Tiddim and was there in March 1944, when he met Norman Kelly again. He described this encounter as a 'Moonlight Sonata', on or around 10 March 1944:

> A year and a half after our first meeting we had another in strange circumstances, which showed that he was a loyal and very brave man.
>
> From the barrier of wire around Tiddim to the unguarded suspension bridge by which I had crossed to the west bank of Manipur, the road had been empty of people. On ascending the hills on the western side, we began to meet very few, and mostly solitary, travellers. The fields which, at this time, should have been occupied with watchers (against plundering animals) and their families were also empty, but one or two villages were noisy when we passed by. Those men whom we did talk to advised caution. 'Do not go in, Japanni mi-nung an um', that is 'there are Japanese people about', a phrase repeated by more than one well wisher. This did not seem likely to me, considering our free progress. Small parties of soldiers, even heavily armed ones, and virtually unprotected wayfarers like we were, never slept in a village house or an empty rest-house. Unfriendly visitors were apt to open fire first to test for the presence of the Army before moving in.
>
> Feeling rather uneasy, I chose before nightfall a useful camping spot. A projecting bend in the road consisted of a high bank on our left hand which enclosed, in between the arms of the curve, a hollow deep enough to hide our mules. From the top of the bank there was an open view of thirty yards or so to the next corner. Half a mile below was a large village, behind the trees and so out of view. A fire was lit and my orderly went to ask whether any egg or chicken could be got to improve our boiled rice. He soon came back. 'No eggs. No chicken. Do not come. In the village are two thousand Japans with guns.' This, of course, was preposterous. There had been no sound of firing all day and this was the west bank of the river. I then thought of the unguarded bridge and the possibility that a small enemy foraging party had crossed. It behoved us to keep quiet and move well before dawn – one medical officer, one orderly, one muleteer and three docile mules need not

make more of a disturbance than a stray bullock wearing its wooden bell or clapper. So we ate and lay down. I must have slept a little, but was awakened in the middle of the night. Beyond the shadow of the trees beneath which we lay the moonlight was astonishingly bright. Some distance away someone tapped gently on a drum and droned a slow song that seemed to be getting closer. I woke up very smartly and very completely – it was no drum, but the clop-clop of a horse's hooves. We all were awake and listening. Our horses had long since been disposed of. Only Japanese officers rode. I did not know that their soldiers sang as they marched. There was no sound of talk nor any tramp of marching feet, but Japanese soldiers did not have metal-clad boots. The singing stopped. A few embers of the fire still glowed a little.

'Cover the fire' I said, and 'Tum, drabi. You, muleteer, keep those mules silent. If they make a sound I'll shoot.' I hope I meant the mule and not the driver, but a threat to his mules might have been more effective than one to himself, and a threat only is what it was meant to be. The almost certain response of the mules to a passing horse was our greatest danger.

'Rami Chand, your rifle!' and he and I placed one rifle and one sten gun (protection of the wounded) on the lip of the bank and pressed ourselves down close behind it so as to be as inconspicuous and as safe as possible.

The hoofbeats padded on. The uneasy atmosphere that had prevailed all day seemed to have changed into a very definite feeling of apprehension. Being aware that medical officers were afforded no special privileges by Japanese captors, and having heard some firsthand accounts of what had happened to some, did nothing to allay mounting anxiety. In fact, it would not be inaccurate to say that it was, if not at its height, verging towards that extreme. The most benign fate that would be afforded us was a long walk to Rangoon jail. Just then, a grey shape came out of the darkness at the nearest corner.

It was a horse with an officer astride. As I peered into the shadow behind him to see what sort of men and how many were following, the horse came slowly forward, looking very white now in the moonlight. Half-way towards us it stopped; the rider started to hum that song again. The nightmare (no pun intended) was over. Here was Norman Kelly, alone but for his own white horse.

I laughed and trembled, but I am not sure which came first, the shivering or the laughter. I had been amply repaid for that broken nose!

Mutual identification followed. I explained why our camp was hidden, that I had to assume that a Japanese foraging party, maybe as many as twenty or thirty, might be in the village below, although some scaremonger frightened my orderly into reporting to me that there were many hundreds there.

'No, Doc' he said, 'there are nearer to two thousand there and in the small villages around. I am on my way down to find out.'

He was in civilian clothes and armed. The proposal was a suicidal venture. I felt bound to oppose it, and a warm, almost heated, argument went on. He said that he would hide his horse nearby, which he did, and came and said:

'I have to go. You don't understand, Doc. Those are my people. They will not give me away', and down he walked to the village.

We never met again, but he survived. Many months later I said to someone 'I've just heard the news from a situation report that 14th Army has recaptured Fort White.' That is the place, near Tiddim, which was much fought over by 17th Indian Division. I got a swift reply – '14th Army, be hanged. It was Norman Kelly riding alone on his white horse with his brass telescope under his arm who first re-entered Fort White and reported to Army that it was empty.'

I cannot remember now if his nose ever did straighten out again, and a fragment of a letter that I have tells me that in 1946 I was not allowed to go to the Chin Hills to see.[12]

Oatts also experienced the same deadly hush as he marched down from Tiddim to the suspension bridge at Tuibel, and described it vividly in his book *The Jungle in Arms*:

> This silence was bad enough when we encountered it last time. Now it fairly got on one's nerves. We did not meet a soul all the way down to the bridge. Before crossing it, I had a good look round with my field glasses and picked up a party of villagers near the crest of the next ridge. They were running like hell – a bad sign. We got to the village at about ten o'clock at night, and found it in turmoil.

He could see in the bright moonlight the Japanese march route, the path road leading north into Manipur.

The Japanese offensive had begun in earnest. Their plan was to capture Imphal and all its supplies. General Mutaguchi and the Fifteenth Army had been ordered 'to destroy the enemy at Imphal and establish strong defensive positions covering Kohima and Imphal before the coming of the rainy season [i.e. before the middle of April]'. [13]

On 12 March 1944 Norman Kelly was sent a personal typed letter (see illustration no. 26) from the Japanese Chief of Co-operation Commissioner, Chin Hills, which is reproduced below with the original misspellings:

Major C. Kelly. Addl. Commissioner.

Nippon troops will arrive near your nest place.
It is so trouble to prsparing for shifting to fogs
place in the jungles with tried mind. *I like you*
very much, so I want to teach you about Bible
before you die. Whole Christian world is
believing the Revelation 16-12-16. Here St, John
has revealed that 'The Kings Of the East' are stirred
to come to the Armagddon War of the great day of
God Almighty. Thus we raed in the final movements
of nations: 'And the sixth angel poured out his vial
upon the great river Euphrates and the water thereof
was dried up, that the way of the kings of the east
might be prepared... Who are these kings of the east?
The Revised version instead of the expression 'the
kings of the east,' says 'the kings that come from
the sun rising' so, on the far east coast of Asia is
Nippon—known as the Land of the Rising Sun.

*This importance to be reported to the Army
Commander. If youll report, the Army will be saved
By God. If you hope to learn more you must visit
Nippon troop with this letter.*

(signed) Moifonta
12th March 44.
Chief of Co-operation
Commissioner Chin Hills

The psychological warfare was uncomfortably specific. The Japanese employed the Tobatsutai, a 'pacification' or 'subjugation' unit for their civil administration. They used some of the same methods as the Kempeitai, a system within a system and renowned for its barbarous severity. It was a specialist department of the Japanese army, an internal intelligence organisation that was ruthless and efficient. Their methods of torture, described by Ian Morrison in his book *Grandfather Longlegs*, were designed to give it 'a name whose lightest mention should strike fear into the hearts of men'. The Chief of Co-operation Commissioner, Chin Hills, was known at the time as Kempeitai Commander Inada. Morrison's book is about Major Hugh Seagrim, GC, DSO, MBE, who fought with the Levies in the Karen Hills in south-east Burma from February 1943 to February 1944. Captured documents showed that the Japanese arrested at least 270 people, including elders and headmen. Many of these were tortured and killed in the most brutal fashion. In spite of this the Karens continued to assist and shelter Major Seagrim, but the enemy conveyed a message to him that if he surrendered they would cease reprisals: 'If within ten days of receiving this letter you surrender to me, I promise that you will not be killed but will be treated honourably as a prisoner of war. Signed KUROKATA INOSUKE.'

To save the Karens from more systematic executions, Major Seagrim gave himself up about 15 March 1944, knowing exactly what the consequences would be. He was immediately taken to the Kempeitai headquarters in Rangoon and on 2 September was sentenced to death with seven of his Levies. That day they were all blindfolded and shot at the Kemmendine cemetery in Rangoon, and buried in a common grave.

The Encirclement of Tiddim

Had the Japanese pulled off another masterstroke? Major-General Ian Lyall Grant commented: 'At the end of February 1944 the Tiddim Road had just been opened to single-way traffic, by 3-ton trucks, up to Tiddim. The 17th Division was the most vulnerable of the British Divisions, 164 miles south of Imphal down the narrow and precipitous mountain road.' [14]

There was a critical bottleneck at Milestone 126 where it crossed the Manipur River on a high-level Bailey bridge (see colour map no. 28). With two brigades, 3,500 animals and 2,500 vehicles, mostly jeeps, but including ambulances, specialist vehicles and trailers, it would not be easy to get the whole division back over the bridge in less than three days. The timing of the withdrawal from Tiddim was critical. To do so prematurely would be disastrous.

On 6, 7 and 8 March the shelling on Kennedy Peak and surrounding areas had been very heavy. On the night of 8/9 March the Japanese had suddenly attacked a patrol base on top of a range overlooking Tonzang. A further attack on the night of 12/13 March had made it obvious that the Japanese objective was Tonzang, and the bridge below it carrying the Tiddim Road.

General Scoones telephoned the order to withdraw to General 'Punch' Cowan in Tiddim at 2040 hours on 13 March. On 14 March the troops began to march out on foot. Only essential equipment, ammunition and petrol went in the vehicles. A company of Madras Sappers was the last out at 2400 hours, leaving Tiddim in flames behind them. Fourteen days' reserved stores and food had to be abandoned. The whole division was clear of the area within twenty-seven hours of the order to withdraw being given.

The day the British left, Stephen Khup Chin Pau, son of the headman Pau Za Kam, remembered, 'The smoke made the sunlight pale and red. I was crying a bit. We had been shelled by those Japanese big guns.' [15] For the Chins it was a very hard and uncertain time. The villagers could not comprehend the strategy of why the British had to retreat to win the campaign and destroy the Japanese 33rd Division. It had been such a short time before when the plan was that the 17th Indian Division was going to drive the Japanese from the Chin Hills, back to Kalemyo. The attack on Tonzang came as a great surprise. When the demolition work was in progress, the Chins, who had little to eat, wanted to salvage as much food as they could, to take it and hide it in the jungle. Men, women and children took part in this operation.

The Levies had agreed to fight to defend their homes and families. Now the British were deserting them. How could they know if they would return? Tiddim was the centre of their world and now part of it was being burned to deny it to the Japanese. During the military build-up for the offensive, Leo Deng Hau, the Tiddim photographer, recalled:

> I was one of the victims of the Second World War, and there are many things I cannot forget. As a young boy at that time, I cannot forget the fighters that dropped bombs [Hurricanes armed with two 250lb bombs]. The aeroplanes called 'Dakotas' came to drop military supplies. I could not think of them as being operated by men, because they came every day. My father was appointed to collect what the military air force dropped to our area. The rice bags dropped from the planes used to be broken. My father used to carry some of the rice. He also used to bring tinned meats that were dropped.
>
> When the British soldiers visited the holy Father Blivet, of the Foreign Mission Society of Paris, I used to follow them when they returned. I accompanied them up to 1 mile. The British soldiers used to give me some bread. I can still visualise the uniforms of the British, Gurkhas and Punjabis.
>
> When the Japanese reached the first stock gate, the Baptist missionary Reverend Nelson said to Father Blivet, 'The Japanese soldiers will soon reach Tiddim and they will kill us. Therefore let us flee to India.' Father Blivet said that he and his family members could flee to India to save their lives, but as for himself he preferred to die with his Catholic Christians in Tiddim. I could judge by myself, from that time, that he was a real good shepherd. [16]

It must have been a dreadful time for Norman Kelly. Tiddim was the place where he had said goodbye to his family nearly two years before and where he had persuaded the Chins, in spite of their internal tribal divisions, to fight with the British in their darkest hour. It was where he had been so happy before the war – but he decided he was not leaving 'his people'.

He could have gone out with the 17th Indian Division, as the rest of the Chin Hills Battalion did, but he had discussed the options with his chief clerk and stenographer, Vum Ko Hau. He wanted to remain behind in the Chin Hills and asked Vum Ko Hau if he would accompany him, or go back to the Siyin Valley to look after his family. Vum Ko Hau's brother, who was also in Tiddim, was on the staff of Major Bobby Peebles of the Chin Hills Battalion and would accompany him out with the division. Vum Ko Hau decided to return to the Siyin Valley; Norman thanked him for serving him and his predecessors honestly, and gave him a signed surplus leave certificate.

Norman also said goodbye to his table-boy, T. H. Go Khan Pau of Tuitum village. He was about sixteen years old at the time, had served in the Pony Levy and had looked after Norman Kelly and his chief Levy officer, Thawng Chin Thang, for three years.

> Your father was very kind and gentle to me. He appreciated me very much. Unfortunately, in the second week of March your father and Thawng Chin Thang had to withdraw. It was the 10th of March 1944, very unforgettable for me, when your father presented me a dining-spoon for remembrance and bid me goodbye, for I had to go back home. We departed since then but I miss your father very much.[17]

On 13 March 1944 Norman Kelly left Tiddim with the Siyin Levies on foot, carrying their rations and rifles only. Thawng Chin Thang, who had been Norman's right-hand man throughout the campaign, came with them.

The 'Heroic Contingent'

Norman Kelly and his 'heroic contingent', in the words of Vum Ko Hau,[18] left Tiddim on the night of 12/13 March and crossed the Manipur River between 14 and 16 March, moving westwards. They were accompanied by Thawng Chin Thang, Suang Lian (a Levy company commander who had received the Burma Gallantry Medal from Mountbatten) and Sien Lian. They nearly encountered a party of the Japanese 215 Regiment, commanded by Colonel Sasahara, which was making its way up the west bank of the river, at Kaptel (see colour map no. 27). The enemy was supported by a battalion of mountain guns and a company of engineers. This was the regiment which had crossed the Manipur 12 miles south of Tiddim, marched north through the hills on the west side of the river, seized the depot at Milestone 109 on the Tiddim Road and formed a roadblock in the area of Singgel, close to Milestone 100 (see map no. 7 on p. 80). It also despatched a company to capture the vital Bailey bridge over the Manipur at Milestone 126.[19]

Norman knew that Kaptel was in the middle of the Japanese line of advance since a villager from there had reported to 17th Indian Division on 10 March that a battalion of Japanese had been there that morning. The 60 Field Company of Sappers had destroyed the two suspension bridges across the Manipur River near Kaptel and Tuibel on 9 and 10 March, Tuibel being the more northerly. Norman's contingent went south from Tiddim to Saizang and crossed the river below the village, knowing that the west bank was alive with Japanese. It was around the time of the full moon.

The 17th Indian Division would have ensured that Norman had a powerful radio with which to communicate with the division and 4

Corps. Thawng Chin Thang, who had been the school inspector before the war, had relatives west of the Manipur. This was the land of the Soktes, who had been represented at the crucial meeting with Norman Kelly in Tiddim on 13 and 14 April 1942, which resulted in the formation of the Chin Levies. The plan was to remain in the vicinity of Kaptel during March, watch the enemy and then move to Champhai in the Lushai Hills, and there to organise another local body of troops to attack the Japanese. They would then continue their guerrilla activities, back in the Chin Hills, based at Sa-ek on the west bank of the Manipur River (see map no. 6 on p. 74). It must have been a lonely feeling for Norman with the 17th Division gone and Tiddim in flames. Living in the jungle amongst the Japanese was a precarious existence to which was added the constant threat of betrayal by a Chin.

Jungle Night

The man with the green cigarette strolls down the path
Waving it in the air in conversation.
The man with the tiny anvil strikes it softly like a bell –
Tink-tink; tink-tink.
The man with the dark blue cloak goes quietly by.
There goes the man with the green cigarette again.

They are not really there. You know quite well
They are not there.
Then one of them whistles softly
You finger the trigger of your Bren.
Half fearing, half desiring the sudden hell
Pressure will loose.
You listen –
Nothing –
Then

The man with the green cigarette strolls by again
Waving it in the air.
Down comes the dew,
Drip-drip; drip-drip.
The man with the tiny silver anvil
Strikes twice; strikes twice
Softly passes the man with the cloak of blue.

Fireflies.
Bell birds
Shadows
Japanese.

'K'
from *Muse in Exile* [20]

The withdrawal of the 17th Indian Division had been initiated just in time. Ian Lyall Grant, a Royal Engineer, described the withdrawal graphically: '17 Division had left Tiddim on the 14th and after a desperately slow march on the very congested road throughout the night and following day, had settled into two harbours [camps] at milestones 142 to 144 before dark on the 15th [see colour map no. 28]. The Tehri Garwal Sappers demolished the Bailey and suspension bridges over the Beltang Lui behind the rearguard.' On 17 March the Japanese entered Tiddim and on the 18th and 19th virtually the whole of the 17th Division had crossed the Manipur River bridge 126 miles south of Imphal, the Japanese objective. Lyall Grant continued, 'The Battle of Tonzang raged from 8–26 March 1944 near Milestone 140.' In five days General 'Punch' Cowan, with great skill, 'had broken a Japanese road-block and got his whole marching division (less the rearguard), together with all its vehicles, animals and equipment, through the bottleneck of the Manipur River bridge.' [21] By this time the Japanese 215th Regiment had seized control of 12 miles of the Tiddim Road between the hamlets of Sakawng and Singgel (see map no. 7 on p. 80). It took two separate battles to clear this stretch. The first, near Singgel, at Milestone 100, was fought by 37 Indian Infantry Brigade of 23rd Indian Infantry Division. The second was fought by the 17th Indian Division close to Sakawng. Both engagements overlapped with the Battle of Tonzang.

The Battle of Tonzang

This battle was well described from the Chin perspective by Khen Za Moong, a Levy sergeant from Muizawl, a village on the west bank of the Manipur River on the Japanese line of advance. He recalled:

Tonzang was flooded with various rumours from 10 March 1944. It was learned that the enemy had arrived at Phaidim due east of Tonzang. From then on all preparations were made for evacuation. Every evening, meetings were held at the chief's house to review the situation. Tonzang villagers had to start evacuating to Ngazo *taungya* fields where temporary shelters were built. The Tiddim Assistant Superintendent Franklin arrived and gave me the responsibility to be with the Tonzang chief. The Japanese troops started attacking Tonzang with mortar bombs from the 13th night Gurkha troops took up positions in and around Tonzang. Allied planes came and machined-gunned enemy positions.

The Japanese troops occupied the highest point above Tonzang and stretched along the ridge on the west going down to the river and surrounded Tonzang. They cut the motor road between Tonzang and Tuitum and set up a roadblock [see colour map no. 28]. We therefore moved to the Brigade area (called 'Richmond') above Tonzang. Chief Pum Za Mang, Hau Chin Pau, Vung Za Chin and Hau Go and I formed a group. The roadblock was cleared on 18

March and the way to the Manipur Bridge was open. Then only the withdrawing troops from Tiddim side were able to proceed to the Manipur Bridge. John Franklin told me that my father and his group had proceeded to the bridge. They had evacuated from Tiddim, were blocked at Tuikawizang near Tualmu camp, and were surrounded by the Japanese. After fighting the enemy and clearing the roadblock they had continued to withdraw along the motor road.

Franklin again reminded me to stay with and look after the Tonzang chief and said he would go round looking for a jeep and when he found one he would come back to fetch us. When there was no jeep to be procured for us, Hau Go went ahead to the bridge with his and my bed rolls carrying them on his head. (Hau Chin Pau and Vung Za Chin had already gone back to the village evacuation camp.) Troops were all around, some proceeding to the bridge, some going to forward areas to relieve the troops in line, some resting and many going about here and there. It was the month of March and it was the hottest time of the day. Fighting was going on around Tonzang. The heat, the excitement and the battle noises were enough to make one mad. [22]

The Tonzang chief was 'unusually heavy'. He could not keep up. 'All available light vehicles had been used to carry important equipment and starting from Kennedy Peak, all officers and soldiers and attached personnel, whatever their status, had walked. Pum Za Mang and I started to walk slowly. Franklin was unable to keep our slow speed and left us. The chief wanted to go to the Ngazo Camp. Pum Za Mang's spirits got so elated that he plunged right down the slope among the bushes and disappeared into the jungle. I waited for a while and then went down to the Manipur Bridge.' [23] Khen Za Moong met his friend Hau Go at the bridge. Nobody was allowed to cross with other than their arms, ammunition and backpack. He then met his father and Franklin.

The chief survived. The party remained at the Nakzang (Manipur) Bridge for about a week. It was bombed, machine-gunned and bombarded with artillery. They stayed in the Divisional HQ and slept at night in the bunkers, when not watching the tracer bullets flying around. After the roadblock was cleared, they crossed the bridge, which was then blown up.

Now 48 Brigade, which had crossed the Manipur River on the night of 17/18 March, broke through a strong roadblock in the Milestone 110 area and appeared to be about to annihilate one of General Yanagida's battalions. Lyall Grant commented: '215 *Regiment* had already lost about half its fighting strength and if the attrition went on there could be no hope of a successful attack on Imphal, which was his main task.' On 26 March the Tiddim Road to Imphal was open to Milestone 105. General

Cowan ordered the rearguard to cross the Manipur River and the big bridge was blown behind them.

In Tiddim, the Japanese set up a civil administration as they had done in Falam and Haka. The first two Co-operation Commissioners, Masada and Imamura, were based in Tiddim. Norman Kelly had received a letter, signed by Moifonta on behalf of the 'Chief of Co-operation Commissioner, Chin Hills' on 12 March 1944 in which he had made the incongruous statement, 'I like you very much, so I want to teach you about Bible before you die.' The enemy's Civil Affairs Officers, escorted by troops, had penetrated into all parts of the Siyin tribal territory round Fort White and were on both sides of the Manipur River, where Norman's Levies were operating.

The Japanese knew that Norman Kelly and his Levies were very active. During their occupation of Tiddim they were ruthless and killed some innocent people without interrogation. Peter Sian Lian Pau, of Tonzang, recalled:

> One such instance was that jungle fire broke out and was burning on the slopes above Kah-gen village in Tiddim sub-division, which looked very like some English writings. Some treacherous people reported to the Japanese officer and they accused Suak Za Dal of Kah-gen village, of sending information to Mr. N. W. Kelly by jungle fires. Suak Za Dal was caught and killed by the Japanese without any interrogation.[24]

During March, April, May and June, Norman Kelly was behind Japanese lines, organising his Levies, and doing the best he could to disrupt their lines of communication through the Chin Hills. The most vulnerable part of the Tiddim Road was the 8 miles between Tiddim and Tonzang where it followed the course of the Manipur River through a steep gorge on the east bank (see map no. 6 on p. 74). From his positions on the west bank any movement of men or vehicles could be shot up. This was an important role because while he was there the Chins did not feel abandoned by the British. He was personally fighting for their homes and families and was the best guarantee they could have that the Allied forces would return.

In the south, where the Union Jack was always flown at Levy headquarters at Lungler, after it had been rescued when Falam was evacuated, Oatts met the Chin chiefs of the Zahows, Khongsais and Hakas. They had a *zu* drunken orgy during which it was explained that the 17th Indian Division had not been driven out of the Chin Hills, as they might suppose. A trap had been prepared by the general at Imphal, who had pretended weakness in order to draw the Japanese to their doom upon which they were now rushing. Even the Klangklang chief who had been so unhelpful during the battle of Haka was impressed. They were told that a brigade was gathering in the Lushai Hills, where

Norman Kelly had his headquarters at Champhai. The Lushai Brigade was ready to fall upon the Japanese when they were driven back from Imphal. The Chins agreed that it was an excellent plan which was bound to succeed. When the time was right, the Chins, British and Indian Army would give the enemy no peace and drive them once and for all out of the hills. Once airdrops resumed the Levies soon recovered their spirits.[25]

Cuthbert Burne, who had done such excellent work in the Tiddim zone before moving south, was approached by Hau Za Lian, paramount chief of the Soktes – a tribe akin to that of the Siyins, which held most of the land west of the Manipur. The chief told Burne that the Soktes would not under any circumstances tolerate the Japanese administration, and asked for arms. They were a long way from Gangaw and had hitherto not served in the Levies. Greatly impressed, Burne arranged for 300 rifles and ammunition to be dropped by air. The Soktes then succeeded in killing all the Japanese Civil Affairs officers and their escorts. They captured another 300 rifles, and even armed their womenfolk. The Levies then set about killing as many Japanese as they could find west of the Manipur. Taking the Zahows to that side of the river, Burne established contact with the Sokte chiefs, Thuam Za Mang, the Mualbem chief (who had been present when Norman Kelly addressed the Chins in April 1942) and Pau Za Kam, the headman of Tiddim. With Kelly's intervention in January, the Siyins, who had been mishandled by the 17th Indian Division, now returned to the battle with a vengeance. A major success was the rescue of 80 Gurkhas, left behind by 17th Indian Division. Because none of his Levies could swim, Burne himself swam the Manipur to take a rope across. He nearly lost his life in the process, but managed to get all the Gurkhas over the river by this means.[26]

The Siyin chiefs of Limkhai and Buanman were joined by the Ngawns from the Vazang area and, later, by Chief Hlur Hmung of Zanniat. The Japanese were hemmed in at Tiddim, Falam and Haka. They could not move except in strength and even then they suffered severely. The 'flag marches' carried out earlier in the campaign had paid handsome dividends. By mid-1944 there were about 1,200 Levies in the field, led by some 20 British officers. Burne was responsible for the Tiddim Zone, Baker for Falam and Harold Braund for Haka. Because of the decisive battles going on at Imphal and Kohima (of which more in Chapter 12), the Japanese did not have the manpower to make reprisals and one or two attempts to seize hostages were easily thwarted. The Siyins, Soktes and some of the Zahows had to live off the country and fight without pay.

The Japanese, as well as their own forces, used the Indian National Army (INA). They had been inspired by Subhas Chandra Bose's mission 'Jai Aza Hind' (Free India from the British). Bose had escaped to Germany and raised a National Army there before arriving in Japan in a submarine.[27] Many of his converts were Indian Army troops captured by the Japanese in Malaya or Singapore, and persuaded to fight for them. A few were loyal to the British and saw the INA as a way of trying to get back to their old units. There was, however, the 'badmash element – freebooters attracted by the open door to loot and rape. The INA were high-handed, brutal and lascivious.'[28] They were hated by the Chins, and had no qualms about trying to literally 'headhunt' British Levy officers.[29]

The Japanese also created the Chin Defence Army. The task of the CDA was to look after the Japanese-occupied territories of the Chin Hills, while the regular Japanese forces and the INA invaded India; the total strength of the CDA was about 200. Many of the Chins who were forced to join the CDA remained loyal to the British at heart; they were waiting for their opportunity, which did come later, to rise up against their oppressors.

There were various categories of personnel who were employed by the Japanese in 1944. The first category were quislings long before the Japanese occupied Tiddim. The second group were patriotic, often young, British government officials who decided to serve the occupation forces in order to look after the interests of the Chins, though in some cases at the cost of innocent lives. The Chin Leaders' League was formed to help those arrested and to persuade the Japanese to use proper investigative procedures.[30] Pau Za Kam, a Levy commander, and Vum Ko Hau, Norman Kelly's stenographer, held the most senior ranks, conferred by the Japanese in Tiddim. Both also held the highest ranks in the CDA and worked in the Japanese headquarters. They kept in contact with Norman Kelly's Levies west of the Manipur, and joined and communicated with their own Chin resistance organisations.

The treatment by the Japanese of prisoners of war, wounded men and civilians, as elsewhere, was barbaric. Norman Kelly had been correct in his prediction. Another Japanese Commissioner in Tiddim, 'Tiger' Inada, later came to the attention of the Allied War Crimes Commission. Some members of the Chin Leaders' League moved themselves from Tiddim to Tuikliang, near Tonzang. After that, there were no more killings in the Tiddim headquarters, and it was easier for Pau Za Kam and Vum Ko Hau to send news to friends on the British side, west of the Manipur River. As a result, a precious petrol dump near Tiddim was blown up by Chins.[31]

The Chin Levies who had gone out with the 17th Indian Division spent a short time at the transit camp at Comilla, where units stayed after returning from the fighting, or on their way to the front line. They then proceeded to Hoshiarpur in the Punjab to join the rest of the Western Chin Levies. The Chin Hills Battalion went to retrain and re-equip in Shillong, Assam, where there was also a refugee camp for civilians from the Chin Hills.

The 17th Indian Division was gaining the upper hand in their fighting withdrawal along the Tiddim Road back to Imphal. General Yanagida, commanding the Japanese 33rd Division, who was an intelligent and experienced soldier, was already dismayed at the lack of success and the heavy casualties at Tonzang. Now General Mutaguchi, from his headquarters some 250 miles away in Maymyo (he was the commander of the Fifteenth Army during the second Battle of Bishenpur), decided to replace Yanagida. [32] The Japanese gamble was not paying off.

Chapter 12

FROM RETREAT TO CONQUEST

General Mutaguchi, commander of the Japanese Fifteenth Army, had thought that if he captured the base of Dimapur, the British could neither reinforce their beleaguered troops in Kohima and the Imphal plain nor use the railway to retreat to India (see map no. 12 on p. 226). While the 17th Indian Division was fighting its way back to Imphal along the Tiddim Road, the situation at Kohima was likely to be even more dangerous. General Slim remarked, 'Kohima, with its rather scratch garrison and what was worse, Dimapur with no garrison at all, were in deadly peril.'[1] He realised he must fly the 5th Indian Division from their triumphs in the Arakan in the south into Imphal (see illustration no. 45). This began on 17 March 1944. During ten hectic days, the troops, guns, jeeps and mules of the 'Fighting Fifth' were loaded into transports and flown to Imphal, nearly 400 miles away. One brigade was sent to defend Dimapur. The 'Fighting Fifth' was one of the most travelled formations of the British Empires's armies, its divisional sign being a ball of fire on a black background. The reinforcements were in place only hours before Mutaguchi's troops arrived.[2]

Kohima

Brigadier D. F. Warren took his 161 Brigade, part of the 5th Indian Division, to Kohima on the 29 March 1944. In the first week in April the Japanese had cut the Kohima–Imphal road to the south. Colonel Richards, with the Royal West Kents under their CO, Lieutenant-Colonel Laverty, and Indian and Gurkha troops were defending the Kohima 'box'. Arthur Swinson commented, in his book *Kohima*, that 'Warren did more than any one man to save Kohima'[3] Warren formed a second 'box' with the other two battalions and eight of his guns at Jotsoma, 2 miles along the road towards Dimapur to the north. Swinson said, 'It was not an ideal defensive position by any means, but it commanded an excellent view of the Kohima Ridge, and was near enough for the guns to give close support to the garrison.'[4] The base of Dimapur depended upon Kohima being held.

On the night of 5/6 April the Japanese had gained control of the water supply. For the garrison inside the Kohima 'box', thirst was the worst blow of all. The RAF, flying low over the treetops, regardless of fire from the ground, dropped motor-car inner tubes filled with water. The Japanese mountain guns were constantly shelling the shrinking perimeter. The troops were involved in close-quarter fighting across the Deputy Commissioner's tennis court. Slim wrote later: 'It was a very miscellaneous garrison of about a thousand who stood-to as the covering troops were slowly forced back, and it was a grim prospect they faced as fifteen thousand raving Japanese closed in on them.'[5]

On 18 April Warren's men finally broke through and joined up with the hard-pressed garrison, clinging grimly to their smoking hilltop. A Punjabi battalion was the first to enter, and at once took over part of the perimeter from the exhausted defenders. Kohima was relieved. On the 20th the rest of the original garrison was also relieved. At six o'clock Colonel Richards handed over the command he had so gallantly held and collected his men. Three hours later they marched out leaving behind the dust, din and stench of death they had lived with for eleven days. Slim commented, 'Sieges have been longer but few have been more intense, and in none have the defenders deserved greater honour than the garrison at Kohima.'[6]

During May fierce fighting took place, with tank 75mm guns, to dislodge the Japanese from their deep bunkers. By 13 May the Deputy Commissioner's bungalow, his garden and tennis court (which had acquired an almost ritual significance) were all finally in British hands. During April, May and June the Japanese had also been attacking Imphal. It was along the Tiddim Road that the 17th Division, after its withdrawal, was engaged with the Japanese 33rd Division.

At Home in India

In March 1944, when the Japanese advance on Tiddim was under way, my mother was having an anxious time in Naini Tal. On 3 March she wrote in her diary: 'Saw reports of Norman in "Statesman".' On 25 March there was a wire from Calcutta about my father (probably saying that he had remained in the Chin Hills).

After his own dramatic escape from Burma, Ian Wallace, who had been my father's best friend at Cambridge, had served first with the exiled government in Simla from 1942 to 1943. He had particular responsibility for the Chin Hills and later this organisation became the Civil Affairs Service (Burma) – CAS (B), with its headquarters in Delhi. In his memoirs he described his work with the officers of the Burma Frontier Service who remained behind, with whom he had constant contact:

> Incidentally, I do not think it is recorded history, but I believe it to be true that Kelly, wearing a top hat, one night 'jeeped' down from Fort White in the Chin Hills into the Kabaw [Kale, in fact] Valley, which was under Japanese occupation, and returned unmolested the next day. (I suppose he had heard from his Chins that the local Japanese were temporarily not in residence, but it is typical of the Kelly I knew.)[7]

On 30 March my mother received letters from Ian Wallace about my father, followed by a wire. She recorded her reactions to it in her diary, 'Very tired and worried'. On 1 April she replied to Ian's wire and asked in her letter what chance there was of her husband being granted leave.

It is likely that the Civil Affairs Service, and especially 4 Corps, were most anxious that my father should stay on the west bank of the Manipur River, gathering intelligence on one of the major Japanese supply routes, the Tiddim Road. The British knew that the Chins needed to be supported at this critical time, when the Japanese were doing all in their power to persuade them that the Allied forces had been completely defeated and would never return. The whole purpose of the withdrawal to the Imphal plain was to expose their lines of communication. My father was indispensable because he was trusted by the Chins and he would have to recruit a deputy before he could go on leave. Fighting during the monsoon, which began in May, and living under canvas in the jungle with the constant risk of being betrayed, would fray the nerves of most people.

It was not until the beginning of June that things began to happen. On 4 June 1944 the Japanese 31st Division began to withdraw from Kohima. According to Ian Lyall Grant 'they left without an order; they were starving'.[8] When it seemed that the tide had turned irrevocably in the Allies' favour, the uplift in morale was enormous. My father applied for and was granted leave in June 1944. My mother recorded in her diary:

1st June	School 'Break' begins [it lasted until 13 June]
2nd June	Desmond's birthday
5th June	Wire to Norman and letter to Ian
6th June	Wire from Norman at 6.30 – took four days from Aijal
7th June	Packed and went to Calcutta
8th June	In train

My mother arrived in Calcutta at 12.50 p.m. on 9 June and met my father at 3.30 p.m. What a reunion that must have been. She had travelled alone halfway across the vast expanse of India to see her man. My father, after nearly three months behind Japanese lines, then marching through the Lushai Hills and following the path we had taken on our trek out, was now reunited with his wife at last. My parents wrote to me on 11 June from the Great Eastern Hotel where they were staying.

Great Eastern Hotel
Calcutta
Sunday, 11th June '44

My dear Desmond,

I hope Patricia [now Maeve] has shown our letters to you. We write to her because there were messages for her to give to people in school.

Daddy and I have been thinking of you a lot and hope you are having a good time during the 'break'. We ought to be with you at the end of the week, so Dad's very exciting adventures can be told you then.

It is most frightfully hot here and difficult to write as one perspires such a lot. We leave for Delhi (all being well) tomorrow. I hope Mr. Forsyth brought your watch from Delhi. I asked him to buy one for you there.

It would appear that I cannot go on teaching if Daddy gets long leave. But if Mrs. Rose cannot get anyone I shall certainly come up each day rather than allow Mrs. Rose and the others to do my work.

Hello old boy,

It is a pity I did not arrive here in time to spend your 'break' with you but I shall be back in Naini with Mummy in a few days when I have finished my work in Delhi. I am looking forward to a long, restful holiday after a very tiring and worrying year's work in the Chin Hills.

I do hope you have got the watch for your birthday. I am sure you will have a great deal to tell me about your school life when I see you. I am very proud indeed to hear you are enjoying your cricket and football, hockey, etc., but do not forget to do the odd spot of schoolwork as well.

Will see you soon, old chap.

Daddy

My parents stayed in Calcutta on 10 and 11 June, before boarding the train to Delhi. There my father would have reported to the Civil Affairs Service Headquarters and met Ian Wallace. My mother next wrote to me from Maidens Hotel, Delhi, on 16 June:

Maidens Hotel
Delhi
16th June 1944

My dear Des,

I do hope everything is going well with you at school and that Mrs. Rose has been able to get someone to teach my form. I have told her that I shall come and carry on until another teacher is found. I hope you are working well, for Daddy is very proud of you and wants to find you working hard.

It is just too hot here, for my taste. One perspires all the time and I'm so glad that you and Patricia are in a cool place. So far as we know it is not necessary for us to go home, as Daddy can take his leave in India. He is still on duty here and his leave begins the day we go to Naini. Daddy wants to take Patricia and you for a lovely holiday in the September break, so it is worth working well until then, don't you think?

We saw Ohn Pe (Tiddim postmaster) and his wife in Calcutta. Both of them were so interested to hear about you and sent their love. You will be thrilled to hear of Dad's adventures when we meet. We hope to reach Naini on Monday and it will be grand to see you again.

With heaps and heaps of love from us both.

Yours,

Mummy

On 18 June my parents left Delhi on the night sleeper and reached Naini Tal at 12.15 the following day. My mother's diary reported, 'Norman ill'. My mother had dropped everything, including her job at the Hallett, when my father's wire from Aijal had arrived on 6 June. Now he had to try and persuade the headmaster to allow his wife to work part-time during his precious leave. He had written to Robert Llewelyn, and he replied on 22 June, the day my mother returned to the school.

From The Headmaster, The Hallett War School, Naini Tal

June 22nd 1944

Dear Colonel Kelly,

Thank you very much for your letter, which makes it easier to free Mrs. Kelly. Naturally I want to meet Mrs. Kelly in any way I can both because she has been so very sporting in coming in to whatever job we asked her to take and that with hardly any notice, and because to release her will be a help towards your recovery after your harrowing experiences of the past few months. On the other hand the job of collecting a Staff, which has never been easy, is made considerably more difficult if I regard too lightly the rules governing notice period, and I have, of course, to regard these matters from the School point of view, so any ideas I have had for bringing Mrs. Kelly back on the premises you must regard as being in your interests as a father if not as a husband!

However, your letter makes it clear that the School's claim is, in the circumstances, the lesser one and that being so I am quite prepared to release Mrs. Kelly at once, or on any date you and she think she should go.

Yours sincerely,

R. C. Llewelyn

My father stayed at Brookhill House during his leave; this was the small guest house overlooking Naini Tal Lake, run by Topsy Bailey. Many servicemen on leave from Burma boarded there as well. There were dances at the Boat House Club, tennis and bridge, sailing on the lake, and many visits to the two cinemas, the Capitol and the Roxy. My father's health steadily recovered. I had been given a watch for my tenth birthday and, on 13 July, my father bought my mother a diamond ring in a white gold setting, which she was to wear for the rest of her life.

By 22 June, while my father was on leave, 'The Imphal-Kohima battle, the first decisive battle of the Burma campaign, was not yet over, but it was won.' [9] On that day the road between Dimapur and Imphal was opened and the siege of Imphal was over after 86 days. Mutaguchi ordered the halt of the Japanese offensive on 29 June and the 214th Regiment began to withdraw. The approval of the Emperor for these orders was given on 2 July and reached the Japanese headquarters on the 5th, one day after my father's fortieth birthday.

The tide had turned and by the end of July 1944 the 17th Indian Division was on its way to a well-earned rest. Slim wrote: 'It had been actively engaged since December 1941, that is for three years and eight months, and almost all that time in direct contact with the enemy. A record I should think.' [10] On 18 July the 5th Division relieved the 17th Division and by 31 July had advanced down the Tiddim Road to a point 42 miles south of Imphal, on its way to Tiddim. The Japanese were in full retreat, but fighting tenaciously all the way.

On 21 July my father went to see the Senior Service Officer (SSO) about when he would return to the Chin Hills. In spite of all the distractions during his leave his thoughts could never have been far away from what was happening in Assam and Burma. On 29 July one of his Levy commanders wrote to him about the fate of his two brothers, from Hoshiarpur in the Punjab, where the withdrawn Levies had been stationed.

> Detachment of Chin Levies
> P. O. No. 91
> Hoshiarpur
> 29 July 1944

My dear Sir,

This is the second letter sent to you since I left Tiddim for India. The first one was sent (posted) sometime in the middle of February last, so it might have not reached you, as the 17th Div. might have started its honourable withdrawal by the time my letter was due to be delivered. A very shocking news to me too.

Now, you will find, I am afraid this letter full of queries. I could not simply help enquiring although I am well aware of your tough and increasing job over there. Before I go on with it please allow me to express my thanks for your every help without which to hold a commission in the forces must have been but a 'wishful thinking' or at least a mere dream.

I am okay myself here, but I have some very deep 'BUTS' within myself. The first 'BUT' is, what has become to my brothers – the latest news about them is that two of them (which two I do not know) were last seen in Tiddim ready to march along with you. Had they come out safe I have no doubt that they would have written to me. So, I just wish to know the fate which has befallen them.

The second 'BUT' is my anxiety to the unfortunate Chin chiefs. Many might have suffered badly from the Japs as a reprisal for their loyalty to the British Government. I am sorry to say this, but I am sure Japs would not leave them unpunished.

My last, but in no ways least 'BUT' is as to the general food situation in the Chin Hills. By now, like Calcutta, many of our folks and kins might have felt the onset of starvation if not already proved fatal. I only hope it has not.

I am fit here and so all the other Levies. Hope to get news from you before long.

With best wishes,
Yours sincerely,

Dal Za Kam

My mother had written to me the day before from Brookhill House:

Brookhill House
Naini Tal
28.7.44.

My dear Tigger,

We are looking forward to seeing both of you on Friday. The idea is to sleep in our room, so you and Rabbit will be able to creep into Daddy's bed in the morning.

On your way down the hill perhaps you could be discussing with Rabbit the things you would like to do most. We have plans made, but it always helps when we know exactly what you like to do.

I wonder are all the marks up yet? It will be grand to find you have done so well, particularly in English.

Cheerio till Friday, and take it easy.

Your Mummy

By August the military situation was moving forward and the Allies were increasing their successes bit by bit at removing the Japanese from their dug-in positions.

The Pursuit of the Japanese

On 23 August the 5th Division had reached Milestone 85 from Imphal on the Tiddim Road. It had advanced at an average of 2 miles a day. The Japanese rearguard positions were stubbornly defended. To eject them, their bunkers would be shelled and strafed from the air, using Hurribombers. While this was going on a wide outflanking movement through the hills would strike behind the enemy. Then a co-ordinated frontal attack with tank support would be launched. This was taking place during the monsoon season, during which 500 inches of rain fell in Assam in 1944.

The Tamu Road through the Kabaw Valley – parallel and to the east of the Tiddim Road – had priority for the engineer resources of the

Fourteenth Army. Down it, the 11th East African Division was advancing towards Kalewa. It was a much easier road to make, had fewer curves and none of the terrible gradients of the Tiddim Road. The 5th Division was largely supplied by air. 'The advance down the Tiddim Road and the Kabaw Valley took place in mid monsoon. At one time it rained continuously for 55 days. The Allied troops marched in rain and sunshine.' [11]

During this period while my father was on leave, a time of momentous events for the course of the war, my mother had been working part time at the Hallett War School. On 9 September the headmaster wrote to her and said:

> I should therefore be glad if you can stay on until the end of September in Hurricane House (boys).
> I can't write this without adding a note to thank you most warmly for what you have done for us. I really do think (and so do others) it is magnificent of you to have come in at such short notice and carried on in the way you have; and I am very glad that things have worked out so that your connection with the school has not been severed. Very many thanks indeed for it all.

The Lushai Brigade

The Lushai Brigade had been formed by the Fourteenth Army to stop Japanese infiltration through the Lushai Hills during their advance. It was composed of spare Indian battalions and some local Levies and contained many Chins. It was commanded by Brigadier Marindin, with its headquarters at Aijal. At the end of June General Slim had ordered Marindin 'completely to dislocate Japanese traffic on the road Tiddim–Imphal from Tiddim northwards, and render it useless as a line of communication'. [12] The Lushai Brigade worked in close cooperation with the 5th Indian Division. The brigade had four Indian battalions, the Lushai and Chin Levies and some V Force detachments. They were spread out along the west of the Tiddim Road for 100 miles, from Milestone 44 to Tiddim, not continuously, but with 15 miles between sectors, with orders to raid the road at least once a day in their area. Marindin, in addition, set out to launch the brigade into the Chin Hills to capture Falam and Haka. The Chin Levies in the Lushai Brigade took their families with them, depositing them in their own villages as they recaptured them one by one. They were overjoyed at the prospect of liberating their own country, for the Chins, in the main, had remained loyal throughout their occupation by the Japanese. [13]

Philip Barton, Norman Kelly's assistant in Tiddim, was the Civil Affairs Officer attached to the Lushai Brigade from April to September 1944. In his recommendation for an award to General Slim, Fourteenth Army commander, Marindin said of him:

I wish to most strongly recommend this Civil Affairs Officer for showing the utmost devotion to duty, and rendering most valuable assistance to the armed forces. This officer worked in close co-operation with O.C. 5 'V' Ops, whose role was to reconnoitre for operations on the Tiddim Road and break the power of the Jap Civil Defence Army. During this phase he rendered invaluable assistance in getting information and fearlessly venturing into enemy held territory, with a small civil police escort only. On several occasions, he did sterling work in encouraging loyal Chins. When large-scale operations started I attached him to my HQ and he was invaluable again in the matter of local information. Also his influence over the Chins had smoothed away transport difficulties which would have held up operations.[14]

Philip Barton was awarded the MBE, a very well-deserved decoration. His recommendation was signed by Slim.

Slim, in *Defeat into Victory*, wrote of the Lushai Brigade:

The two most northerly battalions [of the Lushai Brigade] were in position by the end of July after most difficult marches of eighty and one hundred and twenty miles, over mountains five thousand feet high, and across flooded rivers. They wasted no time. The Japanese soon found movement by day or night was harried [along the Tiddim Road] not only from the air, but also by stealthy ambushes and sudden bursts of fire.[15]

Slim estimated that at least 500–600 Japanese were tied up in this static defence. Over 200 were killed, many wounded and a number of vehicles destroyed – all at a cost of 20–30 casualties to Allied troops.

The greatest success was on a small sector of 8 miles where the Tiddim Road ran along the east bank of the Manipur River from Milestone 142 to 150, through a precipitous gorge between Tonzang and Tiddim. The Lushai Brigade, protected by the raging torrent of monsoon water, kept this part of the road under constant fire from the west bank, at ranges from 150 to 500 yards. The Japanese could not build a diversion to the road through the gorge. Unless they staged a major operation to bridge the river elsewhere or sent a considerable force to deal with the Lushai Brigade, they would have to run the gauntlet. The road was kept under constant Bren and mortar fire day and night. Several hundred Japanese were killed, 100 vehicles destroyed and lorry traffic on this sector of the Tiddim Road ceased.

Return to the Chin Hills

On 14 September the leading troops of the 5th Indian Division reached the west bank of the Manipur River at Milestone 126. Major-General Geoffrey Evans, who commanded the division, had sent his 123 Brigade from Imphal by lorry to Shuganu and thence down the east bank of the Manipur River, to come in behind any Japanese barring the advance of the 5th Division. They arrived in Shuganu in the first week of September and moved south with a mountain battery and a field company of sappers and miners. As the 5th Division reached the west bank of the Manipur River, 123 Brigade seized the high ground opposite it on the east bank. Slim commented, 'The enemy, realising that he was in imminent danger of being cut off, contented himself with shelling our crossing place, and gave up the defence of the river line.'[16]

Norman Kelly was promoted to Lieutenant-Colonel on 19 September and was on his way back to the Chin Hills. On 20 September he had flown from Calcutta to Comilla, one of the main airbases north of Chandpur. He had reached Aijal by the 23rd, and sent a long letter to Betty on the 24th. Because of the censor, he thinly disguised place names.

c/o H.Q. Lushai Brigade, South East Asia Command,
Sunday, 24th September 1944

My darling Pixiekins,

I sent off another wire to you when I arrived here yesterday afternoon (Ai) [code for Aijal] but, as I was told the line was down owing to rain and that it could only go by post to Silchar, there will probably be some delay before it reaches you. However, it will be quicker than this letter anyway.

My whole journey has been, and will be, pretty rushed as I want to be 'in at the death' at Tiddim!! Am leaving tomorrow morning and will follow the exact route you took in May '42.

On the 20th I flew to Comilla to meet Lindop [Kenneth Lindop, ICS, who was working for the Civil Affairs Service and was senior to Norman] and got all the dope from him [see map no. 5 on p. 70]. Poo Nyo is pretty disgruntled that he has to hand over to me and yet remain in the District under my control for the time being (he has tripped himself up by pressing his own personal grievances and has apparently shown rather an excess of bone between the ears.) The Brigadier [Marindin] was apparently howling for my return last month but Freddy Pearce stuck to his guns and said that since he had already let me down in reducing my leave, he was not prepared to break his promise further by recalling me. Pretty decent of him I think, dear.

Net result is, you are still to be Queen of the May, darling, and I still uncrowned kingpeace of my old stamping ground [i.e. DC of the Chin Hills].

I only passed through Silchar on the 21st (having flown in vile weather. The plane which should have gone on North had to turn back for Calcutta owing to the storm).

By pushing on I hoped to be in Ai by the 21st but the road was pretty grim and I only made it yesterday. A most hairy journey!!

Subaltern at S [Silchar] had failed to warn Ai, and everyone was surprised to see me as they thought we were still on leave at home!! Actually, your wire had been sent to Macdonald the Superintendent, who detained it. Incidentally, he wanted to know last night who the

Betty was who sent me her love from Naini when I was thought to be with my lady-wife somewhere in Ireland. Great joke. I had enquired at the P.O. in the afternoon (when I sent off my wire) whether there were any from you and was told no. You can imagine what a heat I was in, love!!

I was invited to the Mess last night to find a regular guest night in progress. Doesn't it make you jealous to know I was dancing with Mrs. Macdonald and Mrs. Williams (wife of the Brigade Commander)? It was only then that I heard about your wire.

Also, another joke. *You know the Nips had ordered that I was to be shot on sight?* Well, this information was wirelessed to all units in the area. One such unit got the message in two parts, or rather only received the second part, which read instead of 'the Japs have ordered', read simply 'have ordered to be shot at sight'.

Naturally they thought this was the Brigadier and, not knowing me well, signalled back to ask what I looked like!! So you see, sweetheart, the fun and games I so narrowly missed by being on leave in the bosom of my family and in your dear arms.

I can't tell you half I would like to say (indeed I hope I haven't already been indiscreet from the Censor's point of view) but great things have been happening, and by the time you get this there will no doubt have been further good news on the radio from this corner of the world.

I'm afraid I couldn't get the sheets in time at Calcutta, or the lipstick, but Gordon is going to do his best about the former. He is also to send me up some camp kit and the balance of my own stuff (I had to reduce weight a bit for the plane), but I can't hope to get this for some time. Meanwhile I'm travelling very light indeed – little better than when I came out on leave.

However, I'll soon build up a few bits and pieces by degrees to make life as comfy as possible in the circumstances.

Do let me know what the September pay-bill amounts to. I shall write to the kiddies as soon as possible, but I've a great deal to do this evening and I leave at 6.30 a.m. I'm sure the kiddies are a great help to you, darling, at the moment, for I can imagine you would find the room unbearably quiet after I had taken all my noise away with me. Life seemed very empty when we parted at Talli Tal, sweetheart, but I was proud of the way you kept your chin up. Keep smiling, darling.

I shall post my next letter from Champhai and for the time being at least you should write to me at the address I have given above. I'm told that parcels are now coming through this channel regularly, so do you think you could send me 10 tins of cigarettes twice a month. Try sending one lot and tell me in a letter the date of its despatch so that I can check up on its arrival.

I hope Topsy got her lunch basket back safely per the bearer. I find I brought away a Club book she had lent me. Its return will be overdue, so will you pay any fine she incurs over it, dear?

Tell her the ham was delicious and we all did great justice to it. Being afraid it would go off in the heat, we just polished it off!!

No other news just now, love. The mere fact of having to write brings home more poignantly the fact of separation and makes me feel horribly blue, but for having the great memories of the wonderful time you have given me.

Yours alone, darling,

Daddy

Norman was returning to the Chin Hills during the drenching monsoon, a depressing time of the year, and his next letter to Betty tells of the rain and mud that so hampered those on the march.

Camp
Champhai
1st October 1944

Darling Pixiekins,

What a relief to get here yesterday after the long tiring march from Aijal – nothing but mud, slush and rain the whole way and then, still more mud! After doing no marching for so long I expected to find myself pretty stiff, but I didn't do too badly on the double marches, though I feel that, given the chance, I could sleep for a week. I was able to get an Arakanese boy to cook for me on the way, and although a poor curry and rice was his limit, I didn't do too badly in the way of local supplies of eggs and chickens. I also managed to pick up a camp bed at Aijal. Incidentally, I forgot to get the umbrella from your bearer so I hope he has duly returned it to you.

It was simply great, love, to get your letter dated the 18th and one from Tigger of the 20th. There will be some little irregularity in my letters to you while I am still moving away from you but once I get fairly well settled you can expect them at least weekly, as air mail arrangements appear to show a marked improvement. Macdonald, the Superintendent at Aijal, is trying to help as much as possible in this.

I see you addressed your letter to me c/o Supt. Aijal. This seems to do quite well, but my correct address will be c/o Lushai Brigade, S.E.A.C [South-East Asia Command]. The latter address is likely to prove better for parcels mail.

I am on the move again tomorrow, as I am naturally anxious to get back into my own district as soon as possible – the little matter of Burma Allowance and Cost of Living Allowance is quite important. Short Street people insist on having a personal cash account of mine for Rs 500/– to cover cost of kit and any supplies I order in future. This they have had in advance so I'm afraid you'll get a hitch in the November pay bill when this is reviewed by the Accounts Director. The cost of kit they supply is recoverable from the Army for the stuff I have lost so things won't be so bad. In fact, to all intents and purposes, Short Street will act as my Calcutta bankers and forwarding agents. I haven't opened an account with the Imperial Bank, Calcutta, as yet.

I have met several old friends here already – all highly delighted to see me. Chief among these is ex. Subedar Thong Za Kai of Tuithang who has given me much reassuring news of the Hills.

Things have been moving more rapidly and I can't say yet when I will establish my HQ. Naturally I shall get as far forward as possible. It will be grand to be back among our own Chin friends once more.

Nothing further at the moment, darling. Will write again at the earliest opportunity. Am sending a note to Tigger and will write to Rabbit (and Topsy, if pos.) in my next mail.

All my love as ever, sweetheart – even tenfold if that is possible.

Yours alone,

> Daddy

> > > Camp
> > > Champhai
> > > 1st October 1944

Dear Old Tigger,

I have just received your letter dated September 20th today, so you see I got safely to Calcutta and am now a long way beyond it. It was a wizard experience flying and I wish you and Rabbit could have been with me.

I am sure you will have had a lovely 'break' with Mummy at Brookhill House and I hope you are looking after her well.

Did you get into trouble at school for throwing pillows at Father Prior? Glad you enjoyed your tea at the Boat House after I left you at Naini. I just feel that I should like another tea there myself now with you all.

I haven't much to tell you as I have been marching for days and start off again tomorrow.

Let me know how you continue to get on at school, old boy. I am sure you will try your best to make things easy for Mummy.

Hope the Wellington turns out a success by the time you have finished it.

Fancy you sleeping in 'my big bed' at Brookhill!!

Give Mummy and the Rabbit lots of big hugs from me, old chap.

Cheerio and be good.

> Daddy

Norman was returning to the Chin Hills at a critical time. As the Deputy Commissioner (although called the Senior Civil Affairs Officer), he had to try and get the civil administration up and running again. Tiddim had yet to be recaptured by the 5th Indian Division. He did not know how much damage there would be in the process. He was to be bombarded with requests and eventually had to set up his headquarters in Falam. The Japanese were fighting every inch of the way from their deep underground bunkers and often mountain guns and tanks were needed to dislodge them as these were designed to resist bombs.

Chapter 13

THE TRIUMPHAL RETURN TO THE HILLS

In the Chin Hills the Lushai Brigade and the Chin Levies had been involved in ambushing and harrying the enemy, and disrupting their lines of communication. Norman Kelly was involved in this work from March until June 1944 when he went on leave, handing over command of the Chin Levies to Captain Burne. Philip Barton was with the Lushai Brigade from April until September 1944. Their task was to help recruit villagers to join up with their private guns and to liaise with the Chins.

When the battles of Kohima and Imphal had been won, and the Japanese were in retreat, the Lushai Brigade was spearheading its advance on the western side of the Manipur River. Members of the Chin Hills Battalion, who had reached India during the withdrawal, joined with the Chin Levies in a joint effort to clear the Japanese from the Chin Hills.

The Chin Rebellion against the Japanese

Chief Hau Za Lian of Suangzang was the first and most important leader of the rebellion. His tribe, the Suktes (or Soktes) held most of the land west of the Manipur (see map no. 6 on p. 74). They had not served in the Levies and asked Captain Burne for arms; 300 rifles and ammunition were dropped by air. The Chins were increasingly alarmed and angered by the behaviour of the Japanese; twelve Chins had been executed by the Japanese in Tiddim without trial. Hau Za Lian said:

> What the Japanese had written and spoken proved to be opposite to each other, ordering food stuff and animals without paying, summarily executing people on suspicion based on false reports, and keeping a list of people they would execute. The Chins were hungry, frightened and groaning, hoping for someone to deliver them from the Japanese.[1]

The Levy commando leader, Chief Hau Za Lian, had been wondering how to procure enough men and equipment to fight the still fearsome Japanese Imperial Army. Help came from an unexpected quarter. The Japanese *vuandok* (subdivisional officer) Za Biak, who had always been very anti-British, assembled all the chiefs and headmen of Tiddim district at the Lawibual headquarters of the Japanese Commissioner and said:

Japanese soldiers have liberated the Chins from the hand of the King of England. Those who have opposed the Japanese government and sided with the British will have their heads cut off. Even now there are three men who side with the British on the west side of the Manipur River, and the case will be investigated. The order has been issued so that all the guns and horses from those *Gungal* [the west bank of the Manipur River] villages shall be sent to Tiddim before 14th June 1944. All those who do not send their guns and horses shall be killed.[2]

Za Biak's speech, instead of cowing the Chins, helped to galvanise them into action. When Hau Za Lian arrived at Suangzang he called a meeting of all headmen and elders who had guns and horses at Heilei village on 14th June 1944. The chief sounded a clarion call: 'Instead of waiting for the Japanese to come and kill us, would it not be more honourable to fight back and die?' [3] All the men at the meeting agreed to fight. He recruited 875 men from various villages in the *gungal*. They were supplied with guns, which the Levies had previously hidden in a secret cache in Leitawhtan. When this was not enough they sent for the necessary guns and ammunition from Sa-ek where Captain Burne and Lieutenant Thawng Chin Thang were stationed.

Chief Hau Za Lian and Thawng Chin Thang conferred and agreed to combine the Chin Levies and Hau Za Lian's men in a single place. The Levies therefore moved from Sa-ek to Taakzang camp above Suangzang village, still on the west of the Manipur. The chief, Hau Za Lian himself, moved into the encampment to train the partisans. When this news reached the Japanese in Tiddim, they dispatched 58 Chin Defence Army (CDA) soldiers to attack Taakzang. Hau Za Lian and Thawng Chin Thang cut them off at Kaptel, captured them all alive and quickly absorbed them into their own force.

News of this success spread rapidly and some CDA Chins who could not stand the ill treatment of the Japanese also decided to defect. They joined 60 Gurkha soldiers left behind by the 17th Indian Division on the east bank of the Manipur. The Chin leaders sent Cuthbert Burne to meet them near Mualbem. Oatts commented, 'Burne managed to get them all across the river by rope, nearly losing his life in the process, for he had to take it over by himself without assistance, as none of his Levies could swim.' [4]

On 14 July another meeting was held of the headmen and elders of villages on the west bank, at which Hau Za Lian was appointed Chief of Operations and Thawng Chin Thang Head of Administration. They decided that at the end of the rains they would cross the Manipur River and drive the Japanese from Tiddim. They called this force the Free Chin Movement. At a meeting at Taakzang Headquarters to discuss future objectives, Tun Thual of Kaptel made this proposal: 'Now that we have initiated the plan to raid the Japanese posts and drive the Japanese from all the Tiddim area, will it not be proper to name this movement after this territory [Suktegam] and call it "Sukte Independent Army", which sounds better than "Free Chin Movement"?'[5] This appealed to their sense of history and the name 'Sukte Independent Army' was unanimously adopted.

Rank badges were designed at once. The shoulder rank was made from red silk on a white background with red SIA letters. Chief Hau Za Lian, as Commander-in-Chief, elected not to wear any rank except the SIA logo. He explained:

> The soldierly name we've just adopted is named after the soil which gave it birth. By this name our men will crush those murderous Japanese overlords who had abused Tiddim people like slaves. We are soldiers who will endeavour to liberate all those who dwell in Tiddim land including Sukte, Sihzang, Saizang, Dim, Vangte, Khuano and Kahau. We dare to put our lives on the line and we will dare to die for our people.[6]

While the SIA commander was travelling around and inspecting his men who were guarding the villages, an urgent letter came from the Sukte chiefs Thuam Za Mang, Thawng Za Khup and Pau Za Kam in Tiddim. It requested that the SIA commander return from Laitu to headquarters post haste. 'Japanese *vuandok* Za Biak will arrive at Mualbem on 14th September 1944 to arrest all chiefs and headmen of East Sukte *gungal*, confiscate all guns and take them to Japanese stronghold at Suahlim.' [7] An urgent meeting was called at Taakzang headquarters of all headmen and elders. Hau Za Lian said, ' Since the Japanese have decided to arrest all the chiefs and headmen of East Sukte *gungal* we must protect their lives.'[8]

On 8 September 1944 the SIA, Chin Levies and porters left Taakzang and camped at the Suk Lui river beach. It was at the height of the rainy season. With the ferry capable of taking only two men at a time, it took three whole days to ferry all the men and equipment to the east bank of the Manipur. This was as hazardous an undertaking as any army could make. The ropes for the ferry were homemade. An Enfield rifle grenade-launcher was loaded with a defused grenade to fire the end of the string across more than 300 feet of the Manipur in full monsoon spate; the attached ferry rope cable was then pulled across.

From the east side of the riverbank the Chins moved to Beelmual, below Mualbem, to assess the strength of the Japanese in the village. When it was known that Za Biak, with fifteen Japanese and thirty CDA soldiers, had arrived at Mualbem on 14 September, the SIA and Levies set off from Beelmual camp and marched to Mualbem. They arrived at midnight and began to surround the village. Za Biak and the fifteen Japanese soldiers had been put up in the house of *Laipianpa* [translator] Pau Cin Hau and the CDA soldiers at Mang Khaw Kam's house. The five Japanese assigned to the task of collecting the guns slept in the horse's stable. H-hour for the attack to go in was to be at dawn, but somebody accidentally fired his gun and the shooting started prematurely. Only one Japanese died and the rest escaped. Za Biak and the CDA soldiers were, however, captured at dawn. The Suangzang villager Phawng Kim was killed and Ngo Nang, Vial Lang, Hau Khual and Khai Za Khup were wounded.

The Sukte Independent Army opened its headquarters in the house of the chief of the Suktes, Thuam Za Mang, in Mualbem and an instruction was immediately sent out for all CDA soldiers in all the villages to report to SIA headquarters. The Limkhai chief Pau Kam and Lam Zam reported in, followed by Kiam Piu from Vangte and Vum Ko Hau, Awn Ngin and Thian Pum (the Buanman chief) from the Japanese headquarters in Tiddim, as well as the young E. Pau Za Kam and many others. Thang Tin Lian (the Zahau chief) who reported from Falam, was sent back home to organise the resistance movement there.

A substantial fighting force attacked the Japanese in Saizang, Lailo and Khum Vum headquarters, as well as outposts at Thangnuai, Phunom and Dolluang. On 26 September Phaipheek was attacked and the enemy routed. Khai Khaw Hau took the opportunity to emulate his warrior forebears and brought back two Japanese heads to Mualbem. This was celebrated by a big *Ngal-Ai* victory feast, which Norman Kelly had predicted in his speech of 25 April 1942. 'It was complete with hornbill feathers, red-dyed goat hair plumes, reed *phiit* pipes, gongs and drums, as was seen in the very *inn sau* [longhouse] in olden days.' [9] It was attended by the son of the Tiddim headman, Stephen Khup Chin Pau, who remarked: 'It was the only Ngal-Ai feast I have ever seen.' [10]

His father, the Sukte Pau Za Kam, who had been the headman of Tiddim before, during and after the war (not to be confused with E. Pau Za Kam above), was an SIA subedar and carried both his Mauser rifle and double-barrelled shotgun to war. He was also one of the East Sukte *gungal* headmen, and led the SIA fighters in assaults against the Japanese stronghold at Suahlim, which was fortified with 'bomb-proof' bunkers. It was attacked on 9 October 1944. Eight Japanese were killed and forty-three CDA soldiers were captured. There they found a Japanese execution chamber intended for the Kamhau Chief Pum Za Mang and Chief Thuam Za Mang. Sukte Pau Za Kam was later to command the attack on Sakhiang in the Siyin area.

In Limkhai, the commander of the SIA, Sukte Pau Za Kam, and others had a long conference with the Siyin leaders, including Awn Ngin and Vum Ko Hau. Later, the latter used the letters SIA to designate the Siyin Independence Army. [11] In fact, there was no such name before 9 October 1944, the day Suahlim fell, and on 27 November 1944 all future operations were handed over to the 5th Indian Division. [12]

Chief Awn Zam of Khuasak asked, 'What does SIA mean?' Commander-in-Chief Hau Za Lian replied, 'Since SIA soldiers were recruited on the Sukte west bank area, they are named Sukte Independent Army after the land and locality.' U Awn Zam then asked, 'Since we Siyins are also participating in driving the Japanese out, since the S is the same in Sukte and Sihzang, can we not just say Sukte/Sihzang Independent Army?' Hau Za Lian replied, 'In our task to drive the Japanese out, we are not working or fighting to gain rank or name; but with love in our heart for our people and risking our very lives in fighting the Japanese who are trying to kill our people, we are working to save the lives of our own people. Since the Sukte Independent Army was named after the land and the locality and with the desire of the people, I cannot, by myself, make the addition.' [13] Norman was delighted with the Chin rebellion and the way the Levies and the SIA cooperated with each other, and he thanked Vum Ko Hau for his part in the SIA. The chiefs of Limkhai and Buanman in the Siyin Valley, the Ngawns in the Vazang area and Chief Hlur Hmung of Lumbang all took part in the Chin rebellion.

The Chin Levies in the south, with their headquarters at Lungler, between Lungding and the Lushai border (see map no. 11 on p. 200), were still under British officers and were being supplied by air. As the Fourteenth Army began to gain the upper hand, airdrops became more generous. They received 100 tons of rice 'as a gift to the Chins in acknowledgement of their gallant services'. This was delivered by Dakotas and fed the Haka and Zahau villages controlled by the Levies.

The Advance of the 5th Indian Division

Meanwhile, the 5th Indian Division was slowly advancing down the Tiddim Road from Imphal:

> Repeated air strikes, backed up by spectacular tank attacks weakened the enemy and steadily the tide of the battle rolled back to the Burma border. As the road became more precipitous, tanks and artillery were winched up hillsides, climbing thickly wooded slopes of 30 degrees, so that the guns could be brought to bear on Japanese positions.' [14]

The 5th Indian Division had reached the west bank of the Manipur River on 14 September 1944. Even with the Japanese driven from its banks, crossing 100 yards of rushing torrent was not an easy operation (see photographs nos. 49 and 50). It was

> flooding through its gorge at a speed of ten to twelve knots, hurling itself against boulders in fountains of spray, bringing down tree trunks in full career. Its roar, audible for miles, was like a football crowd. Not without difficulty, the engineers got a rope across, and a flying bridge – a ferry attached to a cable – was built. The first boat to attempt the crossing was capsized by the fury of the stream. All its occupants were lost. But the cable held and next day, the

16th September, the ferry was working, though a crossing was still a hazardous and nerve-testing experience.[15]

By 19 September a roadblock had been placed behind the Japanese rearguard, which had been shelling the crossing with some 155-mm guns. These were captured, leaving 90 Japanese dead. The 5th Indian Division was pushing on towards Tiddim under the command of D. F. Warren, now a major-general, who had played such an important part in the defence of Kohima. He had replaced Major-General Geoffrey Evans, a victim of scrub typhus, climate and exhaustion.

The Japanese at Tonzang were amazed when 123 Brigade of the 5th Indian Division, after an 80-mile detour with mules through dense jungle and over treacherously steep terrain, appeared out of the monsoon mist. The Punjabis swept into the village, shouting their war cries and creating havoc. They captured eleven guns, all trained to cover the crossing of the Manipur River from deadly artillery positions. The Dogra infantry fought off the desperate attempt of the Japanese to recapture their guns. Surprised by this onslaught from the hills, the Japanese fled. The brigade had climbed seven mountain ranges of 5,000 feet and two of 6,000 feet. Even the mules, which had struggled along almost vertical mountainsides, had to be pushed and pulled to stop them falling over the edge.

Ahead lay the formidable 'Chocolate Staircase', the most infamous part of the Tiddim Road (see photographs nos. 51 and 52). In 7 miles it climbed 3,000 feet from the Beltang Lui, a large tributary which ran into the nearby Manipur River. There were thirty-eight hairpin bends and an average gradient of 1 in 12. The road surface was earth, which became chocolate-coloured ankle-deep mud when churned up by marching men. Slim commented,'No soldier who marched up the Chocolate Staircase is ever likely to forget the name or place.'[16]

The Dogra infantry crossed the swollen Beltang Lui under cover of darkness, climbed through the thick undergrowth and up the steep hillside to straddle the road several miles up. The Japanese had to withdraw to the heights around Hill 160, 10 miles further on. Before the assault on this, the last obstacle before Tiddim, the six General Lee M3 tanks of the 3rd Carabiniers (weighing 28 tons), which had crossed the Bailey bridge miraculously constructed over the Manipur River, were brought to the foot of the 'Chocolate Staircase'. There they were hidden overnight. At dawn, aircraft circled overhead to drown the noise of the armoured vehicles as the tanks made their way up the tortuous track, through the low cloud that hung in the valley. The British and Indian troops were astonished to see the tanks emerge through the mist at the 6,000-foot summit. One can imagine the dismay of the Japanese when the tanks went into action in the final thrust on Tiddim, but the road was mined (see photograph no. 53).

The heights and ridges before Tiddim were only cleared after two weeks of the most intense air and artillery pounding of the campaign. The Dogra infantry stormed the 'Staircase' while two battalions of the Punjabs (3/2nd and 2/1st) swept in a wide left hook through the most difficult terrain and appeared on the road 9 miles beyond Tiddim, on the way to Kennedy Peak. This was to the rear of the Japanese. A third battalion (1/1st Punjab) made an even bigger outflanking movement to swoop upon the bewildered Japanese at No. 3 Stockade. *The 'Fighting Fifth' – History of the 5th Indian Division* recorded:

> They made marches of more than five weeks over some of the steepest mountain ranges in the Chin territory and were among the most arduous made by any troops down the Tiddim Road and beyond. Often the men had to crawl hand over hand up steep cliffs and along narrow ledges, so that even the mules – many of which had been campaigning for nearly four years – became panic stricken and slipped over the edge.[17]

Lieutenant-Colonel Oatts was later to write:

> At the beginning of October 1944 Cuthbert Burne had entered Tiddim with a large force of Levies, killed many Japanese, smashed up their transport and destroyed their telephone lines. He then withdrew. He had been joined by Ken Shaw, and the pair of them did most valuable service.[18]

Back in the Chin Hills

Norman Kelly's first letter to his wife, of 8 October 1944, on his way to Mualbem, described how he had visited Sa-ek, where he had first established his headquarters in March 1944. With him on the west side of the Manipur River were Captain Cuthbert Burne, Lieutenant Thawng Chin Thang, Sing Lian Leh and Lian Dim. This was after the 17th Indian Division had left Tiddim.

Mualbem
8th October 1944

Dearest Sweetheart,

You simply couldn't imagine the thrill I have had on my return here. News of my return to the district had spread like wildfire and all the Siyin and Sokte Chiefs, headmen and lots of villagers have been in to see me already (arrived here yesterday). Their genuine grins of delight and the hand wringing were most touching and even some of the old women were anxious to embrace me in the midst of their tears. All have had a pretty tough time and are praying it is now over – I do hope to God it *will* be shortly. Enquiries after you and the kiddies have been legion and I can't hope to convey half their messages at length. Chief among them have been the Heilei Chief (whose brother was murdered for having helped me), Awn Ngin, Thawng Chin Thang, Pau Za Kam [the Tiddim headman] and Tun Khai [Norman's constable].

Isn't such loyalty just marvellous, darling? Tun Khai is working for me again and Ngin Kum (your original *mali* in 1939) has attached himself to me. Nawk Ngin is still in a tight corner, but I hope to have him back with me in a few days' time.

Pau Za Kam has his family here all safe. The only one who has not yet come to see me is Pum Za Mang, the Tonzang Chief, but I understand he is ill in hospital in his village (now again under our protection).

Poo Nyo is away down in the South and I have assumed charge from him though it will be some time before I can get down there to take over the office from him [in Falam] – there is lots to do here and these are vitally important days. His lack of interest in this important area has been remarked on by all and does not rebound to his credit.

Am with Cuthbert Burne at the moment – a good reunion though we had nothing but a bottle of 'zu' to celebrate it. Gifts of *mithun*, pigs, chickens and eggs are the order of the day from the grateful populace. Spent a day with Smith at Sa-ek and another with Philip Barton at Heilei en route in order to get the picture of what had happened in my absence. It would fill a book but little can be said at the moment.

I have sent a signal through Lindop to the A.C., giving the date on which I crossed back into the district and have asked the latter to expedite adjustment of my Burma Allowance and C.L.A. in my pay-bill. In this way I hope that your finances will soon be on a regular basis again, sweetheart. Do let me know how you stand.

The snaps I brought with me have gone the full rounds of the village and all express surprise at the development the kiddies have made since they last saw them. All are looking forward keenly to the day when you will return to them again, dearest.

Do please try to send me cigarettes by post, dear. Also a decent shaving mirror for travelling (standing-folding type). Otherwise I am as comfortable as can be expected and as fit as a flea, though it is indeed a far cry to those marvellous Brookhill days and nights.

I am thinking of you, darling, back at school again after the 'Break' with the kiddies, and I trust you will be happy there. I haven't had any further letter from you yet, but I can't complain as I have been on the move until now. I hope, however, to be settled in this area for a while so once the letters begin to come, they should be fairly regular. In your case too, love, once you have received this one, my future letters will be regular.

Keep smiling, sweetheart, we both have a job to do and its just got to be done.

All my fondest love,

Daddy

Am writing to Topsy and Rabbit in this same mail.

Camp

Mualbem

15th October 1944

Darling Pixiekins,

I went over to Limkhai, in the Siyin valley, a day or two ago and had a great reception. Other parts of the valley are not yet entirely clear but the locals are doing great work mopping up odd parties. I am sending Tigger a Jap flag and cap which should please him – the result of a successful action near Bamboo Camp on the 10th inst. Hardly a day passes but we have reports of skirmishes. Nawk Ngin was in action the other day at Suangpi, and his uncle – Ngul Khai – Naylor's old cook bagged his man in one. Things have hardly moved as fast as I expected, but with tank and artillery support now operating, we should soon have the Hills cleared – there are indications that the enemy will be pulling out into the plains before long.

I have succeeded in getting a commission in the Civil Affairs Service for Thawng Chin Thang who will act temporarily as 2nd Civil Affairs Officer Tiddim with Philip Barton as No. 1.

Poo Nyo is to go straight out to report at Delhi and will not be returning to the District. Turnbull is also out on leave at the moment and Smith has just gone.

It was just a fortnight since I had your first letter and I was beginning to feel very neglected when, last night, your next letter dated the 26th Sept. arrived. By this time you must have had some of mine, dear, and henceforward I trust we will be in fairly regular communication. The zip bag I have kept with me for odds and ends of kit. I can't understand the two different dates on my wires from Calcutta. We got in there on the 19th afternoon and I left again on the 20th morning. Very decent of Desmond Mayne to write; I may possibly see him sometime in the future. Haven't come across Peter Hoole yet or heard any news of him in this area. I can't place Barry Gilbert, but remember Dennis Wynne quite well. If he is still with you, give him sound cheerios from Cuthbert Burne and myself.

Glad to hear you are getting the odd dance or two, sweetheart; keep it up and let me know all about it. How are you getting on at school? I suppose G. D. [a Hallett War School master] will have removed himself by now and that you will have got settled into your own rooms. I had a very breezy letter from the Rabbit in which she expresses her determination to work hard. I wonder will the Tigger be equally enthusiastic this term, or is he still playing you up in class? [My mother was my form teacher.]

Fancy meeting Arthur Potter in Naini – still the big Brigadier, I suppose.

Sorry to hear Ian Wallace had been ill; hard luck, particularly when he was on leave. I am absolutely 100% fit, darling, so you need have no worry on my account.

I only sent one wire from Aijal, so it looks as though the postal people had duplicated it – they are a pretty woolly lot. I told you of the purely promiscuous way in which I heard from Macdonald of your telegram. But for his chance remark I would never have known about it, dear. I am certain the papers about the 1943 I.T. rebate were registered to Simla. It is most annoying that they have gone astray because they contained the premium receipt without which I cannot renew the claim. The papers you say you were forwarding from Maguire have not turned up in this mail. However, most of the problems raised in Simla are also coming to me through Lindop direct.

No other great news at the moment sweetheart. Here's hoping to get another letter from you soon.

All my love and hugs as ever,

Yours alone,

Daddy

Tiddim was found deserted by Dogra patrols on 17 October (see photograph no. 55). They paid tribute to 221 Group of the RAF for the accuracy of their air strikes. As a mark of their appreciation of the part played by the airmen, the following signal was sent to them from the 1/17th Dogras: 'The 1st Dogras wish to congratulate the RAF on their successful liberation of Tiddim and consider it an honour to have co-operated.'[19] The 5th Indian Division had been largely supplied by air by British and United States flyers, steadily dropping food, ammunition and clothing, medical supplies, signal equipment and even jeep engines and 25-pounder ammunition. The road from Imphal was abandoned behind the division in its non-stop chase of the Japanese. Everything that was needed came in by air, including new tracks for tanks damaged by mines.

The Chins in Tiddim must have been full of wonder to see tanks rumbling through the tiny village, nestling in the 6,000-foot-high shoulder of the Chin Hills, which had given its name to the Tiddim Road. The British had kept their promise to come back and liberate the Chins from the tyranny of Japanese occupation. By this time many of the beaten army were close to starvation, and the Levies reported several cases of finding them eating their dead. In spite of all their tribulations they were still putting up a fantastic fight. They were dug in deep bunkers, with log roofs to protect them from bombs and artillery shells, and required flame throwers, tanks, artillery and grenades to blast them out (see photograph no. 54).

The Levies in the south were fighting fiercely to recapture Falam. In the course of this action, Dick Bennion, a fine young officer well known to Norman Kelly, who had come from the 7/14th Punjabis, was killed while leading an attack on a village. They had been pressing the Japanese hard for weeks and on 15 October 1944 entered Falam. They shot up the Japanese as they retired. The Lushai Brigade arrived on 18

October. There was great rejoicing with the reunion of loyal tribesmen and the recapture of the capital of the Chin Hills. This was enlivened by the free distribution of rice and stores from the Japanese. Haka fell to the Levies and the British two days after Falam.

The Chins hated the Indians of the Bose Brigade almost more than the Japanese. Their animosity towards them seemed to have a kind of dark ferocity, because of their appalling behaviour. The Chins 'thought they came straight out of hell, and had every intention of sending them all back there at the first opportunity'. [20]

Camp
Mualbem
21st October 1944

Dear Tigger,

I was very glad to get your letter written on October 6th, and to hear you had done well in the sack race at the school sports. It was also jolly to learn that you had been dancing and that Rabbit was one of your partners. I hope you didn't quarrel with her over your dancing steps the way I used to do with *my* sister!

Don't forget to be careful of your spelling this term, old boy. You really must learn to spell correctly before you go home or you will be badly ragged by other boys at your English school.

You will have heard on Mummy's wireless that we have recaptured Tiddim, Falam and Haka. Isn't it grand news. I am sending you a Japanese flag and a Jap soldier's cap which were taken near Bamboo Camp on October 10th – after the Jap had been shot, of course.

I am also sending a Jap seal for Rabbit and some Jap 'occupation' money which you can share between you. It is absolutely valueless, of course, except as a souvenir, for it is all printed in Maymyo and you will see that they don't even promise to pay cash for their notes.

The rains are just coming to an end here and the cold weather is just starting. I imagine Naini is getting pretty cold now.

Must stop in order to write to my Rabbit.

Lots of love,

Daddy

Camp
Mualbem
21st October 1944

Darling Pixiekins,

You will see that I still have my base in the same area though I have been doing a good deal of wandering round the area to various villages.

Everything has gone very smoothly and of course you will have heard on the world radio the grand news of our re-occupation of Tiddim,

Falam and Haka. There is no doubt that the Jap is now utterly demoralised and we have been giving him heavy punishment. In this the Chins themselves have played a full part; their morale is excellent and they have been killing Japs all over the place in support of Lushai Brigade's operations well ahead of the 14th Army troops. I suppose I shall shortly have to visit the Falam and Haka areas, but there is still a good deal to be done at this end, liaising with the new divisional command, organising food supplies and getting things back on to a more normal basis in the newly re-occupied zone. Lindop is a great help and I have just had a very successful civil air drop of 80 tons of rice and 20 tons of salt which has stimulated local morale tremendously.

This has caused my own stock to soar considerably as all the locals confidently expected things to happen as soon as their 'father and mother' came back.

I certainly could not have timed my return better, but it is an awful shame you are not with me, sweetheart mio.

Hope to give you news shortly of the extent of the damage to the civil stations of Tiddim and Falam. Preliminary reports indicated pretty widespread devastation at the former place.

Have got your letter of October 6th enclosing those of the children as well.

I suppose you are now settled down completely to the term's work after the excitement of Speech Day, etc. Thanks for sending off the cigs., etc. – they haven't arrived yet of course.

Am worried about what you term the financial crisis – let me have figures to enable me to check up what has happened. Failure to get the 1943 Income Tax Rebate has been a bit of a blow, and there are new regulations about the civil govt. only making up the difference between our pay and that of our present military ranks. It is all damned annoying when letters take so long to pass back and forth. I think Civilian Living Allowance has been finally stopped together with Travel Allowance in favour of a consolidated army field allowance which has to be drawn by me here, but I'm trying to get a definite ruling on this through Lindop.

Am very sorry indeed to hear that Tom Bailey [the husband of Topsy in Naini Tal] has been killed – just the luck of the game, but very sad nonetheless. Hope Ben [Betty's brother] will be OK in France.

It is early yet to advise what you should do about Agra in February, darling, but I suppose you would need to make timely arrangements for accommodation; *I am certainly quite hopeful of getting out to see you before you will be sailing for home.*

I have just fathomed the mystery of my travel allowance out to Calcutta and thence to Delhi. You remember we got a civil coupe from Calcutta. In order to do this Gordon Scott bought the tickets and I had to sign a receipt for their value without having actually handled the cash, which went straight to the railway people. This has been treated as an advance of T.A. [travel allowance] which actually amounted to more than I was entitled to under the claim I put in at Delhi. Hence the claim for refund of the balance. The net result is that we did not travel free from Calcutta as we thought at the time, and they have only allowed my own claim to a duty journey. Apparently you are not treated as having been travelling with me on duty, darling, though I seem to remember that we both found the journey a very pleasant and domestic duty at the time!!

The rains are pretty well at an end now and, with the cold weather setting in, I am feeling absolutely first rate. I do hope you are all keeping equally fit, sweetheart, and that you will not have any further trouble with rheumatism and what not, this cold weather.

With all my love and kisses as ever, darling,

Yours alone,

Daddy

On 25 October 1944, Subedar Ram Sarup Singh (2/1st Punjab) won the Victoria Cross at Sialum Vum, which overlooked the road from Tiddim to Kennedy Peak and Fort White. His company had captured a strong enemy position and sat there for four weeks, miles behind the Japanese forward troops, harassing the enemy's line of communication with their mountain guns. Before the action, to dislodge the Japanese from their bunkers, the subedar said to his company commander: 'Sahib, either the Jap or myself die today,' When mortally wounded by machine-gun fire, which he had drawn on himself, he called with his dying breath to his platoon havildar, 'I am dying, but you carry on and finish the devils.' [21]

In the battle for the peaks and the high ground overlooking Fort White the Japanese were strongly ensconced in old fortified positions. Kennedy Peak, at nearly 9,000 feet high, must have appeared to be an impregnable fortress. From it, the Kalemyo Valley could be seen to the east and Tiddim to the west. The British gunners fired from fantastic positions on the sheer mountainsides, where their guns had to be lowered on ropes, and gave incredible support to the Indian infantry.

The RAF Hurribombers (see photograph no. 46), armed with two 250lb bombs and four 20mm cannon, and the Mitchell bombers of the US Air Force pounded the Japanese positions on Kennedy Peak. Finally, the Punjab infantry of the 'Fighting Fifth' raced up the heights from the east to meet the Mohammedans and Dogra Rajputs of the Jammu and Kashmir State Force on the summit. They had fought their way up the heights from the west. On 4 November Kennedy Peak was in British hands (see photograph no. 59); 4 Troop, C Squadron, 3rd Carabiniers (Prince of Wales's Dragoon Guards) set an altitude record, at over 8,000 feet, when they drove one of their tanks onto the summit (see photograph no. 60).

During the greater part of the day the top of the hill was above the clouds, but generally for about an hour in the early morning and again in the afternoon the clouds lifted, disclosing a scene which would have gladdened the heart of any artist. The plain was clearly visible for many miles and the winding rivers and streams looked like silver threads as they glistened in the sunshine. It was a magnificent picture (see photograph no. 29).

Mualbem
30th October 1944

Darling Mummiekins,

I'm just back today from my visit to Tiddim and am leaving tomorrow for Falam.

We are making excellent progress and there is little doubt that we will have the Kennedy Peak and Fort White area clear within another week or so. Since our recapture of Tiddim has already been announced on the radio, I suppose I can tell you a little about it, dear. The whole story is pathetic and depressing but our bombers have certainly made a job of it in driving the enemy out. The community hospital is largely a mass of ruins, Nelsons' a collection of matchwood, the offices and Post Office uninhabitable and not a single house in the bazaar or Battalion lines that has not been damaged in greater or lesser degree. However, nothing better could really be expected since the place has been fought over twice and we will have plenty of scope for improvement when it ultimately comes to rebuilding the new station.

An old friend of yours arrived at Division H.Q. the day I was there – none other than John Franklin. He has been attached to Division as formational Civilian Affairs Officer as I refused to have him under me territorially. He thereby loses the Lt. Colonel he had hoped to get by going to China – apparently he only got as far as Myitkyina and was there exactly one hour!! So much for your erstwhile boyfriend, darling.

Another interesting piece of news – Roy Ogden is to come in as my Addl. D.C. I'm very pleased about this for he is a first-rate fellow, but I imagine Margot will be pretty sick that he has to play second fiddle to me!! Meow!!

My present movements appear to have upset the delivery of my mails which are probably following me round and are unlikely to reach me now before I get to Falam. I'm dying to have more news of you, sweetheart, in letters, but all the same I'm awfully grateful for your cheery wire dated October 20th, which reached Aijal on the 21st and was waiting for me here, having been sent by post – not bad work.

Expect I'll be at Falam for quite a spell as there'll be lots to do in getting things started again. Here's hoping there'll be mail waiting for me when I get there.

All my love as ever, darling,

Yours alone,

Daddy

Let me know if my letters to you are being opened by the censor.

Norman's next letter came from Falam, in which he described the depredations wrought there by the occupation of the Japanese.

Falam
7th November 1944

Darling Mummiekins,

Not a word from you yet, sweetheart, except your very disturbing telegram of October 30th about the pay-bill. Am very worried about it all for I have now confirmed that under the new regulations I appear to lose Rs 220/– a month. We lose both C.L.A. [civilian living allowance] and our civil travelling allowance, and in lieu only get Field Service Allowance at military rates which amounts to Rs 30/– a month. This will not pay for my local eggs and chickens let alone servants, so it looks as though I won't have enough to manage on here when the military move forward. So bang goes my dream of being able to save for a banking account in Calcutta. Everyone is complaining of the mix-up in the Civil Affairs Service due to the dual system of accounts – military on the one hand and civil on the other. Instead of the civil paying us as hitherto, our pay is now assessed on our military rank, and only if civil pay is higher does Burma Govt. pay us the difference. The trouble is I don't even know what I'm entitled to as a Lt. Col., as I have none of the Army pay manuals. The whole thing is perfectly bloody and I'm fed up to the teeth that I ever came back.

How on earth have you managed this month, darling? I'm worried to death about it all and you simply *must* write every week dearest, if I'm to keep going at all in this bloody place [this is his first letter from Falam].

I arrived here to find the military in crowded possession and 'Titus' Oatts running his damned Levy office in my house [the house of the Deputy Commissioner]. The place is filthy and, as he has officers sleeping all over it, I decided not to occupy it and have moved into the small house – formerly Assistant Superintendent Falam's just beside Moore's [the Commanding Officer of Chin Hills Battalion before he was relieved]. None of the station houses have been greatly damaged but they are indescribably filthy and blackened with soot. Apparently the Japs preferred to light open fires in the middle of the rooms rather than use the fireplaces or the stoves (the latter have all been removed). They also appear to have played about with most of the bathrooms and the water supply is pretty poor. Some of the floorings have been burnt and all the decent furniture has gone – Naylor's piano I found lying in the servant's quarters utterly ruined – all the strings and the ivory keys taken. The Battalion have suffered the worst and they have done a fair amount of damage in the bazaar. The Hospital is fairly OK but the filth and the rats would drive you frantic, love.

We are trying our best to achieve some sort of order out of chaos but it's a pretty grim job without any regular Public Works Department staff and it will be some time yet before I can get regular building contractors, sanitary staff, etc., gathered together.

Fortunately, however, the place has not been bombed to the extent of Tiddim. First reports show that Haka has also suffered badly. I'm just about at my wit's end with the Civil Affairs Officers from Haka, Falam and Tiddim bombarding me with their requirements at a time when I can't get priority air-drops in view of the accelerated military operational requirements.

Major Sawyer of the Burma Medical Corps, whose wife is at the Hallett, has just arrived here. I had not met him before, but it was a pleasant coincidence. Can't say whether I ever met her at Naini. He is obviously Anglo-something and a bit too boisterous – like Col. Rose – to suit my book entirely.

It will be a great help when Ogden arrives; I only have Simpson here at the moment as Civil Affairs Officer Falam.

I'm also up against a big job in assessing the guilt of certain Chiefs who were undoubtedly helping the Japs. How far they did so under duress is a difficult problem to settle. I have Thang Tin Lian, the Zahau Chief, in the lock-up together with my late sub-inspector of schools Shiah Luai (a son of the Tashon Chief) who was leading Chin rebels against us at Jap request.

The deaf old Tashon Chief, with his many wives and other family, I have left in their village but some of them appear to have been pretty deeply involved against us. The dentist's daughter, whom I think you met, was called in by my Jap opposite number to act as his treasurer and bed companion. As she, however, had already had a pretty chequered sex career she doesn't appear to be greatly the worse for wear! It is all very complicated and I am snowed under every day by odds and sods all trying to convince me what good boys they have been in my absence.

The redeeming feature, however, is the genuine delight with which the people have hailed our return. I thought I should never get away from Lumbang for old ladies, who have lost their all, kissing my knees and offering their few eggs and bananas with tears in their eyes! The Lumbang Chief's wife completely broke down, and being unable to speak for her tears, could do nothing more than clasp my two hands to her shapely breast – much to the embarrassment of the Chief and the surreptitious pleasure of your devoted husband!! So you see, darling, just a few of the difficulties with which I am having to contend at the moment. Don't make it harder by denying me the joy of your letters – regularly.

Did I tell you I had succeeded in getting Thawng Chin Thang commissioned as a full Lieut. in the Civil Affairs Service? He is Civil Affairs Officer II at Tiddim with Bob Wilson as No. 1 in place of Philip Barton who goes on his well-deserved war leave. Tuang Hmung is the only one I have in the Haka area as de Glanville is away on operational duty and Turnbull is out on leave. No word of Sayer's return yet.

Your garden, I'm afraid darling, is a complete wilderness but we cannot spare either the labour or the time at the moment to start putting it right. Naylor's rose-plot in front of the house was apparently used for vegetables! It's an awful pity the damned house had not been completely destroyed – but after all there is still the hope of moving the District H.Q. elsewhere.

I'm afraid I'll have to put off writing to the kiddies to another day, love. It is damned trying on the eyes writing at night with only a small hurricane lamp, besides being utterly depressing. I shall make Ogden live with me to break up the loneliness of the long nights.

All my love, hugs and kisses, darling, and here's hoping I shall at least hear from you before I write my next week's letter.

Yours alone,

Daddy

p.s. Cuthbert Burne has got his Military Cross at last. High time!

Falam
14th November 1944

My Dearest One,

It was simply terrific to get your letter last night, darling, for, after a complete silence of three weeks I had begun to wonder how far our mutual promises to write regularly had taken you. More especially as I had letters from the kiddies dated October 14th and 21st, without a line from you, dear. Your present one is dated October 30th so if you did write in the two preceding weeks, it looks very much as though they have gone astray. I *do* hope the kiddies' souvenirs turn up OK at your end. I still haven't received any parcel yet, so it doesn't look as though the mail arrangements are working so smoothly after all. You were quite right about Cuthbert Burne's M.C. – I seem to think I mentioned this in my last or a recent letter to you, dear. He certainly remembered the Loilem days well and it was grand to be with him for a while and to yarn over old times. He is also fond of trying out a powerful wheel-barrow tone voice and as he has a great fund of Gilbert & Sullivan we were able to pass a good deal of time making the night hideous with our cat-a-wauling. Altogether a 'good companion'. Did I tell you Syd O'Donel had sent me his cheerios from Silchar, through a veterinary officer who is attached to us at present? Too much of a trek on foot, however, to expect to see the gallant Kern-hole [light-armed Irish foot soldier] in person up here!!

I'm still very worried about the pay-bills but am hoping to hear better news in your next letter, by which time you should have got the October slip. I don't pretend to understand this new system of military accounting. Substantive pay Rs 1050/– is my ordinary pay as an Assistant Superintendent in the Burma Frontier Service. I can't imagine what the hell they mean by 'commencing balance' 844/5 or how the blue blazes they can show 'payment to Bank' of that account when you don't

55. *A leading scout of the 5th Indian Division looking down on Tiddim as the last Japanese hurry out.*
(Photograph courtesy of the Imperial War Museum, London)

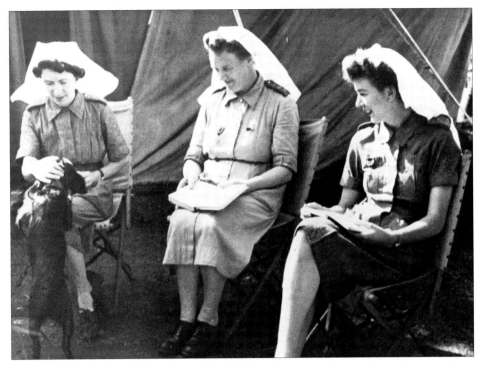

56. Above: *British nurses (Sisters) at Tiddim who were three of the staff of the field ambulance. From left to right: Sister M. Coleman from Staffordshire, Sister-in-Charge N. A. Murison from Perth and Sister E. Stewart from Dundee.*
(Photograph courtesy of the Imperial War Museum, London)

57. Opposite above:
Chin labourers building the road from Tiddim to the airstrip used for the evacuation of soldiers wounded in the fighting. One of them pauses while the road line is checked.
(Photograph courtesy of the Imperial War Museum, London)

58. Opposite below:
This airstrip for the evacuation of Burma casualties was built in four days; the vegetation was removed by bulldozers and local Chin labour. The aircraft shown here is an Auster, known as the 'flying jeep', and is coming in to pick up the wounded from Tiddim.
(Photograph courtesy of the Imperial War Museum, London)

59. *Troops of the 5th Indian Division moving up to consolidate their newly won capture of Kennedy Peak in the Chin Hills.*
(Photograph courtesy of the Imperial War Museum, London)

60. A tank on top of Kennedy Peak in November 1944 – the 'world's highest tank' at over 8,000 feet. It was driven by Malcolm Connolly of C Squadron, 3rd Carabiniers (Prince of Wales's Dragoon Guards) and is the same tank as shown on the front cover of the book. Left to right: Lance-Corporal Innes, Trooper Hovell, Lieutenant Bell, Troopers Thomas, Connolly and Anthony, and Major Morgan.

(Photograph courtesy of Ian Morgan)

61. The recapture of Fort White. Soldiers are here raising the Union Jack.
(Photograph courtesy of the Imperial War Museum, London)

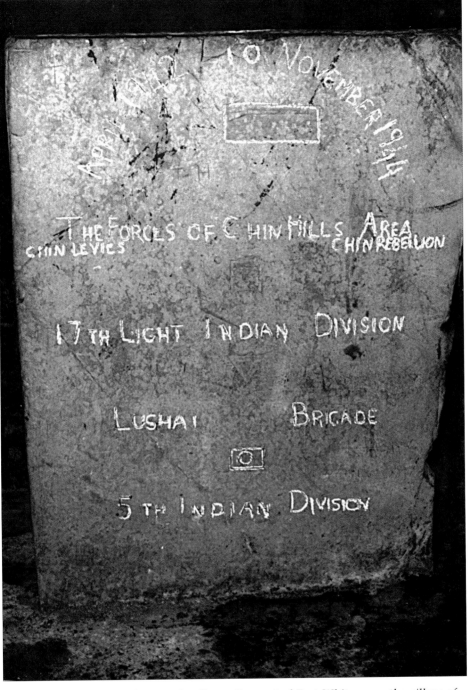

62. *The Chin memorial stone, 3 miles to the west of Fort White, near the village of Taingen, where the forces of the Chin Hills area are commemorated. Included are the Chin Levies, Chin rebellion, 17th Light Indian Division, Lushai Brigade and the 5th Indian Division; the Chin Hills Battalion should not have been omitted.*
(Photograph courtesy of Stephen Khup Chin Pau)

63. The Secretariat Building, Rangoon.

64. Government House, Rangoon.

appear to have received any such sum. Please send me the actual pay slips, dear, or make copies if you can so that we always have the details if the originals go astray in the mail.

So far as I have been able to figure it out the position should be somewhat as follows:

Civil Rates		Military Rates	
Basic Pay	1050	Pay or Rank	1225
Special Pay	300	Indian Army Allowance	100
Burma Allowance	150	Staff Pay	300
Overseas Pay	400	Family Allowance	not known
C.L.A. (140)	stopped		
Total:	1900	Total	1625

Govt. of Burma should pay difference Rs 275/– but of total emoluments Accounts Corps makes allotment of Rs 400/– automatically to Grindlays, London, in lieu of civil overseas pay formerly drawn.

As for funds drawn in the field I lose Fixed Travel Allowance Rs 250/– and get only military rates of Field Allowance Rs 30/–. In addition, I forfeit 5% of total civil emoluments for free accommodation, i.e. 5% of Rs 1900 = Rs 95/–. In addition, there are the regular deductions for Income Tax, Super Tax and Provident Fund.

The 5% deduction for free accommodation is a dreadful twist, for in the front line the only free accommodation officers get is a ground sheet to rig up over mother earth. That hardly seems worth Rs 95/– a month, does it, dear?

However, we will see what this month has brought forth, love. I do hope things have been straightened out because I feel so powerless to help you from this distance. Don't give post-dated cheques to the tradesmen if you can possibly avoid it. Everything will be OK in the end, but it is this damned transitional period from leave to duty which upsets things.

What arrangements are you making for the period after the end of the school term, love? I am wiring to you about this.

Also, what decisions have you reached about the schools for the kiddies at home? I see Desmond's spelling is still pretty grim and I have tried to give him a hint at the end of this week's letter. I think we can feel quite happy about the Rabbit's ability to hold her own in her age class.

There does not appear to be a single Jap left in the whole district now, and our forces are down in the plain and closing in on him at Kalemyo. There are already indications that he is pulling out of there under our artillery fire both from the north and west. He'll certainly have to move quickly or we'll have him in the bag at Kalewa, judging by radio news.

I'm afraid I haven't been quite so fit this week. I have had four nights of low fever (around 101°F) and the Medical Officer, from a blood slide, has diagnosed Benign Tertiary malaria. I have been OK during the day (that's why I'm writing this morning) though a bit washed out, but with the regularity of clockwork the onset of the fever has been heralded by shivering fits daily at 4 p.m. It is nothing to worry about and I shall be perfectly fit again in a few days when I have completed another course of Mepacrine and pamaquin. The M.O. is also giving me a few arsenic injections as a tonic.

We had an unfortunate fatality yesterday: I had ordered the reconstruction of a bridge across the Manipur between Tashon and Lumbang. One of the Tashon Chief's sons was superintending the work and has lost his life together with 5 other villagers. I feel very sorry about it, but the work must be completed for the only alternative means of crossing the river entails a very long detour on the Lumbang side to an old cage-and-windlass crossing we had rigged up much further downstream.

No other news of importance, sweetheart. I trust all is well with you, darling; look well after yourself and have the fair body in A.1. form for my surprise visit in January! I see you don't give me much news of your boyfriends at the dances, and I'm still full of 'ja-lousy' knowing the added attractions which the years have brought you, darling. Don't forget that you are my bundle of joy, and that I am loving you more deeply and with the same passion as ever.

Yours alone, sweetheart,

Daddy

Falam
14th November 1944

Dear old Tigger,

I have been moving about so much and kept so busy, that I have not been able to answer your grand, long, red ink letter of October 21st. And then, last night, I got your next one dated October 28th.

I was *so* glad to hear that you were better and were out of the 'San' again. It must have been pretty dull there, but I am sure Sister Dunne looked after you very well – she was certainly very kind to me when I was ill at Brookhill Guesthouse.

Great work, old boy, getting 8 out of 8 for Arithmetic and no bad marks the whole week. By the time you get this your exams will be over and you will be very near the end of term. Will you be sorry to leave the school or are you looking forward keenly to your school in England?

I'm glad the Wellington has turned out such a success. I *do* hope the Jap souvenirs ultimately reach you safely; I would be most annoyed if they got lost in the post, and I'm sure you would be disappointed. It might have been wiser had I kept them to bring with me when I next see you, as I hope to do before you sail for home.

I am kept busy at present in my capacity as Special Judge trying traitor Chins who were bullied by the Japs into fighting against us. As many of them were compelled to do it against their will it is very hard to punish them severely, but on the other hand I can't let them off entirely – particularly the bunch that attacked my own party at Tibual in March last, or the party who killed a friend of mine (Capt. Bennion) and then cut off his head to take to the Japs. Incidentally, we dug up his head in a Jap camp here – a camp just at the very top of the hill coming up from Tashon where the old summerhouse used to be [just before you get to Falam].

I forgot to tell you, that when I was in Tiddim last month, I found that the horrid Japs had had the cheek to destroy our lovely little Red Rose Cottage.

No more news at present, old boy.

Heaps and heaps of love from,

     Daddy

p.s. Keep an eye on that spelling you young tiger!!

Falam

14th November 1944

My darling Rabbit,

I'm afraid I have not been very regular in writing to you, because I have been moving around so much and have been kept so busy.

Now I find two of your letters (October 14th and 28th) remain unanswered.

There was no letter from Mummy in the mail which brought yours of October 14th but I was thrilled yesterday to get one dated October 30th together with yours of the 28th.

No, I'm afraid I can't make the slightest guess of what Elspeth Naylor said she did for her Daddy when she was eleven, so the surprise you have for me is still complete, old thing.

I'm glad you like Miss Nicholas better than Mr. G. D. [F. Gwynne-Davies, Assistant Master, Hallett War School 1942–4] – she seems to mark your lessons much more leniently, but on the other hand I'm sure you are improving in your Latin by hard work, and that this accounts largely for the better marks you are getting.

I like your joke about Des being quite well again and 'getting round as large as life' (or your handwriting). Your latest letter is really very carefully written and was a real pleasure to read.

Your sketches of the little woolly men were also very jolly. I think I prefer the one with the lots of wee woolly hairs standing up on top of his head.

You seem to be finding your music quite easy and I'm frightfully pleased. It will be great fun if you have to play something at the 'musical recital'.

Keep going at the hockey, old girl – you'll have to play it a great deal at your home school and you will want to be able at least to keep your end up creditably when you first start there.

It is grand to be back in Falam again with the horrid old Jap chased right back to Kalemyo and not a single one of them left in the Hills except dead 'uns. However, they have left all the houses in a very filthy condition, but Mummy will have told you all this from my last letter to her.

I'm afraid I have no exciting news this week, Rabbit, so this is where I ring down the curtain.

Oceans of love and kisses from,

> Your loving Daddy

On 8 November 1944 Fort White had been entered by patrols of the 5th Indian Division. It was empty. The Union Jack was raised as a symbol of victory as it had been when Fort White was first established in the 1880s (see photograph no. 61). But now it was a joint victory of the Chins and the British. On 27 November, at Fort White, the Sukte Independent Army leader Hau Za Lian and his commanders, and the Western Chin Levy leader Thawng Chin Thang and his commanders, handed over their commands to Major-General D. F. Warren, CBE, DSO, Commanding Officer of the 5th Indian Division, and Major John Franklin in a simple ceremony. Franklin, who had been so active in the Levy cause, said:

> We British soldiers of the 5th Indian Division have come to fight the Japanese in India and Burma. I salute you soldiers of the Sukte Independent Army and Western Chin Levies for having driven the enemy from Tiddim district, staking your own lives and carrying your own weapons and eating your own meagre provisions, for the love of your land and your people.
>
> From now on we shall take the responsibility of fighting the Japanese. Please go home and live in the peace you so richly deserve.[22]

Certificates honouring both those who had joined the SIA from 26 June 1944 and had served until 27 November 1944 and those who had joined after the capture of Mualbem and served until 27 November 1944 were given.

All the operations of clearing and driving away the enemy had been possible under the leadership of Hau Za Lian, Thawng Chin Thang and Captain Cuthbert Burne. The Japanese had killed two of Hau Za Lian's cousins without trial; he said, 'We Chins are those who go through suffering, privation and even death to resist foreign rule.'[23] The Sukte composed songs to commemorate Hau Za Lian's plans to rebel against the Japanese and recruit men for the Sukte Independent Army. He had tried to save his own people in the East Sukte *gungal*, and had succeeded in preventing the Chin chiefs from being arrested and their guns confiscated. The SIA helped drive out the Japanese, and this was due to his ability to organise and ally with the people in Sukte and Sihzang tracts. [24]

A fortnight earlier, on 13 November, a patrol of 5th Indian Division had met a patrol of 11th East African Division, which had advanced from Tamu down the Kabaw Valley (see the illustration on p. 24). Together they had entered a deserted Kalemyo on 2 December 1944. [25]

In the course of the 5th Indian Division's advance down the Tiddim Road enemy casualties, excluding those inflicted by the Lushai Brigade, were 1,316 killed and 53 prisoners. The division's own battle casualties in the same period were 88 killed, 293 wounded and 22 missing. Antony Brett-James recorded: 'This had been an outstanding advance in the face not only of an enemy fighting a stiff rearguard action over nearly 200 miles, but of very serious diseases, the worst furies of the monsoon, mud and steep places on a tortuous road, and a host of administrative difficulties.' [26] The division, after clearing its area of enemy stragglers, collected in Kalemyo, and was flown out to refit in the Imphal plain. Slim commented: 'The 5th Indian Division had completed a remarkably fine feat of arms and endurance in its advance from Imphal to Kalemyo.' Now the Fourteenth Army had liberated an area of Burma, including the Chin Hills, twice the size of Ireland. [27] The building of the Tiddim Road, the loyalty of the Chins and the leadership of their British officers had laid the foundation for the successful outcome of the Chin Hills campaign.

Chapter 14

'THERE IS NO JUSTICE'

In Falam, Norman Kelly must have been homesick for the pre-war Tiddim he had loved so much. Antony Brett-James, of the 5th Indian Division, described how he had seen Tiddim for the first time on 23 October 1944:

> This little town, whose inhabitants had numbered little over 150, spread itself below at a point where a saddle of the range formed a plateau. Here, open and without trees, the houses stood, some 50 of them, square-roofed buildings of wood and red-painted corrugated iron sheets, or more solid structures of red brick with paned windows and grills on the lower floor. Certain officials of the Chin Hills administration had lived in Tiddim before the Japanese coming, but now there were no people to greet our entry, though flowers still bloomed in tiny front gardens, roses and honeysuckle and what might have been marigolds, and a dog prowled in the rubbish. Bombs had shattered some homes, yet Tiddim possessed a beauty of its own, derived from this setting 5,000 feet high against the great range topped by Kennedy Peak and Vital Corner, the coming objectives of our Division. As I drove through the upper fringe of the town, I looked ahead to the sunlit ridge and found the peak of which we had spoken so frequently in conference and gossip. White cloud-masses brooded over the eastern hills, though Kennedy Peak rose clearly to the sky like a questioning challenge to our energy and skill. From the summit the Japanese could watch Tiddim and the road south with a simplicity that made our every movement naked and without pretence.[1]

Dr Charles Evans, who also visited Tiddim with the 5th Indian Division, almost certainly found where our home had been: 'In the afternoon I walked a short way back down the ridge to the remains of a bungalow; there was a lawn, a rose border, juniper, geraniums and chrysanthemums, and a white gate that led nowhere.'[2] Betty Kelly had loved her garden. The Chins had built an airstrip with a road leading to it at Saizang, 6 miles south of Tiddim (see photograph no. 57). The hospital was up and running, and serious casualties were flown out by an Auster aeroplane each day to Tamu (see photograph no. 58).

In contrast, Falam did not hold the same memories of family, children's laughter and dogs, and Red Rose Cottage on the lawn looking towards Kennedy Peak. It had its own tradition. The Tashons had called themselves Fahlams before the British so rudely invaded Chinland. They had had their powerful leaders like Pu Con Bik, who had bravely fought against the Imperialists. The present Falam site had a British fort built in 1892 with barracks and official buildings, which later became the headquarters of the Chin Hills Battalion. 'According to hearsay of the Tashon tribes, Fahlam had its meaning. The word "Fa" means sons and daughters (children) or generation, and the word "Hlam" means secure place. Hence, Fahlam's literal meaning is the secure place where people live peacefully.'[3]

The British had brought peace to Falam, and they and the Chins had fought and died to defend it against the Japanese. Indeed, there were those who contemplated ignoring the strategic withdrawal and holding out on their own. Havildar Du Lal of the Chin Hills Battalion was one such hero, who wept at not being allowed to fight on. One of the most remarkable stories about the defence of Falam concerned Bobbie Peebles who, with his company of the Chin Hills Battalion, was committed to defend the east side of the Manipur River. He told Kenny Fraser, the Medical Officer of the battalion, that the paramount headman of the area '…had offered to marry Bobbie into his family if he, Peebles, would stay and help his people to fight on when the British had gone.'[4]

Even Lieutenant-Colonel Roddie Russell, CO of the battalion at the time, writing to Lieutenant-Colonel A. Moore, wondered if things could have been different:

> I am so glad [Tommy] West is doing well – he was always so splendid. Unfortunately when the real crisis came both he and [Jack] Oats were wounded and then [David] Milligan was killed and there was hardly anyone on whom I could rely. Still perhaps if the 17th Division could not hold Tiddim, there was no disgrace in the Chin Hills Battalion not holding Falam. I still sometimes wonder if I could have won that battle, if the Khongsais had been fresh, if West and Oats had been there, if Milligan had not been killed, the people in Falam had not blown up the place while I was hanging on by my eyelids at Laisson, and shown in what a bad way we were. Probably there was nothing to be done anyway. If you had been there we might have done it.[5]

Thang Tin Lian was the Zahau (or Zahow) chief and pro-Japanese. In August 1945 Roddie Russell, again writing to Lieutenant-Colonel Moore, remarked:

> I am glad Thang Tin Lian is dead. His men led the Japs up behind our position, which was on the high hill behind his village, and was responsible for the loss of the position and several lives of the

Khongsais. We subsequently, you will remember, recaptured the place in a night attack and captured Thang Tin Lian's son in a surprise raid on Klau school, where he was sitting talking with a platoon of Japs in the school. No sentries out! We were getting our tails up again.[6]

When Norman Kelly was in Falam in November and December 1944, the Levy commanders were pushing the Japanese down into the Gangaw Valley. Lieutenant-Colonel 'Titus' Oatts was in wireless contact with Cuthbert Burne, who had been seconded to the 5th Indian Division. He was also in communication with Harold Braund and David Cozens. Baker, a regular army officer, who was with Oatts in Falam, was instructed to take the Zahows across the Manipur River and drive the enemy from Webula to Natchaung, and not to stop until they had reached the Chindwin (see map no. 3 on p. 28).

It was not part of the original agreement, which Norman Kelly had made with the Chins in April 1942, to extend the fight beyond their hills. Harold Braund's Hakas were the first into the Gangaw Valley but they were naturally anticipating leave to fall out, so that they could return to their families. They would hand over the chase to the Lushai Brigade, who had the former Levy officer Manning doing their liaison work. Ken Shaw was still in the field and there were two new Levy officers in Falam, one of whom was called Flanagan, who was worse than his friend Wilson for sticking his neck out.

Cuthbert Burne, with Ken Shaw, Johnson and Flanagan, led the Siyins and Zahows into the dense, fever-ridden belt of forest that separates the Gangaw Valley from the Chindwin. With great difficulty they finally reached the river, but Johnson and a number of Levies had died of malaria on the way. Burne's men established several posts along the banks of the Chindwin in the jungle below Kalewa. 'The Japanese river traffic downstream was considerable and the Levies shot up innumerable river craft and sank several.'[7] Flanagan, with thirty men in captured boats, crossed the Chindwin to attack a party of Japanese who had opened up on the Levies with mortar and machine guns from the east bank. Like Wilson, he never knew when to stop. 'It was a fine performance, all the same, for the Levies to have crossed the Chindwin and gone into close action on the left bank. It was an outstanding achievement of which they had every reason to be proud.'[8]

On 10 December 1944 the engineers had completed a floating Bailey bridge over the Chindwin at Kalewa. It was 1,154 feet in length, then the longest Bailey bridge in the world. The Indian sappers had assembled the spans in the Myittha River, between Kalemyo and Kalewa, and floated them down to the Chindwin and put the bridge in position in twenty-eight hours. Barrage balloons, no longer required in Calcutta, were used to protect the bridge from the Japanese planes that attacked two days later.

On 13 December, Shwegyin, on the east side of the Chindwin, was occupied by the 11th East African Division. There was no stopping the Fourteenth Army now, but it still had the Irrawaddy to cross, and it was not until 3 March 1945 that Meiktila in central Burma was recaptured. By 20 March 1945 Mandalay was in British hands and the Union Jack was again flying over Fort Dufferin – the site of the former royal palace of Thibaw, the last Burmese king.

Norman Kelly wrote from Camp Tussak on 18 January 1945, to issue a permit for one of his most loyal Levy commanders:

> Thian Pum, Chief of the Buanman Tracts of the Siyin area is permitted to proceed to Kalemyo to satisfy his curiosity regarding the landing of aeroplanes there. This will have good propaganda value in the Chin Hills and it is requested that he be given reasonable facilities to approach the airport and to see any air activity that may be permitted by the authorities without breach of security.
>
> This Chief took a leading part in the Chin Levy Organisation from April 1942 to date and was wounded in action.
>
> N. W. Kelly
> Lt. Colonel, OBE, B.Fr.S.
> SCAO, Chin Hills, SEAC

Norman, as Deputy Commissioner and Senior Civil Affairs Officer, was beset by problems in trying to differentiate between loyal and disloyal Chins, and rebuilding the houses and roads destroyed by the fighting. He was also bombarded by requests from Assistant Superintendents and, uppermost in his mind, were worries about Betty and the family.

The Intrepid Journey

During January 1945 my mother became convinced that she should visit my father in the Chin Hills. As early as September, my father had expressed the hope that he would be able to get some more leave and see us in India before we sailed for England. The Hallett War School had closed in December 1944 so my mother's job would not stop her travelling in January.

At the beginning of the year my mother was far from well. There were days when she felt washed out and had to stay in bed. It was cold in Naini Tal and there had been a considerable fall of snow. On 12 January this was deep enough for us to go tobogganing. That evening my mother wrote to my father. The following day she filled in the forms to book our passage back to England.

On 28 January she visited Cheena to have a final view of the Himalayan snows. She then had an urgent message from my father telling her that it was safe to visit him in Tiddim. It was a clandestine arrangement because the Chin Hills were still in the war zone and he, as a lieutenant-colonel, was under military command. As Deputy Commissioner, he was the most senior civil affairs officer in the Chin Hills. Although Simpson had joined him in Falam to help with administration, my father was short of staff and desperate to see my mother before we sailed. He would be able to make all the arrangements once she had arrived in his area of jurisdiction. My mother was spurred on by the thought of seeing the Chin Hills again, and the prospect of another long separation.

On Tuesday, 30 January 1945, we left Brookhill House at the north end of Naini Tal Lake and got a rickshaw from the 'The Flats'. We passed the Royal Hotel and the Boat House Club, which had been the social centre of Naini. As we passed down the Mall, with the willow trees on our right and the white sails of the boats on the lake, we looked up to our left to see the Hallett War School at the top of Beetle Hill. It was an emotional farewell. We had been very happy in these captivating surroundings, and the bonds of war and the school had left indelible memories. From the Talli Tal bus-stand we were driven 'down the hill' through Jeolikote and Ranibagh to Kathgodam, in order to catch the train to Lucknow and then on to Gonda. John and Joan Haskins were now stationed at Gonda and John was the ideal person to plan my mother's journey by train halfway across India. She had bought a first-class train ticket from Kathgodam to Manipur Road, the station for Dimapur in Assam.

We arrived in Gonda on 31 January. Travelling as an attractive woman alone on the Indian railways was not without risk. It was small, however, compared with trying to get into Burma, where the war was still raging. My mother said to Joan, 'I am going to see Norman in the Chin Hills – I am going alone – do you mind looking after Maeve and Desmond while I am away? If anything were to happen to me and Norman, could you arrange for them to get back to England so that Berta Talbot, my sister, could bring them up?'

I do not remember – nor does Maeve – if she told us where she was going. She had been to Calcutta on her own in the past, to meet my father, so we were used to her being away. She could not have told us how she was going to get to Tiddim, because she did not know. She had no idea at that time how she was going to get back. I do know she had a carriage, No. BA 4028, the second compartment from the front of the train, as she set out for Assam. I suspect there were tears when she left Gonda on 1 February.

The railway line to Gauhati had major problems on it (see map no. 13 on p. 284). There had been a civil disturbance, known as the '1942 Rebellion', characterised by severe rioting. The sabotage of trains had started shortly after this. The wreckers would merely remove one or more fish plates from the track, usually on a curve, and the centrifugal force generated by the trains would distort the track; derailment followed. There was also a lot of theft and corruption on the line. Although my mother had a first-class ticket, at that time the military were running that portion of the Indian railways because there was so much traffic on a very heavily used main line to the Burma front.

By Friday, 2 February, my mother had reached Katihar. After the second night on the train she arrived at Lalmanirhat on Saturday in the morning. Then followed a long journey to the north of the Brahmaputra, across which there were no bridges. She was still on the single-track metre-gauge line, which she had been on since Gonda. Now she was travelling east, through Golakganj, and at Rangia took the branch line which turned due south to Amingaon on the banks of the great river, where she arrived on Sunday. This was the end of the line, but carriages were loaded on to the rail ferry to make the crossing to Pandu on the opposite bank. It was here that a wagon of blasting powder had been broken into. The train driver, thinking that the stolen case contained tinned food, opened it on the foot-plate and a spark from the firebox had set it off. He and his crew were blown up and killed in the shunting yard of Pandu. Military security must have been very tight following this episode.

My mother was not in uniform and was now entering the bottleneck of supplies to the front, where a saboteur would be revealed by suspicious behaviour. She could hardly say she was going to meet her husband in the Chin Hills. The gods were on her side that Sunday as she left the ferry port of Pandu and made the 5-mile journey to Gauhati, which was the northern rail junction and road-head for Shillong, the provincial capital of Assam. It must have been a relief to get off the train at last after four days and three nights since Gonda. She booked into the YMCA and slept in a bed at last, away from the constant rattle, stopping, starting, jolts, unscheduled stops – and railway station food – with incessant flies and the risk of being laid low at such a critical time in her life.

On Monday, 5 February, she left Gauhati at 3 p.m. She was still a long way from Dimapur. This must have seemed one of the longest days of her life. She was now writing in code in her diary lest it fell into the hands of Japanese, or British for that matter, and they turned her back. At least she had her first-class ticket to Manipur Road. My mother and father could not have been in communication with one another since she left Gonda. He would have driven up the Tiddim Road and headed north for Imphal, a journey of 164 miles. He would then have passed through Kohima on his way to Dimapur, their planned meeting place. He would have wanted to arrive ahead of her. A single woman waiting alone, in a male-dominated environment, would have been vulnerable.

My mother caught the 3 p.m. train from Gauhati for Lumding, via Chaparmukh. This too was single-track metre gauge, which carried fourteen trains a day each way with essential supplies for the Burma front. Each train could carry forty-five four-wheeled trucks. It was the main supply line from Calcutta. I'm sure my father would have found some excuse to be in Dimapur – but how long would he have to wait? Suppose they missed each other – what then? At 1 a.m. on Tuesday, 6 February, Betty's diary recorded: 'Met Nor'. It must have been a

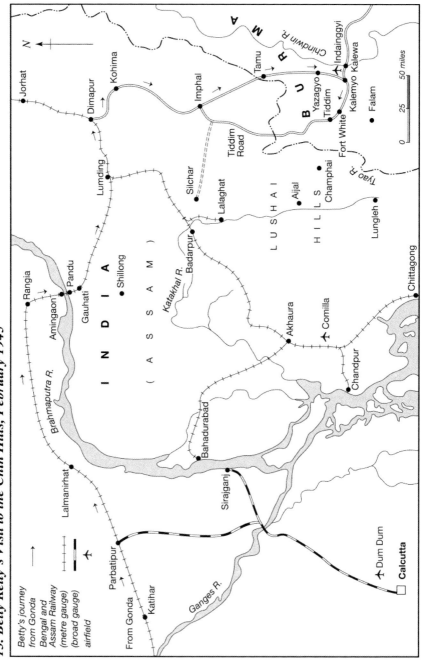

13. *Betty Kelly's Visit to the Chin Hills, February 1945*

wonderful reunion once more. Where in Dimapur had they met? He could not have known her time of arrival.

On Tuesday they were still at Manipur Road railway station. Her diary had in bold: 'McCarthy Igo – may be I go McCarthy. Saw Lt. Col. Norman RAMC [Royal Army Medical Corps]'. Was this another way of hiding my father's identity? Clearly the Army did not want wives visiting their husbands in this way. My father and mother would have to get back to the Chin Hills separately. He was breaking the rules, always a problem if it is the chief adjudicator, as he was on the civilian side. The next part of her journey was going to be up to her intuition.

On Wednesday, 7 February, my mother had reached Imphal 137 miles to the south. There the roads divide: due south to Tiddim along a precarious route or, slightly to the east, to Palel and Tamu on a much better road, which was the main artery of supply to Kalewa (see illustration no. 45), and then across the Bailey bridge over the Chindwin. My mother was in Tamu in the malarious Kabaw Valley on Thursday. The following morning, at 7.15 a.m., she was at No. 2 HQ with the War Graves Commission, where she hitched a ride on a truck going south to Kalemyo.

On Friday, 9 February, my father met her at Joe Ingram's camp north of Kalemyo, near Indainggyi. That same day, Philip Barton had sent a note to Norman from Tiddim warning him to be careful. 'There is a Colonel type here from 14th Army. He'll be returning tomorrow so I hardly see how you can avoid him. If you see his jeep from afar – well and good. You'll be able to stop in time and have a sweet tea, while your luggage [my mother's] lurks in the jungle. Alternatively, let them dress in blankets as Chins! Can suggest no other courses.'

The next day Joe Ingram drove them in his jeep up to Fort White. It must have been a great thrill for my mother to be back in the familiar Chin Hills again. They arrived there at 2 p.m. on Saturday. The old rest house had been destroyed; then they drove on to Tiddim, where Philip Barton, Bob Wilson and Cyril Hazzard were waiting. Pum Za Niong and other Chins must have been so glad to see her. They had a few drinks and talked themselves hoarse. So far they had been able to avoid the Fourteenth Army 'colonel type'.

On the following day, Sunday, 11 February, Betty went to see the hospital, talk to the staff and cheer up some of the patients. Her itinerary included where the Nelsons had lived (the American Baptist missionaries) and Naylor's games' office. In the afternoon she watched a football match on the ground used for so many airdrops (and where my father had been nearly decapitated by a flying bag of rupees) and then there was a quiet dinner with Joe Ingram. Monday was spent recovering from her journey and the emotional turmoil of being back in Tiddim where our home had been burnt down and her beloved garden destroyed.

On the Tuesday she met a lot more Chins. News of her arrival would have spread rapidly and if her welcome home was anything like my father's, it would have been heart-rending. She was much loved by her knitting circle, and so many others, before we had left in 1942. She spent the morning ironing and 'Cookie' (Lieutenant-Colonel E. H. Cooke) threw a party for her that evening. On Wednesday, 14 February, to her dismay, the road to Dimlo (where she was to meet my father) was unjeepable. He had also been dodging the colonel. She spent all morning, in her frustration, with Cookie and at 4 p.m. left Tiddim in a 15cwt truck to drive to Dimlo. She finally arrived after a nightmare journey and 'no kit' at 6.25 p.m. 'Unforgettable Nor' said it all. She had travelled thousands of miles and they were together again.

The next day, 15 February, disaster struck: 'Morale low ebb'. She saw a dead Japanese soldier in a car. Much more devastating, though, was that my father had hoped to take her back to his new home in Falam but that news had leaked out and he had been ordered to get her back to Calcutta immediately – 'Poor darling Norman'. With the road blocked, they had to walk to Fort White. They paused after the first 10½ miles for a rest and then reached Fort White and had tea at the water tank. They then had to walk to No. 3 Stockade; a total of 25 out of 28 miles on foot, two hours of which were in the dark!

On Friday, 16 February (her forty-first birthday), with sore knees, they got to Joe Ingram's camp, and had a 'stream wash' on the road to Indainggyi; my mother had to catch a mail plane to Calcutta. It was number 674 to Comilla in Assam and Dum Dum, near Calcutta. My father must have felt desperate waving goodbye to her after all they had gone through to be together again. Had he disobeyed orders, he could have been court-martialled.

That evening my mother was unable to get a room at the Great Eastern Hotel in Calcutta; she had to make do with the less good Grand. She had accomplished her mission, but what a poignant ending. On Saturday she met the Kennedys in Theatre Road. They had a drink and a laugh and my mother probably had some exciting tales to tell. Her friends must have been a tonic when she was missing her husband so – 'Saw me off. Hurrah.' On Sunday she was on the train for Lucknow, where she arrived the next day to catch one to Gonda.

On Monday, 19 February, we were reunited with our mother. I'm sure we had no idea what jeopardy she had been in. Her anxiety was not unfounded, for the moment higher military command discovered what was going on she was ordered out. My father had a fairly short fuse at the best of times; I hope he never discovered who had blown the whistle on him. He had obtained permission in advance for her to travel to Falam: 'This authorises Mrs. Kelly, wife of Lt. Col. Kelly, to travel in a Civil Affairs Service truck between the hours of 8 a.m. and 8 p.m. on Saturday 17th February 1945.' This permit had been signed by a major –

was he the culprit? My father must have returned to Falam with a heavy heart. We, for our part, were thrilled and I'm sure the Haskins were greatly relieved to see my mother back. She did not tell them a great deal about her adventure – from triumph to disaster in less than twenty-four hours.

Tiddim
18th February 1945

Darling,

I have just had a message from Shillong that you had arrived safely in Calcutta on the 16th. It is a tremendous relief and I am indeed grateful to our Signals people for getting your message through so quickly.

Tiddim is not the same without you, sweetheart, and I have sent off a wireless message today asking for ten days' compassionate leave to see you and the children again before you sail.

I'm afraid our parting (as usual) was very hurried, darling, and I felt utterly beastly at having to hustle you off. As a matter of fact I was half dazed by the suddenness of it all and it was only after you had gone that I fully realised that you had had no lunch, dear. I had posted myself well out on the right hoping you would spot me, and the thrill of getting your final hand-wave was well worth the cloud of dust I got from the slip-stream as you roared off down the run-way. I stood and watched you climb in a long run east and waited until you came back again almost directly over the drome, before setting off for No.2. I felt much too sick at heart, darling, to go and join a lot of strangers in the officers' mess, so I'm afraid I disobeyed your injunction. However, I had only trudged about 10 minutes up the road before Ingram picked me up with his new jeep. He was greatly disappointed at missing you – another conquest of yours, dear. He rushed me back to his camp for lunch and then we set off for Indainggyi. I had several things to do and the activity kept my mind off other things.

Between us we got all our jobs done, but we did not get back to camp until nearly 9 p.m. The Administration Commandant had dinner with us and drove me up here yesterday morning, to spend one night with Wilson and Barton. Joe Ingram followed up later.

There is little more to tell and I am leaving here tomorrow morning. All the local people are dreadfully disappointed that you have gone away again, love.

I shall be glad of a change of scene since you are no longer with me, sweetheart.

God Bless and protect you,

Daddy

Falam
24th February 1945

My own darling,

I arrived back here yesterday to find all the staff eagerly awaiting your arrival, and it brought it home to me very much when I had to tell them that you hadn't been allowed to come. But much more than that has been the signal from Frank Donnison regretting that he can't even grant me ten days' leave to see you before you all sail.

As you can well imagine, darling, it has made me see completely red. When every other fellow in the rear is able to get it, it does seem grossly unfair that I should be stopped. I have therefore sent him a signal saying that in view of his refusal I am seeking a personal interview with Freddy [Major-General Frederick Pearce, Chief Civil Affairs Officer, Burma] at Delhi, will make my own arrangements to get there and will combine the visit with the discussion of many official points of policy which require early decision. I have asked him to wireless his acknowledgement of my message so now I am waiting to see what comes of it.

My Chief Clerk – Mr. Ali – had completely transformed the house in my absence, darling, in preparation for your arrival, and he has been the most disappointed at the breakdown in the arrangements.

He had found some lime in the Jap camp and has had the place white-washed throughout. Also brought back a great deal of furniture and had had curtain rods fitted. Better still, he had retrieved a lot of the glass which had been taken with the furniture to the villages and had all the windows repaired. Had earth-oiled the floors in lieu of polish and had fitted up the bathrooms with thunder-boxes!! I would hardly have known the place, and as soon as the coolies arrived with your boxes, dear, I had to set to at once and get the curtains hung. I couldn't help thinking what a joy it would have been had I only been helping you in the task, darling. Tun Khai was like a hen with chickens and before long – with the two rugs on the floor, the photos on the mantel, the pictures hung and the flower vases filled with cherry blossom, we had the place looking quite homely. In the circumstances I shall certainly not move into the big house. Oatts and his other Levy officers will be back shortly, so they can have that place.

Nothing more at the moment, darling. I'm trying to possess myself in patience for Donnison's reply to my latest move. God bless you, love.

All my deepest devotion,

Daddy

INDIAN POSTS AND TELEGRAPHS DEPARTMENT

26 FEB 45

TO: MRS. KELLY

CARE OF HASKINS GONDA =

RELIEVED LEARN YOUR WIRE SAFE ARRIVAL STOP

MY COMPASSIONATE LEAVE DELHI CATEGORICALLY REFUSED BY 4 CORPS STOP

AM EARNING OUTSIZE IN BOWLER HATS STOP *

LETTERS EXPLAIN STOP

WIRE ME IF ANY DIFFICULTY YOUR SAILING PAPERS STOP

ALL MY LOVE AND THANKS YOUR EPIC EFFORT TO REACH ME STOP THERE IS NO JUSTICE

NORMAN

---

* i.e. running risks with the Army

Chapter 15

FAREWELL TO THE HILLS

Betty Kelly did not know that her husband's health was deteriorating. The categorical rejection of compassionate leave by 4 Corps was to have dire consequences – the thought that he might not see the family before they sailed for England was the last straw. He was now under the care of Captain Ba Pu, Senior Medical Officer, Chin Hills, who wrote the following report on 4 March 1945:

Confidential:
Report on present health of Lieut. Colonel N. W. Kelly, O.B.E. CAS(B)., Senior Civil Affairs Officer, Chin Hills
I have been in personal contact with Lt. Colonel Kelly for the past year.

I am of opinion that owing to long service and continued residence in isolated forward areas (Chin Hills) for the past three years his health and general condition has, and still is, deteriorating.

He has not had home leave (U.K.) since 1936; he suffers from insomnia, and this is, I consider, partially due to anxiety connected with family affairs.

Both myself and Lieut. Joseph, CAS(B) (Medical) consider that he is now suffering from ANXIETY NEUROSIS and that it is desirable for Lt. Col. Kelly to appear before a board empowered to recommend either treatment or leave to United Kingdom. Further continued service in his present state is undesirable.

Signed: Ba Pu, Capt.

C.A.S. (B)

Senior Medical Officer, Chin Hills

Dated Falam

4th March 1945

No. 351/0-1 dated 4/3/45 from SCAO., Chin Hills to Dy.CCAO.[1]

The next couple of letters from Norman Kelly to his wife betray his frustration and increasing irritation with the authorities over the question of leave and his health.

S.C.A.O., CHIN HILLS, S.E.A.C.
[Senior Civil Affairs Officer, South-East Asia Command]
7th March 1945

Darling,

I have just been thrilled to get your first two letters in the mail – one headed The Grand, Calcutta 3.15 p.m., and the other, the Royal Hotel, Lucknow, February 19th. It makes life worth living again, sweetheart, to have got them. The one you refer to as having been posted on the train on the 18th has not turned up. Despite your telegrams by which I knew you were safe, you can imagine how keen I have been to get some details of your journey. I'm glad you enjoyed the air-trip and were looked after on arrival – but then, what male could have resisted looking after you!! It was damned amazing, albeit, that you got no booking at the Great Eastern and had to share a room at the lousy Grand. What a bit of luck running into John and Molly Kennedy! He always seems to be popping up in your young life!!

(This damned ink powder of yours seems full of grease.)

I will certainly write and thank Malcolm for trying to help you, darling. I have had a message that the trunk had been despatched. I'm sure the Kennedys did their best to make you happy while you were hanging around Calcutta.

The luck seems to have held in meeting Meg O'Donel in the office when you went to book for the Gonda train. As Syd has moved much further on, it is unlikely I'll have a chance to see him again now.

By now, of course, you know all about the disappointment of my projected Delhi visit, and the scrape I landed myself in over it [blacked out by censor] two doctors here to give me a health certificate to say 'I've had it' and that I am suffering from an anxiety neurosis on which they recommend I be put before a medical board with a view to home leave. God knows how this one will turn out, darling, but the die is cast so I can only stand by the result, even if this means a bowler hat. It is all very worrying and does seem so unfair that I should have to risk – in order to get away – our whole future, by going so Bolshy, after I have tried for so long to give them loyal service.

However, you and the kiddies come first and always will, sweetheart, so I'm trying not to think about it. I pray God will see that justice is done and that He will see that we are soon reunited.

No great news here, love. Col. Oatts and all the old gang are back in H [Haka] and expected here soon. Tuang Hmung [Assistant Superintendent] from H has been over to discuss a few things and returns tomorrow.

Cookie [Lieutenant-Colonel Cooke] sends his best respects in his usual formal way!

Hope Ian Wallace has been looking after you in Delhi. I have sent off a wire asking your address after March 7th (today) which you mentioned in your wire. It is all very confusing not knowing what your movements are.

Neither of your letters really tell me how you are, sweetheart, as of course you were keyed up in the throes of travelling, but in your next I trust I shall learn that both you and the kiddies are thoroughly well (though still probably unsettled). What a damned life.

All my devoted love as ever, sweetheart.

Yours alone,

Daddy (BOLSHY)

S.C.A.O., CHIN HILLS, S.E.A.C.
8th March 1945

Sweetheart,

A wire from you today! Is this a record reply to mine yesterday, or a telepathic overlap? But, oh, how I would like to know why the delay in your sailing papers!

However, it may all turn out for the best, because, were I 'boarded' and sent on leave, who knows but that I might not be able to join you before the end of the month? Is that too much to hope, love? I feel scared to tempt the Fates by even thinking of it!

From the wire I gather you must have linked up with Dodie Courtenay at Maidens Hotel, Delhi. Give 'em my love (if you can spare a spot of it).

A kick in the pants for Freddy [Major-General Pearce, Chief Civil Affairs Officer, Burma] from me, if you see him. I'm fed up with the whole blooming shootin' match. It's dreadful not knowing fully what is happening at your end.

Only mail today is Grindlay's statement! We seem to have been pretty deep in the red at one stage and only pulled out in Jan. So now you'll have to figure out where you stand over your insurance and the kiddies advance fees. I *do* feel their chances must not be jeopardised and you must go ahead with your best plans for them, even if it means a further overdraft against the security of your Defence Bonds and/or insurance. I'm sorry I'm not there to help you, sweetheart, but I know your decisions will be right and will be God-guided.

You'll have to take every bean there is in the bank (Imperial) when you sail, and draw whatever advances are admissible on sailing. Leave me to work it off somehow. 'They' will either keep my nose to the grindstone milling out the few family shekels or they will take it out of me as soon as they get me back from a begrudged leave.

Riches just don't seem to come our way, darling, other than by way of Love, so keep smiling!

Sweet dreams and God bless you.

All my love,

The Bolshy Dad

In Delhi, on Saturday, 3 March, Betty went to see the Senior Service Officer in the Old Fort. She was doing her best to try and get 4 Corps to grant Norman compassionate leave. On the following day, with the same mission, she visited GHQ (where Freddy Pearce was based) and then had dinner at Maidens Hotel, to press her case. On 6 March she met Ian Wallace again for lunch. At this stage, the Civil Affairs Service, Burma, where Ian Wallace worked, was based in the HQ of Army Land Force South-East Asia (ALFSEA). This was the office to which the Civil Affairs Officers in the Chin Hills reported. Before the war it would have been the Secretariat in Rangoon, which had responsibility for the Burma Frontier Service. Betty, while in Delhi, was getting to know as many people as possible.

On 7 March there was a dinner dance at the Maidens hotel with the 'Contemps Band'. Betty's diary records:

Thursday, 8th March:	Work with Des. [We had not had any lessons since December!]
Friday, 9th March:	Shopping with Dodie Frost, walk with Doreen; Maidens 'Contemps'.
Saturday,10th March	Imperial Hotel, New Delhi, Pauline and Humphrey.

On Sunday, 11 March, Betty met Meta Robinson Cleaves at 4.30 p.m., and at 11 a.m. the next day she met Pauline at New Delhi Station. She saw Stephen de Glanville, whom Betty and Norman had first encountered in Loilem before the war. He had done outstanding work helping Norman during the Chin Hills campaign.

Meanwhile, Norman's health continued to deteriorate in spite of treatment in Falam; towards the end of March Captain Ba Pu wrote a further report for the Medical Board at 88 Indian General Hospital in Imphal. His report was backed by Lieutenant-Colonel Cooke, Indian Army and Deputy Senior Civil Affairs Officer, Chin Hills.

OFFICE OF THE SENIOR MEDICAL OFFICER, CHIN HILLS, FALAM
CONFDL. NO. 152/Med.
Dated Falam, the 29th March 1945.
To: 88 Indian General Hospital

Subject: Medical Board–Lieut. Colonel N. W. Kelly, O.B.E., SCAO, Chin Hills

Since my report regarding Lieut. Colonel N. W. Kelly written on 4th March 1945, I have visited him daily. He complains of palpitations, sleeplessness, loss of appetite and there is apparent loss of weight. I have examined him carefully and though there is no apparent physical disease which I can detect, his condition is deteriorating.

He has been treated with the usual sedative drugs, but these do not appear to do any good; on one occasion 90 minims of paraldehyde had to be followed with 20 grains of bromide.

Insomnia and forgetfulness are becoming more in evidence and difficult to control; I consider this to be due to anxiety connected with family affairs. During my visits he is sometimes attentive, but more often not so, and frequently after a sleepless night it is not possible for him to connect subjects; he repeats the same statement again and again.

Whatever his disease may be I consider that his condition is abnormal and that he is not capable of performing the duties expected of him.

Insomnia, forgetfulness, inability to concentrate are the main signs indicating some form of nervous trouble.

Captain, S.M.O., C.A.S.(B).,

Chin Hills, Falam[2]

H.Q., 4 Corps, SEAC

Subject: Medical report

Medical Report regarding Lt. Colonel N. W. Kelly, O.B.E., SCAO, Chin Hills forwarded herewith.

In anticipation of orders for Lt. Col. Kelly to attend a medical board I am sending a copy of the report to H.Q. 551 Sub Area.

Signed: E. H. Cooke, Lt. Col. Deputy SCAO, Chin Hills[3]

Harold Braund related his farewell to his friend Norman on his departure from the Chin Hills in his book *Distinctly I Remember*, in which he gives a sense of the poignancy of what they had been through together mingled with the sadness of friends lost:

I marched out of Falam, most fittingly, with Norman Kelly. He now was in bad shape physically and was on his way out via Tiddim and Imphal to appear before a Medical Board. It was a sorry trek for both of us, with our memories of the sylvan progress that the traveller along the ridge top had once enjoyed.

At Mangkheng, the last halt before Falam, I spent some time searching for the grave of David Milligan. He had been killed there, and the Japs were said to have buried him superficially on the slope above the now ruined rest house; but I was unsuccessful.

In what once would have been the shade of the Fort White rest house, I said 'farewell' to Norman and watched his still-resilient stride carry him off towards the Tiddim that he knew and loved so well. I stayed long enough to identify from afar the slopes on which Peter Bankes had died, and then dropped down the road that led to the Stockades.[4]

Norman Kelly duly appeared before the Medical Board in Imphal in early April 1945 and was not sent on leave, or treated, as suggested by Captain Ba Pu. He was considered to be 'unfit for active service' for six months and sent back to Falam. Shortly after his return he suffered an acute heart attack. He was only forty-one and had been extremely fit before the war reached the Chin Hills. The strain of the past three years had finally taken its toll.

CONFIDENTIAL:

Office of the Senior Medical Officer, Civil Affairs Staff, Chin Hills District
No. 158/Med.
Dated Falam, the 17th April 1945.

To: 88 I.G.H.

Subject: Lt. Col. N. W. Kelly, O.B.E., C.A.S.(B), SCAO, Chin Hills

I understand Lt. Col. N.W. Kelly O.B.E., CAS(B) was placed in Medical category C2 for 6 months by the Medical Board, held at 88 I.G.H. during early April 1945.

In continuation of my report No. 152/Med., dated 29/3/45, regarding Lt. Col. N. W. Kelly, O.B.E., I now report that he had an acute heart attack on the evening of 16th April 1945. The pain is localised over the precordial region causing restlessness. I am of the opinion that he is suffering from CORONARY THROMBOSIS. He is under my treatment at FALAM, Chin Hills.

He will be evacuated to 88 I.G.H. as soon as he is fit to travel.

Captain, Ba Pu, M.B.B.S., S.M.O.

Chin Hills District, Falam[5]

It is highly probable that prior to the heart attack he was suffering from severe angina with palpitations and insomnia due to chest pain, which was difficult to control. The journey to and from Imphal could not have helped his precarious cardiac state; it is more likely to have aggravated it. The underlying diagnosis had been missed, and he was being treated with heavy doses of sedatives, which would have caused forgetfulness and an inability to concentrate. He would now have to remain in Falam until his heart muscle had healed sufficiently for it to be safe to travel back to the hospital where he had been less than two weeks before. On 16 April Dr Ba Pu advised that when he was fit to travel '...he should use the pony on the whole of the journey'.

Rank	Name and Initials	Corps	Nature and date of casualty	Date	Remarks (in the case of casualties from wounds or disease any available information for communication to relatives should be stated)
Lt. Colonel	KELLY, N.W.	C.A.S. (B)	CORONARY THROMBOSIS	16 April 1945	Heart attack on evening of 16th April '45. Diagnosis by S.M.O. Chin Hills – CORONARY THROMBOSIS. Now under treatment at Falam, Chin Hills, and will be evacuated to 88 I.G.H. when fit to travel, ride S.C.A.O. Chin Hills, signed No. K 4/17 dated 17 April '45, addressed D.C.C.A.O. 505 District.

(date)   17/4/45   Lt. Colonel E. H. Cooke, S.C.A.O. Chin Hills S.E.A.C.[6] [Lieutenant-Colonel E. H. Cooke had now taken over as Senior Civil Affairs Officer from Norman Kelly.]

Eleven days after his heart attack Norman wrote a reference for Vum Ko Hau, who had served him so well throughout the campaign:

> Office of the Deputy Commissioner
> Chin Hills District
> Dated Falam, the 28th April 1945

I have been in close touch with Vum Ko Hau since my first arrival in this district in 1939, and have had every opportunity of forming a fair opinion of his character.

I regard him as being entirely trustworthy, and intelligent beyond the point required for the appointment he holds at present, namely that of Stenographer to the Senior Civil Affairs Officer.

He is a Siyin Chin who commands considerable influence amongst his own people as was evidenced in the active part he took in the organisation and operations of the Siyin Independence Army in its rebellion against the Japanese domination in September–November 1944.

I commend him highly to my successor.

> Lt.-Colonel N. W. Kelly, O.B.E., B.A. (Cantab.)
> Senior Civil Affairs Officer & D.C.
> Chin Hills, S.E.A. Command

In Simla

My mother, Maeve and I moved to Simla; Maeve and I and shared the same tutor, Mr Parker Gilmore, as John and Una, the children of General Slim, then in command of the Fourteenth Army. My mother was bombarding Ian Wallace to try and get my father out of the Chin Hills. She must have known the results of his first medical board from Ian.

```
JHBC V JGJG NR22/PT404/0     IMMEDIATE      10TH MAY1945

FROM: DETARM INDIA 101200

TO: COL IAN WALLACE CIVIL AFFAIRS SERVICE BURMA C/O ALFSEA *

S/37120/SIGS RESTD. FROM MRS. KELLY:-

AM STILL IN SIMLA AND NOT (REPEAT NOT) MOVING. TELL LT
COL N. KELLY TO COME SIMLA (KILSHORE HOUSE). DOING
NOTHING ABOUT PASSAGE ** UNTIL HE ARRIVES. ADVISE HQ
ALFSEA. ONLY PLEASE ENSURE IMMEDIATE DELIVERY.
```

It was not until 1 July, after treatment for his heart attack, that my father appeared before his second medical board and was granted 'release leave'.

> Norman Wilson Kelly OBE, Personal Number ABRO-955 Major 15/2/43, Lt. Col 19/9/44, duly appeared before a medical board and was 'Struck off Duty' on the forenoon of the 1/7/45: to proceed on 84-days release leave pending local release.

A copy of this notification, under Release Regulations, Burma Army, was sent to the Frontier Areas Administration, General Administration Dept., Government of Burma, Secretariat, Rangoon, on 11 July 1945, and a copy to Record Office-Burma Army, Maymyo. My father was on his way back to England at last.

Back in the Chin Hills

There was a new commander at 4 Corps – General Sir Frank Messervy, a first-class officer with a great sense of humour. He had distinguished himself on the Arakan front; when the Japanese went round his flanks he formed a perimeter and fought it out. Air superiority enabled supplies to be dropped into his 'box', and this won the day.

The Lushai Brigade had been relieved by an East African brigade. The Chin Hills Battalion had attacked the Japanese who were in deep bunkers defending Gangaw, but the attack had failed so the RAF had been called in to provide an 'earthquake minor'. The Japanese positions

---

* Army Land Force South-East Asia
** to England

were hit with precision bombing, then Thunderbolts arrived and shot up the ground with cannon. The defenders left in the night, knowing another attack was imminent, and the Chin Hills Battalion thereafter encountered very little opposition.

Za Hu, who had lost an arm when he put a grenade down the back of a Japanese soldier and did not get out of the way in time himself, was the leader of a Chin platoon of Levies. After this episode he was sent to India to be fitted with an artificial limb. He returned with some thirty men and became a gentleman adventurer; he and his men were called the 'Forty Thieves' by Lieutenant-Colonel Oatts, who was still commanding the Levies:

> We always flew the Union Jack at Levy headquarters. It was quite irregular but it was not of my doing – the Chins insisted on it. They had brought the flag away from Falam to prevent its capture, a thing which had never occurred to any of the British officers... The Chins were proud of it, and proud to serve under it and carry it forward to victory in this manner, after all our troubles. So I let it go, and had gradually become proud of it myself.[7]

The brigadier of the East African Brigade came to say goodbye to Oatts and his Levies. He arrived where the 'Forty Thieves' were drawn up for the ceremonial parade in front of the Union Jack. They were in feathers, sworded, with inlaid powder horns slung across their shoulders on embroidered belts, and they were dressed in their Chin ceremonial blankets of dark crimson silk. Oatts recalled:

> On the word from Za Hu they presented arms, with a grave and knightly courtesy which more than made up for any lack of unison. *Ta da da! Ta da da! Ta da da!* sang the trumpet and the Brigadier stiffened like a ramrod and gave his usual drill-book salute. I half expected to be crossly informed that a Brigadier was not entitled to a general salute with trumpet, but he let it pass, being, I think, a little moved, as I was myself. The fine turnout and demeanour of the Forty Thieves brought home to both of us the full extent of the effort made by the brave and loyal Chins. There were no 'reserve occupations' in the Chin Hills; no age limits for active service; no one making profit out of war. Everyone was in the front line, fighting under the British flag, which even now fluttered out behind the Guard of Honour, having been proudly run up by the Chins themselves who, strange as it may seem, could see nothing wrong with the British Empire. I wish that others could have seen this demonstration besides the Brigadier and myself.[8]

The Chin Hills would never be the same again. Harold Braund had

> wondered what the future might hold for these tough, untutored people, whose destiny thus far had been a harshness of living

unknown to the majority of the human race. Would they be better off under the debilitating shield of civilisation or by returning to the demanding life that had bred them? The choice I suppose would not be theirs.[9]

Pioneer Camp and its rest house were a shambles. The PWD bungalows all over the Chin Hills, which had been so attractive before the war with their gardens full of flowers, no longer existed. The mountainsides were scarred by Japanese bunkers, and there were motor lorries rotting down the *khud* (hillsides). In many places the jungle had been blasted out of existence. No. 3 Stockade nearly reduced Braund to tears as he made his way from there to Tahan and Kalemyo. There the only building standing was a latrine-like edifice, where the Subtreasury had once stood before Norman Kelly had spirited away the cash from under the noses of the Japanese. Harold Braund flew out from Indainggyi, on the same route as Betty Kelly, to Calcutta.

The chief of the Lumbang Khongsais had been honoured with an OBE for his loyalty. Although he had been captured by the Japanese, his prestige and high position among the Chins had saved him from ill-treatment and they had finally let him go. He had been of great assistance to Cuthbert Burne and other Levy officers and had been awarded, by His Majesty King George VI, an emblem the size of a soup plate, which he wore around his neck. A veteran of the Western Front from 1915 onwards, he could not have been more delighted. Norman Kelly, as Deputy Commissioner, must have recommended him for his OBE.

The Levies' Victory Celebration in Haka

Three thousand men, all of whom had served the Levy cause, came in from all over the Chin Hills. Some had been travelling for two weeks. There had never been a gathering of this magnitude before, and it was the first and only occasion at which all the Levies assembled in one spot. The Haka, Zokhua and Klangklang villagers had been preparing *zu* for days. Each chief had arranged for a display by his best dancers and the Lomban chief brought 50 girls. The Chin men and women do not dance together but perform separately – the men expressing courage, strength and agility, the women expressing grace and beauty. This was the ultimate demonstration of what victory had meant to the Chins. Some wore their crimson silks, others ornaments and feathers, while shields and spears were much in evidence. The spectacle was entrancing, emanating friendship and enjoyment, and it lasted through the night.'Titus' Oatts described the celebration:

> The Lomban girls swung round in a circle, hand in hand. I do not know whether it was due to the whisky, the general atmosphere, or the fact that they had washed, but I thought I had never seen girls so lovely and so graceful. Each had a flower in her hair and all

were dressed alike in flowing crimson skirts cut tightly round the hips in a manner which disclosed the most admirable figures, but left all the details to the imagination.

It was a strange thing, also, that not a man got drunk and there was no rowdiness or any noise at all, in fact, other than the music. It was a night of quiet happiness and an occasion in which one is fortunate indeed to have taken part, being such as in this life is likely to occur at the most, but once.

As dawn crept up over the eastern hills they began to depart without a word as they rode away, with their rifles slung across their backs. It was a romantic sight, full of emotion and joy and nobody who was present could ever forget it. [10]

Norman Kelly had predicted a victory celebration – he was so proud of the Chins, whom he thought of as 'my people', and now the Levies were to be no more. They had done their job and come through the entire campaign with patience, courage and honour. It was a fitting farewell, steeped in their own customs.

The spirit of the Chin Levies lived on in the 1st and 2nd Chin Rifles. Their badge was the crossed headhunting swords, which the Levies had wielded so effectively against the Japanese invaders (see photograph no. 15). The 1st Chin Rifles marched through Burma in the wake of the Fourteenth Army. 'Titus' Oatts and Ken Shaw were with them. Oatts remarked, 'The Burmese, and inhabitants of numerous villages, were uncommonly glad to see the British back.'[11]

General Messervy, commander of 4 Corps, also paid his personal tribute to the Chins in his Farewell Order of the day, 13 February 1945, to all ranks, Western Chin Levies:

The story of Fort White and its defence by the Chin Levies was a glorious one. I remember so well the splendid efforts of the Chin Levies in our reconquest of Burma.

It will always be a matter of great pride for you and your sons to know that this great result has been achieved to a considerable extent by your own warlike efforts in the defence of your homes and driving the Japanese for ever from your country. I wish you all the best of luck in the future, and thank you for all you have done to bring about the great victory of 1944/45 against the Jap. [12]

In addition, Brigadier Sir Bernard Fergusson, a famous Chindit, had this to say: 'The Chin Levies built up a formidable achievement and tradition of their own, and became a legend in their short lifetime.'[13] He went on to discuss how many of the Levy officers had been

British employees of the Burma firms, which had been engaged for three-quarters of a century in developing and handling the resources of that rich and beautiful country... I came to know them, these men were all in uniform; but the characteristics which they had in common shone and shimmered through the anonymity which the donning of uniform sometimes involves.

They were all quite remarkably resourceful, and no wonder. I soon discovered that almost without exception they had lived up-country for long periods on their own. They had become accustomed in early youth to being self-sufficient, to taking major decisions without troubling their superiors, to dispensing rough medicine and even tougher justice, and to being, in short, responsible far beyond their years. They were that *corps d'elite* of 'Burma hands'... Braund and all the others rose so splendidly to the occasion, and brought to it their virtues of knowledge, experience, confidence, enthusiasm and guts. But it does give me a chance to pay my own tribute to this select group of men, whose endowments and achievements and contributions are not as widely known as they should be. Among these, incidentally, was the extraordinary loyalty, which they inspired in their subordinates from the many races that inhabit Burma. They shared their faith and their fate, hiding them, guiding them, and sharing all the risks, because they had learned to trust them. Many of these were killed, and must not be forgotten. To seek to recapture the atmosphere of those pre-war days might seem like trying to catch the rainbow with a butterfly net; but I think he has done it. Certainly he has done much to explain to me why the 'Burma hands' who became my trusted friends and comrades in those unexpected and gruelling years were so outstandingly good. [14]

The Chin Levies and their British officers were there when others had departed the arena in 'India's most dangerous hour'.[15] Harold Braund recorded that, at the end of the campaign, the Chin Levies had won the following honours:

> They include 1 DSO., 1 OBE, 2 MBEs., 8 MCs, 5 BGMs [Burma Gallantry Medal] (that I can recall).
>
> For the Haka zone probably more than 400 casualties inflicted on the enemy, we lost 8 killed in action or died of wounds, 8 more by drowning, accident or illness, while of 7 wounded in action only 2 were incapacitated for further service.[16]

Noel Stevenson, who was awarded the OBE in June 1944, wrote: 'It is not easy to assess the service they [the Chins] have done us by that lonely stand, but this we can say – that had the Chins let the Japanese pass through on their conquering way into Manipur and Assam, the difficulties that would have befallen India are beyond computation.'[17] Vum Ko Hau had the most distinguished post-war record of all the Chins. He was a cabinet minister in General Aung San's government and later the Burmese Ambassador in Paris and Prague. In his view:

Since the approach of the Japanese Imperial Army to the Chin Hills border the most important man who had worked for the defence of the Chin Hills, with the assistance of the local Chin people, was Lt. Colonel N. W. Kelly, OBE, BA (Cantab.) of the Burma Frontier Service. He was a highly educated man and was not in favour of denying higher education to the Chins. He was very popular with the people as well as with the Chiefs. The Japanese intended to invade India through the Tiddim subdivision so this part was more vitally important than any other part of the Chin Hills. Col. Kelly did his best to organise the Tiddim Chin Levies. In due course the Siyins and the Soktes came forward to give a helping hand.

Col. Kelly had won a name for himself for the many invasions of Japanese outposts in the Kale Valley and his evacuation of the Kalemyo Treasury just before it fell to the enemy.

When Burma was occupied by the Japanese army, the only district that remained defended by the local people themselves and was for a long time unoccupied was the Chin Hills. We were able to defend the last part of British Burma for a few years until March 1944. [18]

A great deal of credit should go to the Chin Hills Battalion, who remained continuously in the front line, without a break, for an inordinate amount of time. Others who played an indispensable role and deserve full acknowledgement include the transport coolies and those who laboured to build not only the Tiddim Road but also the airstrip near Tiddim from which the seriously wounded were evacuated. The support that the wives and children gave their menfolk, and the loyalty of the majority shown to the British cause should also be recorded. Some of the Chin women, like the Russians, carried arms in the defence of their homes. They were living on or near starvation subsistence for much of the campaign. No other indigenous tribe in Burma made such a large contribution, or was so intimately involved in the fighting as the Chins.

Norman Kelly had done his duty and more, for it nearly cost him his life. He had inspired the Chin Levies and had remained in the hills in March 1944, when the 17th Indian Division was fighting its way back to Imphal. As the Senior Civil Affairs Officer 1944–5 he had the responsibility of getting the civil administration back on its feet again, before his health broke down. On 25 April 1942, when the loyalty of the Chins was in the balance, he had said: 'We must all be prepared to help. We must fight each for his own existence, for in that way only shall we conquer and be worthy of our victory.'

Homeward Bound

In April 1945 my father handed over as Deputy Commissioner of the Chin Hills to Jack Leedham, who knew that my father was a very sick man. Harold Braund, who accompanied him on the first part of his journey to Tiddim, described him as 'in bad shape physically', and by the time he got to Calcutta, Marjorie Leedham said she did not recognise him. No wonder my mother sent a wire to Ian Wallace on 10 May, saying she was not moving from Simla, nor arranging a passage to England, until her husband appeared. On 3 May 1945, just three years after the capital of Burma had fallen to the Japanese, the British Fourteenth Army marched into Rangoon.

My father arrived at Kilshore House, Simla, in June and must have been enormously relieved to lay down the burden he had carried since April 1942. As Jack Leedham said in his subsequent letter to my father: 'Your release from Civil Affairs Service Burma must be a great tonic.'

When my father finally reached us there was a tremendous celebration. Burma had been recaptured, the Chins had covered themselves with glory and my father was back with my mother and out of danger – not just until his leave was over but for good. We later moved from Simla to Bombay, and my father wrote to Jack Leedham from there on 14 July. We stayed in Bombay at the Taj Mahal Hotel, described as the most modern in the East. It was massive, standing on the seashore, near the Gateway of India – another impressive piece of imperial architecture. It was erected to commemorate the landing of King George V and Queen Mary in 1911, and looked out over the harbour and the hot muddy ocean. The panorama, which greeted passengers steaming into Bombay, has been compared to the Bay of Naples. The mail boats lay alongside the wharf at Ballard Pier. We were only at the Taj for a night because of the vast expense, before moving on to the Mirima. This was a delightful hotel with a sandy beach, palm trees and its own swimming pool. Here I was bewitched by the ocean and got severely sunburnt.

At last we set sail on the SS *Magdipur* for Plymouth. We took with us Margaret Rose, daughter of Marjorie Rose, one of my form teachers at the Hallett War School. Margaret was my age and it was not unusual in those days for children to be taken home by other families. The three of us had a great time. It was traditional for juveniles – and, I dare say, some grown-ups – to throw their topees over the side as they sailed away from India for the last time. As we left the brown waters of Bombay, there came a time when the sea changed to the dark navy of the Indian Ocean. While sailing across this we had to stay below decks because of the fear of air raids. My mother gave us school lessons daily.

Everything was a novelty – and there was English money on board, instead of Indian. A ten-year-old boy and I decided we would set up a laundry and, with the money earned, we would be able to buy our parents a drink at the bar, the ultimate in sophistication. Neither of us had any experience of ironing shirts, but we soon became proficient. There was also 'housie-housie', now known as Bingo, another distraction to spend our money on, fancy-dress parties, deck games and lots more. It was wonderful having my father with us. His health was restored and he would bribe the dance orchestra to play his favourite tune, 'A Nightingale Sang in Berkeley Square', which he and my mother loved so much.

As we entered the Red Sea the temperature rose appreciably. Our laundry was in the bowels of the ship, but by now we had some regular clients, and in spite of the intense heat, could not let them down. We arrived at Suez and entered the canal. It was an awesome experience to see Egyptians on camels so close to this extraordinary waterway through the desert. It was single file until we arrived at the Bitter Lakes, where there was space for ships to wait in turn to enter the remainder of the canal. The sunsets were out of this world, the vast blazing orb sinking slowly into the sand. From Port Said we entered the Mediterranean. I don't remember *gully gully* men this time. The term is an English corruption of the Egyptian word *gale*, meaning magic. *Gale* men still entertain children with their tricks at birthday parties in Cairo.

On 14 August 1945 the Japanese surrendered unconditionally to the Allies. My father was in party mood on the SS *Magdipur*, steaming across the Mediterranean. He hung out his captured Japanese flag, the one he had given me. It adorned our cabin door. I'm sure he would have recalled the letter from the Chief of Co-operation Commissioner Chin Hills on 12 March 1944: '...I want to teach you about Bible before you die...the Kings Of the East...Nippon...the Land of the Rising Sun.'

The next day it was my father and mother's wedding anniversary. Who could have guessed that in fourteen years of marriage they would have been through so much together? As my father had said, 'Riches just don't seem to come our way, darling, other than by way of Love, so keep smiling!' For us, as a family, we had much to be thankful for. My father had survived the war against all the odds, had stood up for what he believed in and had won the respect and gratitude of the Chins. Now this was the parting of the ways.

We passed the Rock of Gibraltar, sailed through the turbulent Bay of Biscay and finally arrived at Plymouth. Maeve recalls that ' "Home" was a cold and distant land. It was drizzling with rain, an alien culture. There were freezing winters, rationing, English boarding schools, loneliness and isolation. The battles in the Far East were not much regarded by a nation bombed by Hitler just over the water, so we locked up our experiences and silently mourned the loss.'

Lend-Lease by the United States ended abruptly in September 1945; immediate post-war Britain was short of goods and money. Attlee's grim message to Parliament was that with peace comes austerity. We listened to the wireless a few hours a day and here again were the chimes of Big Ben at 9 o'clock, as we had heard them years before in our Tiddim bungalow where our wireless ran off a generator powered by my father or our gardener pedalling a stationary bicycle on the veranda.

Noel Stevenson was now in a senior position with the Civil Affairs Service, Burma, where his experience must have been invaluable. He was referred to in a letter that Jack Leedham had written to my father, dated 19 August 1945.

S.C.A.O., Chin Hills,
Burma, S.E.A.C.
19th August 1945

My dear Norman,

Many thanks for your letter from Bombay (dated 14/7) and received here four days ago. The Simla 'gossip' was most welcome as I hardly ever get any news of what is going on in the haunts of the mighty 'Asoya' [Government]. With Stevenson sitting in the haunts of the mighty I feel that certain gentlemen who shall be nameless are not going to get away with as much as they have in the past, if they get away with anything at all in the future. H. N. C. Stevenson seems to have a hell of a pull there, and though he and I do not get on too well I am glad to see him where he can smite the ungodly.

We have not received the promised reports on the Zahau–Hualngo [19] case, on Tashon, etc. And you have one of the files from the District office with you. I have released Chief Thang Tin Lian [of the Zahau-Hualngo tribes] from close arrest and his return to his tract will have to be permitted in the near future. I did not want to do it till I got your report on the Hualngo business but my hand is rather being forced by the passage of time and public opinion. I cannot justify his detention much longer. You may have submitted your reports at Simla, in which case I will no doubt get them in another 3 or 4 months' time, depending on the 'celerity' of Simla, and the vagaries of the Army Post Office (I am still getting letters from Marjorie written in Calcutta and dated early April). Marjorie mentioned your visit and said she did not recognise you, and I don't wonder for you were a very sick man when you left here. However, your release from Civil Affairs Service, Burma must be a great tonic, and two months with the family as well ought to have done a lot for you – it is less than you deserve for your last three years.

I am pretty definitely not to be here permanently. Who is to relieve me is another question. I am either to go to the Shan States or to the Kachin Hills according to the gossip. This state of suspense is damnable for me as I have to try and keep things dragging along till the permanent man comes up, and for the Chin it is the most unfortunate thing that could have happened. Trust government to give the most trouble to those who fought for them, everyone seems Burman mad just now – and to hell with the hill folk both Kachin and Chin who did so well.

As I am not to be here permanently I have brought in no equipment or household odds and ends, and am still using yours. I will have them packed up and ready to be sent on to you. One of Betty's vases is alas defunct. I will be very grateful if you will let me know what I owe you for its loss and for the wear and tear on your other things, it has been very kind of you to allow me to use them.

The best of luck to you both and the kiddies for your leave.

Yours,

Jack Leedham

This was to be the last letter from the Chin Hills. Jack Leedham became Resident and Special Judge, Lashio, Northern Shan States. Joshua Poo Nyo was appointed Deputy Commissioner, Chin Hills, in Falam. Tommy West joined the Burma Frontier Service and took over my father's old job from Philip Barton as Assistant Superintendent, Tiddim. Roy Ogden had, amazingly, rescued Maureen Baird-Murray (née Rossiter), who had been left behind as a child by her father Edward Rossiter, also of the Burma Frontier Service, during the Japanese occupation. Her mother was a very beautiful Shan lady, Khin Nyun. The remarkable story of her arrival in England, thanks to Ogden, is told in her book *A World Overturned: A Burmese Childhood 1933–47*. Her father was very ill after his trek out and died in India.

The King's Message to Burma

In Rangoon on 17 October 1945 the Governor of Burma, Sir Reginald Dorman-Smith, read a message from King George VI to the people of Burma at City Hall in front of a gathering of eminent citizens, to welcome the Governor back:

> Finally, the King's message had a special word for the hill peoples of Burma, who had with such steadfast courage maintained for three long years the fight against the enemy. A separate arrangement would be made for their administration, so that special attention might be given to their welfare and their indigenous institutions be developed. His Majesty expressed the hope that the day was not far distant when they too would desire of their own free will to take their place in a self-governing Burma. HMG would do all in their power to forward this last step in the historic task of the unification of Burma. [20]

In October 1945 nobody knew what the future would hold for Burma. The British had won a famous victory, thanks to the loyalty of the Empire's troops. They had, to their eternal credit, fought for their core values but the cost in lives was huge. Burma was saved from the Japanese and their atrocities, but the Burmese now wanted their independence (*Epilogue in Burma 1945–48* by John McEnery provides a lucid account of events). Would it be possible to safeguard the interests of the hill peoples before independence came? Norman Kelly was to resume his career with the Burma Frontier Service in Rangoon. When he left England once more he did not know what his new job would be; it was a bitter pill to swallow that his family was to remain behind.

Chapter 16

RETURN TO RANGOON

England seemed cold and drab in 1946. Food and clothing were rationed and in their hearts the British realised that things would never be the same again. The British Empire, which had contributed so much to the prosperity of the United Kingdom pre-war, was now unsustainable. Britain owed millions of dollars to pay off the Lend-Lease debt to the USA; this had been entered into in March 1941, when Britain stood alone, to use US military equipment without paying for it until after the war.

On 26 July 1945 Churchill and the Tories had lost the general election to Clement Attlee; Labour was in power with an overwhelming majority. The new government was concerned with the construction of the welfare state and the National Health Service; the rebuilding of Burma was not on its agenda. However, a White Paper outlining the plans for Burma's independence was published; it protected the hill peoples and honoured the Karenni's treaty rights.

In February 1946 my father set off to return to Rangoon alone. It was with a heavy heart, as his first two letters to my mother and myself indicate.

Adelphi Hotel
Liverpool
12th February 1946, 8 a.m.

Darling,

It's no use trying to say anything for I know you will try your best to keep smiling and to keep a firm upper lip. Things could be a lot worse, and I trust it won't be long before you can join me again. Don't let the old job get you down, sweetheart, and look after your health – you *must* know how precious you are to me.

I shared a carriage up to Liverpool St. with a very decent Scot in the RAF and this conversation and the gin kept me going. Got over to Euston by 10.30 p.m. – too late for a drink – so filled in my time drinking coffee in the hotel. Shared a carriage down with an ICS chap bound for Calcutta, so we both had ample room to stretch out and managed to get some sleep. Arrived here shortly after 6 a.m. and have just had breakfast. Have written letter cards to both the kiddies. I'm sure they'll be interested to know that ex-King Zog of Albania is travelling on the 'City of Exeter'. [1]

We are due to embark at 10 a.m. and there's no other news, dear. It looks as though we'll be a pretty crowded ship, and from first appearances, an average mouldy crowd of elderly folks.

You'll notice that my damned pen has run dry! It would! I *do* hope you get yourself a super one as my birthday gift, love.

My cheerios to Lily [my father's sister] and Bernard and do try to thank them for me, for giving us such a good and homely time.

All my love, sweetheart, as ever and tons of hugs,

Yours alone,

Daddy

On 1 October 1945 I had become a boarder in the junior part of King's School, Canterbury, my first experience of an English school.

Adelphi Hotel
Liverpool
12th February 1946

Dear Old Tigger,

Just a line to say goodbye for a while. Don't be downhearted and try to keep smiling. Mummy will give you instructions about my address, and I do hope you will write to me regularly.

Time will soon pass, and it will be great fun looking forward to our next meeting.

I have just had breakfast here after travelling all night and we are due to join our ship – the 'City of Exeter' – at 10 a.m. Ex-King Zog of Albania is also travelling in the same ship to Port Said.

I'll try to send you Burma stamps regularly. Try your best in your school work, old boy, and *do* try to be more careful of your spelling. I *do* so want you to do well at school for Mummy's sake.

All my love and tons of hugs,

Daddy

S/S *City of Exeter*, At Sea
22nd February 1946

Darling,

This is our 10th day out and we are due to arrive at Port Said early tomorrow, when I will despatch this by air. As this is an old coal-burning ship I understand we will be in port for at least 12 hours for coaling, but it is not clear yet whether we will be allowed ashore or not. I have already written to the two children but I'm afraid I haven't had much heart to write other letters. I don't think I've ever felt more lonely nor would I have believed it possible among a couple of hundred fellow passengers. It is all so desperately different from our homeward voyage when we were all together. I'm just hating these seemingly endless days with the inevitable round of food, games and sleep, dearest, and my one anxiety now is to get back to my job as quickly as possible. Perhaps I'll not feel so bad when I've got something positive to occupy my mind, and to keep me from thinking too long on all the happiness I have left behind in you and the kiddies, sweetheart of mine.

This ship has accommodation for over 200 and the cabins are quite good. I am sharing a two-berth room with an ICS fellow – Lewis – who is Director of Rice Supplies, Calcutta – a very decent chap whose family life has been steadily heading for a bust for the last fourteen years. Naturally he is very down in the mouth so I fear we make a pretty gloomy pair at the moment. We have formed up a quiet bridge four with two other chaps – one P.W.D. and the other a mine manager for Mackinnon Mackenzie.

Deck games and evening amusements are much the same as on the home trip and there is very little variety. The food is quite good, fortunately, and we have both a barber's shop and a laundry. The passengers are a very mixed bag. At one end are the ex-King Zog of Albania with his Queen Geraldine and her three appalling sisters together with a numerous entourage, including a personal bodyguard of thugs!

Then there is the Governor of Cyprus and his Lady Woolley, and two other Indian titled parties – members of the Viceroy's executive council.

There is also a bunch of 75 Indian students – some of the 'Bevin' boys who have been doing engineering courses in England.[2]

Then we have a whole bunch of about 20 earnest women of all ages going out again to western China on various missionary enterprises.

Funnily enough, I haven't come across anyone else on board whose ultimate destination is Burma.

I imagine any Burma crowd must have travelled by the 'Empire Kitchener' direct to Rangoon, and I have a feeling that in view of the delays and expense I'm likely to incur on my onward journey from Bombay, I would perhaps have been wiser to go that way. However, the die is cast, love, so there's nothing more to be said. With any luck I'm expecting a letter from you at Port Said, to put my mind at ease one way or another about your condition, darling. I'll feel a dreadful cad if I've landed you in the soup when I'm not at hand to help you.

I wonder, too, whether the kiddies will have addressed any letters to me at Port Said? I'm full of interest to learn how you are liking your new job, love, and to hear how they are getting on at their schools. I do hope you will be happy at No. 20 Belstead Ave [Ipswich] but you really must pull out at the first sign of friction, and not be imposed upon in any way.

Give my love to Lily, Margaret [my cousin] and Bernard, dearest [we were staying with my aunt and uncle].

We haven't had any violently rough weather, but have been very slow in running into the sunny weather, even after passing Gib. on the night of your birthday. However, for the last two days we have been sailing into perfect weather and blue sea, and I suppose this will continue now.

I do hope you got my birthday greetings cable, dearest. I should love to have been with you, as you know.

No other news at the moment, but I hope you won't want any other than that you are still, to me, the beloved companion and companionable lover that you have ever been. May God bless my darling.

Daddy

S/S *City of Exeter*, At Sea
5th March 1946

Darling,

We should be in to Bombay sometime tomorrow evening and I'm hoping that you will possibly have a letter waiting for me there.

Since leaving Port Said, nothing very startling has happened; the weather has been remarkably breezy and cool throughout and we have not had a tremendous amount of sun. There has been the usual round of Treasure Hunts, Scavenging Parties, etc., and a couple of deck dances. Funnily enough, I didn't compete in the dancing as I have only spoken casually to very few of the women on board, and those were of the elderly type, whose zest was long spent for such pastime. An elderly dame (Mrs. Morse) from the south of Ireland, with a brogue as broad as the bogs, has rather taken me under her wing. She is travelling with her husband to Lahore, and they are a very decent couple indeed.

Another chap on board who claimed to have seen me in Naini Tal is John Bolam of the Police. His wife, I gather, ran some place called Greylands and was coupled up with the Joan Edwards crowd. You probably know more of them than I do, as I believe they had two boys at the Hallett. He seems a good scout and has been my regular partner at deck tennis. Did I tell you that J. C. Poulton's friend Jack Reddy of Scotts was on board? He is bound for Bombay and ultimately Rangoon. Scotts are apparently starting up again there, but apart from telling him what I thought of his outfit, I haven't prosecuted his acquaintance.

I shall stick to the Imperial Bank this time in conjunction with Grindlays at home.

I shan't know until after landing tomorrow what my next movements are, but if there are no instructions awaiting me at Bombay, I propose to catch the night train to Calcutta, which would land me there on Friday the 8th. We at least have our own Govt. representative there who can arrange my onward journey either by sea or air.

Until I get going, darling, I have absolutely no news – everyone is just waiting to get the voyage over.

Have had great fun playing chess with my cabin mate, Lewis, and this has kept us out of possible mischief successfully.

If I can get time tomorrow between landing and catching my train, I shall write giving you any further news I have. Otherwise I'll write on Saturday from Calcutta.

Have written to both the kiddies.

All my love and devotion, sweetheart, as ever,

     Daddy

                   Dhanbad
                      Bihar
           9th March 1946

Darling,

There were no instructions awaiting me at Bombay and no word from Noel Stevenson, so I caught the Calcutta Mail on Wednesday night. We berthed in the afternoon but had a long wait in the Customs sheds before our baggage was sorted out and passed, and this left me no time to drop you a line that evening. Accommodation on the train was very limited and I was lucky to share a coupé with the Dhanbad agent of Mackinnon's who had got it booked in advance. He had invited me to stay with him over the weekend in order to visit some of their collieries and industrial plant, and also to meet some people – Mr. and Mrs. Bowles, whom I had known in Bassein in 1927 and who were very kind to me then. In view of the present disturbances in Calcutta I was glad of the invitation and I can stay with Flannigan, the agent, much more cheaply than in a hotel in Calcutta. I have wired to the Burma Representative in Calcutta re. my passage by sea or air and should hear from him by Monday. My intention will therefore be to pass straight through Calcutta, if possible, only to catch my plane or ship as the case may be.

My host has a grand bungalow here with all modern conveniences and every luxury – rather on the lines of the way the B.O.C. looked after their people.

This place is only about four hours run by rail from Calcutta and is therefore very convenient for my purposes as I also have the use of the Company's telephone and can thus arrange my onward journey direct from here.

Your airmail of February 20th was awaiting me, sweetheart, at Bombay and it is great to know that you were enjoying your school work.

It is most awkward about the kiddies' holidays and your own. I agree that they cannot be left to cross London alone, but perhaps either Carol or Nance Scott could help. If not, surely Lily could go up to meet one or other of them if you paid her expenses?

I'm afraid I hadn't much heart for doing much on the ship and spent most of my time sitting about reading and dreaming of you, darling. I *do* pray that I can arrange for you to join me before very long, sweetheart.

The question in Parliament re. the ex-King Zog and his entourage was rather amusing. They were met in state on arrival at Port Said and certainly had hundreds of packages of baggage including some heavy cases which were closely guarded and must have contained either the royal treasury or ammunition for the bodyguard!!

The report of the discovery of oil in the Chin Hills is really exciting and I shall certainly cable you from Rangoon, darling, if I am going back there. On the other hand, if I am to be stationed in Rangoon, I shall insist on a tour to Tiddim to collect my kit.

I have been speaking to Tommy Bowles on the phone and his information is that conditions there are pretty bloody so far as living is concerned.

He has invited me along to his place tonight (with my host) to give me the 'low-down' so far as he knows it. He and his wife apparently made their exit from Burma in 1942 via Mawlaik and Tamu.

There were no letters for me from the kiddies at Bombay but I suppose they have my Burma address c/o The Director, Frontier Areas Administration, Govt. of Burma, Rangoon.

All my devoted love, as ever, dearest.

Yours alone,

Daddy

Grand Hotel
Calcutta
13th March 1946

Darling,

Arrived here last evening and am standing by now for a plane in to Rangoon either tomorrow or the 15th. All well so far except that the air priorities board are trying to be a bit sticky about my baggage in excess of 65lbs weight. However, Col. Pelly (who remembered me from Bassein days) is the Govt. of Burma representative here, and seems to think he can make it OK for me to take the lot. After all, it doesn't amount to much but I don't want to get separated from it.

On arrival here I rang up Lewis (with whom I shared a cabin on the ship). He picked me up in his car, and after a drink at the United Services Club took me on to the Saturday Club for dinner. Wish you'd been there to dance with me, sweetheart. All the good old 1920–30 tunes and the usual delightfully subdued music which is a feature of the Saturday Club.

This morning the first people who ran into me at breakfast were Mrs. Jennings and Iris Hill! Apparently their house at Kalaw was totally destroyed by RAF bombing and the pair of them are fulminating as ever.

I went to see Pelly this morning and got fixed up with my Burma identity card. He tells me that Bert Mitchell died about a month ago.

This evening I'm going to see the Buzetts who are at the Great Eastern waiting to get away to Canada.

I also ran into John and Mabel Shaw. They are hoping to go to the U.S.A. but are having difficulty in getting their money out of the country.

I bumped into Frank and Phil Nelson who now have a second baby girl. They are on their way to Imphal and then Tiddim where they hope to live on the church verandah, with a lean-to hut alongside! Phil got your address intending to write, but in his usual excitement, Frank left the paper behind in my room when they went off!

Tommy Loadir, the P.W.D. overseer for Loilem, also recognised me here and introduced his wife. He is now a Lt. in the army and is hoping to get his wife in to Burma shortly. They tell me that Toby Leitch, Resident in Taunggyi, has already taken in his wife and 3 children!

At this rate everything should be in order for you to join me in October, love, and the sooner you can do it, the better I'll be pleased.

I'll cable you from Rangoon when my posting is settled, just to let you know what I'm likely to be doing.

At the same time it's damned lonely being in a hotel and, incidentally, Rs 18/8 a day! Shan't be sorry to get settled some place. It's a full month now since I left you, darling, and every day has seemed an age.

You are still my only love and *don't you forget it.*

All my hugs and kisses, dearest,

Yours alone,

Daddy

Norman Kelly flew from Calcutta where the weather was perfect. The plane then overtook a severe storm above the Pegu Yomas mountain range and was subjected to a heavy buffeting, the pilot having to land 32 miles from Rangoon at Hmawbi.

Additional Secretary to the Governor

Norman reported to Government House (see photograph no. 64) and found that he was posted as Additional Secretary to the Governor, Sir Reginald Dorman-Smith, GBE. Norman's job was to last for three months, pending the arrival of Philip Nash from England.

Noel Stevenson, who had been awarded the OBE in June 1944 for his part in the Chin Hills campaign, was Resident and Director, Frontier Areas Administration, Rangoon. Miggy, his wife, gave Norman a great welcome. At 7 p.m. he met Sir Robert Bruce and T. L. Hughes, CBE,

ICS, who was the number one Governor's Secretary, whom he had last met when he was with General Alexander near Kalemyo in 1942.

Norman had never worked in the Secretariat (see photograph no. 63) before and his task was a daunting one. He anticipated a lot of jealousy from the Indian Civil Service (ICS) personnel, who would have been expected to have been chosen for this coveted appointment. He was to live in Government House, and had been promoted to the Resident's grade of the Burma Frontier Service, paid at the same rate as Deputy Director Frontier Administration who had responsibility, among other things, for the Chin Hills. Norman met Jack Haswell, who was now a brigadier and had a DSO for his work in the Chin Hills, as well as L. B. Naylor, who had been awarded the CBE that he so dearly wanted in June 1943 and had talked about with Norman in 1942 (see page 108). Roy Ogden and John Leyden, both Burma Frontier Service men rewarded for their war service with the OBE, were also working in Rangoon.

Norman, who as a Financial Commissioner now rated in precedence above judges of the High Court and Commissioners of Divisions, soon realised that he indeed had the enmity of the Indian Civil Service to contend with. Their clique had the reputation in the Secretariat of being 'whole-time occupied in doing each other down for personal advancement… It will take all my tact (and then some) to steer me safely through the many pitfalls I am sure they will try and set for me', he wrote on 25 March 1946. Shortly after his arrival he dined with the 1st Chin Rifles, at the invitation of Lieutenant-Colonel Oatts, their CO, and met many old Chin Levy officers. Oatts and Sammy Newland had both been awarded the DSO. Although Norman's health was sound, at the end of March he asked for the report on his electrocardiogram to be sent out from England.

Thaung Chin Thang wrote to Betty Kelly in April 1946. He was now Civil Affairs Officer and Assistant Superintendent of Falam subdivision, with magisterial powers. His chief, who only had one wife, had just produced their twelfth child! A friend of Norman and Betty had been murdered on the stairs leading to his flat on the Sule Pagoda Road in December 1945 by an eighteen-year-old Tamil. On 9 April 1946 Norman wrote to Betty saying that

> Military rations and civilian supplies and cloth, etc., are being stolen by the lorry-load in huge quantities and blatantly offered for sale on the black market, which flourishes in Rangoon's Chinatown. The police seem powerless to do anything about it and indeed many of the subordinate force would appear to be in the pay of the black-market ringleaders. In all, some 13,000 buildings have been destroyed or seriously damaged in the town, and thousands of unauthorised squatters have put up their little bamboo and mud huts on these sites with no attempt at sanitary accommodation. Adequate supervision is impossible with our

existing personnel and these areas harbour many organised *dacoit* gangs, well armed as a result of the Jap occupation. There is a tremendous amount of pilfering going on in the docks. General lawlessness and epidemic disease paint the broad outline of the Rangoon picture at the moment and I really don't see that pre-war conditions here will ever be restored again in our time. Hence my wish to get away up country again when you re-join, darling.

The Governor hurried back to Rangoon from Maymyo for the 'Resistance Day' celebrations, in case military action was called for.

On 2 April my father wrote to me to say that a party of VIPs from Bournemouth, England, had arrived by flying boat in Rangoon during the week. The diplomatic bag from London came on the same plane and with it our mail. Peter Courtenay, who had accompanied us out of Burma, had lost his job when the Civil Affairs Service, Burma, closed down and had returned to England. John Franklin, who was in Tiddim with Norman in March 1944, had suffered a nervous breakdown and had been sent home to recuperate. He never returned to Burma. Stephen de Glanville was DC in Falam, but then handed over to Joshua Poo Nyo. A clerk there shot and wounded his boss, and his wife sent Betty Kelly a Laizo Chin blanket, in the hope that her husband's 'five years in the cooler' would be reduced.

One day, as Norman was leaving Government House for the Secretariat, a Burmese rifleman on guard 'presented arms' and then burst out in Chin that he came from Zung, a village near Mualbem, and did Norman remember that as Assistant Superintendent in Tiddim he had enlisted him? 'His obvious joy at seeing me was indeed a pleasure to behold and I really do feel that we have both made our mark in that wee corner of the Empire, dearest' wrote Norman in a letter to Betty on 16 April 1946. In the same letter Norman told Betty that 'Brigadier Marindin, who used to command the Lushai Brigade (now Major General of the 19th Division) phoned me up on Sunday morning to make a date, so I had him along here for lunch. Needless to say we had a great old chin-wag in more senses than one.' In *The Jungle in Arms* 'Titus' Oatts wrote:

> The Rangoon Burmans were greatly interested in the Chin Rifles, which was the only 'native' regiment in the country. By 'native', I mean that it was comprised entirely of natives of Burma – apart from myself and my half-dozen remaining British officers.
>
> I got the impression they were proud of it, indeed they said so for they were continually asking me to dinner parties.[3]

Noel Stevenson and Norman Kelly had told the Governor all about the Chins and, commented Oatts, 'as a result Sir Reginald Dorman-Smith visited the battalion several times'.[4] Stevenson had said:

At one time they stood virtually alone to face an enemy that had just beaten a great army. Aided only by their mountain environment and a small irregular force composed of the local Frontier Force Battalion, itself largely Chin, and disbanded Chin sepoys of the Burma Rifles, the people had succeeeded, in spite of their paltry numbers and inadequate arms, in throwing the enemy back from their borders. [5]

The new Burma was taking shape. Oatts was glad to be back in England after the depressing post-war atmosphere of imperial decay. 'When at last we sailed down the Rangoon River on the evening tide and I saw the gold façade of the great Shwe Dagon Pagoda glittering in the westering sun, I knew very well that I would never set eyes on it again.'[6]

Back in England

Meanwhile, my letters to my father were still full of dreadful spellings. He suggested that my mother should take us to the Victory Parade in London. It was poetic justice that Lieutenant-Colonel Oatts should be chosen to lead the Burma contingent in the Victory Parade and march past before His Majesty King George VI, who took the salute. Oatts later described the event in his book *The Jungle in Arms*. The Americans and Indians went ahead in that order, although the British and the Chins were 'the only ones who had kept the field from first to last. They carried the flag of Burma, a dark blue with the Union in canton and, in the fly, a "peacock in his pride".' It turned out that it had only been invented in 1939 and, as far as Oatts knew, this was the only occasion on which it was publicly displayed. 'The troops lining the route presented arms to it and Attlee and Churchill doffed their hats. As for recognising it, the King did, of course; he had probably designed it himself. Apart from His Majesty, the thousands of schoolchildren also knew what it was. I suppose they had been studying the flags of the British Empire in their atlases... And so, as we marched through London, we were greeted all along the route by shrill and heartfelt cries: "Hurrah! Well done! Good old Burma!"'[7]

The same flag was flown on the Governor of Burma's car in Rangoon. My father sent one to me and I have it to this day.

It was fitting that those who had fought in the Chin Hills campaign should have been so publicly recognised at a time when the sun was going down on the British Empire. Kenny Fraser, among others, had won the Military Cross; when I first knew him he was too modest to tell me how but, shortly before he died, the story came out. He was with the battalion in the thick of the action, and a man in front of him was wounded. Kenny ran out and put him on his back; he could see where the firing was coming from, but saw that 'the Jap was aiming too high'. When Kenny expected to be hit by a bullet the firing suddenly stopped, and he wondered 'Was he going to withdraw or had he run out of ammunition?' Fortunately, Kenny's life, and that of the wounded Chin, were spared.[8]

Events in Rangoon

On 7 May Norman told Betty that he had suffered a bad bout of malaria of the malignant tertian type, which recurs every other day. He was on a course of Mepacrine. The report on his electrocardiogram in England had duly arrived. By 17 June he had fully recovered and was fit enough to play squash on alternate evenings: 'I find that even this strenuous exercise does not knock the old ticker too badly off its beat, so I must be a good deal fitter than when I got home on leave.' In May 1946 the political situation in Rangoon was very tense and the Governor, Dorman-Smith, was due to fly home for discussions with Attlee.

Government House
Rangoon
22nd May 1946

My own darling Lover,

I got off a note in the diplomatic bag yesterday and expected to write at length last night. H.E., however, asked Hughes and myself to his rooms after dinner and we didn't get away until 12.45 a.m. – both of us dead beat. The pace at the moment is terrific, for the country is on the very brink of another and more bloody rebellion than that of 1931 and an unfortunate incident has already occurred in which police have opened fire on a demonstration near Insein. A storm of protest nearly sent the country up in flames. The anti-government 'Pay No Land Revenue' campaign is in full swing and Aung San, who commanded the Burmese puppet army raised during the Jap occupation, is now a political force in the country with the avowed intention of obtaining the immediate total independence of Burma, even if it means fighting for it. He has a well-organised show which calls itself the People's Volunteer Organisation (P.V.O.) and they insist on carrying out military drill. They are well armed with modern automatic weapons and hand grenades so if the country does flare up it will indeed be a bloody struggle. Naturally, we cannot tolerate the formation of private armies and it was found necessary to prohibit the P.V.O. from drilling with even dummy rifles, etc. The situation is complicated by the fact that Aung San has openly admitted shooting, with his own hand, a pro-British headman during the Interregnum. For this murder, the law should take its course but Dorman-Smith had been told that he must not arrest Aung San without advice from the Labour Government, who haven't got one man among them with any *recent* knowledge of Burmese political moves.

Dacoits throughout the country have increased eight-fold and the rice production programme is being held up, with India on the verge of starvation. Unless H.E. can get Aung San into his Govt. we can't prevent a revolt and Aung San can't even be included in the Govt. unless he is given an amnesty against the murder he has committed. The position is most frightfully tense, and while I am writing this, H.E. is having his last interview with Aung San.

Meanwhile the P.M. has agreed that H.E. should go home to discuss the position but has taken the unfortunate step of inviting a complete outsider (Sir Henry Knight, KCSI, CIE, of the Indian Civil Service from Bombay) to act in his absence. This was done without prior reference to H.E. The P.M. has subsequently turned down suggestions that either Wise (already Deputy Governor) should be recalled from his leave in India, or that the acting Chief Justice should take over from H.E. for the three weeks he was at most expected to be away.

Now the bold Knight proposes to arrive here plus wife and two children, so it rather looks that he has been told by Petherick-Lawrence [the Secretary of State] in India that he is coming for some time and that H.E. is unlikely to return to Burma at all.

H.E. was very depressed last night and feels his political enemies at home in the present Government are likely to sell him out completely, and with the present position in India, the Labour Government are quite ready to wash their hands of Burma altogether.

Her Excellency and Pat Dorman-Smith are due from Maymyo next Saturday and it probably won't be long before they leave and we have the new Acting Governor here.

With the political scene shifting every few hours here, you can imagine we are kept pretty busy. It is thought by the CID that there may be some trouble on Saturday when the funerals of the people killed in the recent shootings take place.

It was my intention to get down to answering your grand long three-part letters of the 13th, darling, and here I've filled a whole form with purely my local concerns.

> All my fondest and hottest love, darling, from your only
> Papaduke

With all this pressure, my father wanted my mother to join him in September/October when Maeve and I were back at boarding school.

By 27 May the situation in Rangoon was calmer. Dorman-Smith was due to fly to London on 8 June and Aung San, who was also the leader of the Anti-Fascist People's Freedom League (AFPFL), was doing his best to keep the more unruly elements of his party in check. My father commented:

> The country, however, is still very much on the verge of rebellion and a good deal will depend on Aung San. He certainly has a strong following and all depends on whether he will throw its support in on the side of government or against it. Hitherto he has been anti-government but after negotiations in the last day or two

the position is somewhat more hopeful, although Donnison, the Chief Secretary and Chettle, Inspector General of Police, have threatened to resign if Aung San is brought into H.E.'s Executive Council. To complicate things, H.E. himself has developed amoebic dysentery and is undergoing a course of emetine injections.

Sir Henry and Lady Knight are not bringing their family after all. I've no doubt that he'll have his hands full enough as it is, being entirely new to the present political situation.

The highlight of last week was the re-opening of the old Pegu Club as a Navy, Army and Air Force Indian Officers Club. H.E. was the guest of honour and I was invited as one of the staff. NAAFI has renovated the buildings regardless of cost and ran a very good show – excellent dinner, reasonable orchestra and a cabaret of girls from an E.N.S.A. party. There were about a hundred guests in all including the senior ladies from the services and government.

It was all very reminiscent of the old peacetime club shows and, I thought, seemed just a wee bit unreal in the present state of the country.

I am enclosing a set of the Burma Victory stamps, which I want you to send to Desmond, dear. They look a pretty poor lot to me, but I've no doubt he'll be pleased.

Sir Henry Knight arrived on 10 June and was sworn in the following day; Norman said 'he appeared to be very shrewd and a real live wire'. Dorman-Smith could not fly to England because of his medical condition, so sailed on 14 June on the troopship *Orduna*. In his letter to Betty of 17 June Norman described the temporary Governor as '...a tiger for work and strikes me as a very brilliant Indian Civil Service brain without Reginald Dorman-Smith's political flair and personal charm'. On 25 June he went on to say, 'The possibility of rebellion is still very close and parliamentary interest in the U.K. keeps us at it at all hours. H.E., despite his 60 years, impresses me very favourably with his zest for office work!'

When Philip Nash arrived, he became Secretary to the Governor while T. L. Hughes was on leave; Norman continued in his post as Additional Secretary. Noel Stevenson was due to fly to London to see the Secretary of State at the Burma Office and present their case for better all-round treatment of the hill peoples who had done so well during the war. The Karens in the south-east, according to a letter from Norman on 16 July, had been 'badly massacred by the Burmans during the Japanese occupation, and are sending a deputation to London demanding complete separation from Burma in what they call "Karennistan" – a country of their own'. Norman continued, 'H.E. is now proposing to tour Upper Burma later this month, taking with him both Nash and the Military Secretary plus 2 A.D.C's, leaving me in sole command at this end. In a way I am quite pleased since this gives me another opportunity to show what I can do single-handed.'

On 23 July Norman wrote:

H.E. and party left on Wednesday morning by special train but an hour after I'd seen them off at Mission Road station I got a phone message in the office from the chief Railway Commissioner saying that the train was derailed about ten miles out of Rangoon. This, needless to say, caused considerable consternation and kept me pretty busy at the end of a telephone the best part of the morning. Later news was that only the tender and the first two bag-cars had left the rail and that a relief engine was hauling the rest of the train back to Rangoon.

They were taken back to Government House and set off again the next morning since it took most of the night to repair the track. Norman continued:

By 7.15 p.m. they had reached Toungoo, running about 20 minutes late. Nash, the blighter, has left me a file of arrears to deal with. I can see I'll be working late the whole time they are away in order to keep anything like up to date, as I also have to look after the Military Secretary's office with only one young ADC, a boy of 22, to help supervise the office staff.

Frank Donnison, CBE, Chief Secretary and the official head of the Home and Judicial Department, promised to help but, said Norman, 'he is up to his eyes in his own work with the Communist Party (just declared an illegal association for its subversive activities), staging mass demonstrations tomorrow in Rangoon against what they call the repressive measures of Government'. When Philip Nash got back to Rangoon he and Norman had to decode all the top secret high-level telegrams from London personally, following Dorman-Smith's arrival in London.

On 30 August General Sir Hubert Rance, GBE, CB, the last Governor of Burma arrived, and was sworn in the next day. He had a full year in Burma as Head of the Civil Affairs Service behind him, so he was much more familiar with local problems than Sir Henry Knight. At the dress rehearsal of the 'swearing-in ceremony' Norman had to act the part of His Excellency. Sir Hubert had infinitely more personal charm than his predecessor, Sir Henry Knight, as well as great sincerity of purpose.

Homeward Bound for the Last Time

Norman was hoping to be offered the post of Assistant Director in Noel Stevenson's Frontier Affairs Office. John Leyden, Deputy Director in Noel Stevenson's absence, posted Joshua Poo Nyo to the job. Norman was incensed, had a row with Philip Nash and demanded a day's casual leave. Sir Hubert wanted to know why, saw Norman and recommended that he should be given leave, if he so desired it, at once. It was his wish, so on the following day, 14 September 1946, he handed over his duties to G. E. E. Webster ICS and, instead of Betty going out to join him in October, he boarded the troopship SS *Ormonde* in Rangoon, bound for Southampton. Norman had explained the circumstances in his letter to Betty of 20 September 1946:

> My decision to apply for leave was taken quite hurriedly but I'm sure it was the right one. It came as a result of constant friction with Philip Nash and the ICS generally, plus the jealousy and lack of co-operation from Leyden. In order to do me out of the post of Additional Director, which Steve intended to create for me, Leyden, in Noel's absence, posted Poo Nyo to the existing H.Q. post of *Assistant* Director. This was the post that was to be converted for me into *Additional* Director. Philip Nash has been piling more and more work onto me in a determination to get me tired out to such a pitch that I'd ask to be relieved to make room for his ICS pal Webster.

On 2 October, while his ship was in the Suez Canal, he wrote again to Betty:

> Am feeling very fit myself; sleeping fairly well and my nerves much better. We are due in Port Said tonight about 10 p.m., where we disembark a draft of troops for Palestine. Have had a very good voyage so far apart from the three days' delay in Bombay. Weather good apart from three hot days in Red Sea. Am just living for the day when I'll be with you dearest. All my love as ever.

On the following day he wrote once more, this time from Port Said:

> We went aground last night in the Canal and have been 12 hours late arriving in Port Said. I'm thrilled by the support your letter has given me, darling. I'm completely browned off with government services at the moment and am toying with the idea of throwing my hand in for good if I can find a congenial job. However, I want time to think and talk this out with your help, sweetheart, and the days will be all too long until I'm with you. When we are together just nothing can stop us and nothing else matters. Love is all, sweetheart. All my devotion as ever.

Norman's predictions were correct. In September, after he left Rangoon, the police went on strike and then most of the civil servants, to be followed by university students and key industrial workers. Aung San's Anti-Fascist People's Freedom League (AFPFL) were behind the unrest and he refused any further cooperation with the Governor. The country was soon paralysed; Sir Hubert Rance had to climb down and appoint a new Executive Council in which Aung San was Vice-Chairman with the power of a prime minister. Had Norman's departure been deferred by a few months he would have seen the tide turning against his beloved Chins and the other hill peoples. Their bid for genuine independence was coming to naught; they were being forced into the chaotic mainstream of Burmese politics. It would have been a bitter experience for him to witness all this.

The Panglong Agreement was concluded on 12 February 1947, in the Shan States near Loilem (see map no. 2 on p. 18). General Aung San signed for the government of Burma; leaders of the frontier areas put their full trust in him [9]. The hill peoples, namely Shan, Kachin and Chin, were represented, but the Karens did not trust the Burmese and did not attend. The three Chin chiefs who were all signatories were Hlur Hmung from Falam, Thawng Za Khup from Tiddim (the elder brother of Thawng Chin Thang) and Kio Mang from Haka. Vum Ko Hau attended as the interpreter. They agreed to cooperate with the interim Burmese government as the best way towards independence. Clause 7 of the agreement stated: 'Citizens of the Frontier Areas shall enjoy rights and privileges which are regarded as fundamental in democratic countries.'

The elections of April 1947 gave Aung San and his party a crushing majority in the Constituent Assembly. Sir Hubert Rance had to appoint a new Executive Council in which Aung San and the AFPFL took full control, and in which moderates and ethnic minorities no longer counted.

A meeting was held in Falam for the nomination of Deputy Councillor for the Chins. Thawng Chin Thang, who had played such an important role during the war, gained the highest number of votes. However, he declined the appointment when he learned that accepting it would entail having to give up the Burma Frontier Service, for which Norman had supported him. A second election was held and Vum Ko Hau became Deputy Councillor for the Chins in the Constituent Assembly. While the new constitution was being drafted, and with the army jubilant with Burmanisation, the country was struck with an unimaginable blow of misfortune. [10]

The Assassinations

On 19 July 1947 Aung San and six of his colleagues were gunned down in the Cabinet room of the Secretariat. Vum Ko Hau was in the building, seeing a Chin delegation downstairs, when the long bursts of automatic gunfire began. The killers were speedily arrested. They had betrayed themselves when they returned from the Secretariat, shouting in triumph, to report their success personally to U Saw at his home. He was arrested, found guilty and hanged. Burma could hardly have got off to a worse start. U Nu, the most senior surviving member of the AFPFL, took over as leader. He was a powerful politician with a high reputation for strength and Buddhist integrity.

On Independence Day, 4 January 1948, the Union flag was lowered for the last time to the solemn notes of 'God Save the King' and the new flag of Burma raised in Independence Square in downtown Rangoon. After warm farewells, which left many in tears, including most of the Cabinet as they stood in line in their elegant silken national dress, Sir Hubert and Lady Rance embarked on the cruiser HMS *Birmingham*, which slipped quietly down the Rangoon River to the open sea, bound for Colombo.

***

My father left the Burma Frontier Service in April 1948. He always saw his time in government service in Burma as the pinnacle of his career. He did not discuss his wartime experiences, like many veterans, but he did ask Maeve to write an account of our trek out of Burma, which she did.

My mother had a massive heart attack on my father's seventy-second birthday, while on holiday in Northern Ireland. She was buried in the Megarry family grave in Broomhedge, near her old home. My father bore his loss as well as he could, and grieved silently. Maeve looked after him and was with him when he died, ten weeks later. She said, 'I was fortunate to be with him at the end, and to be his confessor. I listened to his steady breathing through the night until, at dawn, it stopped. Later, as a form of gratitude for what I'd learned of life through my father's travails and example, I became a nurse, one step towards an aspiration to heal others. I always thought of him as a good man, a true gentleman, always courteous and compassionate, though, like all of us, he had his faults. However, I feel his greatness of spirit outshone them and he has been an inspiration – as has our mother – so many times in our lives to Desmond and myself.'

My father was buried in Upper Dovercourt parish churchyard, close to the grave of his parents and his sister Lily. The whole family attended the funeral.

Norman Wilson Kelly OBE
4 July 1904 – 10 September 1976

Inspired and was loved
by the Burmese people of the Chin Hills
and his devoted family

Chapter 17

TIDDIM REVISITED

Into my heart an air that kills
   From yon far country blows:
What are those blue remembered hills,
   What spires, what farms are those?

That is the land of lost content,
   I see it shining plain,
The happy highways where I went
   And cannot come again.

A. E. Housman
from 'A Shropshire Lad'

Like so many people who experienced pre-war Burma, I was drawn back by an irresistible urge to return to the hills and rivers I had known as a child, struck down by a strange malady, the 'exotic love affair' between Britain and the Orient, so well described by Saeed Jaffrey. [1] Burma had been my home until I was seven and then India until I was ten years old.

In 1978 I revisited Naini Tal and the Hallett War School, now Birla Vidyamandir, which had celebrated its Silver Jubilee in 1972 (see photograph no. 31). There was kindness and courtesy all the way. Many of the ideals of a British education had been maintained, but enriched by Indian culture. Naini and its lake had retained their delightful charm.

It was not until 1986 that I returned to Burma for the first time. A seven-day visa was all that was allowed. This enabled me to see Rangoon, Mandalay, Maymyo, Lake Inle and Taunggyi. The country was in a time warp – many of the British buildings were still intact, and the country as beautiful as I had remembered as a child. I met a Chin guide working for Tourist Burma, the only tourist company allowed to escort foreigners. Her father had fought with the 17th Indian Division.

The Irrawaddy had left a deep impression on me, and in 1997 I travelled again to Rangoon and met Vum Ko Hau, who gave me a copy of his PhD thesis, completed in Prague when he was Burmese Ambassador to Czechoslovakia. He had been my father's stenographer and one of the few Chins at that time to write of their culture and the part they played in the campaign.[2] His gratitude to my father was immense. In 1998 I got as far as Kalewa, up the Chindwin, on RV *Pandaw I*'s maiden voyage; she was part of the restored Irrawaddy Flotilla Company (see photograph no. 32). In 1942 nearly all the old paddle steamers, which had been used by the British during the evacuation, were scuttled at Katha, on the Irrawaddy, to deny their use to the Japanese.

But I always longed to see Tiddim again. Foreigners are normally forbidden to enter Chin State. This was only made possible by Nicholas Greenwood, who managed to obtain permission on my behalf. A government official had to accompany me – the one condition of my visit. On 21 November 1999 I set off with a backpack – there were no hotels or guest houses in the Chin Hills – to revisit my 'land of lost content'. Would this be a foolhardy adventure, which I would regret for the rest of my life? If I got ill, at least I was a doctor. At no time did I feel my life was in danger, even when seeing a jeep at the bottom of a crevasse outside Tiddim. I was told the occupant was in hospital with a severe head injury.

Major Myo Khaing was my liaison officer, a Shan who spoke excellent English. After long delays we flew from Mandalay to Kalemyo, now called Kale, just as the sun was beginning to set over the Chin Hills. We checked into the hotel often used by American missionaries for Baptist conventions; one of the staff was a Chin girl.

That evening the Kale Commander took me to meet Monsignor Nicholas Maung Thang, the Roman Catholic Bishop of Haka, now the capital of Chin State; I was surprised that he was living in Kalemyo, in Sagaing Division, rather than in the Chin Hills. His home was surrounded by a barbed-wire fence. When he heard I had been born in the Shan States he said, 'Oh, then you are a Burma boy.' He was a most interesting and well-travelled man.

The following day we hired a car and drove over the boundary into Chin State at Tahan where most of the migrants from the Chin Hills live. We went past '9-mile gate' and No. 2 Stockade, and then began the 3,000-foot climb past No. 3 Stockade up the Vownalu, which rises to 5,000 feet. We stopped to look back at the valley below. Here they were growing coffee and the bushes were irrigated in the time-honoured way by bringing water from a spring up the mountain in split bamboo channels. Three small children were playing happily on a homemade swing, when their father returned with his rifle under his arm,'the hunter home from the hill'. It might have been near here that the road collapsed on 11 November 1944 and the 'Lee' tank of C Squadron, 3rd Carabiniers (Prince of Wales's Dragoon Guards) fell 1,000 feet off a sheer cliff; Trooper Eric ('Dickie') Bird was tragically killed (see photograph no. 44). To this day his brother Bernard has not been able to pay his respects where the remains of the tank still lie.

The next stop was at the 'Tea House', just below the signpost where the road to Fort White and Tiddim goes to the right and that to Falam to the left. It is called Falam Point. Like so many Chin homes it was on stilts on the side of the hill, affording wonderful views over the valley below. While having lunch, I saw a calendar with 'Tedim' in the bottom left-hand corner. I did not know the name had been changed. As we left, the children could be heard chanting at the local school, while a noisy lorry carrying a load of black pigs struggled up the steep incline, accompanied by the occasional squeal.

There used to be a rest house at Fort White, where I must have stayed on many occasions. Now there was a sign on the side of an uninhabited building, with goats grazing beneath it, and written in English was: 'This is Fort White much fought over during World War II'. Our driver picked through a box of metal pieces left over from the campaign to see if he could use any of them in his garage. He picked up the tail fin of a two-inch mortar bomb.

I walked through the gap by the signpost between two hills and found, beyond, the fertile valley that contained the seven Siyin villages (see photograph no. 38). Our driver pointed out their names and we could see the road winding down to Khuasak. When General Sir George White's men established the post, it was of much more strategic significance. Now it could not be defended against modern mountain guns because of the overlooking hills. I very much wanted to visit Kennedy Peak, having seen pictures of it with a tank of C Squadron on its summit (see photograph no. 60). They had achieved the altitude record of over 8,000 feet at the time. I was later privileged to meet their CO, Major Ian Morgan, and Malcolm Connolly, who both appeared in this historic photograph. Connolly was driving the tank shown on the front cover of this book and, after replacing its engine, managed to get it to the top of Kennedy Peak. This is still guarded by the military, as are its approaches. As luck would have it, it was a clear sunny day. We were up above the clouds that drifted lazily across the Kalemyo Valley below (see photograph no. 29). Now there is a pagoda on its summit and a sign as you approach in Burmese: 'May all your wishes be granted'. Looking away from Kalemyo in the opposite direction, there was Tiddim on a distant ridge. I knew the *Nats* were on my side. It was a tremendous thrill to see it again after 57 years. A dream had come true.

Major Min Lwin Oo, Commanding Officer responsible for Chin State, was waiting on the road to escort us into Tiddim. To my great surprise he had found three Chins who had known my father: U Neng Khen Thang, aged 78, the retired Education Officer who spoke good English, Captain Hau Za Gin, who had served in Falam, and La Chin Khup. They reminisced about the war and my father's part in it, and I showed them the book dedicated to them by Professor Kenny Fraser, *'Don't*

Believe a Word of It!' They were delighted that he had written it under his Chin pseudonym 'Sii Boi-pa'.

The next morning I was taken to see the hospital, which was almost empty. Most Chins are too poor to use it. They have to pay for their own medication, and that is beyond them. There was only one doctor, who had trained in Mandalay, to treat everything. Malaria was still by far the most common problem. The village pharmacy stocks drugs mostly with Chinese instructions; like so many goods in Burma, few are homemade.

We took two four-wheel-drive army vehicles down to the Manipur River (see photograph no. 30) to see the suspension bridge. Our party included the ADC, Warrant Officer II [3] Nyunt Aung, as we set off into the depths of the valley near the village of Mamsuang. There are wooden towers at either end with steel cables to support the roadway. In pre-war days creepers were used instead of steel (see photograph no. 20). The bridge could not support a laden lorry; the driver and his crew had to unload it and trundle the goods across on a trolley, in several journeys. I could see the bridge bending as the empty vehicle slowly edged its way across to be reloaded on the other side.

It was a beautiful warm sunny day, light glittering on the water. The hills were full of birdsong. It was a magical time and childhood memories came flooding back. On the return journey to Tiddim I saw Chin graves by the side of the road and some memorial stones, usually with the date in English. I wanted to see the football ground which had been used as a dropping zone during the war. A match was in progress. It was here that the Tiddim headman's son Stephen Khup Chin Pau remembered me as 'Desi-men, a seven-year-old when he was eight'. Tiddim now has twenty-four churches, a remarkable number for a township of 20,000. There had been less than 200 people before the war. There were also cheerful, delightful nuns.

I met Leo Deng Hau, the Tiddim photographer, when visiting the Roman Catholic Church, which Father Blivet would have been proud of. He had stayed in Tiddim during the occupation in spite of being forced to carry bags of rice by the Japanese. The Nelsons would be thrilled to know that the Baptist churches, especially the Cope Memorial, were in such a good state. It was in the grounds of the latter that the Theological College of Tedim put on a 'Sing Spiration' as a pre-Christmas fundraising affair. They were in their different tribal costumes and sang and danced through the cultural evening (see photographs nos. 34, 35 and 36).

U Neng Khen Thang asked me to make a short speech in the middle of the concert. I said, 'I was a Tiddim boy, and left in May 1942 when I was seven. I bring you greetings from London. My father survived the war thanks to your loyalty. I have come back all these years later to thank you in person. What was done during the Chin campaign will not be forgotten.' U Neng Khen Thang translated my words into Tiddim Chin. He described my parents, and how I was as a boy. He said, 'N. W. Kelly was our leader.' The sincerity of their welcome left a deep impression. After it was over a number of the students wanted to be photographed with me, and one of Leo's assistants was there to oblige.

The next day we set off for Tonzang. We went down the side of the mountain where the 'Chocolate Staircase' had once been, to the Beltang Lui. We stopped at the bridge, which now replaced the one the Tehri Garwhal sappers blew up behind the 17th Indian Division as it withdrew and followed the Manipur River for part of the way, as the Tiddim Road had done. We were heading for the Nakzang Bridge over the Manipur River where the Bailey bridge had been at Milestone 126 in March 1944, before it too was blown (see photograph no. 37). We met U Khup Za Mung, now in his eighties, who, although he looked dreadfully thin and frail, had a vivid memory of where the British bridge had been. He had known my father very well and when he talked of him his eyes filled with tears. He was related to the old Tonzang chief, Pum Za Mang. The translation from Chin to Burmese to English was not easy.

We returned to Tonzang to have lunch with Peter Sian Lian Pau, son of the former chief, and U Khup Za Mung. The girls changed into their tribal costumes for our benefit. Conditions were better than in the 1940s; there was electricity, running water and easier communication with Kalemyo through the regular bus service. From the bungalow I could see the Manipur glistening at the bottom of the valley, and the poinsettia and cherry were in blossom among the pine. The village had been bombed by the RAF but all the inhabitants had left to live in the jungle well before and nobody was killed during the British advance in September 1944. Now, to commemorate the war, there is a stone obelisk and a battered tank.

On leaving Tonzang, where they had seemed pleased to see an English face, we stopped to look at the old memorial tablets, which are so commonly seen in the hills. Here the feats of famous Chins were recalled, with pictures of the animals they had killed. That evening we went up to the top of Tiddim ridge to watch the sun go down over range upon range of the Chin hills, stretching to the west and the Lushai border.

The next morning I was woken by cocks crowing. I got up and went out to video the first rays of the sun as they burst over the Letha Range. After breakfast we went to visit the compound where our home had once stood. It had been rebuilt on the original foundations and was now the home of the Tiddim headman. I could imagine being a child again from old photos of the lawn where the Wendy house had once stood. It looked towards Kennedy Peak, which was now easily recognised by the pagoda. There was a young Chin boy who could well have been about seven years old playing with a dog. Could that be a distant relation of Patch, our fox terrier? Wild cosmos flowers grew where once my mother's garden had been. There were far fewer pine trees but it was a beautiful setting, with the top of the ridge behind the house. Here indeed were 'the happy highways where I went', and was so very privileged to see again.

It was time to set off for Falam. The roads in the Chin Hills are pretty rough and maintained by the villagers themselves. Landslides were being repaired. We had lost our exhaust system on day one and, on leaving Tiddim, a wheel-nut came off and we had to return to have it replaced (see photograph no. 33). Although the sun was up, there was still frost on the road in the deep shadow of the hill. Looking back at Tiddim for the last time, I could see smoke from cooking rising in wisps and the morning mist swirling as it had done since the British first came to this isolated village all those years ago. The words of U Neng Khen Thang were in my head, 'If you cannot come back and see us, send your son.'

There was no time to look for the graveyard above Fort White, or the Chin campaign memorial stone. We had lunch at Falam Point. The road ran round the rim of another mountain range and could be seen stretching into the distance, and I imagined what a journey it would have been on foot, or even with a pony. Our destination lay on the west of the Manipur River; there were many hairpin bends on the way down to the bridge and on the left was a pipe from a hydroelectric plant discharging into the ravine. We got out and walked onto the bridge before crossing it. I thought of Noel Stevenson blowing the old one as he left Falam burning after its evacuation. Now all was peace and tranquillity.

The sun was beginning to set as we climbed up the other side and entered what had formerly been the capital of the Chin Hills – the home town of the Chin Hills Battalion. The township had expanded tremendously since colonial days and the graveyard had been dug up to make room for much-needed housing. Here, too, were churches in abundance. The first visit was to the old administration offices where my father had worked as Deputy Commissioner. I looked through the bookshelves hoping to find the records of the British administration, but they had gone. General Ne Win, the former Burmese dictator, had ordered their return to Rangoon. [4]

I met U Van Kyi, the retired Inspector of Schools, who spoke faultless English, and he gave me a copy of the Falam centenary magazine, 1892–1992, in Chin and English. He knew a great deal about the history of Falam and remembered my parents. I also met U Kiam Si, a retired DC of Falam, and Lal Taithaanga, the tribe leader. We talked into the night and then met again the next morning before visiting the hospital; this used to have a school of nursing, but it had been transferred to Haka. After a brief call at the Roman Catholic Church we set off for the new Chin capital.

On the way I was shown an irrigation pumping station which had been attacked by the Chin National Front; four people, including a policeman, had been killed. The CNF have their bases in Mizoram in the Lushai Hills. They are fighting for the restoration of democracy in Burma and self-determination for the Chin people, and the organisation comprises many Chins who have fled across the border since the democracy uprisings of 1988. [5] On the outskirts of Haka, Major Min Lwin Oo told me how he had apprehended some CNF men who were carrying bombs into the town at the time of the National Student Games two years previously; one of them had blown himself up. The roads in Chin State had been improved in anticipation of the games and a sports stadium constructed with the necessary accommodation for the competitors.

I also met two YMCA officers, U Lian Hmung Ling and U Thla Kio Lian as well as another former Levy leader, Siang Uk, who had been a member of the Western Chin Levies. They remembered my parents playing tennis together. We were taken to a school, a language academy where they were learning English, spoke to the headmaster and were shown students doing a computer course. At the hospital I met a very able surgeon, Dr Tun Aung, the Medical Superintendent, and his wife, who was a pathologist. You need enormous ingenuity to practise hospital medicine in the Chin Hills. Dr Tun Aung showed me his operating theatre; there was one patient on a quinine drip for malaria, the commonest illness, which had accounted for 37 per cent of admissions to the adult medical ward in the previous year.

The Baptist Church is where the first missionary, the Reverend Arthur Carson, is buried. He was born in 1860 in America and died in 1908 in the Chin Hills. It took him seven years before he had his first convert, who happened to be a Tiddim Chin.[6] Laura, his wife, described their life and work in *Pioneer Trails, Trials and Triumphs* (1927). There is a picture of the first baptism by total immersion in the Haka Lake, with the Reverend Carson in the lake, wearing a topee during the ceremony! There are also photographs of the mission compound in Haka village, a Chin chief with his flintlock and an Easter lily, emblem of the Resurrection and a native flower of the Chin Hills. Both husband and wife are buried in Haka; I saw their tombstones and later the baptism lake and the orphanage run by the church. I was shown the lake, dug out by Chins who had been involved in the rebellion in 1918–19. It had been punishment for those who had refused to go to France with the Chin Labour Corps.

The Reverend Joseph Cope, to whom the Baptist church in Tiddim is dedicated, is also buried in Haka. He was born in Philadelphia in 1882 and died in Haka in 1938. There is a memorial stone to the Zomi Baptist Convention, which celebrates 'Chin for Christ in one century 1899–1999'. During that time they had 20,524 converts and seven missionaries died of illness, accidents and old age.

On returning to Falam the next day we met, purely by chance, the three Chins I had talked to previously. We had lunch together and they presented me with 'Shan' bags and a Chin *longyi* (a cotton sarong, also worn by men in Burma, all woven locally on hand looms). It is difficult to convey my feelings of regret as we parted because I felt I was seeing them for the last time. We crossed the Manipur River on leaving Falam and the memory of it will always be with me. At the 'Tea House' just below Falam Point, we stopped again. By now the mist was beginning to gather and there were spots of rain. Little boys were outside on the road with their favourite Chin toy – a small wooden cart that is pushed up the hill, and then, with four or five aboard and one steering, trundles down the road to shrieks of delight.

Soon we were back in Kalemyo. The balcony of my hotel room looked out on to the main road, and just on the other side was the airport runway. While waiting for our plane the next day I watched, from my room, an array of extraordinary lorries in different stages of disrepair, honking their way through the bicycles with *longyi*-clad girls gracefully riding pillion, protecting themselves with their parasols from the midday sun. Then came the *gharries*, preceded by the sound of their trotting hooves. As the Myanma Airways Fokker slowly climbed into the sky and crossed the Chindwin I looked back at the Chin Hills for the last time – now I had to come down from 'the land of lost content'.

As a consequence of my visit to Tiddim and Tonzang I wrote to those I had met, including Peter Sian Lian Pau. He sent a copy of my letter to his cousin, Stephen Khup Chin Pau, who wrote to me in March 2000. Stephen, who is writing a book on Kamhau customs, had trained as an engineer and is a retired major. He told me that he had a copy of my father's speech to the Chins assembled in Tiddim on 25 April 1942. His father, who was the Tiddim headman at the time, had died, and Stephen was now living in Singapore. We have been corresponding ever since and I met Louise C. H. Ciin, his daughter, a doctor working in England, who is now a Member of the Royal College of Physicians. Stephen, his wife Rita, and Louise returned to Tiddim and Tonzang in November 2000. They were able to take letters and donations from me back with them. Stephen found and photographed the Chin campaign memorial stone near Falam Point, by the village of Taingen (see photograph no. 62); across the top is written:

APRIL 1942 TO NOVEMBER 1944
THE FORCES OF CHIN HILLS AREA
CHIN LEVIES   CHIN REBELLION
17TH LIGHT INDIAN DIVISION
LUSHAI BRIGADE
5TH INDIAN DIVISION

The Chin Hills Battalion should have been included. The Sukte Independent Army played a major part in the Chin Rebellion and helped the Lushai Brigade clear the Japanese from the west bank of the Manipur River in 1944. The Siyin Independence Army also fulfilled a very valuable role, but neither are named on the memorial stone as Vum Ko Hau thought in his thesis *Profile of a Burma Frontier Man*. Stephen sent me a copy of the pamphlet *Sukte Beh Leh Tedimgam Tangthu* (1996) and also introduced me to Colonel (retired) Khen Za Moong in Rangoon, who had been active in the Chin campaign. He was an overseer for the building of the 'Chocolate Staircase', looked after Chief Pum Za Mang at the Nakzang Bridge when the 17th Indian Division withdrew across the Manipur River and was a Chin Levy sergeant.

My last journey to Burma was in November 2001. The main aim was to visit the National Archives in Yangon (Rangoon), where I hoped to find some records of the British administration of the Chin Hills. It is not possible to see these without special permission. It was a great relief to hear, when I arrived, that there was a message for me from Major Ko Ko Oo to phone and meet the Director, Daw Khin Khin Tun, on Saturday morning at 10 a.m. at the National Archives. I had to write a formal letter of application to the Director General, U Kyaw Zaw. This met with his approval and to my delight I found that the Director had instructed two of her staff, the Deputy Director (Archives Section) Daw Hla Kyi, and Daw Khin Khin Mya, Assistant Director (Records Section). They had already found some files that referred to my father and the Chin Hills campaign. It was on that Saturday morning 3 November that I learned for the first time that my father had suffered a heart attack in Falam, for here was the evidence. I was shocked by the thought that he could so easily have died in 1945. They told me I could photocopy certain pages if the Director General gave his permission, which he did. I collected the valuable photocopies and saw Colonel Khen Za Moong, who told me about his reminiscences, which he had made into a series of descriptions for his relatives called *Tedim to Yangon* and *Lest We Forget*.

I was also to meet Dr Go Za Kham, a Baptist Doctor of Divinity, living in Rangoon, with whom I had been corresponding for some time. It was his brother, T. H. Go Khan Pau from Tuitum, near Tonzang, who had been my father's table boy during the campaign. When they parted on 10 March 1944 my father had given him a spoon. When I had visited Tonzang in 1999, Go Khan Pau did not hear of my visit until later; then he wrote to me and sent me a photograph of the spoon. He asked if I would help him financially to extend his fish-breeding pond, now that he had thirteen mouths to feed, to which I agreed. He fulfilled his part of the bargain and sent me a photograph (no. 40) of the dedication he had made to my father:

N. W. KELLY'S FISH BREEDING POOL

The name N. W. Kelly is given to this pool in dedication to him as it was constructed under financial support of his loving son Desmond Kelly of London. The pool is owned by T. H. Go Khan Pau who once served his master N. W. Kelly as a table boy during World War II from October 1942 to March 1944.

May his soul be with God forever.

Erected by,
T. H. Go Khan Pau
Pool owner
Tuitum Village
Chin State
Burma
Date 1.5.2001

I had said to his brother that he must not make the effort to travel all the way from Tuitum to Rangoon to see me. In spite of that he came – saying that his brother would look after him if he became ill with his heart problem. I was to meet them both at the Inya Lake Hotel; he had come to thank me in person (see photograph no. 39). He said this would be the first and only time in his life that he would see me. I told him that we both loved the same man and that my father would have wanted me to repay him for the loyalty and service he had given him. When they had said goodbye my father had crossed over the Manipur River to stay with the Levies after Tiddim was evacuated, and Go Khan Pau returned to his family. His brother Dr Go Za Kham wrote to me on 9 January 2002:

> In my trip to the hills, I visited Tonzang, Tuitum and Nakzang, in Nakzang where we have the whole village belong to our Evangelical Baptist Church, I helped them start a new church building which was burnt down in the last summer. I also see the bridge and old memories comes back as to the old bridge built by the British Force engineers. Those are still vivid in my mind. I also noticed still in my mind your father, the Honourable Kelly, riding his Norton motorbike and its horrible sound like thunder, ha ha ha.
>
> In Tuitum I also look and saw my brother T. H. Go Khan Pau's fish pond with some friends and it is real good and fantastic. Some of the fish are big enough now that he caught some and we ate,

very good. I wish I could be with you and witness his accomplishment.

I could believe that you are almost nearing to the book you would publish and I could believe that it will be thrilling for modern man for such a time as in those days. I wish you could come back once more and have good fellowship again. But its all depended upon time and circumstances and God's will.

I shake hand with your wife and children – Happy New Year. May the Lord bless you and keep you. Thank you.

I think this would have made my father smile. It would certainly have brought a twinkle to his eye – especially if accompanied by a *chota peg sahib que wasti* – 'a small whisky for the Master!'

Appendix A

CHIN TRIBES

There were about 36 tribes in the Chin Hills in the 1940s. The principal Chin tribes of the Tiddim area were Kamhau, Sokte, Siyin and Thado (known as Kuki in Assam and Manipur). Confusingly, many of the tribes had alternative spellings for their names, such as Kamhau/ Kamhow, Sokte/Sukte, Tashon/Tarshon, Khongsai/Khongzai/ Kongzai/ Kongsai/Khonzai and Whelngo/Whelgno (who were also known as Hualngo). This is reflected in the literature and documents of the time and can seem misleading. The Kamhau, Sokte and Siyin were the dominant Tiddim tribes in 1942.

Principal Chin tribes (with alternative spellings)

Tiddim subdivision

Kamhau/Kamhow
Sokte/Sukte
Siyin (their seven villages were Tuklai, Khuasak, Lophei, Buanman, Limkhai, Voklak and Pumva; village headmen were often called chiefs).
Huite (they lived in the north-west, near the Lushai border).
Zo
Thado/Thadow (called Kuki in Assam and Manipur).
Lithu (under the Kamhaus).
Ngawn

In addition, 'Tiddimland' included Sihzang, Dimpi, Vangte and Khuano.

Falam Chins

Tashon/Tarshon
Lumbang/Lombang/Lomban
Zahau/Zahow/Zahaw (from Zanniat).
Whelngo/Whelgno (also called Hualngo).
Yahow
Khongsai/Khongzai/Kongzai/Kongsai/Khonzai
Khuangli
Laizo

Southern Chins

Haka
Zahow/Zahau (from Zokhua)
Klangklang
Mi Er
Zophei
Than Tlang

Laizo was the language of the Falam Chins; in the north the language was Kamhau or Siyin while Lai Zo was spoken in the centre and Lai in the south. The Zahow Levies generally spelt their name thus, rather than Zahau.

Some of the Chin chiefs in 1942

Chief Pum Za Mang, ATM (Kamhau tribal area, Tonzang/Tiddim)
Chief Hau Za Lian (Sukte tribal area, Tiddim)
Chief Thawng Za Khup, ATM (Saizang tribal area, Tiddim)
Chief Hlur Hmon, ATM, IDSM (Lumbang/Lomban tribal area, Falam)
Chief Van Hmung (Tashon tribal area)
Chief Thang Tin Lian, ATM (Zahau tribal area, Falam)
Chief Kio Mang (Mi Er tribal area, Haka)
Chief Thuam Za Mang (Mualbem tribal area, Tiddim)
Chief Lam Kho Mang (Tuklai tribal area, Tiddim)
Chief Suang Hau Thang, ATM (Lophei tribal area, Tiddim)
Chief Lian Thawng, ATM (Khuasak tribal area, Tiddim)
Chief Thian Pum (Buanman tribal area, Tiddim)
Chief Mang Cung Nung (Khuangli tribal area, Falam)
Chief Mar Thio (Than Tlang tribal area, Haka)
Chief Tha Min, ATM (Lungngo tribal area, Haka)
Chief Pau Kam (Limkhai tribal area, Tiddim)
Chief Van Kio (Shurkhua tribal area, Haka)

Appendix B

MILITARY RANKS

There were two kinds of officers in Burma and India. Most of the King's Commissioned Officers (KCOs) were British and had gone through Sandhurst Military Academy; very few Burmese or Indians gained a King's commission, except Indians who had gone through Sandhurst prior to 1932. Their ranks were:

> Second Lieutenant
> Lieutenant
> Captain
> Major
> Lieutenant-Colonel
> Colonel
> Brigadier
> Major-General
> Lieutenant-General
> General
> Field Marshal

The Governor's Commissioned Officers (GCOs) were the native officers commissioned by the Governor of Burma, not King George VI. In the Indian Army the equivalent of a GCO was a Viceroy's Commissioned Officer (VCO). Their ranks below second lieutenant (which had no equivalents in the British Army) were:

> Jemedar (one small star or pip, in command of platoons)
> Subedar (two small stars)
> Subedar Major (small crown)
> Naib Commander (an honorary title, given to, e.g., Pau Chin of the Chin Hills Battalion)

A Warrant Officer (WO) had a warrant signed by a government minister or representative of the Army Council. A WOII was typically a company sergeant major. The subedar major in the Indian Army oversaw the jemedars and subedars and assisted the Commanding Officer (CO).

Non-Commissioned Officers (NCOs) were:

> Lance Corporal or Lance Naik
> Corporal or Naik
> Sergeant or Havildar
> Company Sergeant Major or Havildar Major
> A private (ordinary soldier) was a sepoy in India.

NOTES

Chapter 1: Shan States to the Chin Hills

1. John L. Christian, *Modern Burma* (University of California Press, Berkeley, 1942).
2. Andrew Marshall, *The Trouser People* (Viking Penguin, London, 2002). The Scott Line is reproduced in Marshall's map of the Wa Hills.
3. J. George Scott, *Gazetteer of Upper Burma and the Shan States*, Part 1, Vol 1 (Superintendent of Government Printing, Rangoon, 1900).
4. L. B. Naylor, *A Practical Handbook of the Chin Language (Siyin Dialect)* (Government Printing, Rangoon, 1925). Naylor was assisted with this book by Rev. J. H. Cope, American Baptist Mission and the Honorary Inspector of Schools.
5. F. K. Lehman, *The Structure of Chin Society* (University of Illinois Press, 1963).
6. F. M. Rundall, *The Siyin Chins* (Superintendent of Government Printing, Rangoon, 1893).
7. Stephen Khup Chin Pau, *Northern Chin Sukte-Kamhau Customs and Architecture* (in press).
8. H. N. C. Stevenson, *The Economics of the Central Chin Tribes* (The Times of India Press, Bombay, 1943).
9. H. N. C. Stevenson, *The Hill Peoples of Burma* (Longmans, London, 1944).
10. Sir Charles Crosthwaite, *The Pacification of Burma* (Edward Arnold, London, 1912).
11. Bertram S. Carey and H. N. Tuck, *The Chin Hills* (Government Printing, Rangoon, 1896).
12. *Sukte Beh Leh Tedimgam Tangthu* (Sukte Clan and Tiddimland History), 1996.
13. Khen Za Moong, *Tedim to Yangon* (private pamphlet, Yangon, 1995).
14. Ibid.
15. Ibid.
16. Lieutenant-Colonel L. E. L. Burne, CIE, CBE, IA, first came to the Chin Hills in 1917 as a captain during the Chin rebellion. While he was Deputy Commissioner he abolished the *shilla* slave system and retired after some twenty years as DC in July 1937. He was a just and respected administrator.
17. 'Customary law' was a system by which some tribal chiefs were appointed by the British government to rule over their own people. The tributes by the villagers, described on p.31, were in return for protection by the chiefs. This system worked reasonably well, although there were some Chins who were anti-colonial and some chiefs who were regarded as oppressors.
18. Rangoon authority.
19. *History of the Chin Hills Battalion, 1894–1949* (Mss Eur E250, The British Library's Asia, Pacific and Africa Collections).
20. Khen Za Moong, op. cit.

Chapter 2: A Lone Outpost of the Empire

1. Ian Lyall Grant and Kazuo Tamayama, *Burma 1942: The Japanese Invasion* (The Zampi Press, Chichester, 1999).
2. Major Anthony McCall was in the Indian Army before he joined the Indian Civil Service in 1935, and became Deputy Commissioner of the Lushai Hills in Aijal. He had devised a scheme for the defence of his district and later wrote a book called *Lushai Chrysalis* (1949).
3. Huites live in the far north-west, near the Lushai border.
4. Many Chins saw the Labour Corps as fulfilling the treaty signed at Fort White in 1891 where the signatories vowed to render aid in time of war.
5. 'The Japanese had released some prisoners of war as a goodwill gesture. This was attributed to Pum Za Mang's contact with the Japanese. He was well informed about the use of Japanese military might and the Nationalist spirit of the Burmese through his younger brother G. Lian Cin Thang who was in college at the same time as Aung San and the 'young patriots'. He had asked the Japanese not to molest the Chin women and burn their houses. I remember that one, Luan Cin Suan, arrived in Tiddim and was arrested by the authorities, which made his brother Khaam Za Thang furious.' (Stephen Khup Chin Pau, personal communication.)
6. *Sukte Beh Leh Tedimgam Tangthu* (Sukte Clan and Tiddimland History), 1996.
7. Field Marshal Sir William Slim, *Defeat into Victory* (Cassell, London, 1956; Macmillan, London, 1999, paperback edition).
8. Ibid.
9. *History of the Chin Hills Battalion* (Mss Eur E250, The British Library's Asia, Pacific and Africa Collections).
10. Sally and Lucy Jaffé (eds), *Chinthe Women: Women's Auxiliary Service Burma 1942–1946* (Chipping Norton, 2001).

Chapter 4: Letters from Tiddim

1. Vum Ko Hau, personal communication.
2. Harold Braund, *Distinctly I Remember* (Wren, Mount Eliza, 1972).
3. Ibid.
4. Saeed Jaffrey, *Saeed, An Actor's Journey* (Constable, London, 1998).
5. Leslie Glass, *The Changing of Kings: Memories of Burma 1934–1949* (Peter Owen, London, 1985).
6. For a discussion of hill tribes, see Ian Morrison, *Grandfather Longlegs*, Appendix 7.

Chapter 5: Waiting and Watching

1. Harold Braund, *Distinctly I Remember* (Wren, Mount Eliza, 1972).
2. Jack Oats, letter to Prue Bankes, 1944.
3. *History of the Chin Hills Battalion 1894–1949* (The British Library's Asia, Pacific and Africa Collections).
4. Harold Braund, op. cit.
5. *Frontier Administration July 1943–November 1943* (Mss Eur E250, The British Library's Asia, Pacific and Africa Collections).

Chapter 6: A Conflict of Loyalty

1. R. S. Wilkie, telegram in the National Archives, Yangon, 22 September 1942.
2. L. B. Naylor, telegram in the National Archives, Yangon, 29 September 1942.
3. Frank George, telegram in the National Archives, Yangon, 16 October 1942.

4. R. S. Wilkie, telegram in the National Archives, Yangon, 17 October 1942.
5. Frank George, telegram in the National Archives, Yangon, 20 October 1942.
6. Jack Haswell, telegram in the National Archives, Yangon, 22 October 1942.
7. *Frontier Administration July 1942–November 1943* (The British Library's Asia, Pacific and Africa Collections).
8. 1 lakh of rupees was approximately £7,500. From *A Handbook for Travellers in India, Burma and Ceylon* (John Murray, Calcutta, 1938).
9. R. S. Wilkie, letter in the National Archives, Yangon, 13 December 1942.
10. L. B. Naylor, letter in the National Archives, Yangon.
11. L. B. Naylor, letter in the National Archives, Yangon, 4 November 1942.
12. *Frontier Administration July 1942–1943* (The British Library's Asia, Pacific and Africa Collections).

Chapter 7: The Lifeline with India

1. G. W. Towers, 'The Tiddim Track' in *Journal of the United Service Institution of India*, No. 317, Vol. LXXIV, October 1944, pp. 462–7.
2. Jack Oats, letter to Prue Bankes.
3. Sii Boi-pa (Kenny Fraser), '*Don't Believe a Word of It!*' (Culross, 1999).
4. Ibid.
5. Ibid.

Chapter 8: 'There's a Boy Coming Home on Leave'

1. L. B. Naylor, letter in the National Archives, Yangon, 3 January 1943.
2. L. B. Naylor, letter in the National Archives, Yangon, 10 February 1943.
3. Jack Oats, letter to Prue Bankes, 1944.
4. L. B. Naylor, letter in the National Archives, Yangon, 20 April 1943.
5. *Naini Tal: A Historical and Descriptive Account* (Government Press, Allahabad, 1928).
6. Patrick Gibson, *Childhood Lost* (London, 1999).
7. Harold Braund, *Distinctly I Remember* (Wren, Mount Eliza, 1972)
8. All of these were officers in the Burma Frontier Service, three of whom were later to be awarded the MBE. Philip Barton was appointed to the Burma Frontier Service in 1940 and worked as an assistant to Norman Kelly. He was a gourmet cook and an accomplished painter who had worked at Kutkai in the Shan States where he first met Harold Braund. Gilbert Turnbull had worked with the hill tribes of Burma before the war. John Franklin first came out to Burma in 1935 and Toby Leitch had been appointed as Assistant Superintendent in 1930; he was the same age as Norman Kelly.
9. Ian Lyall Grant, *Burma: The Turning Point* (The Zampi Press, Chichester, 1993).
10. Ibid.
11. Ibid.
12. Ibid.
13. *History of 17 Indian Division: July 1941 to December 1945* (Thackers Press, Calcutta, n.d.).

Chapter 9: The Storm Breaks

1. Anthony Gross, 'Chins at War' in *India in Action* (National Gallery, London).
2. H. N. C. Stevenson, *The Economics of the Central Chin Tribes* (The Times of India Press, Bombay, 1943).
3. H. N. C. Stevenson, report in the National Archives, Yangon, 8 April 1943.

4. *The Story of Gurkha VCs* (The Gurkha Museum, Winchester, 1993).
5. Ian Lyall Grant, *Burma: The Turning Point* (The Zampi Press, Chichester, 1993).
6. Harold Braund, *Distinctly I Remember* (Wren, Mount Eliza, 1972).
7. Balfour Oatts ('Titus'), *The Jungle in Arms* (William Kimber, London, 1962).
8. Jack Oats, letter to Prue Bankes.
9. H. N. C. Stevenson, report in the National Archives, Yangon, 8 June 1943.
10. Telegram from the Governor of Burma to the Secretary of State, Burma Office, London, 4 June 1943 (The British Library).
11. H. N. C. Stevenson, letter in the National Archives, Yangon, 8 June 1943.
12. Ian Lyall Grant, op. cit.
13. Field Marshal Sir William Slim, *Defeat into Victory* (Cassell, London, 1956; Macmillan, London, 1999, paperback edition).
14. Laurie O'Hara, letter to author, 6 June 2000.
15. Professor Kenny Fraser, letter to author, 8 March 2001.
16. H. N. C. Stevenson, report in the National Archives, Yangon, 15 June 1943.
17. H. N. C. Stevenson, letter in the National Archives, Yangon, 26 June 1943.
18. Jack Oats, letter to Prue Bankes.
19. Harold Braund, op. cit.
20. H. N. C. Stevenson, letter in the National Archives, Yangon, 1 August 1943.
21. H. N. C. Stevenson, letter in the National Archives, Yangon, 20 August 1943.
22. *History of 17 Indian Division: July 1941 to December 1945* (Thacker's Press, Calcutta, n.d.).
23. *History of the Chin Hills Battalion 1894–1949* (Mss Eur E250, The British Library's Asia, Pacific and Africa Collections).
24. Haka b was a small village 3 miles south-west of Natchaung, not the same place as the subdivision Haka.
25. Lieutenant-Colonel A. C. Moore, letter, 14 May 1948.
26. Professor Kenny Fraser, personal communication.
27. H. N. C. Stevenson, letter in the National Archives, Yangon, 30 October 1943.
28. H. N. C. Stevenson, letter in the National Archives, Yangon, 30 October 1943.
29. H. N. C. Stevenson, letter in the National Archives, Yangon, 30 October 1943.
30. Oatts, op. cit.
31. *History of the Chin Hills Battalion 1894–1949* (Mss Eur E250, The British Library's Asia, Pacific and Africa Collections).
32. H. N. C. Stevenson, report in the National Archives, Yangon, 22 December 1943.
33. Oatts, op. cit.
34. Ibid.
35. Ibid.

Chapter 10: On the Run

1. Geoffrey Evans, *The Johnnies* (Cassell, London, 1964).
2. Balfour Oatts ('Titus'), *The Jungle in Arms* (William Kimber, London, 1962).
3. Ibid.
4. Ibid.
5. Ibid.
6. Ibid.
7. R. S. Wilkie, letter in the National Archives, Yangon, 19 November 1943.
8. C. F. B. Pearce, signal in the National Archives, Yangon, 23 November 1943.
9. Lieutenant-General G. A. P. Scoones, letter in the National Archives, Yangon, 21 December 1943.

10. L. B. Naylor, letter in the National Archives, Yangon.
11. Lieutenant-General G. A. P. Scoones, letter in the National Archives, Yangon, 21 December 1943.
12. L. B. Naylor, letter in the National Archives, Yangon, 17 December 1943.
13. D. W. Rae, report in the National Archives, Yangon, 4 March 1944.
14. John Franklin, report in the National Archives, Yangon, 21 February 1944.
15. Rachel Brown and Alison Anne Whiting, personal communication.
16. Prue Bankes, personal communication.

Chapter 11: The Japanese Advance on Tiddim

1. Ian Lyall Grant, *Burma: The Turning Point* (The Zampi Press, Chichester, 1993).
2. Ibid.
3. Balfour Oatts ('Titus'), *The Jungle in Arms* (William Kimber, London, 1962).
4. T. H. Go Khan Pau, personal communication. The seven villages were Tuklai, Khuasak, Lophei, Buanman, Limkhai, Voklak and Pumva.
5. Harold Braund, *Distinctly I Remember* (Wren, Mount Eliza, 1972).
6. Philip Ziegler (ed), *Personal Diary of Admiral The Lord Louis Moutbatten: Supreme Allied Commander, South-East Asia, 1943–1946* (Collins, London, 1988).
7. Vum Ko Hau, *Profile of a Burma Frontier Man* (Kilatmadju Press, Bandung, Indonesia, 1963). The ATM was the Burmese Good Service Medal and was invariably only awarded to chiefs in the Chin Hills.
8. *History of the Chin Hills Battalion, 1894–1949* (Mss Eur E250, The British Library's Asia, Pacific and Africa Collections).
9. Ibid.
10. Lyall Grant, op. cit.
11. S. W. Kirby et al., *History of the Second World War. The War Against Japan*, Vol 3, *The Decisive Battles* (HMSO, London, 1961).
12. Sii Boi-Pa (Kenny Fraser), *'Don't Believe a Word of It!'* (Culross, 1999).
13. Lyall Grant, op. cit.
14. Ibid.
15. Stephen Khup Chin Pau, personal communication.
16. Leo Deng Hau, personal communication.
17. T. H. Go Khan Pau, personal communication.
18. Vum Ko Hau, op. cit.
19. Lyall Grant, op. cit.
20. 'Jungle Night' was published in *Muse in Exile: An Anthology from Fighting Men of South East Asia*, published by SEAC in June 1945. It vividly portrays the tension of the jungle warfare experienced by soldiers in Burma.
21. Lyall Grant, op. cit.
22. Khen Za Moong, *Tedim to Yangon* (private pamphlet, Yangon, 1995).
23. Ibid.
24. Peter Sian Lian Pau, personal communication.
25. Oatts, op. cit.
26. Ibid.
27. S. G. Chaphekar, *A Brief Study of the Burma Campaign 1943–45* (Maharashtra Militarisation Board, Poona, 1958).
28. Braund, op. cit.
29. Ken Shaw, personal communication.
30. Vum Ko Hau, op. cit.
31. Ibid.
32. Lyall Grant, op. cit.

Chapter 12: From Retreat to Conquest

1. Field Marshal Sir William Slim, *Defeat into Victory* (Cassell, London, 1956; Macmillan, London, 1999, paperback edition).
2. Ian Lyall Grant, *Burma: The Turning Point* (The Zampi Press, Chichester, 1993).
3. Arthur Swinson, *Kohima* (Cassell, London, 1966).
4. Ibid.
5. Slim, op. cit.
6. Ibid.
7. Ian Wallace (Mss Eur F180/41B, The British Library's Asia, Pacific and Africa Collections). After the war Ian Wallace wrote *Some Personal Recollections of Events in Burma*. During the war years he served first in the Secretariat of the exiled government of Burma in Simla and was responsible for the Chin Hills. Later he moved to the Army and became Senior Staff Officer of General Administration at the HQ of the Civil Affairs Service Burma, CAS(B), under the Chief Civil Affairs Officer (Burma).
8. Ian Lyall Grant, personal communication.
9. Slim, op. cit.
10. Ibid.
11. S. G. Chaphekar, *A Brief Study of the Burma Campaign 1943–45* (Maharashta Militarisation Board, Poona, 1958).
12. Slim, op. cit.
13. Ibid.
14. Tom Barton, personal communication.
15. Slim, op. cit.
16. Ibid.

Chapter 13: The Triumphal Return to the Hills

1. Hau Za Lian, *Sukte Beh Leh Tedimgam Tangthu* (Sukte Clan and Tiddimland History), 1996.
2. Ibid.
3. Ibid.
4. Balfour Oatts ('Titus'), *The Jungle in Arms* (William Kimber, London, 1962).
5. Tun Thual, *Sukte Beh Leh Tedimgam Tangthu*, 1996.
6. Hau Za Lian, op. cit.
7. Thuam Za Mang, *Sukte Beh Leh Tedimgam Tangthu*, 1996.
8. Hau Za Lian, op. cit.
9. Stephen Khup Chin Pau, *Northern Chin Sukte-Kamhau Customs and Architecture* (in press).
10. Stephen Khup Chin Pau, personal communication.
11. Vum Ko Hau, *Profile of a Burma Frontier Man* (Kilatmadju Press, Bandung, Indonesia, 1963).
12. *Sukte Beh Leh Tedimgam Tangthu*, 1996.
13. The Suktes formed their army first and called it an 'Independent' army; the Siyins formed their army second and called it an 'Independence' army, but they both had the same initials. Chief Hau Za Lian could not agree to them fighting under the same name, but he was democratic and could not accept responsibility for a change of direction on his own. In the event, the SIA only existed for two months.
14. *The 'Fighting Fifth' – History of the 5th Indian Division*, n.d.
15. Ibid.

16. Field Marshal Sir William Slim, *Defeat into Victory* (Cassell, London, 1956; Macmillan, London, 1999, paperback edition).
17. *The 'Fighting Fifth'*, op cit.
18. Oatts, op. cit.
19. Antony Brett-James, *Ball of Fire* (Gale and Polden, Aldershot, 1951).
20. Oatts, op. cit.
21. *The 'Fighting Fifth'*, op. cit.
22. John Franklin, *Sukte Beh Leh Tedimgam Tangthu*, 1996.
23. Hau Za Lian, op. cit.
24. *Sukte Beh Leh Tedimgam Tangthu*, 1996.
25. John Nunneley, *Tales from the King's African Rifles, A Last Flourish of Empire* (Askari Books, Petersham, 1998).
26. Brett-James, op. cit.
27. Slim, op. cit.

Chapter 14: 'There Is No Justice'

1. Antony Brett-James, *Report My Signals* (Hennel Locke, London, 1948).
2. Charles Evans, *A Doctor in XIVth Army: Burma 1944–1945* (Leo Cooper, London, 1998).
3. *Falam Centenary Magazine 1892–1992*.
4. Professor Kenny Fraser, personal communication.
5. Roddie Russell, personal communication (from Lieutenant-Colonel Patrick Cardwell Moore).
6. Ibid.
7. Balfour Oatts ('Titus'), *The Jungle in Arms* (William Kimber, London, 1962).
8. Ibid.

Chapter 15: Farewell to the Hills

1. Captain Ba Pu, report in the National Archives, Yangon, 4 March 1945.
2. Captain Ba Pu, report in the National Archives, Yangon, 29 March 1945.
3. Lieutenant-Colonel E. H. Cooke, report in the National Archives, Yangon, 29 March 1945.
4. Harold Braund, *Distinctly I Remember* (Wren, Mount Eliza, 1972).
5. Captain Ba Pu, report in the National Archives, Yangon, 17 April 1945.
6. Lieutenant-Colonel E. H. Cooke, report in the National Archives, Yangon, 17 April 1945.
7. Balfour Oatts ('Titus'), *The Jungle in Arms* (William Kimber, London, 1962).
8. Ibid.
9. Braund, op. cit.
10. Oatts, op. cit.
11. Ibid.
12. Vum Ko Hau, *Profile of a Burma Frontier Man* (Kilatmadju Press, Bandung, Indonesia, 1963).
13. Bernard Fergusson, in his Foreword to Harold Braund's book *Distinctly I Remember*.
14. Ibid.
15. *India's Most Dangerous Hour* is the title of volume 2 of *The War Against Japan* by S. W. Kirby et al (HMSO, London, 1958).
16. Harold Braund, op. cit.
17. H. N. C. Stevenson, *The Economics of the Central Chin Tribes* (The Times of India Press, Bombay, 1943).

18. Vum Ko Hau, op. cit.
19. The chief of the Zahau-Hualngo tribe, Thang Tin Lian, and the Tashon chief, Van Hmung, were accused of siding with the Japanese.
20. *The Statesman*, 19 October 1945.

Chapter 16: Return to Rangoon

1. King Zog of Albania was deposed on 2 January 1946 and a republic declared on 12 January.
2. In the early years of the war Ernest Bevin, the Minister for Labour in the coalition government, had recruited 'Bevin boys' to work in the mines to help the war effort.
3. Balfour Oatts ('Titus'), *The Jungle in Arms* (William Kimber, London, 1962).
4. Ibid.
5. H. N. C. Stevenson, *The Economics of the Central Chin Tribes* (The Times of India Press, Bombay, 1943).
6. Oatts, op. cit.
7. Ibid.
8. Professor Kenny Fraser, personal communication.
9. Khen Za Moong, *Tedim to Yangon* (private pamphlet, Yangon, 1995).
10. Ibid.

Chapter 17: Tiddim Revisited

1. Saeed Jaffrey, *Saeed, An Actor's Journey* (Constable, London, 1998).
2. Vum Ko Hau, *Profile of a Burma Frontier Man* (Kilatmadju Press, Bandung, Indonesia, 1963).
3. Warrant Officer II is typically a company sergeant major. See Appendix B.
4. John H. McEnery, *Epilogue in Burma 1945–48* (Spellmount, Tunbridge Wells, 1990).
5. Shelby Tucker, *Burma: The Curse of Independence* (Pluto Press, London, 2001).
6. Laura Carson, *Pioneer Trails, Trials and Triumphs* (Baptist Board of Education, New York, 1927).

GLOSSARY

anyein pwè	variety show.
atta	wheat flour.
A V school	Anglo-Vernacular (native tongue) school.
ayah	nanny.
'Ayo-Gurkhali'	'the Gurkhas are upon you'.
badmash	bandit.
basha	thatch or leaf hut, often made of bamboo lattice.
bawi-pa	British officer.
beh	clan.
Bose Brigade	The Indian National Army (INA) led by Subhas Chandra Bose, part of Jai Aza Hind (the 'Free India' movement). He was a former president of the Congress Party.
Bombine	The Bombay-Burmah Trading Corporation.
Chai-hpa-rau	a group dance with bamboo poles moved together and apart, and clapping in time with the music. The girls dance between the poles.
chapati	Indian bread made from whole-wheat flour *(atta)*.
chapper	bed made with sticks and leaves, with a tarpaulin.
charpoi	wooden framed bed.
chaung	stream, small river or waterless gully (in the dry season).
chinlon	Burmese game with a small wicker ball kicked aloft in all directions.
chinthe	mythical Burmese lion, a pagoda guardian.
chota-hazri	little breakfast.
chota peg	a small measure.
coolie	hired labourer.
dacoit	bandit, armed robber.
dah	Chin, Kachin or Burmese knife.
dak	government bungalow or mail.
dandy dhooli or *dhooly*	a strong cloth slung like a hammock between two bamboo staffs and carried by two or more men.
Daw	Madam, Mrs, a term of respect (lit. Aunt).
dhani	type of palm used for thatch.
Durbar	a court, state reception.

gal gau	the curse of an enemy killed in battle.
gam or ram	territory, tract of land.
gamsa	wild jungle animal.
gataam	sulphur bean.
gaung	supervisor (lit. head).
gharry	horse-drawn carriage.
ghooral	antelope.
godown	storage building.
gully gully man	magician, a corruption of the Egyptian word *gale*, meaning magic.
gungal	other side of river; the west bank of the Manipur River.
gyi	big animal or Barking deer.
harbour	to create a camp for defence.
helio/heliograph	a method of signalling in Morse code by a mirror reflecting sunlight or a lamp from the top of one mountain to another.
hiang	a type of tall, straight tree used for planking *(Alnus nepalensis)*.
inn sau	a type of Chin longhouse or the home of a chief.
Kempeitai	Japanese secret police.
khin khot naam	a special headhunting sword.
khud	precipitous hillside.
kukri	curved knife, a weapon used by the Gurkhas.
kwet-thit	hutments, shanty town, new quarter.
kyat	Burmese currency, which replaced the rupee. Rupee was the Indian name and *kyat* the Burmese.
lai los	permanent fields.
Laipianpa	translator, lit. a script inventor.
lakh	currency, 1 *lakh* = 100,000 rupees.
Lamgui	a Tiddim Chin dance.
leh	and.
longyi	sarong.
lugale	young man or lad.
mali	gardener.
maung	younger brother, a prefix used before the name.
Mar	Tiddim Chins who tie their hair in a bun at the nape of the neck.
Mills bombs	grenades.
Mithun or mythun	a type of ox found in the Chin Hills.
Mithun/mythun sial	a *mithun* reared for meat or prestige.
mufti	civilian clothes.
myook	a treasury or township officer.
Nats	Burmese spirits of trees, houses, etc.
nattang or gataam	banana plantain.
Newland Fawn-voi	Newland corn.

nga-pi	spicy dried fish condiment, known for its pungent smell.
Ngal-Ai	a special victory feast to celebrate the killing of an enemy.
Nips	slang for Japanese.
paddy	rice in the husk, rice plant.
panjis	sharpened bamboo stakes.
Pawi	Falam and Haka Chins who wear a top-knot bun of hair.
peeng	small bamboo pipes to drink *zu* with.
phiit	a form of musical reed (vibrating) pipe.
pi-dog	ownerless or pariah dog.
punkha	a swinging fan of cloth suspended from a ceiling.
pwè	performance, party or show.
pya	small Burmese coin, 100 to the *kyat*.
que wasti	whisky.
ramsa	a designated part of a wild animal due to a chief as a form of tribute.
rupees (Rs)	Indian coin used in Burma.
sa-ai	a ceremony to commemorate the killing of a wild animal.
sahib	master.
saing	wild ox.
saliang	a shoulder of meat given as a tribute.
Sawbwa	hereditary Shan ruler, chief.
sepoy	native soldier, disciplined and dressed in European style *or* a British Indian soldier.
serang	boatman.
serow	wild jungle goat.
shilla	slave.
sial/siah	a full-grown female ox given by a village every three years as a *mithun* tribute.
sial ban	to cut (kill) *mithun* in order to seal an agreement, e.g. to render aid in time of war.
Sii Boi-pa	doctor, medical officer.
sowar	mounted orderly, soldier.
syce	groom, mounted attendant.
tangthu	story, history.
taung	hill, mountain.
taungya	a field of shifting cultivation (using the slash-and-burn method).
Tedimgam	Tedim (Tiddim) land.
Thakin	'Master', a term of superiority. The Thakin Party (*Do-bama Asi-ayone* – 'We Burmans Association') was a political party.

tobatsutai	pacification/subjugation unit used by the Japanese for the civil population.
Topa	'Master', 'Lord'.
topee	pith helmet.
U	Mr, a term of respect used for an older man (lit. Uncle).
V Force	Those who, undercover, watched for the Japanese west of the Chindwin, mainly north of Tamu (Assam Rifles and the Naga villagers); 5 V ops were part of V Force.
va	river.
Verey lights	used to illuminate the enemy and fired from special pistols.
vuandok	Burmese subdivisional officer, the equivalent of an Assistant Superintendent.
wallah	one employed on a specific type of work.
yoma	mountain range (lit. backbone).
zayat	small rest house.
zo los	fields where maize is cut every year in the cold mountaintops
zu	Chin national drink made from fermented grain (millet, maize or rice).
zu-riel	rice spirit.

ABBREVIATIONS

ABRO	Army Burma Reserve Officer
AC	Accounts Commissioner/Assistant Commissioner
ADC	aide-de-camp
AG	Accountant General
AFPFL	Anti-Fascist People's Freedom League
ALFSEA	Army Land Force South-East Asia
APM	Army Pay Master
APS	Assistant Political Superintendent
ARP	air-raid precations
AS	Assistant Superintendent
ATM	*Ahmudan gaung Tazeik ya Min* (Burmese Good Service Medal)
BFrS.	Burma Frontier Service
BGM	Burma Gallantry Medal
BIA	Burma Independence Army
BOC	Burmah Oil Company
Burdef	Burma Defence
CAS(B)	Civil Affairs Service Burma
CB	Companion of the Order of the Bath
CBE	Commander of the British Empire
CCAO	Chief Civil Affairs Officer
CDA	Chin Defence Army
CID	Criminal Investigation Department
CIE	Companion of the Order of the Indian Empire
CLA	civilian living allowance/compensatory local allowance
CMG	Companion of the Order of St Michael and St George
CNF	Chin National Front
CO	Commanding Officer
CVO	Commander of the Royal Victorian Order
DC	Deputy Commissioner
DCCAO	Deputy Chief Civil Affairs Officer
DSO	Companion of the Distinguished Service Order
Dy CCAO	Deputy Commissioner Civil Affairs Officer
EGM	Empire Gallantry Medal
ENSA	Entertainments National Service Association
FSS	Federated Shan States
GBE	Knight (or Dame) Grand Cross of the Order of the British Empire

GC	George Cross
GCMG	Knight (or Dame) Grand Cross of the Order of St Michael and St George
GCO	Governor's Commissioned Officer/Gurkha Commissioned Officer
GHQ	General Headquarters
GOC	General Officer Commanding
G1(O)	Staff Officer (Ordnance); a lieutenant-colonel or colonel
HE	His Excellency
HMG	His Majesty's Government
HQ	Headquarters
IA	Indian Army
ICS	Indian Civil Service
IDSM	Indian Distinguished Service Medal (Military Medal)
IGH	Indian General Hospital
INA	Indian National Army
IOM	Indian Order of Merit
KBE	Knight Commander of the Order of the British Empire
KCB	Knight Commander of the Order of the Bath
KCSI	Knight Commander of the Order of the Star of India
KCO	King's Commissioned Officer
KPM	King's Police Medal
KSM	*Kyet thaye zaung shwe Salwe ya Min* (King's Service Medal)
LA	local allowance
M&B 693	May and Baker: makers of the first antibiotic – numerical code 693
MB.BS	Bachelor of Medicine/Bachelor of Surgery
MBE	Member of the British Empire
MC	Military Cross
MM	Military Medal
MO	Medical Officer
MVO	Member of the Royal Victorian Order
NAAFI	Navy, Army and Air Force Institutes Club
NCO	Non-Commissioned Officer
QT	'on the quiet'
O&T	Oudh & Tirhout Railway Company
OB	Order of Burma
OBE	Officer of the Order of the British Empire
PVO	People's Volunteer Organisation (a private army of General Aung San)
PWD	Public Works Department
RAMC	Royal Army Medical Corps
R and R	'rest and recreation'
RE	Royal Engineers
RGR	Royal Gurkha Rifles
Rs	rupees

RSM	Regimental Sergeant-Major
RV	River Vessel
SCAO	Senior Civil Affairs Officer
SEAC	South-East Asia Command
2i/c	second-in-command
2/Lt	Second Lieutenant
SMO	Senior Medical Officer
SIA	Sukte Independent Army/Siyin Independence Army
SS	steamship
SSO	Senior Service Officer
TA	travel allowance
TAB	typhoid inoculation
TDM	*Thuyegaung Ngwe Dah Yah Min* (Sword of Honour)
UP	United Provinces of India
USAAF	United States Army Air Force
VC	Victoria Cross
VCO	Viceroy's Commissioned Officer
VE	Victory in Europe (1945)
VJ	Victory over Japan (1945)
WAS(B)	Women's Auxiliary Service Burma

BIBLIOGRAPHY

Baird-Murray, Maureen, *A World Overturned: A Burmese Childhood 1933–47* (Constable, London, 1997)

Braund, Harold, *Distinctly I Remember: A Personal Story of Burma* (Wren, Mount Eliza, Australia, 1972)

Brett-James, Antony, *Report My Signals* (Hennel Locke, London, 1948)

Brett-James, Antony, *Ball of Fire: The Fifth Indian Division in the Second World War* (Gale and Polden, Aldershot, 1951)

Briggs, Maurice, *The Story of Gurkha VCs* (The Gurkha Museum, Winchester, 1993)

Brooke-Wavell, Derek (ed), *Lines from a Shining Land* (The Britain-Burma Society, Caversham, 1998)

Carey, Bertram S. and Tuck, H. N., *The Chin Hills: a History of the People, our Dealings with Them, their Customs and Manners, and a Gazetteer of their Country* (Government Printing, Rangoon, 1896)

Carson, Laura, *Pioneer Trails, Trials and Triumphs: Personal Memoirs of Life and Work as a Pioneer Missionary among the Chin Tribes of Burma* (Baptist Board of Education, New York, 1927)

Chaphekar, S.G., *A Brief Study of the Burma Campaign 1943–45* (Maharashtra Militarisation Board, Poona, 1958)

Christian, John L., *Modern Burma: A Survey of Political and Economic Development* (University of California Press, Berkeley, 1942)

Crosthwaite, Sir Charles, *The Pacification of Burma* (Edward Arnold, London, 1912)

Evans, Charles, *A Doctor in XIVth Army: Burma 1944–1945* (Leo Cooper, London, 1998)

Evans, Geoffrey, *The Johnnies* (Cassell, London, 1964)

Falam Centenary Magazine 1892–1992

The 'Fighting Fifth' – History of the 5th Indian Division, n.d.

Fergusson, Bernard, *Beyond The Chindwin: Being an Account of the Adventures of Number Five Column of the Wingate Expedition into Burma, 1943* (Collins, London, 1945)

Fleming, Lawrence (ed), *Last Children of the Raj* (Radcliffe Press, London, 2003)

Frontier Administration July 1942–November 1943 (The British Library's Asia, Pacific and Africa Collections)

Gibson, Patrick, *Childhood Lost: A Boy's Journey through War* (London, 1999)

Glass, Leslie, *The Changing of Kings: Memories of Burma 1934–1949* (Peter Owen, London, 1985)

Gross, Anthony, *India in Action* (National Gallery, London)

A Handbook for Travellers to India, Burma and Ceylon (John Murray, London, 1938)

Harvey, G. E., *History of Burma* (Longmans, London, 1925)

Herbert, Patricia M., *Burma*, World Bibliographical Series, Vol. 132 (Clio Press, Oxford, 1991)

History of 17 Indian Division: July 1941 to December 1945 (Thacker's Press, Calcutta, n.d.)

History of the Chin Hills Battalion 1894–1949 (Mss Eur E250, The British Library's Asia, Pacific and Africa Collections)

Jackson, Len (ed), *Muse in Exile. An Anthology from Fighting Men of South East Asia* (SEAC Publication)

Jaffé, Sally and Lucy (eds), *Chinthe Women: Women's Auxiliary Service Burma 1942–1946* (Chipping Norton, 2001)

Jaffrey, Saeed, *Saeed, An Actor's Journey* (Constable, London, 1998)

Khen Za Moong, *Lest We Forget* (private pamphlet, Yangon, n.d.)

Khen Za Moong, *Tedim to Yangon* (private pamphlet, Yangon, 1995)

Khup Chin Pau, Stephen, *Architecture of Northern Chins and Sukte-Kamhau Customs* (in press)

Kirby, S. W. et al., *History of the Second World War. The War Against Japan*, Vol 2, *India's Most Dangerous Hour* (HMSO, London, 1958)

—, *History of the Second World War. The War Against Japan*, Vol. 3, *The Decisive Battles* (HMSO, London, 1961)

Lehman, F. K., *The Structure of Chin Society: A Tribal People of Burma Adapted to a Non-western Civilization* (University of Illinois Press, 1963)

Lyall Grant, Ian, *Burma: The Turning Point – The Seven Battles on the Tiddim Road Which Turned the Tide of the Burma War* (The Zampi Press, Chichester, 1993)

Lyall Grant, Ian, and Tamayama, Kazuo, *Burma 1942: The Japanese Invasion. Both Sides Tell the Story of a Savage Jungle War* (The Zampi Press, Chichester, 1999)

McCall, Anthony G., *Lushai Chrysalis: Land of Tranquillity and Upheaval* (Luzac, London, 1949)

McEnery, John H., *Epilogue in Burma 1945–48: The Military Dimension of British Withdrawal* (Spellmount, Tunbridge Wells, 1990)

Marshall, Andrew, *The Trouser People: The Quest for the Victorian Footballer Who Made Burma Play the Empire's Game* (Viking Penguin, London, 2002)

Morrison, Ian, *Grandfather Longlegs: The Life and Gallant Death of Major H. P. Seagrim, G.C., D.S.O., M.B.E.* (Faber & Faber, London, 1947)

Naini Tal: A Historical and Descriptive Account, 1927 (Government Press, Allahabad, 1928)

Naylor, L. B., *A Practical Handbook of the Chin Language (Siyin Dialect)* (Government Printing, Rangoon, 1925)

Neild, Eric, *With Pegasus in India: The Story of 153 Gurkha Parachute Battalion* (Birch & Co., Singapore, n.d.)

Newland, A. G. E., *The Image of War or Service on the Chin Hills* (Thacker, Spink & Co., Calcutta, 1894)

Nunneley, John, *Tales from the King's African Rifles*, *A Last Flourish of Empire* (Askari Books, Petersham, 1998)

Oatts, Balfour ('Titus'), *The Jungle in Arms* (William Kimber, London, 1962)

Rundall, F. M. *The Siyin Chins* (Superintendent of Government Printing, Rangoon, 1893)

Scott, George, *Gazetteer of Upper Burma and the Shan States*, Part I, Vol.1 (Superintendent of Government Printing, Rangoon, 1900)

Sii Boi-pa (Fraser, Kenny), *'Don't Believe a Word of It!"* (Culross, 1999)

Slim, Field Marshal Sir William, *Defeat into Victory* (Cassell, London, 1956; Macmillan, paperback edition, 1999)

Stevenson, H. N. C., *Burma: The Economics of the Central Chin Tribes* (The Times of India Press, Bombay, 1943)

—, *The Hill Peoples of Burma* (Longmans, London, 1944)

Sukte Beh Leh Tedimgam Tangthu [Sukte Clan and Tiddimland History] (1996)

Swinson, Arthur, *Kohima* (Cassell, London, 1966)

Thompson, Julian, *The Imperial War Museum Book of the War in Burma 1942–1945* (Sidgwick & Jackson/Imperial War Museum, London, 2002)

Towers, G. W., 'The Tiddim Track' in *The Journal of the United Service Institution of India*, October 1944, Vol. LXXIV, No. 317.

Tucker, Shelby, *Burma: The Curse of Independence* (Pluto Press, London, 2001)

Vum Ko Hau, *Profile of a Burma Frontier Man* (Kilatmadju Press, Bandung, Indonesia, 1963)

Vumson, *Zo History* (Mizoram, India, n.d.)

Wallace, Ian, Mss F180/41B (The British Library's Asia, Pacific and Africa Collections)

Wavell, A. P., (ed), *Other Men's Flowers* (Penguin, Harmondsworth, 1944)

Williams, J. H., *Elephant Bill* (Rupert Hart-Davis, London, 1955)

Ziegler, Philip (ed), *Personal Diary of Admiral The Lord Louis Mountbatten: Supreme Allied Commander, South-East Asia, 1943–1946* (Collins, London, 1988)

INDEX

Page numbers in *italic* refer to maps. Numbers in **bold** refer to illustrations. NK is Norman Kelly. Some Chin names have an alternative spelling.